WILLIAM WAKE
ARCHBISHOP OF CANTERBURY
1657–1737

WILLIAM WAKE

ARCHBISHOP OF CANTERBURY

1657–1737

BY

NORMAN SYKES, F.B.A.
*Dixie Professor of Ecclesiastical History, and
Fellow of Emmanuel College, Cambridge*

VOLUME II

CAMBRIDGE
AT THE UNIVERSITY PRESS
1957

PUBLISHED BY
THE SYNDICS OF THE CAMBRIDGE UNIVERSITY PRESS
Bentley House, 200 Euston Road, London, N.W. 1
American Branch: 32 East 57th Street, New York 22, N.Y.

Printed in Great Britain at the University Press, Cambridge
(*Brooke Crutchley, University Printer*)

CONTENTS

THE PLATES

Plate II shows part of the rough draft of Wake's letter to Profsssor Jean Alphonse Turrettini of Geneva dated, by the covering letter, 25 July 1718. (From Arch. W. Epist. 25, f. 76.)
Plates III and IV show part of the fair copy of the same letter, sent to Geneva. (From the Bibliothèque Publique et Universitaire, MSS. Inventaire 1569, f. 177.) The contents of this letter are described on pp. 34–7.

Plates II, III and IV are between pp. 32 and 33.

CHAPTER VI

THE CARE OF ALL THE CHURCHES: THE UNION OF PROTESTANTS

Discretion puts a difference betwixt things absolutely necessary to salvation to be done and believed, and those which are of a second sort and lower form, wherein more liberty and latitude is allowed. In maintaining whereof, the stiffness of the judgment is abated, and suppled with charity towards his neighbour.

THOMAS FULLER, *The Holy State*, Book III, chapter 20. 'Of Moderation'

'As to what concerns the union of Protestants', wrote Wake to Dr Daniel Ernst Jablonski, 'how much I have it at heart is sufficiently plain from the sermon which I preached before our most excellent King on the solemn anniversary of his accession, and which when printed by royal command proclaimed publicly to the whole realm my prayers and hopes.'[1] In the sermon to which reference was made, preached before the King on 1 August 1715, being the first anniversary of His Majesty's accession, Wake (then bishop of Lincoln) had animadverted on the blessings of the Protestant succession in the House of Hanover, and on the deliverance brought thereby to the Church of England from the threat of Rome, 'the most corrupt of any Christian church in the world'; and had drawn the moral of the necessity of unity amongst Protestants both at home and abroad.

As becomes a people professing itself the head of the Protestant interest, and that is indeed of all others the most worthy so to be, we should endeavour, yet farther, to unite all the reformed churches and states abroad, in the strictest bonds of love, and peace (Oh! that I might add, and of church-communion too), both among themselves, and with us; as our surest defence against our common enemies.[2]

This zeal for Protestant union was no new enthusiasm on his part. In a sermon preached before William III and Mary on 21 May 1689, when he was still preacher at Gray's Inn, and published under the title of *An exhortation to mutual charity and union among Protestants*, he had adumbrated the

[1] Arch. W. Epist. 25, f. 38b. 'Quod ad unionem spectat Protestantium, quantum ea res mihi cordi fuerit, vel ex illa concione quam coram serenissimo rege nostro habui in solemni inaugurationis ejus annali die, satis apparet, quae, cum jussu regio publice fuerit impressa, haec mea vota, has spes meas, toti regno palam annunciavit.'

[2] 'A sermon preached before the king, on 1 August 1715', in *Twenty-Two Sermons preached upon several occasions*, by William Wake (2 vols. London, 1737), vol. I, pp. 298–9.

principles of his eirenic proposals. In refutation of the argument of Bossuet's famous *Histoire des Variations des Églises Protestantes*, he had argued that

either we must say that all, even the least points, relating to our religion, are so clearly and plainly revealed, that no honest man can possibly be mistaken, if he will but impartially enquire into them; which from the differences of whole parties concerning these things, 'tis plain they are not; or else men's different capacities, and opportunities, and tempers, and education considered, 'tis in vain to expect that all good men should agree in their notions of religion, any more than we see they do in any other concerns whatsoever.

Accordingly the answer to Bossuet was that Protestants 'amidst all our other divisions, are on all sides agreed in whatsoever is fundamental in the faith, or necessary to be believed and professed by us in order to our salvation'. Their differences were in non-essential articles; and these should be no barrier to unity.

For us whom it has pleased God, by delivering us from the errors and superstitions of the Church of Rome, to unite together in the common name of Protestant, reformed Christians, would we but as heartily labour after peace, as we are all of us very highly exhorted to it; I cannot see why we, who are so happily joined together in a common profession of the same faith, at least I am sure in all the necessary points of it, and I hope amidst all our lesser differences in a common love and charity to one another, should not also be united in the same common worship of God too.

On the one hand, the custom of occasional communion on the part of domestic Dissenters was itself evidence of their fundamental agreement with the Church of England; whilst on the other hand, the foreign Reformed churches likewise communicated with it.

Blessed be God, who has abundantly justified both the purity of our doctrine, and the innocency of our worship, not only by the general approbation of the reformed churches abroad, who both freely communicate with us in our religious offices, and have often given testimony in favour of them; but in the happy conviction of many at home, who were once enemies to our constitution, but who now go with us into the same house of God as friends.[1]

When the author of these words was elevated to the primacy it was not surprising that his preferment 'ad supremam et (ut vere a vobis appellatur) patriarchalem hujus nostri orbis Britannici sedem', was greeted by a volume of letters of congratulation from the chief Protestant churches of Europe. Their contents indeed were as florid as formal in compliment and superlative; but their provenance was of interest as illustrating the range of influence of the contemporary Church of England. From Professors Turrettini and

[1] 'An Exhortation to Mutual Charity and Union among Protestants', in *Sermons and Discourse on Several Occasions*, by William Wake (2nd ed. London, 1716), pp. 184, 186, 197.

Pictet at Geneva and from the Venerable Company of Pastors and Professors corporately; from Professor Jean Le Clerc at Amsterdam; from Jean Frédéric Ostervald, 'Pastor et Decanus' at Neuchâtel and from the pastors of that Church; from Gottfried Wilhelm Freiherr von Leibnitz at Hanover; from the Ecclesiastical Senate of the Palatinate; from Balthazar Winkler at Magdeburg; from the Antistes of Zürich, Peter Zeller; from Daniel Ernst Jablonski at Berlin; and from the Senatus Academicus at Berne, there flowed a stream of messages and greetings. More serviceable as evidence of the reputation already enjoyed by Wake in foreign circles than these official felicitations was a private letter addressed to Dr John Rudolf, Professor of Theology and Dean at Berne by one of his brethren, Professor Samuel Schürer on 28 March 1717 from London, which he was then visiting. Schürer wrote to rebuke Berne for having allowed a year to pass without following the example of other Swiss churches and universities in sending a letter of congratulation to the new Archbishop of Canterbury, whom he described as not only eminent for learning and merit, but of friendly disposition towards union, and well esteemed both by the great men and by the generality of the nation.[1]

Wake did not allow such overtures to pass without cordial reciprocation; and perhaps the most important feature of his replies was the immediate advances which he made towards the practical realisation of his hopes of Protestant union. To Le Clerc he avowed his championship of liberty of interpretation, provided that the proportion of the faith was preserved, his earnest desire for the restoration of episcopacy in the foreign Reformed churches, which nevertheless he recognised as true churches, and his hope of union.

Liberty of prophesying, provided only that it is pious and sober, joined with charity and gentleness, and not contrary to the proportion of the faith once delivered to the saints, I should consider ought not to be aspersed but rather approved. Concerning things indifferent I hold that there should be no dispute with anybody. I freely embrace the Reformed churches, though differing from our Church of England in some things. I could wish indeed that the episcopal polity, duly moderated and divorced from all unjust domination, as it stands amongst us and (if I know anything of these matters), as it has been received in the church since the times of the apostles, had been retained by all of them; nor do I despair that posterity will see it in due time restored, even if I do not see it myself. Meantime far be it from me to be so iron-hearted that because of a defect of this kind (if

[1] Staatsarchiv, Berne. B. III. 98, p. 571. I am particularly obliged to Dr E. Meyer, Adjunkt des Staatsarchivars at Berne for drawing my attention to this letter, and for sending me a copy of it. Schürer describes Wake as 'ein Herr und Prelat, der nit nur viel gelehrtheit, merite, und zur brüderlichen einigkeit geneigten humor, sonder auch an dem Hooff und by der gantzen nation grossen Credit hat, welches by allen unseren Kirchen und Staat vorfallenden begebenheiten nichts shaden Könte, da dissmahl Engelland in so grossen ansehen ist'.

I may be allowed so to call it without offence), I should hold that any of them ought to be cut off from our communion; or that (with some vehement writers amongst us) I should declare them to have no true and valid sacraments and therefore to be scarcely Christians. At all costs I desire to procure a closer union amongst all the Reformed. If this could be secured in ecclesiastical government and in the public services of the churches, it would lead unless I am greatly mistaken, in a short time to the fostering of an union of minds amongst them and would pave the way to the establishment of a full agreement in all doctrines of major importance.[1]

In this letter Wake's conscious echo of the phrase of Lancelot Andrewes to Du Moulin ('nos non sumus illi ferrei') and his explicit recognition of the foreign Reformed churches as possessing 'vera ac valida sacramenta' (whilst admitting the repudiation of his view by 'quibusdam furiosis inter nos scriptoribus'), are particularly noteworthy. To the Antistes of Zürich, Peter Zeller, the primate went further. After lamenting the divisions among Protestants, and particularly enlarging on the blame attaching to Protestant Dissenters in England for separating from the reformed national church, he affirmed his desire and hope for the restoration of episcopacy amongst the foreign Reformed churches (drawing a clear distinction between them and domestic Dissenters); and formally allowed and encouraged members of the Church of Zürich visiting England to communicate with the Church of England, and members of the *Ecclesia Anglicana* visiting Zürich to communicate with the Reformed church there.

Meanwhile we, whilst rightly defending our own discipline against these fanatics, at the same time think altogether temperately of the Reformed churches, and as becomes brethren, freely allow to them their own customs. We wish, indeed we fervently desire, that the ancient and (so far as we can gather from the sacred record) apostolic government of the church, that is the episcopal, as it prevails amongst ourselves, had been everywhere retained. We pray our common Lord that in his own time he would restore this order to all the Reformed churches; and having restored it, preserve it until the end of the world. We are confident that this indeed will be granted to them in due time by our most merciful Saviour. In all other

[1] Mosheim-MacLaine, 4 April 1716 (misdated 1719); vol. v, Appendix: No. XIX, p. 169, from Arch. W. Epist. 25, f. 9. 'Libertatem prophetandi, modo pia ac sobria sit, cum charitate ac mansuetudine conjuncta, nec contra analogiam fidei semel sanctis traditae, adeo non vituperandam ut etiam probandam, censeam. De rebus adiaphoris cum nemine contendendum puto. Ecclesias Reformatas etsi in aliquibus a nostra Anglicana dissentientes, libenter amplector. Optarem equidem regimen episcopale bene temperatum et ab omni injusta dominatione sejunctum, quale apud nos obtinet, et si quid ego in his rebus sapiam, ab ipso apostolorum aevo in Ecclesia receptum fuerit, ab iis omnibus fuisse retentum; nec despero quin aliquando restitutum si non ipse videam, at posteri videbunt. Interim absit ut ego tam ferrei pectoris sim, ut ob hujusmodi defectum (sic mihi absque omne invidia appellare liceat) aliquas earum a communione nostra abscidendas credam; aut cum quibusdam furiosis inter nos scriptoribus, eas nulla vera ac valida sacramenta habere, adeoque vix Christianos esse pronuntiem. Unionem arctiorem inter omnes Reformatos procurare quovis pretio vellem. Haec si in regimine ecclesiastico ac publicis ecclesiarum officiis obtineri potuit; aut ego plurimum fallor, aut id solum brevi conduceret ad animorum inter eos unionem conciliandam, et viam sterneret ad plenam in omnibus majoris momenti dogmatibus concordiam stabiliendam.'

matters we allow to every Church its own liberty to establish that discipline for itself which is best adapted to its own usages or which its rulers, guided by reason or taught by experience, shall have decreed. Thus all the wiser ministers of our Church think of you, venerable Antistes; and we both know and rejoice that you also likewise so think of us. We both allow and encourage those of our members going abroad to you to receive the Holy Communion with you in accordance with this opinion. Those of your members who live here, we freely admit to our sacred offices; nor do you forbid it. May we ever preserve unimpaired this holy fellowship thus entered into; and may we so think mutually of each other as of most dear brethren in Christ.[1]

In this remarkable advance made by Wake, once again his principle of unity in essentials and difference in non-essentials was exemplified by his readiness to allow considerable local divergencies in ecclesiastical discipline, granted the restoration of episcopacy. But what was of greater moment was his formal authorisation of mutual intercommunion. Nor was this a departure from his customary rule, owing to exceptional circumstances at Zürich. In a letter to the pastors, professors, and doctors of the church and university of Basle on 17 July 1719, after emphasising the urgency of Protestant union, alike on ecclesiastical and political grounds, he affirmed the principle once again that in his eyes differences on minor points were no bar to communion between churches.

Assuredly we in our Church are generally so minded that we cultivate peace with all who profess with us the same belief in those things which are necessary to salvation. Nor do we refuse communion to such of them as are present with us, on account of difference in other articles of lesser importance; nor separate ourselves from their communion when residing amongst them. This your members who have been in England have experienced. Our members dwelling in Switzerland demonstrate it every day. Thus so far as concerns ourselves, nothing farther in this respect remains to be desired.[2]

[1] Arch. W. Epist. 25, f. 29, 1 March 1716/17. Staatsarchiv, Zürich. E. II, 432, no. 112 for the original of this letter. 'Nos interim uti contra hos homines fanaticos disciplinam nostram jure defendimus, ita de Ecclesiis Reformatis prorsus moderate, et ut decet fratres, sentimus, suosque illis mores libenter permittimus. Optamus, et vehementer quidem optamus, vetus illud ac quantum ex historia sacra colligere possumus, Apostolicum Ecclesiae Regimen, episcopale, quale apud nos obtinet, ubique fuisse retentum. Oramus communem nostrum Dominum, ut suo tempore omnibus Reformatis Ecclesiis hunc ordinem restituat; et restitutum usque ad finem saeculi conservet. Confidimus hoc iis a clementissimo Servatore nostro aliquando concedendum fore. In caeteris unicuique ecclesiae suam libertatem concedimus eam sibi disciplinam instituendi quam suis usibus maxime accommodatam, vel ratione ducti vel experientia edocti rectores ejus judicaverint. Haec de vobis, venerande Antistes, sentiunt omnes saniores ecclesiae nostrae symmystae. Haec de nobis etiam vos pariter sentire et scimus et gaudemus. Quotquot e nostris peregre ad vos proficiscuntur, ut juxta hanc sententiam una vobiscum communicent, et permittimus et hortamur. Vestros hic agentes libenter ad sacra nostra admittimus; nec vos prohibetis: Hanc sanctam communionem illibatam semper conservemus; sic de nobis invice sentiamus ut de fratribus in Christo charissimis.'

[2] Arch. W. Epist. 25, f. 146. 'Nos sane in hac nostra ecclesia, adeo plerumque animati sumus, ut cum omnibus pacem colamus, qui eandem nobiscum fidem in his quae ad salutem sunt necessaria,

Indeed in urging upon the Lutheran and Reformed churches of Europe the necessity of union amongst themselves, Wake pointed to the examples of the King and of the Church of England as illustrating the moral and the way to such union. For just as, following the illustrious example of George I, both Lutheran and Reformed churchmen when in England communicated with the Church of England, so they might establish reciprocal communion amongst themselves.

God has given us a most excellent and most powerful king, who is beyond doubt the chief amongst all the reformed princes; and who, having been brought up amongst the Lutherans and having never renounced their sacred rites, now with all his royal family has joined the communion of the Church of England; and therein, by his own example (by far the most illustrious that can be imagined by the human mind), has clearly demonstrated that there is no obstacle to all Protestants being able to gather, and, as it were, to coalesce in the same church with us. So far as the Reformed are concerned, I believe there is no one amongst them who would decline our communion. In these circumstances it seems to me that the union of the Protestants and the Reformed has thus so far nothing impossible in itself, that it has already practically been realised on both sides; for both Protestants and Reformed admit, if not in words yet (what should be reckoned more significant) in deeds, that they can both agree with us as with a third party, and therefore can be mutually united with each other.[1]

Since the ultimate goal and indispensable condition of union was the restoration of episcopacy in those foreign churches which lacked it, the English primate was not unmindful of the responsibilities of the Church of England in helping towards this end; and the practical means of translating his wishes into actual fact was by offering to ordain to the ministry candidates tor ordination in these Reformed churches. Accordingly he wrote to J. F. Ostervald (already well known for his eirenic efforts by the publication in 1702 of his *Catéchisme ou Instruction dans la religion Chréstienne*, and in 1713

profiteantur; neque aliquibus ob dissensum in aliis levioris momenti articulis, aut communionem denegamus nobiscum praesentibus, aut ab eorum communione nos separamus cum in eorum partibus una versamur. Hoc vestri qui in Anglia fuerint, experti sunt. Nostri qui in Helvetia commorantur in dies ostendunt. Adeo ut quod ad nos spectat, nihil amplius in hac re desiderari posse videatur.'

[1] Arch. W. Epist. 25, f. 115, Wake to the Pastors and Professors of Geneva, 8 April 1719. 'Regem nobis concessit Deus optimum, potentissimum, inter omnes Reformatos principes absque controversia praecipuum. Hic inter Lutheranos enutritus, neque ab eorum sacris ullatenus alienus, ad Ecclesiae tamen Anglicanae communionem, cum tota sua regali familia, accessit; adeoque exemplo suo (omnium quae humano animo concipi possunt longe illustrissimo) plane demonstravit, nihil obstare quominus alii omnes Protestantes in eandem nobiscum Ecclesiam convenire, et quasi coalescere, valeant. Quod ad Reformatos spectat, nullos ego inter eos esse credo qui communionem nostram abfugiat. Quae cum ita sint, mihi quidem videtur Protestantium atque Reformatorum unionem adeo nihil in se impossibile habere, ut jamdudum ex utraque parte tantum non reipsa facta sit; tam Protestantibus quam Reformatis, si non verbis at (quod magis quiddam reputari debet) factis, confitentibus, posse se nobiscum, quasi in tertio aliquo consentire, ac proinde inter se ipsos mutuo uniri.'

of his *Liturgie de Neuchâtel*) urging him to complete his work by restoring episcopacy to the Reformed churches and as a first step thereto by ensuring episcopal ordination to future ministers of his own church.

It will be our part to provide that, if for this reason they come here, they may receive ordination with the minimum of difficulty and expense from our bishops and presbyters (for our discipline associates both orders in this action). O, what a happy and fortunate beginning this would be of the closest union of the Reformed churches. How much would it conduce to conciliate the minds even of the most perverse men.[1]

In one of the foreign Protestant churches, however, that of the Unitas Fratrum, there was already an episcopate which the primate was able to recognise fully and without reserve. Dr Jablonski, who had himself received episcopal consecration from the Bohemian Brethren, sent to Wake on 22 March 1717 a letter designed to prove the uninterrupted episcopal succession in this Church, in view of reports which had reached him from England of doubt, if not denial, of this fact. From his letter he hoped that

it will be clearly evident that the Churches of the Bohemian Brethren have not only preserved the legitimate episcopal order and its succession to this very day, but also that no other church in the entire Reformed world approaches so closely in this respect to the Church of England as the Bohemian Church. For although the other Reformed churches in Brandenburg, Hesse, the Palatinate and in the churches of Lesser Poland and of the Grand Duchy of Lithuania in the kingdom of Poland (including some even of the Swiss churches) enjoy likewise a hierarchical order and reverence their Antistites, Superintendents and Inspectors (who in Hungary and Transylvania are sometimes called Bishops); yet none save the Bohemian Church situated in Greater Poland either has had or has preserved the unbroken thread of episcopal and apostolic succession.[2]

In returning thanks on 6 April for this memorandum the Archbishop professed himself completely satisfied, and hoped that any Anglicans hitherto doubtful, would be also convinced.

[1] *Ibid.* f. 12b. 'Nostrum erit providere, ut si ea de causa huc appulerint, quam minimo labore et sumptu ab episcopis et presbyteris nostris (utrosque enim nostra disciplina in ea actione conjungit) ordinarentur. O quam felix faustumque hoc foret initium unionis conjunctissimae Ecclesiarum Reformatarum; quantum ad conciliandos etiam perversissimorum hominum animos conduceret.'

[2] *Ibid.* f. 32. 'Liquido patebit, non solum Ecclesias Fratrum Bohemorum legitimum ordinem episcopalem ejusque successionem ad hunc usque diem conservasse, verum etiam nullam in toto orbe Reformato Ecclesiam Anglicanae hac quidem in parte tam prope quam Bohemicam illam accedere. Quamvis enim Ecclesiae aliae Reformatae, Brandenburgicae, Hassicae, Palatinae, et in ipso Poloniae regno Ecclesiae Minoris Poloniae et Magni Ducatus Lithuaniae, ne Helveticis quidem penitus exceptis, etiam hierarchico ordine gaudent, suosque Antistites, Superintendentes, Inspectores venerantur (qui in Hungaria et Transylvania nonnunquam Episcopi appellantur); nulla tamen filum successionis episcopalis apostolicae nunquam interruptum, praeter unam illam Bohemicam, in Majore Polonia hospitantem, vel habuit vel conservavit.'

You have clearly demonstrated in your short treatise the episcopal succession in the Bohemian Churches; which for myself I had held to have been sufficiently proved by earlier writers. If there are any persons amongst us to whom your affairs are either insufficiently known or differently conceived, I hope that by this work of yours they will be better informed, so that henceforth they will judge more fairly of yourselves and your episcopate.[1]

At the other extreme stood the Reformed churches in the Grand Duchy of Lithuania, on whose behalf M. Boguslaus Kopijewicz approached Wake in respect of their desire for episcopacy and the uncertainty of its preservation amongst them. For since some scruples had been raised as to whether in the troubled vicissitudes of their history these churches in Poland and Lithuania had preserved the episcopal succession under the name of Superintendents, they had delegated M. Kopijewicz, minister at Vilna, to appeal to the English primate privately (according to the precedent of Nicodemus who came to Jesus secretly), for the determination of the matter. Accordingly their request was that the Archbishop, with the co-signatures and seals of his episcopal brethren, after examination of the case, should either pronounce themselves convinced of the uninterrupted succession of episcopacy, or else should confer the succession on them by diploma as it were, which would be sufficient without consecration by imposition of hands.

If therefore Your Eminence is doubtful whether either or both of the Churches there is certainly adorned with that inestimable benefit of apostolic succession (a treasure which cannot be overvalued), may it please you now, having compared opinions with the illustrious concert of your brethren, to bless our Church with this power by one and the same instrument, which should bear the seal and accustomed mark of the Church of England and be fortified by the signatures of yourself and your illustrious episcopal colleagues. For this will be an imposition of hands to both Superintendents and Ministers, although by a different and respectively sufficient faculty. It is evident from ecclesiastical records that such a dignity has been conferred on many by a written document; and that it is not the ceremony of laying-on of hands (though we should esteem this if it could conveniently be had), but the intention of those conferring (who possess it themselves and have received it from their blessed fathers or predecessors) which bestows on others the episcopal dignity or the priesthood of the new covenant. For holy scripture testifies that all the believers in Christ received imposition of hands from the apostles themselves in Samaria, but were not thereby all made ministers of the word and sacraments, much less bishops; and that therefore this power resides solely in the intention and consent of those conferring it, which without question can be effected as much by the words of a written instrument as by those spoken by word of mouth. If

[1] Arch. W. Epist. 25, f. 33. 'Successionem episcopalem Ecclesiarum Bohemicarum...brevi tuo tractatu clare demonstrasti; et ab aliis antea, quod ad meipsum attinet, satis probatam censueram. Si qui apud nos sint, quibus res vestrae vel minus cognitae, vel sequius acceptae, etiam illos spero tua hac opera melius fore informandos; et de vobis ac episcopatu vestro in posterum aequius judicaturos.'

however Your Eminence is convinced that both or either of these churches is adorned with this treasure, may it please you to confirm this to either or both by an apostolic letter.[1]

Upon receiving this unusual missive, Wake conferred with his brethren, and briefly summarised their conclusions as follows:

I have consulted my brethren upon the proposal you made to me on the part of your Church in Lithuania, and find it to be their opinion as it is my own, that having no authentic account of the state of succession of ministers among you, we are not able to pass any judgment upon the regularity of it; and that we are much less able to supply any defects in it, if there should be any, by the method you propose, for which there is no precedent in ecclesiastical history. We are besides very apprehensive, even from your own account, that were we able to do what you desire, it might be attended with ill consequences among yourselves, and therefore all we can do is to treat you with the same candour and brotherly love that we do the rest of the Reformed churches abroad.

This opinion was communicated to the Lithuanian delegate formally by the primate 'nomine suo atque episcoporum confratrum suorum', in these terms.

Venerable Sir and Delegate, Having taken counsel with my brethren and fellow-bishops concerning the articles which your lordship laid before us, we declare our agreed opinion as follows: That since the state of your churches is completely unknown to us, and since no public or authentic instruments have been laid before us, by which we could obtain any certain information as to the succession of your Superintendents, it is impossible for us without temerity to pass any judgment concerning it. We hope indeed that the ecclesiastical ministry has been preserved inviolate amongst you; but if any defect in it should have been incurred, we consider that such a defect could in no wise be supplied by the method suggested to us by you, which is neither supported by any canonical rule, nor (as we believe) by any precedent extant in the history of the church. In these circumstances we can do nothing more than treat you and your churches with the same brotherly love

[1] *Ibid.* f. 245, 11 September 1712. 'Si itaque celsitudo vestra dubitat alterutram vel utramque Ecclesiam ibidem hoc inenarrabili beneficio successionis apostolicae, talento nunquam satis aestimando, pro certo esse ornatam, placeat jam ad praesens collatis suffragiis cum illustri collegarum choro, uno eodem scripto quod sigillum et solita Ecclesiae Anglicanae ostendat, subscriptionibusque celsitudinis vestrae et illustrissimi collegii episcopalis munitum sit, dictam Ecclesiam tali potestate beare. Et haec erit impositio manuum utrisque Superattendentibus et Ministris diversa quamvis et utrinque non nisi competenti facultate. Constat ex historiis ecclesiasticis scripto talem dignitatem multis collatam fuisse, non enim ceremoniam impositionis manuum (quamvis et hanc veneremur si commode fiere potest) sed voluntatem conferentium eorum qui ipsi habent, et a beatissimis majoribus seu antecessoribus acceperant, aliis episcopalem dignitatem vel sacerdotium novi foederis conferre. Scriptura sancta testatur omnes credentes in Christum Dominum impositionem manuum ab ipsis apostolis Samariae obtinuisse, at non ideo omnes ministros Verbi et Sacramentorum multo minus episcopos, factos, unice ergo potestas haec consistit in voluntate et consensu conferentium, quod aeque per literas verbis scriptis quam ore tenus verbis prolatis procul omni dubio perfici potest. Si vero celsitudo vestra convicta est utramque vel alterutram esse hoc talento ornatam, placeat eam vel eas ibidem uno scripto apostolico in hoc confirmare.'

as we do the other Reformed churches; and pray that by the grace of God you may enjoy peace and tranquillity from those amongst whom you dwell; which we do with all our heart.[1]

The vigorous initiative towards Protestant union which Wake thus launched at the very beginning of his primacy represented another, and perhaps more concrete and specific, episode in the long history of similar movements towards the healing of the divisions of Protestants, in which the seventeenth century had been particularly prolific. From the standpoint of Anglican tradition the Archbishop was convinced that he stood in the line of leading and representative Caroline bishops and presbyters, alike in his staunch assertion of the episcopal succession in the Church of England and of the necessary restoration of episcopacy amongst the Reformed churches of the continent as a condition of corporate union, and in his recognition of the validity of presbyterian ministry and sacraments in those foreign churches whose loss of episcopacy had been inculpable because due to historical necessity.

During the sixteenth and seventeenth centuries indeed, the Church of England by the pressure alike of ecclesiastical and political circumstances, had been led in the persons of representative divines to ponder the particular relevance of its ecclesiastical position *in via media* to its relationship with the foreign Protestant churches; some of which had maintained, like itself, an uninterrupted succession of bishops, as in the Church of Sweden, others were governed by superintendents who did not constitute a separate and higher order of ministry than the presbyterate but exercised an administrative function of oversight, as in Denmark and many German Lutheran churches, and others followed the Genevan model of a purely presbyterian order of ministry with the attendant affirmation of the parity of ministers, as in the Reformed churches. Moreover with the turn of the sixteenth century the Protestant churches of the continent came increasingly to look to the Church of England as the head and pattern of the Protestant interest in its struggle against both the ecclesiastical and political onslaughts of the counter-reformation. Conscious of this identity of interest and fortune against the

[1] Arch. W. Epist. 25, f. 246. 'Venerabilis Domine Delegate: Consilio cum fratribus et co-episcopis habito de articulis a dominatione vestra nobis propositis, in hanc quae sequitur sententiam communiter convenimus: Quod cum Ecclesiarum vestrarum status nobis penitus sit incognitus, neque ulla publica, sive authentica instrumenta nobis exhibeantur, unde de successione Superintendentium vestrorum certi aliquid nobis constet; fieri non potest ut de ea judicium aliquod absque temeritate feramus. Speramus equidem ministerium ecclesiasticum a vobis intemerate conservatum esse: sin vero aliquis in illo defectus acciderit, censemus haudquaquam suppleri posse illum defectum ea quae a vobis proponitur methodo: quae neque ullo jure canonico sustinetur, cujusque nullum omnino exemplum in historia ecclesiastica extare credimus. Quae cum ita se habeant, nihil amplius nobis restat, nisi ut vos, vestrasque Ecclesias eadem fraterna charitate excipiamus qua reliquas Ecclesias Reformatas, vobisque cum Dei gratia pacem, ac tranquillitatem ex parte eorum quibuscum vivitis, quod ex animo facimus, apprecemur.'

new aggressiveness of Rome, Anglican divines had sought to discover an ecclesiastical *modus vivendi* with the non-episcopal continental churches. 'We were glad at first of abettors against the errors of the Roman Church', wrote Jeremy Taylor: 'we found these men zealous in it; we thanked God for it, as we had cause, and we were willing to make them recompense by endeavouring to justify their ordinations, not thinking what would follow upon ourselves.'[1]

In part this search for a *modus vivendi* took the form of the application of the distinction between things *necessary* and *accessory* (which was a fundamental Anglican principle in controversies against both papists and puritans) to the question of church order. Hooker affirmed 'that matters of faith, and in general matters necessary unto salvation, are of a different nature from ceremonies, order, and the kind of church government'; and he expressly reckoned ceremonies 'and matters of government, in the number of things accessory, not things necessary in such sort as hath been declared'. Thus he argued that 'the necessity of polity and regiment in all churches may be held without holding any one certain form to be necessary in them all'; and although the later books *Of the Laws of Ecclesiastical Polity* affirmed of episcopacy that 'if anything in the church's government, surely the first institution of bishops was from heaven, was even of God, the Holy Ghost was the author of it', yet this claim was not exclusive of exceptions. Hooker appealed in his defence of episcopacy in the Church of England to the unbroken historical tradition, whereby for

a thousand and five hundred years and upward the church of Christ hath now continued under the sacred regiment of bishops. Neither for so long hath Christianity been ever planted in any kingdom throughout the world but with this kind of government alone; which to have been ordained of God, I am for mine own part even as resolutely persuaded, as that any other kind of government in the world whatsoever is of God.

Notwithstanding, in the case of certain of the foreign Reformed churches, he accepted the plea of historical necessity.

In which respect for mine own part, although I see that certain Reformed churches, the Scottish especially and the French, have not that which best agreeth with the sacred Scripture, I mean the government that is by bishops, inasmuch as both those churches are fallen under a different kind of regiment;...this their defect and imperfection I had rather lament in such case than exagitate, considering that men often times without any fault of their own may be driven to want that kind of polity or regiment which is best, and to content themselves with that, which either the irremediable error of former times, or the necessity of the present hath cast upon them.

[1] Jeremy Taylor, *Of the Sacred Order and Office of Episcopacy. Works* (10 vols. London, 1883), vol. v, p. 118.

Similarly, developing his argument from the distinction between what is most agreeable to scripture and what may be allowed, though defective and imperfect, he affirmed that acceptance of episcopal government and ordination as the ordinary and normal rule of the church was consistent with recognition that exceptional circumstances might justify extraordinary and abnormal expedients.

Whereas...some do infer, that no ordination can stand but only such as is made by bishops, which have had their ordination likewise by other bishops before them, till we come to the very apostles of Christ themselves;...to this we answer, that there may be sometimes very just and sufficient reason to allow ordination made without a bishop. The whole church visible being the true original subject of all power, it hath not ordinarily allowed any other than bishops alone to ordain; howbeit, as the ordinary course is ordinarily in all things to be observed, so it may be in some cases not unnecessary that we decline from the ordinary ways.

Of such extraordinary circumstances he specified two examples:

One is, when God himself doth of himself raise up any, whose labour he useth without requiring that men should authorise them....Another extraordinary kind of vocation is, when the exigency of necessity doth constrain to leave the usual ways of the church, which otherwise we would willingly keep; where the church must needs have some ordained, and neither hath nor can have possibly a bishop to ordain; in case of such necessity, the ordinary institution of God hath given oftentimes, and may give, place. And, therefore, we are not simply without exception to urge a lineal descent of power from the apostles by continued succession of bishops in every effectual ordination. These cases of inevitable necessity excepted, none may ordain but only bishops; by the imposition of their hands it is, that the church giveth power of order, both unto presbyters and deacons.[1]

With this position of Hooker, the argument of Whitgift was in agreement:

So that, notwithstanding government, or some kind of government, may be a part of the church, touching the outward form and perfection of it, yet is it not such a part of the essence and being, but that it may be the church of Christ without this or that kind of government, and therefore the 'kind of government' of the church is not 'necessary unto salvation'.[2]

In view of the authority carried by Hooker's *Of the Laws of Ecclesiastical Polity* in the tradition of Anglican apologetic, it is little surprising that his defence of episcopacy as the norm and ordinary rule of the church yet with the admission of extraordinary exceptions in case of necessity, should have been followed by some of the leading Caroline divines. Most particularly Lancelot Andrewes was regarded as having given the seal of his express approval to this position in his interchange of letters with Du Moulin, in

[1] R. Hooker, *Of the Laws of Ecclesiastical Polity*, III. x. 8; ii. 2; ii. 1; VII, v. 10; i. 4; III. xi. 6; VII. xiv. 11.

[2] John Whitgift, *Works*, vol. 1, p. 185. (Parker Society, 3 vols.)

which he accepted the principle that a church could be properly so called though lacking episcopacy. In view of the circumstance that Wake twice explicitly quoted Andrewes in support of his own position, as well as echoing his sentiments and sometimes his phrases in his correspondence, it is worth while to cite the statements of Andrewes.

> Nevertheless if our form be of divine right, it doth not follow from thence that there is no salvation without it, or that a church cannot consist without it. He is blind who does not see churches consisting without it; he is hard-hearted who denieth them salvation. We are none of those hard-hearted persons; we put a great difference between these things. There may be something absent in the exterior regiment which is of divine right and yet salvation to be had.... To prefer something better is not to condemn a thing. Nor is it to condemn your church if we recall it to another form, namely our own, which the better agrees with all antiquity.[1]

Similarly Andrewes accepted Hooker's plea of historical necessity.

> You ask whether your churches have sinned in the matter of divine law. I did not say that. I said only that your churches lacked something which is of divine authority; but the fault is not yours but that of the evil of the times. For your France did not have kings so favourable to the reformation of the church as did our England; but some time, when God shall grant better things, that which is now lacking will be supplied by his grace. Meantime, however, the name of 'bishop', which occurs so often in the scriptures, ought not to have been abolished. Although indeed what does it matter if you abolish the name so long as you keep the thing? And you have retained the thing without the name.[2]

The authority attaching to Andrewes' words was emphasised by their citation *verbatim* also by Archbishop John Bramhall in his statement of the Anglican position in regard to the foreign Reformed churches; and by his interpretation of this position in phrases reminiscent also of Whitgift and Hooker. 'This mistake proceedeth from not distinguishing between the true nature and essence of a church, which we do readily grant them, and the integrity or perfection of a church, which we cannot grant them without swerving from the judgment of the catholic church.' Bramhall indeed 'liked

[1] L. Andrewes, *Opuscula*, 191. Nec tamen si nostra [forma] divini juris sit, inde sequitur, vel quod sine ea salus non sit, vel quod stare non possit Ecclesia. Caecus sit qui non videat stantes sine ea ecclesias. Ferreus sit, qui salutem eis neget. Nos non sumus illi ferrei; latum inter ista discrimen ponimus. Potest abesse aliquid quod divini juris sit (in exteriore quidem regimine) ut tamen substet salus....Non est hoc damnare rem, melius illi aliquid anteponere. Non est hoc damnare vestram ecclesiam, ad formam aliam, quae toti antiquitati magis placuit, id est, ad nostram revocare.

[2] *Ibid.* 211 (Library of Anglo-Catholic Theology). 'Quaeris tum peccentne in jus divinum Ecclesiae vestrae. Non dixi. Id tantum dixi, abesse ab Ecclesiis vestris, aliquid quod de jure divino sit; culpa autem vestra non abesse, sed injuria temporum. Non enim tam propitios habuisse reges Galliam vestram in ecclesia reformanda, quam habuit Britannia nostra; interim, ubi dabit meliora Deus, et hoc quoque, quod jam abest, per Dei gratiam suppletum iri. At interea episcopi nomen, quod tam saepe in sacris est, abolendum non fuisse. Quanquam quid attinet abolere nomen, retinere rem? Nam et vos retinetis rem sine titulo.'

well' the distinction 'of the nature and essence of a church from the integrity and perfection thereof', and also, like his predecessors, laid great weight on the circumstance of historical necessity: 'necessity is a strong plea: many Protestant churches lived under kings and bishops of another communion; others had particular reasons why they could not continue or introduce bishops'; and he affirmed the good fortune of the Church of England in having adhered to episcopacy, 'the via tutissima—the safest way', so that 'it is charity to think well of our neighbours, and good divinity to look well to ourselves'.[1]

On several occasions Wake appealed to these seventeenth-century divines in support of his own policy and principles; and it is important to observe that he defended this position both in negotiation with Gallican theologians (before whom he was affirming in the strongest terms the preservation of the episcopal succession in the Church of England) and in his relations with foreign Protestants.

In his correspondence with Wake concerning the validity of Anglican orders, Père Le Courayer was much disconcerted to discover during his researches that Archbishop Grindal had apparently recognised the validity of presbyterian ordinations.

> Je viens de trouver, my lord, dans la vie de Grindal publiée par Strype une pièce qui me fait peine. C'est une reconnaissance de la validité de l'Ordination d'un ministre Écossais ordonné selon le rite presbytérien d'Écosse, et une permission à lui de prêcher et d'administrer les sacrements, comme s'il avait été ordonné selon le rite Anglicane....Cette pièce est embarrassante, car cela prouve ce qui parait d'ailleurs, que ce prélat était purement presbytérien; et ne faisait nulle différence entre les ordinations des episcopaux et celles des simples consistoires.[2]

In his reply Wake admitted the fact but denied the inference.

> The licence granted by Archbishop Grindal's vicar-general to a Scot presbyterian to officiate here in England, I freely own, is not what I should have approved of, yet dare not condemn. I bless God that I was born and have been bred in an episcopal church, which I am convinced has been the government established in the Christian church from the very time of the apostles. But I should be unwilling to affirm that where the ministry is not episcopal, there is no church, nor any true administration of the sacraments. And very many there are among us who are zealous for episcopacy, yet dare not go so far as to annul the ordinances of God performed by any other ministry. See for this in Bishop Andrewes' *Opuscula*, his letters to Du Moulin; you will there find one of the most tenacious asserters of the episcopal government, nevertheless far from un-churching all the other reformed churches for the want of it. And in the case you mention, who can say how far a bishop may have power to license a person, not rightly ordained, to

[1] J. Bramhall, *Works*, vol. III, pp. 518, 475 (L.A.C.T.). N. Sykes, *Old Priest and New Presbyter*, chs. I and III.

[2] Arch. W. Epist. II, f. 30, 11 March 1724 (Postscript).

officiate in the church committed to his jurisdiction? In the meantime you know your schoolmen have been far from censuring presbyterian ordinations, and yet their opinions had no influence to prejudice the episcopacy of your church in which they lived. And should I (erroneously) think such ordination in some circumstances valid, yet I do not see how that would affect my own orders, which I must always prefer exceedingly before the other. At present our constitution is otherwise settled; nor can any archbishop or bishop licence any man to officiate or administer the holy sacraments, especially that of the blessed Eucharist, who is not by an episcopal ordination qualified for it.[1]

In Père Le Quien's reply to Courayer's defence of Anglican orders, the learned Dominican laid considerable emphasis upon the alleged circumstance that the seventeenth-century Anglican divines had adopted a different attitude towards the ministry of their own Church and that of the foreign Reformed churches from their sixteenth-century predecessors. Beginning with Francis Mason they had argued for an uninterrupted episcopal succession in the Church of England, whereas their predecessors, particularly William Whitaker, had urged an extraordinary vocation of the Elizabethan bishops, equating them thereby with the foreign Reformed churches and their ministry. Le Quien alleged this as evidence that the Lambeth Registers were forged, so far as related to Parker's consecration, and had been unknown to the Elizabethans.[2] Wake however was equally at pains to deny both the minor and the major premiss of this argument.

Is Father Le Quien sure that our writers since that period he refers to, of 1615, have given up the principles they allowed of before; not indeed with regard to the Church of England, but with respect to the Reformed churches abroad? We do, and we ought to value our own happiness that the Reformation was carried on regularly among us; that our princes and parliaments came in to it, and that thereby the succession and order of our bishops was happily preserved. But have our writers therefore abandoned the defence of the other Reformed churches, which can hardly be done upon any other principles than those which Le Quien says are now given up by us? No, by no means. Our writers still continue to affirm that their orders are not null, though they be not canonical; that their necessity excuses them; and that, though we think them defective in that respect, that they want an episcopal ordination, yet not so defective as utterly to un-church them. I have before shown how Bishop Andrewes defended our own episcopacy; let us see how he apologises for the French churches' presbytery.

There followed the well-known quotation from Andrewes; upon which Wake commented:

Thus cautiously did this great man allow of their presbyterian orders. But Mr Mason (the same Mason who produced the Registers of our episcopal con-

[1] *Biographia Britannica*, vol. VI, part 2, p. 4094. 9 July 1724.

[2] Michel Le Quien, *Nullité des Ordinations Anglicanes*, vol. I, pp. 330–3; *supra*, vol I, pp. 326–7, 335–6.

secrations, and so well defended that cause) was more bold and free. He wrote a treatise on purpose to maintain the validity of their presbyterian orders, and thought it no way inconsistent with his defending the succession of our English bishops by other measures, to vindicate the truth of the foreign churches' polity, by such principles as Le Quien imagines, but without any just ground, our divines from Mr Mason's time had utterly abandoned. And when in the year 1610 King James restored episcopacy in Scotland, and brought the persons he designed for their first bishops to be consecrated in England; and Bishop Andrewes moved, against their presbyterian orders, that they should first be made priests by episcopal ordination, before they were consecrated bishops, Archbishop Bancroft and the other bishops opposed it, and allowed the ordination they had received at home to be sufficient to qualify them for episcopal consecration. It is true this was some little time before Le Quien's period, but it shews what opinion our bishops had of this matter then; and I do not find they changed their principles afterwards. It is plain Bishop Andrewes, one of the most scrupulous among them, did not; for his letters to Du Moulin were written long afterwards, anno 1618.

And for the method of deducing the succession of the true church, not through the episcopacy of the Church of Rome, but through other separate societies, our learned Archbishop Ussher wrote a book, as Archbishop Abbot had done before, on purpose to show how the true doctrine had been continued in several countries by other faithful servants of Christ without passing through the channel of the Roman Church. How this and the other principles came to be more generally received soon after the time Le Quien marks for it than they had been before, may, I believe, be better accounted for from our own history than by Father le Quien's ungrounded supposition. Towards the end of Queen Elizabeth's reign, as there were several rigid professors in both our universities that went into the Puritan notions, such as Whitaker and Fulke at Cambridge, and Holland and Humphreys and Reynolds at Oxford; so were there others no less eminent that began openly to espouse the other way, more agreeable to the constitution of our episcopal church. Such were Bilson, and Andrewes, and Bancroft, but especially Buckeridge afterwards bishop of Rochester, and Laud, who beyond any other undertook the defence of it. The examples and influence of these great men, and especially of the last of them who in the following reigns was advanced to a very great height of power and authority in the church, influenced many more to espouse and defend these notions; so that by degrees it became a kind of party distinction. Those who followed the church-prelates and were for a strict conformity to the government and discipline of the Church of England, generally forsook the way of extraordinary vocation and an invisible church, and derived the succession of our bishops through the lineal descent of their Romish predecessors; they owned their priesthood to be true, though the Church in which they received it was corrupted with many dangerous errors and superstitions; that their orders were therefore valid and those who were consecrated by them, endued with a power to order and consecrate others. On the other hand such as were puritanically-inclined and enemies to the bishops and their government, and but half-conformists, if any at all, went into the other method; they followed the principles of Whitaker and Fulke, held the pope to be anti-Christ, and the Church of Rome to be anti-Christian, renounced not only the errors of it in doctrine, but its bishops and government, and thought they could be never more in the right than by running at the greatest distance that was possible from everything that belonged to it. The sum of all is: that in these particulars our divines have from the beginning gone their several ways; but yet so as not to have either given up our own episcopal succession and consecration on the one hand, or to have utterly condemned the establishment of the Reformed churches abroad on the other.[1]

But if the English primate in his correspondence with Le Courayer refused to abandon the cause of the foreign Reformed churches because of their lack of episcopacy, in his negotiations with representatives of those churches he omitted no opportunity of urging on them the desirability of receiving episcopal ordination both in individual cases and as an essential condition of corporate union. As a particular token of his zeal for such union and of his favour to the continental Reformed churches, he resolved to take one or two of their younger members into his household at Lambeth. In a letter of 1 March 1718/9 Professor Schürer referred enthusiastically to the Archbishop's expressed wish 'ad unionem et pacem cum exteris Ecclesiis fovendam et colendam identidem, se velle inter suos habere unum et alterum extraneum pro aliquo tempore'.[2] The experiment was begun in 1717 in the person of John Henry Ott, son of John Baptist Ott archdeacon of Zürich, who came to England to complete his theological studies at Oxford, and whom the primate proposed to take into his household,—'in familiam ac clientelam meam recipere'. Accordingly Ott was placed in the archiepiscopal library under the supervision of Dr Wilkins, and proved so apt in learning to speak and to write English and so acceptable personally, that Wake resolved to admit him to holy orders. In due season, therefore, Ott was ordained by the Archbishop personally at a private ordination in Lambeth Palace chapel to the diaconate on 4 June 1721 and to the priesthood on the 25th, and received the degree of M.A. on 27 March 1722.[3] It was the original intention both of the primate and of Ott that the latter should return to the service of the church at Zürich; but owing to contemporary Swiss controversies about subscription to the *Formula Consensus*, he preferred to remain in England, where his preferment was considerable and rapid. For his patron collated to him on 26 June 1721 the rectory of Blackmanstone in Kent, and during the following year also that of East Horsley in Surrey, which he resigned in 1723 on receiving presentation to the archbishop's option of the vicarage of Bexhill in Sussex. In 1723 also he was presented to another option as prebendary of Whittington and Berkswych in Lichfield cathedral, in 1728 he became a Six Preacher in Canterbury cathedral, and in 1730 there was collated to him a further option

[1] Arch. W. Epist. 11, f. 56. 13c–14.
[2] *Ibid.* Epist. 25, f. 147.
[3] Lambeth Act Books, VI, 370, 372; Arch. W. MSS. 330. (A list of ordinations, preferments, and consecrations performed by Wake.)

of the third stall in Peterborough cathedral. In return he rendered valuable service by his frequent visits to France and Switzerland, where he carried both letters and oral messages from the Archbishop and whence he brought back information on matters concerning union and theological discussions relating to reunion. The importance attached by Wake to this venture was expressed in a letter to Turrettini of 22 July 1719.

> I have often declared my intention, whenever Mr Ott leaves me, to take another gentleman of your country in his place, by whom to keep up a good correspondence with the Helvetian churches. Monsr Schürer has a brother, an ingenious and learned young man, whom he much desires may succeed Mr Ott; and indeed I shall not be averse to it. I have by Mr Ott got some interest in Zürich, which, whenever he returns, I hope he will increase rather than suffer to diminish there. If by Mr Schürer I can obtain the same at Berne, it may enable me to do the more good, if occasion should require, in those parts; which is all I desire or propose to myself by this management. And I verily believe those whom we breed, will carry back with them such an ingenuous notion and custom of thinking freely, and not censuring any for differing in matters not fundamental from themselves, as may in time enlarge the minds of others at home, and embolden them to search all things impartially, and so with good understanding hold fast to that which is right.[1]

The compliment was highly valued by the Antistes and ministers of Zürich, who sent several letters of thanks to the primate for his favour to Ott; and Professor Schürer and Berne much regretted that Ott's decision to stay in England deprived them of the privilege of establishing a Bernese as his successor.

Similarly James Horner, a Genevese who had received presbyterian ordination according to the order of the Reformed church and who subsequently became chaplain to Sir Luke Schaub in Paris, came to England to receive episcopal ordination, being admitted to the diaconate by the Archbishop at a private ordination in Lambeth Palace chapel on 25 November 1722 and to the priesthood on 2 December, and receiving likewise the degree of M.A. on 7 March 1724.[2] Nor was Wake's encouragement to foreign divines to receive episcopal ordination confined to those desiring to minister in the Church of England. He warmly approved of the practice by which students of the foreign Reformed churches who had come to England to complete their education, should be ordained according to the Anglican Ordinal, preliminary to their return to serve in the ministry of their native country. Thus he commended cordially to Turrettini in a letter of 25 March 1717 the example of the Genevese M. Jean Sarasin in this respect; expressing

> la satisfaction que j'ai eu de voir Monsr Sarasin commencer son Ministère dans l'Église Anglicane, et d'être Prédicateur de la Parole de Dieu à Londres, avant

[1] Geneva MSS. Inventaire 1569, ff. 69 *seq.*

[2] Lambeth Act Books VI, 421, 422; VII, 50.

qu'à Genève. C'est le meilleur preuve que nous pourrions avoir souhaité de votre Communion Fraternelle avec nous; et que bien loin de croire notre Episcopat un reste du Papisme qu'on n'a pas encore suffisament aboli, vous le regardiez plutôt comme un Ordre veritablement sacré et qui ne doit donner le moindre offence à aucun bon Chrétien.[1]

Likewise on 2 December 1719 he wrote to Bishop Robinson of London to ask him to ordain by letters dimissory on his own behalf Mr Paul L'Escot 'examinatus ad diaconatum', for the service of the French church at Dover.[2] These cases were typical of others in which Wake recommended the same course of action.

In the case of Mr Horner, some criticism was evoked by his re-ordination, as the Archbishop informed Père Le Courayer in pointing out to him that though the Anglican tradition recognised the foreign Reformed churches as having the essence of a church, it did not hesitate to recommend all opportunities of adding by episcopal ordination what belonged to the perfection of the church. 'I have ordained Mr Horner both deacon and priest', he wrote on 14 January 1722/3; 'and thereby received him into the ministry of the Church of England. This is a work that gives the most offence of any to the other reformed churches; but I must agree with you that I know no government older than Calvin's time, but what was episcopal, in the church of Christ.'[3] It is interesting therefore to observe the grounds on which Wake defended his practice to the foreign churches. In a letter to William Beauvoir of 2 June 1719 he bade him to inform the Dutch ambassador's chaplain that

though our constitution suffers no man to minister the Sacrament of the Lord's Supper who is not in priest's orders, nor otherwise to officiate in the church who has not the order of deacon by episcopal ordination; yet no one when he receives these orders, renounces his own which he had before taken, either in the foreign churches abroad, or even by our own dissenting ministrations at home. Nay, till the last Act of Uniformity, Casaubon, Vossius and many other foreign divines were actually preferred in our Church, and had no other besides their own orders.[4]

To the Genevese, however, in a letter of 5 December 1720 he offered a distinctly minimising interpretation of the Anglican doctrine of episcopacy. 'I believe the Church of Geneva has no exceptions against either our liturgy or our Thirty-nine Articles, even the 36th not excepted; which only asserts the validity of our Book of Ordination, but does not affirm the necessity of the three orders which we retain in our Church.'[5]

[1] Geneva MSS. Inventaire 1569, f. 43. [2] Rawlinson MSS. B. 376, f. 171.
[3] *Biographia Britannica*, vol. VI, part 2, p. 4094.
[4] Wake-Beauvoir Correspondence, Letter XXIX.
[5] Geneva MSS. Inventaire 1569, ff. 85 *seq.*

Closely associated with the question of the validity of presbyterian orders in the foreign Reformed churches was that of intercommunion between the Church of England and the continental Protestant churches in regard to the members of each church sojourning in the country of the other. In the case of Lutheran and Reformed churchmen from Europe visiting England, there was a general consensus that they should be welcomed to communicate with the Church of England. Bishop Peter Gunning of Ely, according to the account preserved by his chaplain, mentioned the prince of Orange and his retinue as joining in communion with the Ecclesia Anglicana 'as often as they have occasion to come over hither', and likewise 'any of their ministers and others of the Dutch churches' who were 'publicly permitted to come to our communion'. The same he affirmed of the French Protestants, adding that 'the same charity and concord is always shown to the Lutheran churches', and that 'the like concord I can show with the Helvetian, Hungarian, and Transilvanian churches'.[1] John Cosin during his exile in France maintained close relations with the Huguenots at Charenton, baptising their children, receiving them at the Anglican Holy Communion, and presenting Brévint and Durel, exiled pastors from the Channel Islands, for ordination as deacons and priests according to the Anglican Ordinal by Bishop Sydserf, as well as himself attending their public worship.[2] Similar testimony was given by Wake of his own custom when chaplain in Paris.

> As to our practice abroad, we went ordinarily every other Sunday to Charenton, but none of us ever received the Holy Eucharist there. In this way they were more free with us. I have given the Sacrament to some of their ministers publicly in their own chapel, and to Monsieur Menard in particular, while he was actually one of the pastors of the church at Charenton. By certificates from their ministers and antients (without which I never did it) I have baptised their children and buried their dead. And I never heard any exception taken against it.[3]

This religious practice became the basis of such political enactments as the Act of Settlement of 1701, which required that 'whosoever shall hereafter come into possession of this Crown, shall join in communion with the Church of England as by law established'; and in accordance therewith William III, Prince George of Denmark, the husband of Queen Anne, and George I of Hanover joined in this communion without renouncing their respective allegiance to the Reformed and Lutheran churches in which they had been bred. Similarly when in 1709 an Act was passed to naturalise foreign Protestants, there was a conflict between the Whig low-churchmen who

[1] W. Saywell, *Evangelical and Catholic Unity*, pp. 302–4; *A Vindication of Peter, Lord Bishop of Ely* (London, 1682).

[2] J. Cosin, *Works*, vol. IV, pp. 397–8 (L.A.C.T.).

[3] Ballard MSS. III, f. 40, Wake to Charlett, 21 April 1707.

desired as a condition of such naturalisation that the foreign Protestants should 'receive the Sacrament in any Protestant church' in Great Britain, and the Tory high-churchmen who wished them 'to receive that Sacrament according to the usage of the Church of England'.

All those that appeared for this comprehensive way [i.e. the Whig proposal] were reproached for their coldness and indifference to the concerns of the Church. Of this the bishop of Sarum [Burnet] had a large share; for when the bill was brought up to the Lords, he spoke copiously for it; whilst the Bishop of Chester [Stratford] spoke as zealously against it, who seemed resolved to distinguish himself as a zealot for that which was called high-church.[1]

The consensus of opinion concerning the admission of foreign Protestants to communion with the established Church in England disappeared, however, in regard to the vexed question of the reciprocation of this custom by Anglicans living abroad. In favour of reciprocity may be quoted Archbishop Ussher's affirmation that 'he would receive the blessed Sacrament at the hands of the Dutch ministers if he were in Holland, as he would do at the hands of the French ministers if he were at Charenton';[2] and the parallel statement of Archbishop John Sharp of York that 'if he were abroad, he would willingly communicate with the Protestant churches where he should happen to be'.[3] In like manner during the Interregnum, Cosin counselled communicating with the Huguenots in France, as did also Dean Granville of Durham during the later non-jurors' exile after 1689.[4] On the other hand, many of Cosin's fellow-exiles, including such influential names as George Morley, Bishops Bramhall and Sydserf, and Richard Steward gave much umbrage to the French Reformed by refusing all communion with them; whilst George Hickes illustrated in his own person the varying attitudes of English churchmen by communicating first with the Huguenots in 1673 at Blois and Charenton, and later declining at Montpellier, 'having by reading and conferring about the mission of the French Protestant ministers, altered his opinion'.[5] It is noteworthy that Wake during his chaplaincy at Paris never communicated with the Reformed church; and in 1707 he gave his reasons to the Master of University College, Oxford:

Our case as to a full satisfaction of communion with the foreign churches is in my opinion very different from theirs with respect to us. They cannot except against our ministry, nor the validity of the ordinances which may be supposed to depend upon it. Our clergy are certainly duly ordained, whatever theirs are who want

[1] *Parliamentary History* (ed. W. Cobbett), vol. VI, p. 783.

[2] A. J. Mason, *The Church of England and Episcopacy*, p. 122, citing Elrington, *Life of Ussher*.

[3] T. Sharp, *Life of John Sharp* (2 vols. London, 1825), vol. I, pp. 377–8.

[4] J. Cosin, *Works*, vol. IV, p. 407. R. Granville, *Life of Dennis Granville* (Exeter, 1902), pp. 200–3.

[5] A. J. Mason, *op. cit.* p. 322.

episcopal ordination. And though the case be vastly different between communicating with the Protestants abroad and our Separatists here at home, yet I believe no one who could have the opportunity of an episcopal church even in foreign countries, would make any doubt whether he should choose to partake of some of the gospel ministrations with that or with those of the presbyterian way. My charity leads me to think, and hope, and judge the best of them. But yet I cannot think them so conformable to at least the apostolical pattern and establishment, as if they were settled on the same episcopal constitution as our church is.[1]

It was a considerable step forward, therefore, from this position when as primate he inaugurated his rule by a formal approval and encouragement of reciprocal communion between members of the Swiss Reformed churches coming to England and members of the Church of England sojourning in Switzerland. By so doing he expressed in practical form his persuasion of the validity of the ministry and sacraments of the foreign Protestant churches. Moreover his action gave such a degree of formal approval as could attach to an express declaration of the archbishop of Canterbury, to a custom which had commended itself to some, though not to all, of his Caroline fellow-churchmen. So great was his zeal for Protestant union that he was prepared to offer this remarkable advance as a means of demonstrating his own sincerity and as an encouragement to his foreign brethren to go forward to the consideration of corporate union.

On their side also the half-century since the Peace of Westphalia had been fecund in projects and schemes of reunion, not only between the several Protestant churches, but also between Lutherans and Roman Catholics. During the first half of the seventeenth century John Dury had been an indefatigable and itinerant pilgrim in behalf of union, both on the European continent and in England, making himself too literally all things to all churchmen; since in England he had received episcopal ordination (having been already ordered according to the Reformed pattern abroad), had taken the Covenant and accepted membership of the Westminster Assembly, and had taken the Engagement when Independency ousted Presbyterianism! But although a tireless 'traveller in the cause of peace', he was too much a free-lance and too little supported by contemporary godly princes to bring any of his proposals to fulfilment. A more promising approach was that of the Spanish Franciscan, Christopher Rajas de Spinola, titular bishop of Tina in Croatia and afterwards bishop of Neustadt, who visited the court of Hanover in 1679 with the formal authorisation both of the emperor Leopold I and of Pope Innocent XI to seek means of healing the breach between Lutheranism and Rome. The elector of Hanover, John Frederick, appointed Lutheran theologians to meet him in conference, especially Gerhard Walter Molanus, abbot

[1] Ballard MSS. III, f. 83, Wake to Charlett, 4 June 1707.

of Lokkum; and although an interruption in the discussions was caused by the death of the elector in the same year, Spinola renewed his overtures in 1683 with the encouragement of the new elector, Ernest Augustus, and of the Duchess Sophia. Proposals were drawn up on both sides, and some agreement appeared to have been reached in the search for a compromise between their respective standpoints, as a means of establishing an interim programme of union pending the summons of a General Council to determine the bases and conditions of ultimate reunion. Meanwhile the lay theologian and historian Leibnitz had compiled in 1683–4 his *Systema Theologicum*, which has been justly described as 'the closest approach that Protestantism has ever made to Rome', being virtually a Protestant apologia for Roman Catholic doctrine and practice, and making considerable concessions on such controverted questions as the Real Presence in the Eucharist, the sacrificial character of the Mass, and the papal headship of the church.[1]

Moreover an even greater contemporary figure, namely Bossuet himself, had been drawn into the discussion from the Roman side, partly in the hope of enlisting the support of Louis XIV, and partly with a view to securing assent to the Gallican view of the papal supremacy based on the famous decree of the Council of Constance; and a protracted correspondence ensued between Leibnitz and Bossuet. From the outset the latter adopted the position that, whilst Rome might make concessions on matters which were not fundamentals of faith and on points of discipline, it could not allow any compromise on defined doctrines, including the definitions of the Council of Trent. It was upon this question of recognition of the oecumenical character of Trent that the interchange of views foundered; Leibnitz refusing to accept it as an oecumenical council, and insisting that Protestants could not consider union on the basis of the decrees of an assembly directed against themselves and without their having been represented in its deliberations; whilst Bossuet was equally emphatic that its decisions could not be called in question, acceptance of them being an 'articulus aut stantis aut cadentis' of the infallibility of the church. Notwithstanding the failure of practical results, the episode had been important for the very considerable concessions offered by Molanus and Leibnitz; and with its waning prospects of a successful outcome, the latter had turned his thoughts to the less comprehensive but more urgent question (thanks to international events during the last quarter of the seventeenth century) of the reunion of Protestants.

Within this narrower field the hopes and efforts of Leibnitz were directed chiefly to the Lutheran state of Brunswick and to the Calvinist Brandenburg; where success would evidently depend upon the leadership of the two

[1] G. J. Jordan, *The Reunion of the Churches; A study of G. W. Leibnitz and his great attempt*, (London, 1927), p. 109.

electors and upon the willingness of their principal theologians to co-operate, for the end envisaged was civil and ecclesiastical unity. It would be necessary therefore to establish agreement in fundamental matters of faith and to allow an agreement to differ on such theological questions as the doctrines of the Eucharist and of Predestination. In 1698 Bishop Ursinus and Daniel Ernst Jablonski from the side of Brandenburg conferred with Molanus and Leibnitz from the other side to seek a common ground in relation to doctrine, ceremonies, and the suggested name of 'Evangelical' for the united Protestant church; though toleration of not inconsiderable differences both of belief and practice would be essential to success. Unfortunately various circumstances combined to frustrate this endeavour; including the events of war, the consequent rise to positions of greater importance and influence of Brandenburg as the kingdom of Prussia and of Hanover by its succession to the crown of Great Britain, and also the reluctance of theologians to surrender the distinguishing doctrines of their denominational confessions. The university of Helmstedt indeed was the exception rather than the rule in the liberal sympathies of its professors; and the experience of previous conferences at Thorn in 1645 and at Cassel in 1661 was repeated, when Lutheran and Reformed theologians alike refused to approve differences of opinion on matters which they believed severally to be of importance. By the time of Leibnitz's death in November 1716 the bright hopes of even Protestant union had faded.

Before this date, however, Wake had become archbishop of Canterbury, and had assumed gladly the mantle of champion of Protestant unity. At the outset, unfortunately, he was confronted by formidable obstacles resulting from the recrudescence of theological controversy amongst Protestants, particularly within the Reformed churches of Switzerland concerning subscription to the *Formula Consensus.* This *Formula* had its origin in the general movement for the maintenance of sound doctrine which characterised the chief Protestant states and churches in the seventeenth century, as a defence on the one hand against Rome and on the other against rival Protestant confessions and especially against the sectaries; whilst in the background were the fears aroused by the philosophical and scientific trends of the latter half of this century. To this general tendency the Swiss Reformed churches and cantons were no exception; indeed they rather led the way in theological conservatism, and in particular Berne was pre-eminent in defence of orthodoxy. For, although the decrees of the Synod of Dort had not received official adoption at Berne as articles of faith, they acquired an increasing authority and influence amongst the leading Swiss theologians. Furthermore the relations between the Swiss academies and those of the French Reformed churches were close, and orthodox Swiss divines became alarmed lest the doctrines of Moses Amyraut and of other professors of the academy at Saumur, together with those of Coccius at Leyden and the general vogue of the philosophy of Descartes, should infiltrate into their own circles. Nor was this concern confined to the clergy. The civil authorities at Berne and Zürich espoused the cause of Calvinist orthodoxy, and the Venerable Company at Geneva took steps to safeguard purity of teaching amongst their number. Thus in 1669 the study of the works of Descartes was prohibited at Berne Academy; and in 1680 Berne extended this ban to the academy at Lausanne. The idea of formulating a further standard of doctrine as a means of opposing the propagation of novel teaching in theology came from Basle and Geneva; and accordingly, after deliberate correspondence between the theological professors of the leading Swiss faculties, there was constructed the famous *Formula Consensus Ecclesiarum Helveticarum Reformatarum circa Doctrinam de Gratia universali et connexa, aliquaque nonnulla capita*, which received formal sanction from the Diet of the four Reformed cantons at Baden in June 1675.

This *Formula* embraced a preface and twenty-six articles. The preface defined its purpose as the prevention of erroneous opinions tending to heresy and unorthodoxy in the Swiss Reformed churches, without reflecting upon or creating a schism from the unity of the Reformed churches abroad. The first three articles treated of the inspiration of the holy scriptures and the providential preservation of their text in such wise that the Old Testament books were authentic both in respect of consonants and vowels, as well as being divinely inspired alike in form and content. Articles 4–6 dealt with universal grace, stating the rigid Calvinist doctrines of predestination, election, and reprobation and refuting the mediatising position of Amyraut. Articles 7–9 were concerned with God's covenant with Adam before the Fall; and articles 10–12 with the divine imputation of Adam's sin to all his descendants. Next, the predestination of Christ as the mediator of salvation to and the redeemer of the elect only, was expounded in articles 13–16; and this was followed by the treatment in articles 17–20 of God's means of calling men to a saving knowledge of his will by natural religion and by the revelation through the Jewish and Christian dispensations. Articles 21 and 22 dealt with the impotence of that portion of mankind to whom the gospel had been preached, to repent and embrace its promises of their own will and power apart from the grace of the Holy Spirit; and articles 23–25 set forth the relationship of works and grace, in regard to the doctrine of justification, and to the dispensations of the Old and New Covenants. Finally the 26th article affirmed the general purpose of the *Formula* to preserve an orthodox profession of the Christian faith according to the Word of God, the *Confessio Helvetica*, and the decrees of the Synod of Dort, in the churches of Switzerland. Such was the main content of the *Formula Consensus* of 1675; and, although care had been taken deliberately to refrain from naming the authors of the heterodox and erroneous opinions therein refuted and therefore from any formal condemnation or anathematisation of them, there could be no doubt against whom its articles were directed. 'Son vrai titre, ainsi qu'on l'a remarqué avec raison, aurait dû être Formula AntiSalmuriensis, c'est à dire: formulaire opposé aux doctrines de Saumur.'[1]

The diet at Baden formally approved the *Formula* as a law and rule of the Swiss Reformed churches, and decreed that it should be added as an appendix to the *Confessio Helvetica*, that all professors and ministers must subscribe it, and that subscription should be required henceforth of all candidates for the ministry. Since, however, the document concerned only the Swiss Reformed churches, and was not intended to come to the official notice of foreign Reformed brethren, the diet decided that it should not be printed, but that its text should be communicated in writing to the civil and ecclesiastical authorities represented at the diet. By the end of 1675 the document had been generally accepted, almost without dissent, throughout the cantons and allied regions of German Switzerland, including Grisons; though at Basle the renowned Professor J. R. Wettstein refused his signature and was allowed to continue in office in virtue of a promise not to teach against its articles. More resistance was encountered in Romance Switzerland; where at Neuchâtel it was only agreed in 1676 after pressure from Berne that candidates for the ministry henceforth should sign a declaration engaging to preserve silence on the questions treated in the *Consensus* and to tolerate differences of opinion amongst their number; whilst at Geneva it was not until January 1679 and in consequence of considerable pressure from other cities, that the Venerable Company resolved to require signature in the following terms: 'Sic sentio, sic docebo, contrarium non docebo', and with a considerable latitude of interpretation of the first three articles relating particularly to the Hebrew text of the Old Testament. At Lausanne, however, upon receipt of mandatory orders from Berne, all the ministers signed the *Formula* by the middle of 1676 and the academy had accepted it by the end of 1676. Even so unanimity was not attained, nor controversy stilled. For the practice became increasingly tolerated by which ministers subscribed with various reservations, such as that allowed by the rector of Lausanne academy, in 1682: 'quatenus Scripturae consentaneae'.[2] Further difficulties followed with the influx into the neighbouring Swiss Reformed cantons of

[1] Henri Vuilleumier, *Histoire de l'Église Réformée du pays de Vaud sous le Régime Bernois* (4 vols. Lausanne, 1927–33), vol. II, p. 519. I have drawn freely on this authoritative and exhaustive history for details of the controversies in the Swiss Reformed churches concerning the *Formula Consensus*. Cf. Jacqueline E. de la Harpe, *Jean Pierre De Crousaz et le Conflit des Idées au Siècle des Lumières* (Geneva, 1955).

[2] [*Scil.*] huic Consensûs Formulae subscribit, *ibid.* p. 525.

Huguenot refugee-ministers after the revocation of the Edict of Nantes in 1685; and as a defence against the danger of infiltration of unorthodox pastors, Berne in June of the same year placed upon the Lausanne academy the duty of ensuring their subscription to the *Formula Consensus*, the *Confessio Helvetica*, and the Heidelberg Catechism as a condition of the exercise of their ministry; and in September required this subscription to be without reservations of any kind, both by natives and by strangers. This proceeding brought upon the Swiss evangelical cantons a formal diplomatic protest from Frederick William, elector of Brandenburg, the chief prince of the Reformed faith in the Empire, and an appeal not to divide the forces of Protestantism in its hour of crisis by insistence on subscription. In reply to this *démarche* Zürich explained politely that subscription simply placed the exiles on the same basis as natives of Switzerland, that it merely bound the signatories not to ventilate opinions contrary to the doctrine of the *Formula*, without requiring them to accept its provisions in conscience, and that such action was in no wise prejudicial either to the unity of the Reformed churches or to concord between Reformed and Lutherans. Under the influence of the elector's lead, however, Basle in 1686 silently ceased to require subscription to the *Formula*; whilst Zürich and Berne held stoutly to their practice of compelling signature. Not until 1706 did the qualifying reservation, 'quatenus S. Scripturae consentit Formula', reappear at Lausanne; and in the same year Geneva formally abolished the requirement of subscription; so that the *Formula Consensus* remained in suspended animation, with Berne watchful against any novel evidences of heterodoxy as a result of these concessions.

During the interval since the framing of the *Formula* moreover, the Swiss Reformed churches had experienced the rise of a movement, called by the historian of the pays de Vaud *l'orthodoxie libérale*, which was closely akin in fundamental principles to the latitudinarianism of the contemporary Church of England. The leaders of this movement were a triumvirate from west Switzerland, Samuel Werenfels (1657–1740), professor first of rhetoric and then of theology at Basle, Jean Frédéric Ostervald (1663–1747), pastor of the collegiate church at Neuchâtel and supervisor of a company of ordinands of that city, and Jean Alphonse Turrettini (1671–1737), professor first of ecclesiastical history (the chair in which subject was established for his occupancy) and then of theology at Geneva. Of this triumvirate Turrettini perhaps enjoyed the widest influence and reputation, thanks to his travels in Holland, France, and England, where he had enjoyed the entrée to the most distinguished society of the several capitals and in England had made the acquaintance of Tillotson and Burnet, and to the oecumenical correspondence which he maintained after his return home. Each of these divines distinguished between fundamental and non-essential doctrines in theology, and on this basis all were champions both in writing and by personal example of Protestant union, and entered into correspondence with Wake. Turrettini played an important part in securing the abolition of subscription to the *Formula* at Geneva; and the influence of the triumvirate had repercussions in various spheres of ecclesiastical activity, some of which gave rise to alarm at Berne. Thus at Geneva a new version of the metrical psalter (the work of Professor Pictet) was introduced in 1698, and Berne forbade its use within the territories subject to its suzerainty; and this was followed at Geneva by the publication in 1705 of a collection of about fifty Christian hymns for use as supplement to the psalter. At Neuchâtel in 1713 Ostervald introduced a new liturgy, which showed marked tendencies to decline from the standards of Calvin and to copy those of the Book of Common Prayer, and which was itself the culmination of a decade of liturgical experiment. When Ostervald had published at Geneva in 1702 a new catechism, dedicated to the S.P.C.K. (of which he had been admitted a corresponding member), his action had provoked the riposte from Berne of an order insisting on the exclusive use of the Heidelberg Catechism and the Little Catechism of Berne throughout its sphere of influence. Similarly Berne had instituted in 1698 a detailed enquiry into the theological orthodoxy of teachers and students at Lausanne; and upon receiving the report of its commissioners, ordered individual students whose opinions were suspect either to renounce their heresies, sign the *Formula Consensus*, and take a new oath in regard to doctrine, or to go into exile and suffer the removal of their names from the register of the academy. Two years later a new law for the regulation of the academy was promulgated, a considerable purge of its theological professoriate effected, and acceptance required henceforth of a new oath, *le Serment d'Association*, against novel opinions (specified as Pietism, Arminianism, and Socinianism) on the part of professors and ministers without any qualifying reservations. Despite this stricter supervision, conditional subscription reappeared at Lausanne from 1706 and in 1712 it was resolved to require signature in the form '*Non contrarium docebo*'; but in 1715 a new and more embittered phase in the long-standing controversy between Berne and Lausanne about subscription broke out, which was to involve the chief Protestant churches and rulers of Europe.

The occasion of this new dispute was to be found in the divergence of opinion on theological questions between a section of the ministers of the pays de Vaud and the academic professoriate of Lausanne. The predominant complexion of the academy was that of the new school of liberalism: 'On peut bien dire que dans le corps professorial, la supériorité qualitative non moins que la majorité numérique revenait aux amis du triumvirat helvétique, à ceux que leurs adversaires qualifiaient à tort ou à raison d'Arminiens.'[1] The pastorate on the other hand was orthodox and conservative; and various minor occasions of friction had occurred, such as the episode in the spring of 1715 when sixteen candidates for the ministry made only a conditional subscription to the *Formula Consensus*, 'quatenus Sanctae Scripturae consentit', before their ordination. This incident became the subject of a formal appeal on 13 June from the Classis at Morges to Berne for help in preserving orthodoxy of belief; and when Berne asked for details of the alleged offences, Morges replied on 24 September with the necessary information, but also with the recommendation that subscription only to the *Confessio Helvetica* without condition or reservation should henceforth be required as a sufficient test of all ministers. Meantime the Lausanne Academy, having been informed by Berne of these suspicions of its orthodoxy, sent a formal reply on 25 January 1716, defending conditional subscription to the *Formula Consensus* and rebutting the charges of Arminianism. The responsibility of decision between the professors and pastors was remitted to the academic senate at Berne, whose personnel comprised ten laymen, members of the Grand and of the Petit Conseils, and ten ministers, including both professors and pastors; and upon its recommendation the Lesser Council would determine what action should be taken. Accordingly by order of this Lesser Council in September 1717 a copy was taken from the register of the Lausanne Academy of all signatures and subscriptions to the *Formula Consensus*, by permission of the rector, David Constant, who acted, however, without consulting his colleagues. This was followed by the despatch early in December to the academy of five questions for answer: whether candidates for admission to the ministry took the Serment d'Association at their ordination; how it came to pass that the academy had authorised a conditional subscription to the *Formula Consensus*; under whose rectorship the practice of subscription with the qualifying *Quatenus* had begun; why the academy had not informed Berne of this; and what the opinion of the academy was on this matter? In its reply the academy affirmed that all its members, senior and junior, were under obligation to uphold the *Confessio Helvetica* (an implicit admission that the Serment d'Association was not required of ordinands at their admission to the ministry); that the first conditional subscription to the *Formula Consensus* had been on 5 October 1682 under the rectorship of M. Currit; that the academy had accepted such conditional subscription, and had informed the appropriate governing authority of its practice; and that a memorandum was being prepared in regard to the opinion of the academy on the whole question of subscription. The general tenor of this memorandum, sent to Berne about the middle of December, is sufficiently indicated by

[1] Vuilleumier, *op. cit.* vol. III, p. 633.

M. Vuilleumier. 'Il tendait à supplier le souverain de ne plus obliger ceux qui seraient reçus au saint ministère à signer le *Consensus*; ou à obtenir du moins qu'il leur fût permis de le faire sur certaines réserves.'[1] In particular, it affirmed that the differences of opinion between universalists and particularists did not touch the fundamentals of faith and were therefore questions on which divergencies of belief were legitimate; and it offered a trenchant and detailed criticism of several articles of the *Consensus*, defended conditional subscription, and argued that unqualified subscription would place an intolerable burden on the conscience of ordinands as well as creating barriers not only between Lutheran and Reformed churches but also between the Reformed churches themselves.

On receiving this bold and frank expression of the claim to liberty of interpretation in theological questions which did not concern the fundamentals of faith, the Bernese academic senate approved in February 1718 a formal rejoinder; which, however, owing to some unexplained oversight, was not communicated formally and officially to the Lausanne Academy, but became known there through the unofficial circulation of a private translation into French. This version expressed the regret of Berne that Lausanne should have challenged the authority of the *Consensus*, the provisions of which were especially necessary at a time when libertinism, Arminianism, indifferentism and naturalism were more than usually prevalent; and the articles of which, even if not directly relating to the fundamentals of faith, were ancillary and essential buttresses thereto. Moreover it was emphasised repeatedly that the distinction was well recognised between a *formula fidei* and a *formula doctrinae*, and that the *Consensus* did not aspire to compel belief but only to regulate teaching (as was evident from the terms of subscription: *sic docebo*, or *contrarium non docebo*). Therefore the maintenance of the *Consensus* was recommended, with a side-glance at the ill effects which had followed its abolition at Geneva. Notwithstanding the informal manner of transmission of this report, the Lausanne Academy resolved to return a formal reply, which was approved and despatched to Berne towards the end of March. In this rejoinder there was no cession of ground, but its tone was more ironical and provocative than hitherto; and accordingly the Bernese magistracy had to proceed to an authoritative pronouncement.

On 13 June 1718 the Petit Conseil announced its decision, which, deploring the outburst of controversial writings on both sides of the dispute and without entering into the merits of the arguments for and against the *Consensus*, imposed an absolute silence henceforth on both parties, and required that all persons ordained to the ministry must sign the *Consensus* without condition

[1] Vuilleumier, *op. cit.* p. 644.

or qualification on pain of exclusion from the ministry of the church. An unofficial interpretation, issuing from a well-informed personage at Berne but unconfirmed by authority, intimated that the *Consensus* could rightly be regarded as a *formula doctrinae*, not a *formula fidei*, subscription to which did not imply acceptance of its articles as a matter of interior belief but simply a pledge not to teach or preach in a contrary sense. On this understanding, the Lausannois candidates for the ministry, whose ordination had been deferred pending the decision of Berne, made their subscription and received imposition of hands. With this compromise it appeared as if the episode might have been ended. 'L'orage paraissait s'être dissipé.' Instead, 'ce ne devait être qu'un armistice'.[1]

The renewal of strife was due to a decision of Berne to hold a formal visitation of the Lausanne Academy, including both the professoriate and the pastorate of the city. During May 1719 four Bernese commissioners spent a fortnight in intensive examination, enquiring particularly about signature of the *Consensus*, about the Serment d'Association, and whether ordinands who had studied elsewhere were required to offer a confession of their belief and to subscribe to the *Consensus*. When the visitors, however, sought to engage the teachers of the academy in oral discussion of the suspicions of heterodoxy entertained against them, the academicians refused to allow this method of procedure, whilst expressing readiness to receive and reply to any written accusations. Although the delegates completed their visitation by the end of May 1719, their report was not ready until the beginning of 1720; after which an extraordinary series of complications and obstacles delayed the consideration of its recommendations by the Lesser Council for a further two years! Not until January 1722 did this body present to the Council of Two Hundred for confirmation its recommendations that subscription to the *Consensus* and the Serment d'Association should be enforced on all teachers and pastors of the pays de Vaud in the same manner and sense as they were accepted at Berne; and that a deputation should be sent to Lausanne to execute this decision. But the unprecedented protraction of the dispute had ensured for it meantime the widest publicity. A vigorous and extensive debate of the principles at issue had been conducted in book, sermon, pamphlet and article, not only within the Swiss confederation but also without, notably in Holland and Germany. Even more important, the friends of the Lausannois, both in Switzerland and in other countries, regarding the continuance of the conflict as unseemly in itself and particularly harmful to the cause of Protestant union, hastened to offer their counsel and good offices as mediators; and amongst those desirous of helping in so good a cause none were more prominent or more influential than Turrettini at Geneva and Wake

[1] *Ibid.* p. 664.

across the English Channel. Nor was ecclesiastical authority alone invoked. For, true to the Westphalian principle of *cujus regio*, *ejus religio* the leading princes of Protestant faith were drawn into the controversy in support of their common tradition; and in particular the sovereigns of Great Britain and of Prussia were induced to lend their official countenance to the endeavours to bring Berne, if not to reason, at any rate to compromise.

The interest and thereby also the intervention of Wake in these distressing controversies was a natural and almost inevitable consequence of his friendship and correspondence with the leading divines of Berne, Zürich, Geneva, Lausanne and Basle. Granted the degree of intercourse which he maintained with these Swiss universities, it was to be expected that he would be informed of the conflicts from their early stages, that he would express, privately at first, his concern for their settlement and his opinion of the principles of such solution, and that from private counsels he would pass insensibly to more formal advice and official intervention. During the visit of Professor Schürer of Berne to England in 1717 and his reception by the Archbishop, it would appear that the incipient disputes were discussed; and that the visitor carried home a letter of salutation to his brethren in which Wake expressed his conviction that in the interests of peace and the hopes of unity amongst Protestants, it was unwise to insist on unanimity in obscure points of theology which could not be regarded as fundamentals of faith.[1] In the following year, however, Turrettini brought this question into the forefront of interest by a long letter of 6 January 1718, in which he gave a brief sketch of the history of the *Formula Consensus* and of the beginnings of the Lausanne-Berne bickerings concerning subscription.[2] In his reply of 24 February, the Archbishop outlined the position which he was to expand in many subsequent and longer letters and to reaffirm with inexhaustible patience and diligence to all parties to the controversy.

I am very sorry for the controversie you mention, which is risen up in the Evangelical Cantons. I heartily wish it may come to a peaceable end; which in my opinion such affairs can never do, unless more libertie be allowed in point of subscription of such sort of formularies than most churches seem willing to consent unto. The moderation of the Church of England has been very exemplary in this respect; and we have felt the good effect of it in that peace we enjoy among our ministers, notwithstanding their known difference of opinion in many considerable articles of Christian doctrine. The 39 Articles, published about the beginning of the reign of Queen Elizabeth and collected from those which had been set forth in the last year of King Edward VI, with several prudent amendments with respect to the end I am now speaking of, have been subscribed more than once in our public synods, indifferently, by bishops and clergy of different persuasions. We have left every one to interpret them in his own sense; and they are indeed so generally

[1] Vuilleumier, *op. cit.* p. 659.   [2] Arch. W. Epist. 31, f. 53. 6 Janvier 1718.

Plates II, III, IV

Plate II shows part of the rough draft of Wake's letter to Professor Jean Alphonse Turrettini of Geneva dated, by the covering letter, 25 July 1718.

Plates III and IV show part of the fair copy of the same letter, sent to Geneva.

(The contents of this letter are described on pp. 34–7)

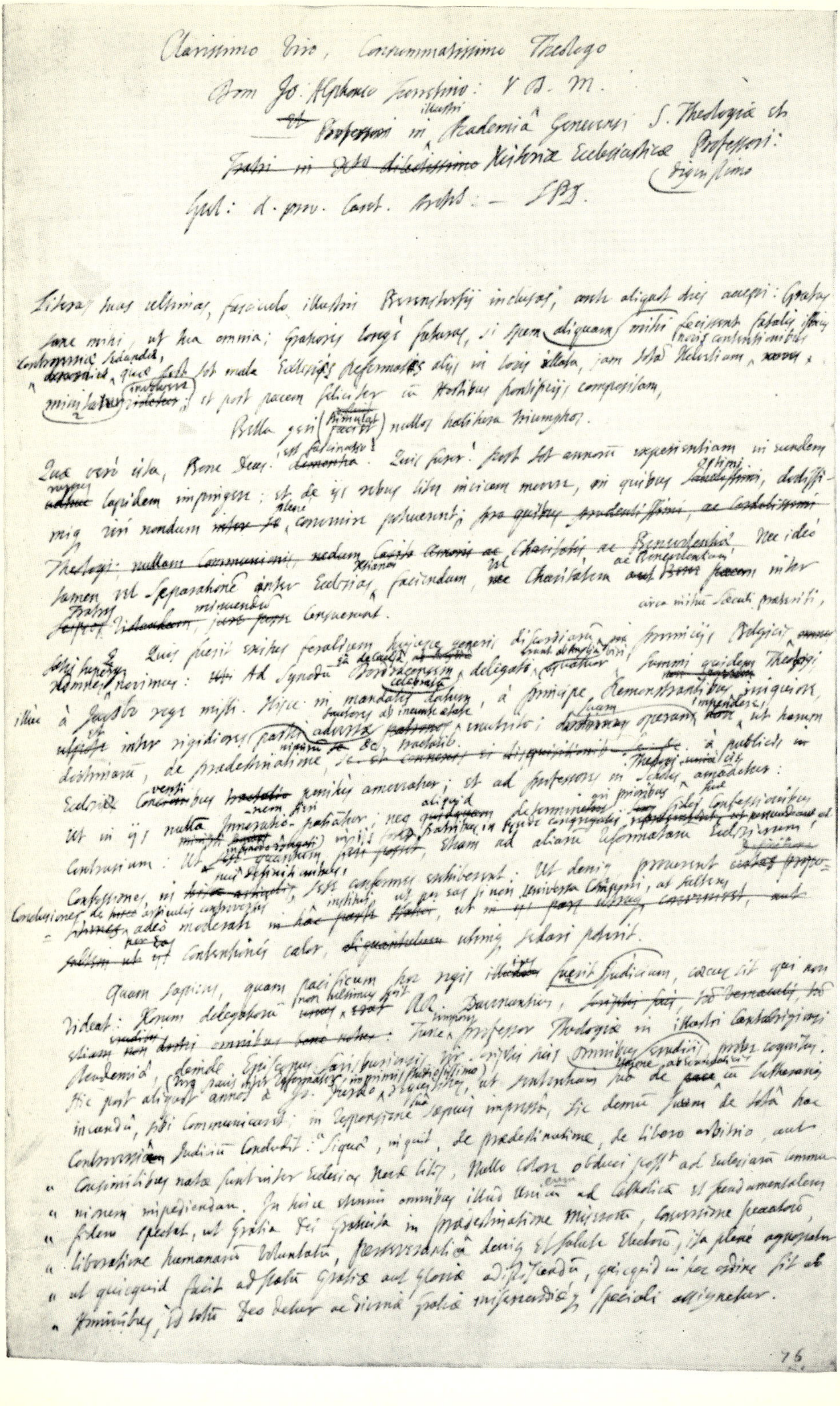
Clarissimo Viro, Consummatissimo Theologo

Dom. Jo. Alphonso Turrettino: V. D. M.

in illustri Academiâ Genevensi S. Theologiæ et Historiæ Ecclesiasticæ Professori: dignissimo

Guil. d. prov. Cant. Archiep. — SPD.

Literas tuas ultimas, fasciculo illustri Bernstorfij inclusas, ante aliquot dies accepi: Gratas sane mihi, ut hæc omnia; Gratiores longè futuras, si spem aliquam mihi fecissent fatalis istius Controversiæ sedandæ, quæ post tot mala Ecclesijs Reformatis alijs in locis illata, jam ipsam Helvetiam novis contentionibus [illegible] minitatur turbare; et post pacem feliciter cum Hostibus pontificijs compositam,

Bella geri (simulat / placet) nullos habitura triumphos.

Quæ verò ista, Bone Deus! est fatuitas! Quis furor! Post tot annorum experientiam in eundem lapidem impingere; et de ijs rebus liti iterum movere, in quibus optimi, doctissimique viri nondum alone convenire potuerunt, [illegible] Charitatis, ac Benevolentiæ. Nec ideò tamen vel Separationem inter Ecclesias Christianas faciendum, vel Charitatem ac Benevolentiam inter Fratres minuendam [illegible] consuerunt.

Quis fuerit exitus feralium hujusce generis dissidiorum et simultatum, Belgicæ, circa initium Seculi præteriti, [illegible] Ad Synodum Dordracenam [illegible] delegati [illegible] summi quidem Theologi, illuc à Jacobo rege missi. Hisce in mandatis datum, à principe, Remonstrantibus iniquiores, [illegible] ut tamen [illegible] doctrinam de prædestinatione, [illegible] à publicis in Ecclesiâ concionibus amoveatur; et ad professores in Scholis amandetur: Ut in ijs nulla innovatio fieri patiatur; neq aliquid determinetur [illegible] Confessionibus [illegible] Contrarium. [illegible] Confessiones [illegible] Conclusiones de hisce articulis controversis [illegible] adeò moderati [illegible] per eas contentionis calor utrinq sedari possit.

Quam sapiens, quam pacificum hoc regis ipsius fuerit Judicium, cæcus sit qui non videat: Horum delegatorum [illegible] fuit Ad. Davenantius, [illegible] Tunc temporis professor Theologiæ in illustri Cantabrigiensi Academiâ, deinde Episcopus Sarisburiensis, vir [illegible] omnibus eruditis probe cognitus. Hic post aliquot annos à Jo. Duræo [illegible] ut sententiam suam de pace cum Lutheranis ineundâ, ipsi communicaret; in Expositione sæpius impressa, sic demum suum de totâ hac Controversiâ Judicium concludit: "Siquæ, inquit, de prædestinatione, de libero arbitrio, aut
" consimilibus natæ sunt inter Ecclesias Nostras lites, Nullo colore obduci possunt ad Ecclesiarum commu-
" nionem impediendam. In hisce etenim omnibus illud unicum ad Catholicam et fundamentalem
" fidem spectat, ut Gratia Dei Gratuita in prædestinatione miserorum, conversione peccatorum,
" liberatione humanarum voluntatum, perseverantiâ denique et salute Electorum, ita plenè agnoscatur,
" ut quicquid facit ad statum Gratiæ aut Gloriæ adipiscendum, quicquid in hoc ordine fit ab
" hominibus, id totum Deo debeatur ac divinæ gratiæ misericordiæ speciali adscribatur.

76

Clarissimo Viro, Consummatissimo Theologo, 177
Domno Jo: Alphonso Turretino, V. D. M.
In illustri Academiâ Genevensi S. Theologiæ, & Historiæ Ecclesiasticæ,
Professori dignissimo:
Gulielmus providentiâ divinâ Archiepiscopus Cantuariensis &c
S. P. D.

Literas tuas ultimas, fasciculo illustris Berenstorfij inclusas, ante aliquot dies accepi: Gratas sane Mihi, ut tua Omnia; Gratiores longe futuras, si Spem mihi aliquam fecissent fatalis istius Controversiæ Sedandæ, quæ post tot Mala Ecclesijs Reformatis alijs in Locis illata, jam Illam Helvetiam novis Contentionibus involvere minitatur; Et post Pacem feliciter cum Hostibus Pontificijs compositam,

Bella geri placuit, nullos habitura Triumphos.

Quæ vero ista, Bone Deus! est fascinatio! Quis furor! Post tot annorum Experientiam in eundem rursus Lapidem impingere: Et de ijs Rebus lites invicem movere, in quibus Optimi, Doctissimiq Viri, nondum plene Convenire potuerunt: Nec ideo tamen vel Separationem inter Ecclesias Xtianas faciendam, vel Charitatem ac Benevolentiam, inter Fratres minuendam, censuerunt.

Quis fuerit Exitus feralium hujusce generis discordiarum in provincijs Belgicis circa initium Sæculi præteriti, Omnes satis superq novimus. Ad Synodum Dordra=
= cenam, eâ de causâ celebratam, delegati erant ab Angliâ quatuor Viri, Summi quidem Theologi, illuc à Jacobo rege missi. Hisce in mandatis datum, à Principe Remonstrantibus iniquiore, et inter rigidiores adversæ partis fautores ab ineunte
„ ætate enutrito; Operam suam impendere,* ut harum Doctrinarum, de Prædestina
„= tione nimirum &c. tractatio, à publicis Ecclesiæ Conventibus penitus amoveatur,
„ et ad Professores in Scholis Theologicis amandetur.* Ut in ijs nullam Innovationem

"fieri patiantur; nec aliquid determinari prioribus fidei suae Confessionibus Contrarium.
*"Ut quantum in iis foret, Fratribus in Synodo Congregati persuadeant, ut etiam ad
" aliarum Ecclesiarum Reformatarum Confessiones, in suis definitionibus, sese Conformes
" exhiberent.* Ut denique procurent Conclusiones de Articulis Controversis adeo moderate
" institui, ut per eas si non universa componi, at saltem Contentionis Calor utrinque
" sedari poterit. Quam sapiens, quam pacificum, hoc Regis illius Judicium
fuerit, Caecus sit qui non videat. Horum Delegatorum non ultimus fuit RR. D.
Davenantius, tunc temporis Professor Theologiae in illustri Academia Cantabrigiensi, deinde
Episcopus Sarisburiensis; vir Scriptis suis omnibus Eruditis probe cognitus. Hic
post aliquot annos a Jo. Duraeo, viro pacis inter Reformatos imprimis Studi-
=osissimo, requisitus, ut Sententiam suam de Unione ab Evangelicis cum Lutheranis
ineunda, Sibi Communicaret; in Responsione sua saepius impressa, Sic demum
suum de tota hac Controversia judicium concludit. —"Siquae, inquit, de
" Praedestinatione, de libero Arbitrio, aut Consimilibus, natae sunt inter Ecclesias
" novae lites, Nullo colore obduci possunt ad Ecclesiarum Communionem impedien-
"=dam. In hisce etenim Omnibus, illud Unicum ad Catholicam, et Fundamentalem
" fidem, spectat, ut Gratia Dei gratuita in Praedestinatione Miserorum, Conversione
" Peccatorum, liberatione humanarum voluntatum, perseverantia denique et salute
" Electorum, ita plene agnoscatur, ut quicquid facit ad Statum Gratiae aut Gloriae
" adipiscendum, quicquid in hoc Ordine fit ab Hominibus, id solum Deo detur,
" ac Divinae Gratiae Misericordiaeque speciali assignetur. E contra, Quicquid ad
" Corruptionem Humanae Naturae, quicquid ad Obstinationem in peccato, quicquid
" ad liberi Arbitrii vitiositatem et Servitutem spectet, quicquid denique ad
" Ultimam Damnationem ducit miseros Mortales, et in Gehennam praecipitet,
" id Omne Nobis, nostrisque demeritis imputetur, et a Deo longe facessere jubeamus.

framed, that they may, without an equivocation, have more senses than one fairly put upon them.

When in zeal against Arminianism, our learned Whitaker then professor of divinity at Cambridge, would have had a more decisive subscription to the five articles and by his interest got even my great predecessor Archbishop Whitgift into the design; and at a meeting at Lambeth-house some articles were drawn up by a select number of persons chosen for that purpose, all the interest of the Archbishop could not bring the Queen to allow of it; nay, they had all of them like to have paid severely for the attempt.

In the University of Oxford, Archbishop Laud being at the head of the Arminian and Archbishop Abbot of the other party, lectures were read and disputes held, and the sense of the Articles of the Church of England alleged on both sides. The learned men in their sermons treated of these points; and a ferment was raised which might have thrown us into great confusions. But the King interposed, commanded a cessation of war on both sides; and orders were issued that these matters should not be preached upon by any but men of the first rank either in the academical degrees or in the dignities and preferments of the Church.

It was for the same reason that King Charles I caused the 39 Articles to be republished by his authority, with the famous declaration before them, forbidding private persons to interpret them in any one determinate sense of their own imposing; and requiring all subscribers to do it in the general words of the Articles, as they were drawn up by our synod. And our most eminent divines have many of them thought, and even declared it in writing, that these Articles were designed by the Church rather as articles of public peace, and to set bounds to men's preaching or writing or instructing the people, than as doctrinal points to be professedly believed by every minister of our Church; a sense which, if allowed, no one can complain of any hardship put upon him, by his being required to subscribe to them.

I do not mention these things, as if I equally approved myself of them. But this I own, that the main articles of Christianity being secured by the creeds of the church; the public worship by a sound and orthodox liturgy; and the clergy by a larger formulary obliged not to preach or write anything contrary to what has, in the judgement of the body of the ministers and pastors of every church, been approved of, as most agreeable to the holy scriptures; I think it sufficient for men to be obliged to declare their own faith and assent only to what is most clear, and certain, and necessary for every one who is to be admitted to any office in the church; and for matters of a more doubtful nature, to be obliged not to make any opposition, nor by preaching, writing or otherwise, to contradict the received doctrine or usages of churches with which he communicates, without being forced to an explicit declaration of his own judgement in such matters; in which he may innocently differ from others of his brethren and yet be a very useful man in the church of Christ.[1]

This letter made so profound an impression on Turrettini that he urged the Archbishop to cast his thoughts into a more formal composition, so that,

[1] Geneva MSS. Inventaire 1569, f. 41. 24 February 1717/18.

if occasion offered, they might be communicated to some persons at Berne with a view to securing an amicable settlement of the trouble. Accordingly on 30 June 1718, in a covering note to accompany a formal Latin memorandum, Wake described his purpose in taking this further and more official step towards intervention.

In pursuance of your desires more than out of any vain conceit that either my reasons or authority will have any weight with the contending parties in the Canton of Bearn, I have here enclosed a Latin letter upon that occasion, to be wholly disposed of as you think it will best answer the ends of peace and mutual forbearance which are aimed at in it. I have adjoined some extracts out of our public Acts which may serve to shew what has been the sense of our Church and nation as to these points, ever since the Reformation. If they may be of any use on this unhappy occasion, I shall heartily bless God for whatever good I am able through his grace to do in any part of his church. If they are of none, it is but a little trouble lost to both of us; and I am sure you will have the goodness to excuse what I have in great measure attempted at your own desire.[1]

The enclosure was a Latin letter of six sides, with *pièces justificatives* covering four sides, which began by lamenting the prospect of further troubles and divisions within the Reformed churches, thanks to the recrudescence in Switzerland of controversy on matters wherein theologians had never been unanimous and which in themselves were not sufficient grounds for breach of ecclesiastical unity or Christian charity. The Archbishop then recited the instructions given by James I to the four English delegates to the Synod of Dort, which were set down first in Latin and with the English original in the appendices. The purpose of this citation was to show James' zeal to prevent such abstruse theological points from being the subject of popular sermons, to avoid innovations, to preserve harmony between the several Reformed churches and to ensure that any definitions made were 'moderately laid down' and such as tended 'to the mitigation of heat'. To enforce this lesson, Wake next transcribed a lengthy quotation from Bishop John Davenant (one of the original delegates at Dort), in which the author contended that the essential purport of the decrees of the synod was as follows:

For in all these matters this alone concerns the catholic and fundamental faith; that the grace of God freely given in the predestination of the wretched, the conversion of sinners, the liberation of human wills and finally in the perseverance and salvation of the elect, should be so fully acknowledged, that whatsoever makes for the attainment of a state of grace or glory, and whatever of this nature is done by men, should be ascribed wholly to God and assigned to special divine grace and mercy. On the other hand, whatever leads wretched mortals to the corruption of human nature and casts them into Hell, all this we should impute to ourselves and

[1] Geneva MSS. Inventaire 1569, f. 49. Arch. W. Epist. 25, f. 77. The former is dated 30 June (O.S.) 1718; the latter 25 July 1718. The content of both is identical.

our demerits, and should deem to be far from God's doing. So long as these points remain fixed and unmoved (as in truth they do remain), although men may have different ways of thinking and speaking concerning doctrines built upon this foundation, nay even though they pursue different opinions, errors of this nature are not therefore so fundamental that on account of them mortal hatred should be developed between churches or a perpetual schism fostered.[1]

Furthermore, decrees of French Huguenot synods could be cited in support of the same position; and when in England, which also had its 'rigidiores quosdam theologos quibus nihil moderatum in hac parte placeret', similar controversies arose, authority intervened to control the protagonists. In illustration of this the primate again cited the episode of Dr Whitaker, Archbishop Whitgift and the Lambeth articles of 1595, and the interventions of James I and Charles I to stop the spread of controversy (of which excerpts were given in the appendices); and rejoiced in the success attending their efforts to put an end to vain disputations.

Blessed be God, who by such a care for these matters has so ordered the issue that no public disagreement now remains any further amongst us concerning these inscrutable mysteries of divine wisdom and power; nor is it reckoned an offence in any one privately to differ in opinion on these matters. In our churches a complete silence is preserved before the faithful in regard to the divine decrees. The issues of predestination, election, reprobation, and the universality, efficacy, resistibility or irresistibility of grace are rarely treated, except incidentally and without any spirit of contention.[2]

In proof of which Wake recalled his undergraduate years at Oxford when the Regius Professor of Divinity, Dr William Jane, not only declared in his inaugural lecture his intention to avoid such subjects and not to reveal his own opinion, but succeeded in doing this; so that, 'although this most worthy professor was always regarded as inclining to the stricter side, yet as a prudent man and a lover of peace, he would not suffer anything to be deter-

[1] In hisce etenim omnibus illud unicum ad catholicam et fundamentalem fidem spectat: ut Gratia Dei gratuita in praedestinatione miserorum, conversione peccatorum, liberatione humanarum voluntatum, perseverentia denique et salute electorum, ita plene agnoscatur, ut quicquid facit ad statum gratiae aut gloriae adipiscendum, quicquid in hoc ordine fit ab hominibus, id totum Deo detur ac divinae gratiae misericordiaeque speciali assignetur. E contra, quicquid ad corruptionem humanae naturae ducit miseros mortales et in Gehennam praecipitat, id omne nobis nostrisque demeritis imputemus et a Deo longe facessere jubeamus. Dum haec fixa manent immotaque (uti revera manent) quamvis in doctrinis fundamento superstructis diversos habeant concipiendi aut loquendi modos, imo quamvis diversas sententias sequantur, non sunt hujusmodi errores adeo capitales ut propter eosdem capitale odium inter Ecclesias foveri aut perpetuum schisma nutriri oporteat.

[2] Benedictus sit Deus qui hac eorum cura eo res perduxerit, ut nulla jam amplius supersit inter nos publica discordia de inscrutabilibus istis mysteriis sapientiae ac potentiae divinae; neque in illis privatim ab invicem dissentire alicui crimini datur. In ecclesiis nostris de decretis divinis altum coram populo silentium. De praedestinatione, electione, reprobatione, de universalitate, efficacia, resistibilitate, irresistibilitate gratiae, raro, nec nisi obiter et absque spiritu contentionis, tractatur.

mined publicly which might give occasion to any one for reopening a dangerous controversy'.[1] In order that this recital might not be purely historical and impersonal, the Archbishop stated unequivocally his own agreement with Davenant. 'If you wish to know my own opinion on this matter, for what it is worth, I will declare it plainly. I agree entirely with Davenant, and I freely subscribe to his above-cited words. Would that we might all think the same, and that, granted the fundamental articles of religion be always preserved, we might require nothing further to be subscribed by any one.'[2] Such restraint indeed was essential to the Protestant churches in view of their common enemy, Rome, which rejoiced in every sign of disunion amongst its rivals; and the Swiss cantons should recognise their responsibility in regard to Protestant unity and the danger of giving further advantage to Rome by their actions in respect of the *Consensus*.

If therefore these articles concerning which a dispute is already being waged between the citizens of Berne and Lausanne may to all appearances not only cause factions, hatreds and enmities in the Swiss churches, but also prove an obstacle to that union of all the reformed churches which is so greatly desired by every one; if all the Lutherans in Germany, Denmark and Sweden, and by far the greatest part of the Churches of England and Ireland will most certainly demand a greater freedom of opinion in these matters; and if even in the Evangelical churches themselves of Belgium, Switzerland and Germany, very many will find an occasion of offence, if not actually of schism, it may be left to the consideration of any discerning judge of these things whether it would not be much wiser to forestall those evils betimes, than, as the saying is, to be wise too late, and when the disease has grown too grave, to apply remedies in vain.[3]

Accordingly the other Swiss Reformed churches, both professors, pastors and magistrates, beginning with Geneva and drawing others to follow their lead, should mediate to restore peace between Berne and its neighbours; seeking to establish the sufficiency of subscription to the Helvetic Confession of 1566,

[1] Tamen professor hic dignissimus in duriorem partem inclinasse semper habitus fuit; sed vir prudens, ac pacis studiosus, noluit quicquam publice determinari, quod periculosae litis movendae occasionem alicui praeberet.

[2] Quod si meam etiam qualemcunque opinionem in hac causa scire cupias, aperte dicam. Cum Davenantio nostro prorsus sentio, verbisque ejus supracitatis lubens subscribo. Utinam sic sentiremus omnes. Et, fundamentalibus religionis articulis semper salvis, nihil ultra ab aliquo subscribendum requireremus.

[3] Si igitur hi articuli de quibus jam inter Bernenses et Lausannenses disceptatur, non tantum in ecclesiis Helveticis factiones, odia, inimicitias, excitare verisimiliter possint; verum etiam unioni omnium ecclesiarum Reformatarum, ab omnibus tantopere exoptatae, impedimento esse; Si Lutherani in Germania, Dania, Suecia, omnes; Ecclesiarum Angliae at Hyberniae pars longe maxima, his in rebus liberiorem sentiendi facultatem certissime postulabunt; et in ipsis Ecclesiis Evangelicis, Belgicis, Helveticis, Germanicis plurimi hinc offensionis, si non et schismatis, occasionem captabunt; cuivis aequo rerum aestimatori considerandum relinquitur, an non multo consultius foret malis istis mature occurrere, quam sero, quod aiunt, sapere; et ubi morbus nimium ingravescerit, medicinam frustra adhibere.

and prohibiting under severe penalties the maintenance in public speech or writing of opinions contrary thereto, whilst avoiding the multiplication of forms of subscription and too close enquiry into the private opinions of theologians and pastors, provided they refrained from public expression of contrary doctrines. In conclusion Wake defended this expression of his judgment as being that of a sincere friend of peace and of all the Reformed churches: 'sententiam quidem hominis nulla authoritate muniti...verum hominis pacifici, Ecclesiarum omnium Reformatarum, ac praecipue Helveticarum, amatoris fidelissimi'.[1]

By the time this memorandum had reached Turrettini, the episode at Lausanne appeared to have ended pacifically, by the subscription of candidates for the ministry to the *Consensus* as a *formula doctrinae* not a *formula fidei* in accordance with the decree of the Petit Conseil of Berne of 13 June 1718. No immediate use was made of Wake's letter therefore; and the Archbishop might have been spared further labours and intervention, had not the dispute flared up again by the decision of Berne to hold a formal visitation of Lausanne in 1719. When this decision threatened not only to destroy the delicate compromise but also to rekindle the controversy with much greater fury, renewed pressure was put upon him on this occasion to indite a more solemn remonstrance. In September 1718 Professor De Crousaz of Lausanne had informed Turrettini that in his opinion the subscription matter was far from settled, and that since the authority of Wake was much regarded at Berne, it would be necessary to persuade him 'nous prêter son secours'.[2] In December, therefore, Turrettini suggested that the Archbishop should take advantage of the forthcoming celebration of the bicentenary of the Reformation at Zürich to emphasise the urgency of Protestant union, and to add 'qu'un des meilleurs moyens serait de s'adoucir sur les matières de la Prédestination'.[3] On the other hand, the primate maintained his correspondence with Schürer, who assured him that the disputed articles were in agreement with Articles VII (Of the Old Testament), XVII (Of Predestination), XVIII (Of obtaining eternal salvation only by the Name of Christ), and XX (Of the Authority of the Church) of the Anglican Thirty-nine Articles, and defended them as being not *dogmata fidei* but only *docendi formulae*.[4] Notwithstanding, in view of the gravity of the position, Wake decided to accede to the request of Turrettini.

It may be doubted perhaps whether either De Crousaz or Turrettini anticipated the thoroughness or length of the treatise which resulted from

[1] Geneva MSS. Inventaire 1569, f. 177. Arch. W. Epist. 25, f. 76. Two short extracts are printed in Mosheim-MacLaine, vol. V, pp. 174–5.

[2] Arch. W. Epist. 31, f. 59. 4 September 1718.

[3] Arch. W. Epist. 25, f. 58. 1 December 1718.

[4] *Ibid.* f. 70. 'Idus April: 1718.'

their prompting. For the memorandum covered nine folio sides, mainly in Latin, but including some citations in English. It was described by its author indeed as 'farraginem incompositam'; but the modern reader will marvel rather at the pains and time bestowed upon its composition by one who was immersed in public business, as he said: 'perturbatus, interpellatus, raro solus, nunquam ab inquietantium turba securus, vix uno momento ad cogitationes colligendas concesso'. After an apology for his delay in replying to Turrettini's request of 1 December (his letter being dated 26 February 1718/19), the Archbishop expressed his regret that the dispute between Berne and Lausanne had not been allowed to drop, since the experience of the Church of England demonstrated the unwisdom of controversy on such obscure and doubtful matters. He was at pains to insist that it was no part of his intention to declare his own opinion on the points at issue:

> What may be my own opinion of these matters I have not hitherto openly declared to any one, nor will I lightly suffer myself to be induced to disclose it hereafter....In justice to myself therefore I require this of you at the outset, that you will in no wise deduce my own opinion on this question from what I am about to write hereby. I will set forth briefly what our most eminent bishops and theologians have concluded concerning the disputed articles of the *Consensus*; and that which, following their example, I believe it is necessary for your Bernese to do, I will candidly relate.[1]

This statement of the attitude of the Church of England, however, involved a sketch, in not inconsiderable detail, of the theological history of England from Elizabeth to Wake's own time, beginning with the Lambeth Articles of 1595. In order that the exact purport of these Articles might be understood, it was necessary to preface a record of the controversy at Cambridge between Whitaker, Baro, and Barret, of the appeal to Archbishop Whitgift, and of his measures to silence public disputation on these questions in pulpit and schools. The text of the Lambeth Articles followed; with the pointed reminder that even these articles were not designed for subscription or formal assent, but simply to ensure in the university

> that nothing should be publicly taught to the contrary; and that also in teaching them, discretion and moderation should be used; that such as should be in some points differing in judgment, might not be of purpose stung or justly grieved;...and that the propositions nevertheless must be so taken and used as their private judgments, thinking them to be true and correspondent to the doctrine professed in the Church of England, and established by the laws of the land; and not as laws and decrees.

[1] Quae mea sit de iis sententia, nec adhuc cuiquam aperte declaravi, neque ut deinceps patefaciam, facile me patiar induci....Pro jure igitur meo, hoc imprimis a te postulo, ne ex iis, quae deinceps scripturus sum, de mea in hac parte opinione omnino judices. Quid praestantissimi nostri episcopi atque theologi de controversis Consensus capitibus judicaverint, breviter ostendam; quid, eorum exemplo, Bernensibus vestris factu opus esse credam, candide referam.

In addition, Wake gave the full text of Baro's strictures on these Articles, and observed that notwithstanding this diversity of interpretation, no schism ensued within the church. Furthermore, when at the Hampton Court conference in 1604, Dr Reynolds in behalf of the Puritan delegates asked that the Lambeth Articles should be added to the official Confessions of the Church of England, and was opposed by Dean Overall from the other side, James I refused the request; and later issued a prohibition against the treatment of these themes by any preacher under the degree at least of bishop or dean, thereby in effect reserving all discussion of them for the universities.

Shortly afterwards controversy waxed furious concerning the opinions of Richard Montagu (of which the memorandum gave a detailed account with some quotations from his writings, in order to show the extent of the Arminian reaction against the Calvinist standpoint); until Charles I in turn prohibited further discussion, and reissued the Thirty-nine Articles with a preface forbidding any private interpretations of their doctrine to be offered. On this matter the King came into acute conflict with the House of Commons, which maintained the Calvinist position. Meantime the Irish Articles of 1615, adopted by the Convocation at Dublin, were strongly Calvinist in tincture and embodied the Lambeth Articles; and they remained the official standard of the Church of Ireland until Strafford compelled a later Convocation in 1634 to accept the English XXXIX Articles: 'ideoque illam Ecclesiam a manibus istorum Praedestinatianorum, quibus nihil moderatum placere potuit, penitus eripuit'. Since the Restoration, the Church of England had been virtually free from controversy on these points.

> In our universities and in our churches rarely, if indeed ever, are these topics treated, except in so far as it should be thought necessary for the practice of the Christian life. If any persons discuss them in writing, they have done so without any disturbance of public quiet and in most cases without any breach of private charity. Therefore to bring to an end at last this narrative which is already overlong, may I be allowed to apply to your situation one or two observations from what I have written, if indeed the judgment or example of our church has any weight with you?[1]

Principally, Wake wished to emphasise the moderation and reserve of the Anglican reformers of the sixteenth century in treating these recondite doctrines.

> They did not think that anything should be conceded to any one's curiosity; nor did they think it right to bind the faith of any one to the pious though uncertain

[1] In Academiis, in Templis raro, si tamen unquam, de iis tractatum, nisi quatenus ad praxin vitae Christianae necessarium judicaretur. Si qui de illis in scriptis disputarunt, id tamen absque publicae pacis violatione fecerunt; et plerumque absque privatae charitatis dispendio. Ideoque ut huic narrationi, jam nimium prolixae, finem aliquando imponam, liceat mihi unam aut alteram observationem, in rem vestram (si quam tamen vobiscum authoritatem habeat Ecclesiae nostrae vel judicium vel exemplum) ab iis quae supra scripta sunt, deducere.

hypotheses of men concerning the divine decrees. For they knew how inscrutable are the counsels of God, and by how great a distance they exceed all our thoughts. Therefore no less piously than wisely they confined themselves within their just limits, being neither wanting in those things necessary for the confirmation of our faith concerning these mysteries, nor officious in the definition of non-essentials.[1]

Wisdom herein had been justified of her children; for experience had taught the Church of England that this was the only way of preserving peace and avoiding schism; and the melancholy history of continental Protestantism reinforced the lesson. Thus the lengthy recital of Anglican history had a practical point. 'Such was our prudence, most beloved brother, and such should be yours. By this moderation we have preserved unbroken the peace of our Church from the very beginning of the Reformation. With the like reasonableness also your Bernese may compose their own disputes.'[2]

In the second and shorter part of his memorandum, the primate turned to continental Protestantism, pointing out that even amongst the delegates at the Synod of Dort, and likewise amongst subsequent expositors of its canons, differences of opinion had been recognised between supralapsarians and sublapsarians; in illustration and support of which contention he quoted from the published works of Bishop Davenant on the English side, and from the examples of Cameron and Amyraut on the Scottish and French sides. Moreover, the preface to the *Formula Consensus* admitted that both parties to the controversy were agreed in the fundamentals of belief on these very points, so that it was the more lamentable that the *Consensus* should endeavour to establish one interpretation, and that the more rigid, as alone legitimate. Even if it were granted, for the sake of argument, that the positions stated in the *Consensus* were true, nevertheless differences of opinion on such matters could not be reckoned as dangerous errors.

The greatest part of these articles therefore are of such a kind that it is allowable for all of us to differ from one another concerning them without loss of truth. For they are of such a kind in which God has not revealed his counsel either so clearly or precisely but that the most learned and perspicacious men may err in their statements of them, or rather cannot be sure that they have not erred.[3]

[1] Non illi curiositati cujusvis aliquid indulgendum putarunt; non piis, sed incertis hominum hypothesibus, de Decretis divinis, alicujus fidem alligare fas esse censuerunt. Sciebant quam inscrutabilia sint consilia Dei, et quanto intervallo omnes nostras cogitationes exuperent. Ideoque non religiose minus quam sapienter, inter justos terminos sese continuerunt, neque in necessariis ad fidem nostram de hisce mysteriis stabiliendam deficientes, neque in non-necessariis determinandis officiosi.

[2] Haec nostra, frater dilectissime, prudentia fuit; haec vestra esse debet. Hac moderatione nos pacem Ecclesiae nostrae ab ipso Reformationis exordio, sartam tectam conservavimus. Eadem ἐπιεικείᾳ etiam Bernenses vestri discordias suas componere valeant.

[3] Sunt igitur horum Articulorum pars maxima illius generis, in quibus ab invicem dissentire nobis omnibus liceat, absque dispendio veritatis. Sunt ejusmodi de quibus Deus consilium suum non adeo clare aut praecise revelaverit, quin etiam eruditissimi atque perspicacissimi viri in suis de iis determinationibus, errare possint; aut potius nunquam certi esse possint, se non errasse.

The severest censure therefore fell upon those who in such obscure matters denied to their fellows the liberty of interpretation which they claimed for themselves. Indeed some of the points of the *Consensus*, especially touching the text of the Holy Scriptures, were incapable of individual determination.

Who is of greater authority in Hebrew studies than Buxtorf and Capellus? and who can determine the issue joined between them about the authority of Hebrew points? Who can know exactly how far the holy scriptures as we possess them at this day, both as to content and as to their very words, are divinely inspired? Who will dare to pronounce what is the authority of the Septuagintal version, so much extolled by Isaac Vossius and others? Or what is the pre-eminence of the Samaritan codex?[1]

In such circumstances the path of wisdom for the Bernese would be to rest content with the Helvetic Confession of 1566, requiring all to adhere to its definitions, and leaving liberty of judgment in other points, even as the Synod of Dort itself recognised and allowed difference of interpretation. For, in conclusion, the Archbishop iterated that the matters here in dispute were *minutiora*. 'Indeed these points are too small for the unity of the church to be broken on account of them, or the conscience of any upright man to be burdened; and yet upon these *minutiae* almost the entire controversy amongst our Bernese brethren turns.'[2] It therefore behoved the Churches of England and Geneva, themselves happily free from such controversies, to mediate. 'For I indeed think it to be reckoned not the least part of my good fortune to preside over a church in which no dissensions about these abstruse questions are allowed....On other matters, indeed, we have frequent disputes, agitated with no small zeal of parties. But on these issues almost complete silence reigns.'[3] And so with a prayer to God to compose the minds of men to conciliation, and a reminder to the civil magistrates of Berne of their duty,

[1] 'Qui[s] in Hebraicis plus Buxtorfio atque Capello valeat, et de punctorum Hebraicorum authoritate litem inter illos contestatam definire? Qui[s] praecise sciat quousque S. Scripturae, uti eas hodie habemus, tum quoad res, tum quoad verba ipsa, sint θεόπνευστοι? Qui[s] pronuntiare audeat quae sit authoritas Versionis Septuaginta-Viralis, tantopere ab Isaaco Vossio et aliis depraedicatae? quae codicis Samaritani praestantia?'

[Johannes Buxtorf, junior, 1599–1664, Professor of Hebrew at Basle, maintained the antiquity of the Massoretic system of vowel-points; whilst Ludovicus Capellus, 1586–1658, Professor of Hebrew at Saumur Academy, contended that the Hebrew vowel points and accents were introduced some centuries after the beginning of the Christian era. Isaac Vossius, 1618–89, of Leyden, royal librarian at Stockholm, 1649–52, canon of Windsor, 1673–89, hon. D.C.L. of Oxford, supported the Septuagintal against the traditional Hebrew chronology. The Samaritan Pentateuch is that part of the Old Testament recognised as authoritative by the Samaritans at the time of the schism, probably about the middle of the fourth century B.C., and represents a Hebrew text maintained independently since the schism.]

[2] Sunt haec quidem minutiora, quam ut pro iis aut Ecclesiae unitas violetur, aut cujusvis probi hominis conscientia oneretur; et de his tamen minutis tota fere controversia inter fratres nostros Bernenses versatur.

[3] Ego sane in parte non ultima felicitatis meae ponendum censeo, quod in Ecclesia praesideam, ubi nulla de his tam abstrusis quaestionibus dissidia tolerantur....De aliis frequentes inter nos disputationes, nec absque nimio partium studio agitatae. In his altum fere silentium.

more Anglicano, to put an end to the unprofitable strife of theologians, Wake expressed the hope that 'brevis haec mea narratio' might be of some avail to this end. If so, he assured Turrettini, it would not have been written and read in vain; 'nec me operae meae in hac tam prolixa epistola scribenda poenitebit, nec te in perlegenda'.[1]

There can be no doubt that the memorandum was a remarkable document; not only, as Turrettini observed, for its 'détail très exact et très curieux', but also in certain other respects, which the Archbishop was to realise later, if not at the time of writing. On the one hand it stated unequivocally his own belief in the wisdom of allowing a wide latitude of opinion on matters not fundamental to salvation; but on the other it bore the implicit admission that only the strong arm of the civil magistrate had been able to impose peace by silence on the theologians of the Church of England. Moreover, though controversy concerning predestination had been stilled, other disputes were continuing, some of which related to the fundamentals of faith, such as those raised in the Deist and Trinitarian controversies; and Wake laid himself open to the rejoinder (which was to come from Zürich) that its latitudinarian policy of comprehensiveness had not saved his church from these dangers, which threatened the very citadel of revelation. Meantime Turrettini on 3 April wrote to the Avoyer of Berne to inform him in general terms of the two letters which he had received from the English primate and to offer an exact copy if desired.[2] On 8 April the Avoyer replied welcoming this offer, expressing the hope that he might be able 'en faire bon usage dans le dessein qu'on a de visiter l'Académie de Lausanne', and avowing himself in favour of moderation.[3]

But, as Turrettini observed in thanking the primate for his memorandum, Zürich, though not directly involved in the dispute with Lausanne, was strongly in support of Berne and even more rigid in its insistence on unconditional subscription to the *Consensus*. At Zürich indeed during the celebrations of the bicentenary of the Reformation, the Antistes had drawn somewhat painful parallels between the Anabaptists whom Zwingli combated in 1519, the Arminians whom the Züricher delegate at Dort, Breitinger, opposed in 1619, and the dangers in 1719 of 'un bouleversement général' of the church by a mixed multitude of heretics, pietists, enthusiasts, Amyraldists, Arminians, Socinians, rationalists and atheists![4] But worse was to follow; for Professor Hoffmeister, continuing the melancholy theme of the flood of heresies which menaced the church, quoted some passages from a letter of

[1] Geneva MSS. Inventaire 1569, f. 53; a foul copy in Arch. W. Epist. 25, f. 57; and a few short extracts in Mosheim-MacLaine, vol. v, pp. 176–7.

[2] Arch. W. Epist. 31, f. 68.

[3] *Ibid.* f. 68b.

[4] *Ibid.* f. 65. Turrettini to Wake, 19 April 1719.

Wake to the Antistes, in which the primate had expressed vigorous disapproval of the protagonists in the Bangorian and Trinitarian controversies, and whose testimony the professor used to demonstrate the necessity of such barriers as the *Consensus* to preserve orthodoxy in the Swiss churches. Nor did the episode lack piquant consequences when a report of the speech, including its citations from the primate's letter, obtained circulation in England.[1]

On 10 January indeed the Antistes, J. L. Neuschler, who had succeeded the late Peter Zeller in that office, had insisted that in face of the number and variety of contemporary heresies, the Zürich theologians would not consent to the abolition of the *Consensus*: 'Ecclesiae saltem nostratis theologi consentient nunquam,...ut subscriptio Formulae Consensus tollatur a medio.'[2] In his reply of 8 April, the Archbishop, whilst lamenting the troubles caused in England by theological disputes which affected the foundations of faith, contrasted the position in the Swiss Reformed churches, where controversy centred in minor points. He challenged his correspondents to show where for twelve hundred years past agreement had been unanimous on these matters of predestination and grace. Let them compare the opinions of the ancient Fathers before Augustine with those of writers after the rise of Pelagianism; or let them examine the differences of opinion during the Reformation and since, including those of members of the Synod of Dort itself; and let them observe the moderation of the Confessions of the Protestant churches.

> In these circumstances I can hardly be too much amazed why your Bernese fight so fiercely amongst themselves for such a cause; or what advantage they propose to themselves in imposing a *Consensus*, such as hardly any other Reformed church to my knowledge lays upon the conscience of its members; for your own Swiss churches when formulating their own Confession did not think proper to impose it upon their ministers.[3]

Finally Wake emphasised the urgency of Protestant union and the obstacle thereto raised by this dispute, and his own anxiety to remove it from the path of the peacemakers.

Having thus declared his judgment on the theological issues in dispute in two long Latin letters, and expanded it in private correspondence with his friends, there was little left for the primate to do, save to watch the course of events and repeat his advice whenever opportunity offered. The modern reader may justly marvel at the extent of his correspondence, and at his

[1] See chapter VIII, pp. 150–3.
[2] Arch. W. Epist. 25, f. 117.
[3] *Ibid.* f. 123. Extracts from the letter are in Geneva MSS. Inventaire 1569, f. 64. 'Quae cum ita se habeant, non possum satis mirari, cur hac de causa vestri Bernenses adeo acriter inter se digladientur; aut quid demum commodi sibi proponant in exigendo Consensu, qualem nescio an aliqua alia Ecclesia Reformata unquam conscientiis suorum imposuit; neque Ecclesiae vestrae Helveticae, cum Confessionem suam fabricaverint, a suis symmistis exigendum fore censuere.'

patience in reaffirming his standpoint and exhorting to moderation. For in addition to his frequent interchange of letters with Turrettini at Geneva, he maintained regular communication with De Crousaz at Lausanne, with Werenfels and with the Antistes, Jerome Burchard, at Basle, with Schürer at Berne, with the Antistes at Zürich and also with J. B. Ott, father of his protégé J. H. Ott; whilst from his chaplain's periodical visits to Switzerland also, the Archbishop derived first-hand impressions of the variations in ecclesiastical temperature in the chief Swiss cities. Some idea of the burden of this correspondence may be gathered from the covering letter to Turrettini which accompanied the second Latin memorandum in February 1718/19.

I have, though with some difficulty, followed your good example; and together with this letter, send you a short historical account of the judgment of the Church of England with respect to the controverted points among your neighbours of Berne.... This narration I was forced to write at a great many several times, and in the midst of a thousand interruptions. You will therefore be pleased to excuse the inequality of it; and consider it as the production of a busy man, who has not leisure to do anything so correctly as he ought, and would be glad, to do.... I shall leave it to your prudence to make such use of it as may be of service to the Churches of Berne, without prejudice to my own reputation; which I justly fear may be likely to suffer, should such a rude, barbarous and unfinished piece be made public to the world. It was the only concern I had for my former letter, and even this I shall give up, if you think it needful, for the public good; to which I can be content to be made serviceable, with some prejudice to myself. I have been forced to make use of another hand in copying my papers, having not time from my present hurry of business to do it myself.... If you communicate this long letter to any of your friends, I must desire the English passages may be carefully translated into Latin. They are some of them but old-fashioned English, and will for that reason, be the more hard to be rightly understood.[1]

Further on 17 June, the Archbishop replying to Turrettini's information of the despatch of copies of both his Latin letters to the Avoyer at Berne, wrote:

I cannot be so vain as to think my two long letters on the subject of the *Consensus* ...should be worthy the regard of the Avoyer of Berne; neither my own capacity, nor the infinite hurry of my business, nor the method I have always used of employing nobody else to make any such drafts for me, and seldom to copy them, will permit me to offer anything exact or curious to you.[2]

Amidst so extensive and varied a correspondence it is little surprising that Wake should have repeated, line upon line, his arguments and persuasions, with difference of emphasis according to the particular circumstances of his several correspondents. It would be as tedious as unnecessary to cite extracts from all his voluminous exhortations; but it may be profitable to notice some qualifications which he was ready to introduce into his dislike of subscription

[1] Geneva MSS. Inventaire 1569, f. 47. [2] *Ibid.* f. 67.

to the *Consensus*. Both from Berne and Zürich the argument *tu quoque* was directed against him; and it was urged that the *Consensus* was in fact intended to serve the same purpose as the Anglican Thirty-nine Articles, as expounded by him in his formal memoranda, namely to restrict public preaching and teaching within the limits prescribed in the *Formula* but not to compel interior belief and assent *in foro conscientiae*. Thus Schürer on 1 March 1718/9 described the *Consensus* as 'fraenum aliquid calami et oris' to prevent teachers and preachers from advocating abolition of all subscription to confessions of faith, and to arrest dangerous tendencies towards libertinism and indifferentism.

> Freedom will be given to every one to think as his conscience dictates, but for the good order of the church, for the securing of uniformity of doctrine, or rather for the avoidance of open contradiction thereof and of the ensuing confusion, our official teachers are obliged not to write or teach anything contrary to the official confession and doctrine hitherto received amongst us from the Word of God.[1]

This was indeed the argument of the primate himself; and in reply he admitted in good measure its legitimacy.

> If your magistrates confine themselves within these limits and require nothing more from the Lausannois than that to this end they should subscribe to the *Formula Consensus*, it is to be hoped that no schism will occur amongst you for this reason. The Christian magistrate both can and should defend the public peace even in matters relating to belief. But he neither can nor should impose on men's consciences articles of belief, unless upon matters which are both clear and perspicuous and altogether necessary to salvation.[2]

Similarly the Antistes of Zürich assured him that the *Consensus* was 'nil aliud quam norma consensus in doctrina, fundamentum quoddam unionis, remedium schismatis, tessera fraternitatis'.[3] In reply Wake conceded the main point of principle and urged moderation in its application.

> If the matter is undertaken with prudence and due reasonableness, it is certainly both useful in itself and almost essential to preserve sound doctrine. No lover of peace will try to teach publicly anything against a rule of this kind. If any man of turbulent spirit should venture anything of this sort I should esteem him justly to

[1] Arch. W. Epist. 25, f. 147. 'Liberum ergo erit cuilibet sentire quod conscientia dictat, sed ad εὐταξίαν Ecclesiae, doctrinaeque uniformitatem servandam, vel saltem apertam ejus contrarietatem et inde nascituram confusionem vitandam, adstringuntur doctores publici ne quid scribant aut doceant publicae confessioni et doctrinae hactenus ex Verbo Dei inter nos receptae contrarium.'

[2] *Ibid.* f. 148. Quoted in Mosheim-MacLaine, vol. v, p. 175. 'Intra hos igitur limites si steterint magistratus vestri, neque aliquid amplius a Lausannensibus requirant, nisi ut hoc demum fine Formulae Consensus subscribant; sperandum est nullum schisma, ea de causa, inter vos exoriturum. Pacem publicam tueri, etiam in rebus ad fidem spectantibus, magistratus Christianus et potest et debet. Conscientiis hominum credenda imponere, nisi in rebus claris et perspicuis, et ad salutem omnino necessariis, nec potest nec debet.

[3] Arch. W. Epist. 25, f. 157. 'VI Id. Sept. 1719.'

be coerced. But it is one thing (and a very different thing) to teach what is thus commanded by lawful authority; and another not to teach anything contrary to it. To this latter a good man will readily suffer himself to be bound, for the sake of peace and concord. On the other hand I believe that nobody will be of such a perfidious effrontery as to think it allowable for himself to propound to others as true, things which he either certainly knows or firmly believes to be false. Therefore it seems to me the same thing to impose on the consciences of men such articles to be believed and to command them to be taught.[1]

On this basis, as the Archbishop confided to Turrettini, a compromise might be arranged which would preserve the peace of the church.

I have lately received a very long and obliging letter from Monsr Schürer...in which he positively affirms that it never was the intention of their magistrates or others, to impose the *Consensus* as a formulary of faith to be professed; but only as a rule of peace, and to hinder imprudent persons from publicly teaching anything contrary to the received doctrine and confession of the Helvetic churches. If the professor be in earnest, and that this is what they have thought fit at last to acquiesce in, I shall rejoice to see all the late struggles and fears brought to so easy and moderate an end.[2]

On the other hand, when the terms of the primate's letter to the Antistes of Zürich were communicated to Geneva and to the other Reformed churches of Switzerland, Turrettini perceived how they might be interpreted as approving not only the principle but the actual form of the *Consensus*.

Messieurs les ecclésiastiques de Z[ürich] nous ont communiqué la nouvelle lettre dont votre grâce a honoré tout le clergé Protestant de Suisse [he wrote on 22 February 1719/20]. Les rigides font courir le bruit que votre grâce approuve le *Consensus*: sous ombre qu'elle convient que *formula docendorum res est in se utilis et ad sanam doctrinam conservandam paene necessaria*. Mais ils ne prennent pas garde que votre grâce explique très bien quelle doit être cette Formula, lorsqu'elle dit, *si quidem cum prudentia atque ἐπιεικείᾳ debita concipiatur*. Or il est bien certain, et votre grâce l'a bien démontré dans les lettres précédentes que le *Consensus* de Suisse n'a point ces qualités.[3]

Unfortunately also the desired compromise did not result; and when, after the lull produced by the protracted deliberations of Berne on the report of its delegates who had visited Lausanne in 1718, the Little Council in

[1] Arch. W. Epist. 25, f. 159. December 1719. 'Si quidem prudentia concipiatur atque ἐπιεικείᾳ debita, res certe est et in se utilis et ad sanam doctrinam conservandam paene necessaria. Contra hujusmodi normam aliquid publice docere nemo pacis amator attentabit. Si quis turbulenti ingenii homo aliquid ejusmodi auderet, merito ego talem coercendum censerem. Sed alia longe res est, quod sic publica authoritate statutum fuerit docere; alia non docere contrarium. Ad hoc pacis ac concordiae causa vir bonus facile sese astringi patietur. Cum e contra neminem esse credo tam perfidae frontis, ut licere sibi putet ea aliis tanquam vera proponere, quae ipse falsa esse aut certe cognosceret aut firmiter crederet. Adeo mihi videtur idem esse, conscientiis hominum tales articulos credendos imponere atque docendos statuere.'

[2] Geneva MSS. Inventaire 1569, f. 69. 22 July 1719.

[3] Arch. W. Epist. 31, f. 89.

January 1722 presented to the Council of Two Hundred its recommendations as to the executive action to be taken, immediate pressure was again brought to bear upon Wake in order to secure the intervention in this new crisis of the king of Great Britain, if possible in conjunction with the king of Prussia. On 5 February 1722, Turrettini sent a detailed account of what was brewing at Berne, and not only pressed for the despatch of a letter from George I but also included a suggested draft of such a communication.[1] But such matters were more readily despatched in Prussia, and on 21 February Frederick William I proved himself first in the field with an official letter addressed to the cantons of Zürich and Berne; in which he followed the example of his predecessor, the Grand Elector of Brandenburg who in 1686 had pointed out to the Swiss Protestant cantons the obstacle raised by the *Consensus* to good relations between the Lutherans and Reformed.[2]

Events in Switzerland, however, did not wait upon the measured pace of British diplomacy; and neither Zürich nor Berne was moved by the initiative of the Prussian sovereign. On 15 April the Bernese Council of Two Hundred, after a debate lasting between five and six hours, ratified the recommendations of the Lesser Council by 70 votes to 62, and remitted to the latter body the responsibility for their execution. Two months earlier, on 14 February Wake had assured Turrettini that immediately upon receipt of the latter's letter of 5 February, he had sent its contents to Lord Townshend.

I am indeed very apprehensive [he added] that our ministers will not concern themselves, nor speak to the King of any of these matters. And I know His Majesty's temper too well to expect that he will do anything in them without their advice. I have had some trials of late that quite discourage me, and make me despair of obtaining anything from them upon this business. I wish I may be deceived; it will be a great joy and consolation to me.[3]

No complaint indeed could be laid against the primate of lukewarmness in the matter. After talking to Townshend about the affair, he wrote formally on 21 February, enclosing a letter from James Horner, secretary and chaplain to M. Schaub in Paris, and urging that diplomatic action should be taken. With this be sent extracts from letters reaching him from Lausanne, in order to make plain 'how much the whole country of Lausanne is alarmed at what the rigid Calvinists are now pushing on, to their utter ruine, at Berne'. He enclosed also the suggested draft of such a *démarche*, written by Turrettini.

By such a letter as Mr Turrettini proposes to be sent from His Majesty, the late King of Prussia (or rather I believe his father, the Elector of Brandenburg) put a stop to the like troubles at Basle, where they have continued in perfect peace as to

[1] *Ibid.* f. 121. [2] A copy *ibid.* f. 131.
[3] Geneva MSS. Inventaire 1569, f. 87.

these matters ever since. They are much divided at Berne upon this procedure, the old Avoyer with a great number of the more prudent and peaceable magistrates being utterly averse to such a violent procedure as the rest with the new Avoyer carry on. I have taken out of Mr Turrettini's letter to me the substance of what is desired. It will be easy to put it into a better form, and prepare it for His Majesty's approbation. Give me leave only to add, that as this affair presses, no time should be lost, lest such a letter, if sent, should happen to come too late, after the resolution of the Council of Two Hundred is taken. I have therefore made the more haste to send it to your lordship, submitting it entirely to your judgment to make such use as you please of it. This is certain, that we have no better friends in all that country, than those who will be ruined if this affair be not moderated, or rather entirely put a stop to.

The *Projet d'une Lettre de Sa Majesté aux Cantons Évangéliques*, which Wake had drafted from Turrettini's suggested form was at once delicate and diplomatic.

Que Sa Majesté, étant informée qu'un écrit nommé *Formula Consensus*, établi en quelques endroits de Suisse depuis 40 ou 45 ans, est une pierre d'achoppement à l'égard d'un grand nombre de Protestants d'Allemagne, et un obstacle à leur Réunion, verrait avec plaisir que les louables Cantons Évangéliques, et surtout les louables Cantons de Zürich et de Berne, levassent cet obstacle, et n'imposussent plus de signature à cet égard; se contentant de leur Confession de Foi établie dans le tems de la Réformation; et à l'égard des questions obscures, difficiles, et non nécessaires à salut, comme sont celles du *Consensus*, défendant seulement sous des très-grièves peines de troubler la paix sur ce sujet par des disputes et contestations hors de saison; ce qui, au jugement de Sa Majesté, suffirait pour entretenir la paix dans le pays, et ne donnerait aucun sujet de plainte à personne. Que Sa Majesté est persuadée que les-dits louables Cantons, par un effet de leur piété et de leur sagesse ordinaire, voudront bien entrer dans ce tempérament, et ôter un des plus grands obstacles de la concorde des Protestants; qui est à présent plus nécessaire que jamais, pour leur commune conservation et pour le bien et l'avancement de la Religion Protestante. Qu'en cela ils fairont un plaisir très sensible au Roi.[1]

At first the Archbishop was optimistic of the success of his intervention. On Good Friday, 23 March, he informed Turrettini:

I have been agreeably mistaken in my expectations from our court. My Lord Townshend not only readily agreed to propose what you desired to His Majesty, but got the other ministers to join with him in it. His Majesty presently consented to send such a letter to the cantons; and I was moved to furnish the subject of it. I copied exactly the plan you sent, and left it to them to put it into such form as they thought proper. They have done so, the King has signed it; and I believe it is at this time on its way to Berne. I write the more doubtfully because having not been abroad for some time, I have not had an opportunity to know precisely when

[1] S.P. Domestic, 35. George I, vol. 30, ff. 38, and 38 (1), (2), and (3).

it was sent; only my Lord Townshend assures me the thing is done. I heartily wish it may have a good effect; and that the two kings joining thus together in the same request, may not be refused what they so reasonably desire.[1]

Unfortunately, however, the gulf between resolution and execution was more considerable than the primate expected; and not until 13 April did Lord Carteret signify to him that

His Majesty's letter concerning the *Formula Consensus* was sent by the last post to Geneva, to be transmitted to the governments of Zürich and Berne by Count Marsay. I cannot forget Your Grace's commands upon so important a subject, in which the King does interest himself so much, in regard to what Your Grace has represented to His Majesty upon that head.[2]

Actually the letter of George I, signed by Carteret and addressed not to Zürich and Berne only but to all the Swiss Reformed cantons, bore the date of 10 April 1722. It was a shorter document than that of the Prussian king, but, like the latter, approached the matter of the *Formula Consensus* not from the theological standpoint proper to an archbishop, nor from considerations internal to the Swiss cantons, but from the point of view of its effect on Protestant union. It began therefore by an expression of the zeal of George I for the union of Protestants, and his concern that the *Consensus* was causing such alarm to Lutherans in Germany in particular, and thereby raising up a barrier to concord and unity. On this ground the request was made that subscription without conditions should not be demanded; but rather that steps should be taken to restrain those who through zeal for orthodoxy were disturbing the peace of the church.

That you may consent to make this concession to the peace of the Reformed Church: namely, that no one shall be required to sign the above-mentioned *Formula Consensus* contrary to your customary indulgence in matters of this kind. Further that it should on the contrary be forbidden by you that any one, under the pretext of setting forth a true profession of faith, should disturb the peace of the church, and by untimely controversies concerning a question too difficult and obscure and (as some consider) in no wise affecting the true end of eternal salvation, should inflict much hurt on religion and the state. How useful, salutary and at this time especially how necessary this advice is, your eminent piety and prudence will readily indicate to you; since in carrying it out, it is a matter equally affecting your own affairs and the common cause of Protestantism. Nor have we any reason to doubt that you will gladly embrace it, since you will thereby both gratify us and in the best manner consult the quiet and safety of the Reformed Churches.[3]

[1] Geneva MSS. Inventaire 1569, f. 91.

[2] Arch. W. Epist. 31, f. 133.

[3] Arch. W. Epist. 26, f. 20. 'Ut velitis paci Ecclesiae Reformatae id concedere, ne aliquis ad signandam Formulam Consensus supradictam, contra usitatam vestram in rebus hujusmodi indulgentiam, adigatur; verum e contrario ut a vobis interdictum sit potius, ne quis sub verae fidei confessionis propagandae praetextu tranquillitatem ecclesiae conturbet et controversiis intem-

Since this letter was addressed to all the Protestant cantons, its circulation, consideration, and the drafting of a common reply inevitably involved considerable delay, the more especially since, for example, Basle and Schaffhausen (where subscription to the *Consensus* had fallen into desuetude) did not see eye to eye with Zürich and Berne on the controverted matters. Moreover on 12 May the Diet of the Corpus Evangelicorum at Ratisbon likewise addressed a communication to Berne and Zürich, emphasising the disservice to the Protestant cause of insistence on subscription to the *Consensus* and the danger of exacerbating both Lutheran and Reformed sentiment in the Empire.

Meantime, however, events had been taking their course at Lausanne; where, during the three weeks' interval before the arrival of the Bernese commissioners, the professors and pastors examined the alternative courses of action open to them. A moderate middle party was willing to accept both the *Consensus* and the Serment d'Association (if a reasonable latitude of interpretation was allowed) in the interests of unity and for the avoidance of schism, and so to sacrifice private respects to the public good of church and state. At different ends of this moderate opinion were the smaller minorities, on the one side of rigidly orthodox conservatives who welcomed the decision of Berne and insisted on unconditional signature; and on the other of liberal divines who found difficulty in subscription at all. Little encouragement was given to this last company by the reply of Zürich and Berne towards the end of April to the king of Prussia, which mingled compliments for his zeal for Protestant union with assurances of the purely domestic character of the *Consensus* in relation to the internal affairs of the Swiss Reformed churches, and insistence on its maintenance in the interests of public order. On 10 May the Bernese delegation, consisting of two select commissioners attended by a secretary, reached Lausanne to execute the decrees of the Council of Two Hundred. In their preliminary conferences with the academic professoriate, both corporately and individually, they were left in no doubt as to the strength of opposition both to the *Consensus* and to the oath; and in turn they were at pains to emphasise that the former was a *formula doctrinae*, not a *formula fidei*, and that therefore acceptance of it and of the oath was a matter of obedience to the decrees of lawful authority, which sought only the unity and peace of state and church. On the eve of the day appointed for the formal communication of the decrees of Berne to the

pestivis super re nimis ardua et obscura, et (ut nonnulli aestimant) ad verum aeternae salutis scopum minus spectante, religioni et reipublicae multum afferat incommodum. Quam utile sit hoc consilium, quam salutare, et hac praecipue tempestate, quam necessarium, summa vestra pietas et prudentia vos facile monebunt, cum et vestris propriis rebus et communi Protestantium causae in eo exequendo aeque prospiciatur; neque est quod dubitemus, quin idem lubentissime amplectamini, cum et nobis simul pergratum feceritis, et quieti salutique Ecclesiarum Reformatarum optime consulatis.'

Lausanne Academy corporately, the members of this body met to record in writing their understanding of the explanations offered orally by the Bernese commissioners; and on the basis of these interpretations, decided to accept the decrees. '"Il fut résolu de faire ce qui était exigé." C'est en ces termes que le procès-verbal de l'Académie relate sa peu glorieuse capitulation.'[1] Accordingly on 15 May the Academy, through the mouth of its rector, the liberal Professor J. P. De Crousaz, accepted the demands of Berne, each member appending his individual signature to the *Consensus* and taking the Serment d'Association. Much greater difficulty was experienced in dealing with the twenty-five young ministers, not yet provided with a cure, who were likewise required to subscribe and sign, but who were exceedingly reluctant to do this without a written official statement of the interpretation accepted as satisfactory by the commissioners. Finally seventeen were persuaded to sign; and the rest, joined by a ninth companion hitherto absent from Lausanne, were summoned to make a final appearance before the commissioners on 23 May, the day fixed by the latter for their return home. After further exhortations, two signed; but there remained seven refusing all submission, who were deposed from the ministry and whose names were removed from the roll of the Academy. It was a melancholy spectacle; the more particularly since the professors who had conformed now witnessed the spectacle of the greater firmness of their younger brethren, the junior ministers who had learned their liberal principles at the academy. The episode, as Wake confessed to Turrettini on 9 July 1722, had made

but little less noise in the Protestant churches, than the bull *Unigenitus* in those of the other communion. I entirely agree with you in the judgment you pass upon the conclusion of that affair. I wish it had been better, yet am glad it was no worse. I am sorry our king's letter came no sooner to you; it was ordered in due time; but our court was then very full of business, and with all my sollicitations, I could not get it despatched sooner.

It is a wonderful thing to consider how very perversely we church-men generally act towards one another. I do not excuse the laity. I am sensible they have their parties and passions as well as the others, and often follow the movements of those rather than of reason. Yet generally speaking in matters of religion they are more easy to be persuaded than the ecclesiastics; and are more ready to indulge men their liberty of opinion, without offering violence to men's consciences, than the others are. As to myself I cannot but think that, excepting in points essential to salvation and therefore necessary to be taught to and received by all, nothing is more reasonable than to allow men to judge freely and determine impartially, at least for themselves, in all other points; and to lay no other restraint upon them than what is necessary to the ends of public peace and charity. When it comes to be our own case, we are all of the same mind. No one cares to be persecuted for his opinions,

[1] H. Vuilleumier, *op. cit.* vol. III, p. 688.

nor thinks it reasonable he should be so. How then can we justify ourselves in departing from this rule when we deal with others; and forget the great duty of doing to them as we would have them under the like circumstances do to us?[1]

The comparison with the bull *Unigenitus* was echoed from another side by M. Lullin at Geneva, who lamented to the Archbishop in the following year, when further distressing events had been added to the melancholy story, 'de voir chez nos ecclésiastiques la même faiblesse que j'avais si fort blâmée chez les Jansénistes à Paris'.[2]

Unfortunately neither the history of the Berne-Lausanne dispute, nor that of the diplomatic interventions of the Protestant powers, came to an end with the submission of the Lausanne Academy in May 1722. The reply of the Protestant cantons to the letter of George I, dated 1 September 1722, after thanking him for his zeal for Protestant union and solicitude for their churches, with many superlative and fulsome compliments interspersed, assured him of their desire for unity and of the purpose of the *Consensus*, 'to no other end than that peace and tranquillity in our church and state may be preserved, and also that unanimous agreement in that evangelical doctrine, resting on the Word of God and handed down by our pious predecessors, may be maintained'.[3] Although there were variations within the cantons in the manner of receiving the *Consensus*, its imposition involved no violation of conscience, nor did it constitute any impediment to union with other Reformed or Lutheran churches.

We therefore most earnestly beseech Your Majesty to be assured that the aforesaid *Formula Consensus* cannot possibly present any barrier to the most laudable endeavours for ecclesiastical unity in Germany now being undertaken; and we further humbly request that of your most kind inclinations towards us, you will not refuse further favour to the profit of our church and commonwealth.[4]

It was indeed a soft answer to turn away wrath; but neither to Turrettini nor to the Archbishop did it seem adequate or sufficient. The former observed that the Berne-Lausanne episode had contributed neither to the peace and concord of the church nor to amity between the cantons, that the remonstrances of Prussia and of the Corpus Evangelicorum at Ratisbon were sufficient refutation of the claim that the *Consensus* was no impediment to

[1] Geneva MSS. Inventaire 1569, f. 101.

[2] Arch. W. Epist. 31, f. 170. 24 December 1723.

[3] Non alium in finem quam ut pax, quiesque in ecclesia et republica nostra, nec non unanimis consensus in Verbo Dei innixa et a piis majoribus tradita doctrina Evangelica, conservaretur.

[4] Arch. W. Epist. 26, f. 70. 'Rogamus itaque majestatem vestram studiosissime, ut saepius dictam Formulam Consensus laudatissimis consiliis unioni ecclesiasticae in Germania agitatis nullum impedimentum injicere posse, persuasum habere velit; eamque obsecramus denique humillime, ut benignissima in nos propensione, ecclesiae atque reipublicae nostrae commodis ulterius favere haud dedignetur.'

union with the Lutherans, that the consciences of many Lausannois teachers and pastors were vexed by the requirement of subscription, and that the reply offered no hope of more moderate measures to solve the problem.[1] In a letter to De Crousaz of 14 November, Wake admitted that the reply was a compromise between the rigid views of Berne and Zürich and the moderate attitude of Basle, but intimated that in view of its unsatisfactory character, a new approach on the part of the King was being considered, in the hope of persuading Berne to suspend subscription, if not to abolish it altogether.[2] In applauding to Professor Iselius of Basle the policy of his city, the primate regretted that its efforts to secure abolition had not succeeded: 'sed adhuc manet scandali petra, non, ut decuit, sublata'; and promised a further letter from George I, which, he hoped, would be more successful.[3] To Turrettini he wrote on 1 November:

> I am encouraged by others, as well as by yourself, to hope that matters may yet be softened by fresh applications; and am sorry to hear (what yet I can easily believe) that the ministers are much more bigoted to the imposing of the *Consensus* than the laity; and that the latter would appear more moderate, if the former did not use all their interest to keep up a spirit of imposition in them. So powerfully does the spirit of popery prevail even over those who would be thought to be the farthest from it.[4]

Towards the end of the same month, he observed again:

> I have lately written my thoughts very freely about the present situation of your affairs to Zürich, Basle, and Lausanne. How my letters will be received by some to whom I doubt my friends will communicate them, I cannot tell. I have discharged my own conscience, and shall leave the event to the divine providence. I am in great hope we shall procure a second letter from the King to the cantons upon this occasion. I wish in such a case, the king of Prussia would also renew his instances to the same effect.[5]

To Professor J. J. Scheuchzer, professor of medicine at Zürich and therefore outside the ranks of the contending parties of that city, who had notwithstanding expressed to the primate, in a letter of 5 July, his sympathy with the policy of moderation, Wake replied on 20 November, urging him to use his position and influence as a neutral on the side of compromise. The Archbishop confessed his disappointment with the outcome of the intervention of the kings of Great Britain and Prussia, but believed it not to have been entirely unavailing. 'Optarem equidem serenissimorum regum atque principum reformatorum interventu, res aliquanto magis sedari ac componi

[1] *Ibid.* Epist. 31, f. 141. 14 October 1722.
[2] *Ibid.* Epist. 26, f. 77.
[3] *Ibid.* f. 81. 'xvi Kal: Nov. 1722.'
[4] Geneva MSS. Inventaire 1569, f. 103.
[5] *Ibid.* f. 105.

potuisse. Neque tamen omnino inutilem eorum intercessionem fuisse existimo; cujus ope contentionis occasionem si non penitus tolli, minus tamen et propius felicem exitum reduci componimus.' He repeated his conviction that the best solution would be a return to the Helvetic Confession and the abolition of the *Consensus*, and his opinions concerning the wisdom of comprehensiveness in things of secondary import.[1]

There remained the drafting of the proposed second letter from George I and the better synchronising of action with Prussia than had been achieved on the former occasion. The draft was made by Wake in December 1722, and despatched, over Carteret's signature, on 10 February 1722/3. It began by expressing regret that the cantons still adhered to the *Consensus*, despite the divisions and disputes which its enforcement had produced. 'However we cannot but lament to find you so tenacious in defending your *Formula Consensus*, which is both so great an offence to the majority of Protestants and also for this reason has been practically abolished by some districts amongst yourselves.'[2] Moreover, notwithstanding the moderation with which subscription had been required, the facts remained that contention had resulted and scruples of conscience had been aroused; and therefore the king urged that the example of those cantons which had abolished subscription, should be universally followed. In this second letter, unlike the former, definitely theological issues were mentioned; and Wake's own sentiments found expression. 'The most learned men whom we have consulted on this matter are unanimously of opinion that the articles treated of in this *Formula* are both very obscure in themselves and also not necessary to be believed for salvation.'[3] Therefore a definite request was made for abolition of the requirement of subscription.

This one thing remains, which we desire, and which you should do, and how small a matter it is you yourselves may judge: namely, that you will make this concession to the public peace and to our intercession, not to require subscription to this *Formula* of any one, and that no one shall either raise any controversy with anyone or bring any action against any other persons concerning its articles. By so decreeing you will perform an action most welcome to us, honourable to yourselves, profitable to your subjects, most desired by all lovers of union and concord amongst Protestants, and burdensome to nobody. This, therefore, we greatly hope of your friendship, piety and prudence.[4]

[1] Zürich MSS. H. 293. A foul copy in Arch. W. Epist. 26, f. 85.

[2] Tamen non possumus non dolere quod vos adeo tenaces reperiamus in tuenda illa vestra Formula Consensus, quae et majori Protestantium parti tanto est offendiculo, et a quibusdam inter vos ipsos pagis, ea de causa, penitus aboletur.

[3] Articulos in illa Formula determinatos, et in se admodum obscuros esse, nec ad salutem creditu necessarios, eruditissimi viri quibuscum de hac re communicavimus, uno ore affirmant.

[4] Arch. W. Epist. 26, f. 71. 'Illud unice nobis optandum, vobis agendum, restat; quod quam parum sit vos ipsi judicate; ut publicae paci nostraeque intercessioni concedatis, ne qua omnino

On 6 April the second letter of the king of Prussia was despatched from Berlin, which, like the British counterpart, after expressing regret that the former intercession had not had the desired result, embarked on a more severe criticism of the theological content of the *Consensus*, protested against its quasi-popish compulsion of conscience, and requested its utter abolition.[1]

These second letters, much more definite in recommendation and positive in tone than the former, could leave no doubt at Zürich and Berne of the disapproval which their policy had evoked in London and Berlin. It might be more doubtful however whether their open censure would induce the recipients to accept their demands for abolition, since to do so would involve an evident loss of face. Turrettini thought George I's missive 'belle et excellente', and hoped that Berne would now persuade its ally to drop the matter.[2] Certainly the composition of an agreed reply was only achieved after protracted and animated interchange of views between the several cantons; though its belated appearance was due in part to the *émeute* and execution of Major Davel at Lausanne and the preoccupations resulting therefrom. Not until 17 June 1724 was the Swiss reply sent to George I; which, beginning with a cordial recognition of His Majesty's efforts for Protestant union and an assurance of their equal zeal and sympathy with this objective, passed to its main theme in regard to the *Consensus*. In its internal relationship, the *Consensus* was then officially defined as not a formula of faith but only of teaching, binding nobody to interior belief, but only to abstention from teaching anything contrary to its doctrine. In its external reference, the cantons offered to abolish it, if and when it should prove to be the sole remaining barrier to Protestant union.

We have determined to offer a just occasion for complaint in this matter to no one in our church; nor to give any molestation to any of our ministers on this account; nor to coerce the conscience of any or to constrain him in any other thing. To this end the *Formula Consensus* is required and retained not as an article of faith to be believed by any one, but only as a rule of doctrine, against which our ministers are forbidden to teach; and for the maintenance of that agreement in doctrine observed amongst us since the Reformation, upon which our public tranquillity and ecclesiastical peace depend. But if indeed even with this moderation, subscription to this *Formula* may seem to delay the union which we earnestly desire, we declare now as an evidence of our sincere wish to promote this union, that when the union

subscriptio Formulae illius ab aliquo exigatur, neque de ipsius Articulis aliquis alteri aut controversiam moveat aut litem intentet. In quo statuendo rem nobis pergratam, vobis honorificam, subditis vestris utilem, omnibus unionis et concordiae inter Protestantes amatoribus desideratissimam, nemini gravem, facietis. Hoc igitur a vestra amicitia, pietate atque prudentia jure speramus.'

[1] *Ibid.* Epist. 26, ff. 106, 107 (German text and English translation)

[2] Arch. W. Epist. 31, f. 118. 9 April 1723.

has been established, subscription to the *Formula*, which in fact has not been required for several years in some cantons, shall be forthwith abrogated in the others.[1]

Although the reply substituted for the desired immediate abolition of the *Consensus* a conditional and proleptic removal when the terms of Protestant union should have been otherwise satisfactorily settled (which to Turrettini 'paraitrait une raillerie, si on l'écrivait à une personne d'autre rang'),[2] during the interim, of admittedly uncertain duration, it offered a conditional subscription, which opened the way to a compromise settlement of the actual dispute at Lausanne. Indeed Wake had written to his Genevan friend on 24 June in this sense: 'I take the obligation of the *Consensus* to be also in a fair way of being, if not expressly repealed, yet the force of it abated, by the little care that will be taken to enforce the subscription of it.'[3] This was perhaps too optimistic; but the verdict of the historian of the Pays de Vaud may be accepted as just.

C'est que, à la face de toute l'Europe qui, dans la mesure où elle y était intéressée, avait eu connaissance des péripéties de cette correspondance diplomatique, elle venait confirmer, de manière solennelle, les 'explications' de plus en plus restrictives que la résistance des membres de l'Académie de Lausanne et l'opiniâtreté de certains membres des Classes du Pays de Vaud avaient fini par arracher à leur souverain. Le Formulaire n'était donc prescrit à personne comme article de foi qu'on serait tenu de croire, mais simplement comme une règle d'enseignement contre laquelle nul ne devait parler, ni écrire, aux fins de maintenir l'ordre et la paix dans l'Église et dans l'État. En d'autres termes, comme s'exprime fort bien Alexandre Schweizer, la formule dogmatique était rabaissée au rôle et au niveau d'une simple mesure de police ecclésiastique, ce qui était aussi contraire que possible à son texte et à l'intention de ses premiers auteurs.[4]

To this end also events at Lausanne had been moving. The task of bringing the pastors into conformity with the line taken by the academy was considerably assisted by the formal issue of the explanations and interpretations acceptable to Berne in respect of the *Consensus*, so that they might be sure that the sovereign authority understood the sense in which they subscribed.

[1] *Ibid.* f. 155. 17 June 1724. 'Nemini in ecclesia nostra hac de re conquerendi ansam justam praeberi, neque ministrorum nostrorum ulli propterea molestiam creari, siquidem neque illius conscientiae neque alio modo vim inferre statuimus. Proinde Formula Consensus, nemini pro Articulo Fidei credendo, verum pro Norma Doctrinae tantum, contra quam ministri nostri docere prohibentur, atque pro conservando unanimi inde a Reformatione inter nos observato consensu in doctrina, a quo etiam quies nostra publica et pax ecclesiastica pendent, imperatur et retinetur. Sin autem etiam hac cum moderatione subscriptio Formulae hujus unionem, quam sincere exoptamus, quodam modo morari videretur, jam nunc, pro argumento veri nostri hanc promovendi desiderii, declaramus, Unione Stabilita Formulae subscriptionem, quae re ipsa, multis ab hinc annis, in quibusdam Cantonibus non amplius requiritur, etiam caeteros penitus abrogaturos esse.'

[2] *Ibid.* f. 174. 19 June 1724.

[3] Geneva MSS. Inventaire 1569, f. 118.

[4] H. Vuilleumier, *op. cit.* vol. III, p. 737.

Naturally this led to a demand for similar conditions in regard to the oath. On 30 November 1722 the Lesser Council had issued a decree requiring every minister to take this oath in the sense of promising conformity to it 'suivant le devoir de sa charge et suivant l'exigence de sa profession et de son emploi'.[1] On 9 February following the Berne authorities also sanctioned officially the various explanations and interpretations, hitherto privately conveyed, by which subscription and signature had been obtained. By this conciliatory step three of the deprived Lausannois ministers were able to conform and were restored; and therewith the dispute promised to end. Unfortunately a further *contretemps* was yet to arise; for the Lausanne Academy was emboldened to enter in its official register of signatures the text of these explanations and interpretations, and when this came to the knowledge of Berne, a demand was made for the delivery of the register. In its stead Berne sent another register containing, in addition to the text of the *Consensus* and of the oath, only the official Bernese letter of 16 June 1722 and the later orders of 30 November; and this was further accompanied by a rebuke of the conduct of the academy, and an order that henceforth subscriptions must be recorded simply without the addition of any other explanatory matter. It was natural that Lausanne should resent this gratuitous exercise of authority; and the trouble, which had seemed on the point of extinction, threatened to flare up again, especially when the second letters from the kings of Great Britain and Prussia were received.

Actually Berne was becoming more than a little wearied by the protraction of the controversy; and on 13 April 1723 issued a decree, forbidding absolutely all discussion whether oral or printed of the matter on both sides of the dispute. Thereby at least it had taken one step advocated by Wake according to the Anglican pattern, namely of the compulsory silencing by the civil magistrate of all public discussion of the matters at issue. When in the following year a conciliatory reply was sent by all the Swiss Protestant cantons to the king of Great Britain, it was generally interpreted as signifying a desire to allow the matter to fall into oblivion. Thus subscription to the *Consensus* and signature of the Serment d'Association continued to be required of all candidates for the ministry prior to their ordination; but the necessary explanations and interpretations were allowed to bring relief to scrupulous consciences. Matters continued in this state until in 1746 the oath was replaced by the so-called Serment de Religion, prescribed by a decree of 15 April 1746, by which candidates promised to conform to and to maintain the Helvetic Confession, and to oppose all who deviated therefrom. The significant feature of the new oath was its omission to mention the heresies of Pietism, Arminianism, and Socinianism which had been specified in the

[1] *Ibid.* p. 707.

former oath. In regard to the *Consensus*, it was tacitly and almost imperceptibly dropped in the Ecclesiastical Ordinances of 1758, which contained no mention of it.[1]

Thus the long and acrimonious dispute closed, so far as Wake's interest and lifetime were concerned, in an inglorious truce of exhaustion. From the practical standpoint and in regard to contemporary circumstances, this was probably the most realistic solution which could be achieved. From the point of view of the Archbishop himself, the episode had given clear evidence of the theological and confessional barriers to his cherished ideal of Protestant union, in the interest of which alone he had been drawn into the Swiss controversy. It had certainly involved him in a great deal of trouble and correspondence; and his contributions to the discussion, if they had not been crowned with the success he desired either in relation to the internal settlement of the Berne-Lausanne quarrel or in regard to the wider problem of the unity of Protestants, had at least afforded opportunity for a full statement of the Anglican principle of comprehensiveness as he understood it. In fact the chief interest and importance of his intervention lie in his exposition of the tradition of the Church of England in relation to these specific controversies, and in regard to the wider question of its toleration of differences of opinion amongst its ministers on matters not necessary to salvation nor fundamental to the faith. In a letter of 10 May 1723 to De Crousaz, he ventured the opinion that the majority of Anglican theologians were of the Lutheran rather than the Reformed persuasion in these points.

> Our Church of England so framed its Articles on these matters that they can be accepted sincerely by men of both opinions; and although on these questions our theologians have always been nearer to the Lutherans than to the Calvinists, yet by the care and prudence of our princes, it has been so provided that for the last hundred years past there has been scarcely any occasion left for controversy on these issues, and none at all for schism or more serious dispute.[2]

Throughout the dispute, however, Wake had resolutely refused in his official letters to pronounce any individual opinion on these theological issues, contenting himself with a historical recital of the administrative policy of the Church of England to preserve peace and order and to avoid public controversy. It is therefore of particular interest to observe that in a private letter to De Crousaz he laid aside this reserve, and essayed the delicate and difficult task of outlining his personal belief.

[1] H. Vuilleumier, *op. cit.* vol. IV, pp. 194–6.

[2] Arch. W. Epist. 26, f. 114. 'Ecclesia nostra Anglicana...Articulos suos de his rebus ita fabricavit ut ab utriusque sententiae hominibus sincere recipiantur; et quamvis in his questionibus theologi nostri Lutheranis magis quam Calvinistis semper appropinquaverint; adeo tamen principum nostrorum cura atque prudentia cautum est, ut per saeculum jam proxime elapsum, vix aliquis his de rebus controversiae, nullus schismati, aut graviori contentioni locus fuerit relictus.

Concerning fatalism, which you mention in your letter, I am so persuaded as entirely to believe that for me there is no dogma more inimical to piety. Since I am unable to reject individual election, so I think it should be thus understood: that to nobody who is called to Christian belief is sufficient grace denied for the attainment of eternal salvation through the merits of the Saviour. God is the Lord of his own gifts; and as in the distribution of the goods of this life he has constituted various grades of men, giving to some more riches and to others less, yet graciously providing to all the things necessary to sustain life; so also in the bestowal of his grace, he has had the right to act justly entirely according to his good pleasure, and in my judgment, has truly so acted. Now, if no one is excluded from the kingdom of heaven by any final and irreversible decree, and if there is no impediment against all who are called to Christian belief being able to attain to it by his grace, I may venture to ask of him why he has given a greater measure of his grace to another person than to myself; or why of his own mere will he has given to some an easier and more assured way of attaining glory than to others of the faithful. I so freely accept that some have been chosen by God before others, but I can with difficulty agree that any are absolutely reprobate. But why should I dwell on this matter with you, who both think so piously of the goodness of God and have so bright a hope of the future happiness of men? Would that every one might follow this rule in determining these abstruse questions, and would not in explaining those things which are obscure, overthrow those which have been handed down clearly and plainly; nor would determine that the divine decrees should be so maintained as to contradict the one and infinite goodness and mercy of God and to turn men away from zeal for piety. Both which things those persons seem to me to do, who so open the kingdom of heaven to some that they cannot fall from it by any negligence on their part, nor indolence, nor (I had almost said) vices and sins; whilst others they so exclude that they cannot attain to it by their most earnest prayers, zeal and endeavour. Since moreover a great many persons today are so infatuated with these articles that they can hardly endure those who differ from them even in the slightest degree, I would that you may keep to yourself what I have here written to you, or at least that you do not communicate it to others without the utmost caution. I am altogether weary of controversies, especially theological. I am hastening towards the end of this life, and I desire to enjoy in tranquillity and peace whatever further time God may grant me. I am, and wish to be, an enemy to no one; nor by my own fault or imprudence to make any one an enemy to myself. I know in Whom I have believed; and I am persuaded that by his infinite mercy I shall obtain from him through the merits of Christ forgiveness, however numerous and great my sins may notwithstanding be. Would that all others might obtain the same. This is sufficient both for the tranquillity of my mind now and for my hope hereafter. Thus I continue to live and thus I hope to die.[1]

[1] *Ibid.* f. 307. 11 October 1725. 'De Fatalismo, cujus in literis tuis mentionem facis, ita sum persuasus ut prorsus credam mihi nullum dogma pietati magis esse inimicum. Electionem etiam particularem uti rejicere nequeo, ita eam sic recipiendam esse sentio, ne cuivis ad fidem Christianam vocato, sufficiens gratia denegetur ad salutem aeternam per Servatoris merita adipiscendam. Deus donorum suorum Dominus est; et ut in bonorum hujus vitae dispensatione varios hominum gradus constituit; his plus divitiarum dedit, aliis minus; omnibus tamen ea quae ad vitam sustinendam necessaria sunt benigne exhibuit; sic et in gratiae suae distributione juste omnino pro suo

In this moving *confessio fidei* may be traced not a few of the springs of the Archbishop's untiring work and zeal for Christian unity (if possible with the liberal Gallicans, certainly amongst the various Protestant churches) no less than salient traits of his personal character. His charitable belief that God wills all men to come to the knowledge of the truth and to be saved, led to his earnest desire that all who professed and called themselves Christians should become in actuality what they were ideally, brothers, and that the churches should attain union. His own aversion to theological controversy made him underrate the attachment of others to confessional standards; just as his conviction of the danger to the fundamentals of Christianity as a revealed religion from the contemporary Deist and Trinitarian controversies led him to relegate to the category of non-fundamentals, matters which to others seemed of primary importance. But despite the setback of the Swiss disputes, his zeal for unity and his conviction that it could be attained by a wise and wide comprehensiveness of belief and worship in all non-fundamental points, led him to continue his efforts to reconcile and unite continental Protestants; and in this eirenic task he was led into an intimate association with Daniel Ernst Jablonski, the religious counsellor of the Prussian king.

The correspondence between Wake and Jablonski had its roots far back in the acquaintance which they had cultivated during the former's residence as Student of Christ Church and the latter's sojourn in Oxford in 1680; and its strength derived from their common interest in and devotion to the cause of union amongst Protestants.[1] Jablonski had been engaged in schemes for the

beneplacito agere potuit, ac revera, meo judicio, egit. Nec, si nullus a regno caelesti decreto aliquo fatali atque immobili excludatur, nec aliquid impediat quominus omnes qui ad fidem Christianam vocantur, Ipsius gratia eo attingere valeant; ego ab illo exposcere audeam, cur alteri majorem suae gratiae portionem, quam mihi concesserit, aut illum faciliorem certioremque aditum, ex mera sua voluntate quibusdam ad gloriam consequendam dederit, quam caeteris fidelibus. Adeo ego aliquos prae aliis a Deo electos esse libenter amplector, ullos absolute reprobatos aegre agnosco. Sed quid ego de his tecum ago, qui et de Dei Bonitate adeo pie sentias et de hominum futura felicitate adeo candide speras? Utinam in his abstrusis quaestionibus determinandis hanc regulam sequerentur omnes: nec in illis quae obscura sunt explicandis ea subvertant quae clare atque aperte tradita sunt; nec adeo de divinis decretis sentiendum statuerent ut una et infinitae Dei bonitati atque misericordiae contradicant, et homines a studio pietatis abducant. Quorum utrumque mihi facere videntur qui adeo regnum caelorum quibusdam aperiunt ut nulla sua negligentia, sive socordia, pene dixeram neque vitiis atque peccatis, ab illo excidere possint; aliis adeo occludunt ut nec ardentissimis suis votis, studio, labore ad illud pervenire valeant. Cum vero de his articulis plurimi adeo hodie insaniant, ut ferre nequeant vel minimum a se dissentientes, quae hic ad te scripsi, ut tibi soli serves, velim; saltem non absque summa cautione aliis communices. Controversiarum praecipue theologicarum omnino pertaesus sum. Ad finem hujus vitae propero, quod reliquum mihi aetatis concesserit Deus tranquille atque pacifice exigere cupio. Nemini ego aut sum aut esse velim inimicus; neque aliquem mea aut culpa aut imprudentia mihi inimicum reddere. Cognosco in quem credidi; et persuasus sum me summa Illius misericordia etiam peccatis meis quantumvis pluribus atque ingentibus non obstantibus per Christi merita veniam ab illo consecuturum. Utinam alii omnes idem consequantur. Hoc et praesenti animi mei tranquillitati sufficit, et spei futurae. Sic vivere pergo, sic mori cupio.

[1] N. Sykes, *Daniel Ernst Jablonski and the Church of England* (London, 1950).

union of Lutheran and Reformed churches in the territories of Brandenburg since 1697; and his admiration for the liturgy and polity of the Church of England had led him to the conclusion that the unity which he sought could best be realised by modelling the worship and constitution of the Prussian church on the pattern of England. Accordingly during the reigns of King Frederick I of Prussia and of Queen Anne in the United Kingdom, he had been drawn into a considerable correspondence with Archbishop John Sharp of York about practical steps to this end. The northern primate had been engaged in this correspondence because of the failure of Archbishop Tenison to reply to an overture from Prussia; and having been interested, had championed the project with enthusiasm. Into the details of the proposals and the reasons for their failure it is not necessary now to enter, beyond observing that the troubled state of international affairs during the war of the Spanish Succession and the fluctuating fortunes of Anglo-Prussian relations, did not constitute a stable background for discussion of details of an ecclesiastical *rapprochement*. Moreover, the deaths during 1713–14 of the Prussian king, the English queen and the archbishop of York removed the chief parties to the negotiation. It may be noted, however, that Jablonski gave particular attention to the twin foundations of his desired ecclesiastical union by drawing up several projects for the introduction of a modified version of the Book of Common Prayer and of episcopacy into Prussia. During the course of the negotiation also the question of familiarising the House of Hanover with the Anglican liturgy and church-order came to the fore, owing to the prospective succession of that dynasty to the British crown in accordance with the Act of Settlement of 1701; and thereby Leibnitz and Molanus were admitted to a knowledge of the proposals. When therefore the uncertainties which surrounded the Protestant succession in England were dissipated by the peaceful and unchallenged accession of George I, the situation both in this country and in Prussia seemed to promise well for a renewal of the former negotiation.

Accordingly Leibnitz addressed a long letter to Caroline of Anspach, now Princess of Wales (whose interest in theological and ecclesiastical questions was as acute as unusual in the royal house into which she had married), in which he urged her to renew the project for Protestant union which had been formerly begun but allowed to lapse. After giving a brief recital of this former attempt and of the reasons for its failure (chief amongst which, it is interesting to observe, he placed the vacillation of the Prussian king: 'il était fort sujet à changer: il se dégoûta d'une affaire qui ne pouvait pas courir la poste'), he emphasised the religious significance of the Hanoverian succession to the British throne, by which George I had become supreme governor of the Church of England without ceasing to be in communion also with the

Lutheran Church of his native Hanover. What was proper for the sovereign was also right for his subjects; and the discussions between Lutheran and Reformed divines might now be renewed with the participation of Anglicans, who had points of contact with both these foreign churches and were well fitted for the office of mediator. The problem was to secure the interest of George I and to persuade him to take the initiative; and to this end Leibnitz desired the impulse to come from the archbishop of Canterbury himself, if Caroline could find some bishop, perhaps Robinson of London or Wake (though Leibnitz was doubtful about the propriety of his being approached owing to his official relationship to the king as lord almoner), to induce Tenison to broach the question with the sovereign. But before this letter was despatched news had reached Hanover of the death of Tenison and of the nomination of Wake as his successor; and Leibnitz added a postscript.

Cela doit faire changer les mesures à l'égard des personnes; et je crois que si Votre Altesse Royale veut prendre l'affaire en main, il faut qu'Elle parle en elle-même au nouveau primat, mais sans faire paraître que j'y aye la moindre part.... Comme le nouveau primat est d'un âge, comme je crois, à se pouvoir promettre d'achever l'ouvrage s'il le commence, je crois qu'il en sera d'autant plus disposé. Il sera bon qu'il paroisse que l'affaire vient entièrement des Anglais; et elle en sera mieux reçue du roi et de la nation. Mais je crois que le secret sera toujours bon au commencement.[1]

Foremost undoubtedly amongst Leibnitz's calculation of favourable circumstances was the accession to the primacy of Wake himself. For just as the coolness of Archbishop Tenison had given a sharp setback to the first approaches from the Prussian king during the reign of Anne in England, so the zeal of his successor was an evident encouragement; and the former intimacy between Wake and Jablonski was easily re-established. Furthermore the two remaining Protestant electorates in the Empire, those of Brandenburg and Brunswick, had recently received an accession of dignity respectively by the recognition of the former elector as King of Prussia at the peace settlement at Utrecht and by the accession of the House of Hanover to the crown of the United Kingdom. Whereas George I, by virtue of the circumstance that his house had acquired the electoral title only in 1692, had previously been of inferior status to Brandenburg, now he could negotiate with his brother Protestant monarch on terms at least of equality. When therefore Jablonski learned that the new Prussian king, Frederick William I, was deeply interested in the union project, the way seemed open for a more promising approach to this intractable question; and the initiative came again from the Prussian side, not from England as Leibnitz had desired.

[1] J. M. Kemble, *State Papers and Correspondence* (London, 1857), pp. 541 *seq.*

On 25 October/5 November 1717 Mr Charles Whitworth, British envoy extraordinary and plenipotentiary at Berlin, despatched to Wake a substantial packet of letters, entrusted to his care by Jablonski, concerning Protestant union. The first item was a copy of a letter from Jablonski to the King of Prussia, occasioned by an episode in February 1716 when, after receiving the Holy Communion on Septuagesima Sunday, Frederick William had introduced at breakfast the matter of religious unity.

The godly discourse about the union of the reformed churches, with which Your Majesty was pleased to honour me, when you last received the Holy Communion at Charlottenburg, has made a very deep impression upon my mind; and I cannot but consider it as the work of God in your royal heart, for the common advantage of Christianity. And since Your Majesty then ordered me to lay before you my most humble opinion both by word of mouth and in writing; that I might not appear negligent in a matter of this importance or give any interruption to Your Majesty's holy zeal, I thought myself obliged on the near arrival of the King of Great Britain to propose with all possible submission if Your Majesty might not think proper to concert this work of the union with the said King; and if for this end it might not be convenient that some persons of trust, though very few at the beginning, should be appointed on both sides to correspond together, and to propose the ways and means whereby this great work...might be carried on. As soon as these commissioners should have agreed on the preliminary methods of treating this affair, they should then make their report to their respective courts, and wait for further orders. It might be particularly deliberated how the Church of England might in due time, by means of his British Majesty, be engaged in this affair; for being highly esteemed by both parties in Germany, she might be a mediator to unite them to one another and to herself.

There followed the lengthy memorandum compiled by Jablonski, dated 31 July 1716 and dealing with two questions: 'in what the said union should consist'; and 'what might be the proper means to obtain it?'

In considering his first point Jablonski examined the chief differences between the Lutheran and Reformed churches in doctrine, ceremonies, and nomenclature.

In the doctrine, we do not agree on several points: as in the Lord's Supper, the Person of Christ, and the omnipresence of Christ's body, Predestination, and Grace, etc. In the ceremonies of the church, in which one party useth exorcism in baptism, wafers in the Lord's Supper, auricular confession, the sign of the cross, surplices, etc.; and the other not. In the name: the one call themselves Lutherans, from Luther; the other will not allow the name from any particular person, but content themselves for a distinction, to be termed Reformed.

If these differences could be removed or composed, the cause of separation would be ended. Therefore Jablonski proposed the following principles of accommodation.

First, concerning the difference in points of doctrine: the dispute must not be as to the truth of them; but it is enough that both parties acknowledge and declare that the differences in question do not concern the body and ground of religion, let the errors lie on which side they will, nor are against any fundamental article of faith; and therefore are not of such importance as to cause a schism in the church, and may be tolerated in it; there being no church in the world in which some different opinions are not suffered. Secondly, the ceremonies of the church, as they only regard the outward forms of religion, might be left to the free disposal of each Church. But yet a commission of several godly and moderate men and well experienced in Christian antiquity, might be appointed of both sides to examine the ceremonies and forms of each of the Evangelical churches, and to propose what might be laid aside as giving offence, or what might be received as serviceable to the edification of the church and for the propagation of godliness. Thirdly, the names taken from particular persons must cease, as many Lutherans are already not willing to receive that appellation. Both the churches might therefore be comprehended under the name of *Evangelical*, in opposition to that of Rome, which relies most on tradition.

By these means the author of this memorandum hoped to restore the unity existing before the famous Colloquy of Marburg in 1529 which had divided the Protestants on the doctrine of the Eucharist; and he commended particularly the *Consensus Sendomiriensis* of 1570, 'whereby both the Evangelical parties throughout the whole kingdom of Poland united themselves in a very edifying manner, which is worth perusal and may serve as a model for the proposed union'.

From these suggestions Jablonski passed to practical steps to set the negotiation in motion. It should be begun by two considerable states of the Empire, the one Lutheran and the other Reformed; and 'Providence seems to point out the two states which should be employed on this occasion, viz. his Prussian Majesty as Elector of Brandenburg, and His Majesty of Great Britain as Elector of Brunswick'. Of these, 'this pious care has been, as it were, hereditary' in the house of Brandenburg since the electorate of John Sigismund in the early seventeenth century; whilst in the electorate of Brunswick the university of Helmstedt had been traditionally favourable to union. If therefore these two sovereigns would appoint two or three moderate divines to confer and draw up a practical project, their conclusions, after being approved by the respective courts, might be communicated to a wider circle of Lutheran and Reformed divines, especially to 'the most moderate Superintendents and Rectors that they might by degrees dispose the minds of the clergy who are under their care and thereby prevent all untimely heats and cabals'. When this stage had been reached, the two sovereigns should consider the entry of other states into the agreement, Prussia commending it to Hesse-Cassel, the Churches of the Palatinate, and 'if it be thought fit', also to Holland and Switzerland; and George I to Saxony, Württemberg, and the imperial cities. Finally, it was Jablonski's dearest hope to bring the Church of England officially into the project; since he believed that the English clergy were 'already well-disposed for it', and the omens particularly propitious, 'since, not to mention others, the Archbishop of Canterbury and Bishop of London [Robinson], who now sit at the helm of that Church, are well-intentioned, experienced, active, public-spirited men, who have real affection for the foreign Reformed churches and are well-informed of our affairs'. If the Church of England could be formally engaged, she

> might be regarded and received by both parties as a mediator. She has something in common with each. In the doctrine she comes nearer to the Reformed; in some ceremonies to the Lutherans. She is loved and esteemed by both sides; and by her means the kingdoms of Sweden and Denmark might in time be so much the easier disposed to concur in this holy work.

Such was the ambitious goal and such the practical proposals of Jablonski. In order to secure as much support as possible, he communicated them to his associate in previous reunion negotiations, the philosopher Leibnitz at Hanover, who in turn made them known to Abbot Molanus, another apostle of unity. Accordingly on Michaelmas Day 1716 Leibnitz wrote to Baron de Printz, president of the council for ecclesiastical affairs at Berlin, to express the cordial approval of Molanus and himself for Jablonski's scheme, a copy of this letter being also enclosed for Wake's information. After stating his conviction 'que Dieu a donné pour cette affaire la conjoncture la plus favorable du monde', Leibnitz urged that Jablonski should be given a formal authorisation to visit George I at Hanover and to discuss the renewal of the negotiation for union. Finally the packet of letters sent to Wake included a copy of the formal commission of the King of Prussia, to be presented to George I by Jablonski and bearing the date of 13 October 1716; in which after recalling the earlier negotiation between the two courts, Frederick William expressed his earnest wish to see the matter now carried to a speedy conclusion, and to this end authorised his chaplain's visit to confer with George I and with such theologians as might be called into conference 'de ratione et modo conciliandae unionis'. Armed with this missive, Jablonski set off for Hanover (George I having left England for his German dominions on 7 July); but on his arrival there found that the English king had gone to his hunting estate at Göhrde, where he was expected to stay for six weeks, and whither Leibnitz and Molanus did not advise Jablonski to follow. Thus the first venture proved unsuccessful.[1]

Notwithstanding the undoubted sincerity of this overture, the great door

[1] Arch. W. Epist. 28, n.f., embracing the four documents specified in the text; *ibid.* Epist. 25, f. 48, Jablonski to Wake, 18 September 1717; H. Dalton, *Daniel Ernst Jablonski* (Berlin, 1903).

and effectual which it opened towards union was attended by many obstacles. Wake received the dossier on 28 November 1717 and immediately acknowledged its receipt to Whitworth, then at the Hague. In his reply to the Archbishop of 31 December/11 January 1717/18, Whitworth wrote cautiously and critically of the possibilities of a result.

It is certain the union of the Lutheran and Reformed churches is a work of very great difficulty, and rather to be wished than hoped; but attempts which from frequent disappointments might seem impracticable, meet sometimes with unexpected success; and when we have used all proper and reasonable endeavours, the event must be left to Providence. If ever this important point be brought about, it will probably be, as Your Grace observes, by Brunswick and Brandenburg, who are the most powerful Protestant princes in the Empire, and whose subjects are so little inflamed by the several different tenets they profess that there is scarce a show of animosity amongst the better sort on this occasion.

He added that the theologians of Saxony who had previously shown themselves hostile to *rapprochement* with the Reformed, might now realise that the defection of their elector to Rome had seriously weakened their position, and that without the support of their Reformed neighbours of Brandenburg and Cassel they might not be able to maintain themselves. However, there was no sure ground for confidence in the Prussian court, since 'some unhappy counsels have such influence there that 'tis hard to see how any overtures of this nature can be made'.[1]

Meantime Jablonski approached the primate directly in a letter of 21 January 1717/18, enquiring if the dossier had been received and asking particularly for advice as to the wisdom of a personal approach to George I on his next visit to Hanover.[2] The Archbishop replied with the assurance that he had read the documents forwarded by Whitworth, and had consulted the Prussian Resident in London, M. Bonet, and also Dr Thomas Bray about their contents. He affirmed his own zeal for unity, whilst insisting that the churchmen could effect nothing unless the two kings and their political advisers were willing to lend their authority to the matter, and observing somewhat ruefully that the latter were singularly loth to attend to ecclesiastical issues. 'Certainly I should hope that the time was even now near, had I not been taught by too long experience how difficult it is to persuade the chief persons, to whom political affairs are wont to be their sole concern, to give their care and authority in earnest to matters relating to the church.'[3] As proof of his own zeal Wake informed his friend Turrettini on 30 June 1718 of the steps he had taken during the previous six months.

[1] Arch. W. Epist. 28, n.f.

[2] *Ibid.* Epist. 25, f. 55.

[3] *Ibid.* f. 56. 'Et sane tempus illud jam prope adesse...sperarem, nisi longa nimium experientia didicissem, quam difficile sit principes viros (quibus res politicae unice curae esse solent) inducere ut in iis quae ad ecclesiam spectant, suam operam atque authoritatem serio impendant.'

As for the other noble design of uniting the Protestant and Evangelical churches in Germany, I have had many considerations about it this last year. It is near six months since our envoy at the Hague, Mr Whitworth, sent me the thoughts of Mr Jablonski upon the same subject. That worthy man has taken great pains in this affair; and Mr Whitworth, who is also himself zealous for it, brought his papers from Berlin to the Hague, and from thence transmitted them to me. I communicated them, as I have since done yours, to Monsr Bonet, the king of Prussia's minister here; who is also by that prince's direction, very hearty in the promotion of it. He has been with Monsr Bernstorff; and, at my request, has put freely to him to say whether he will enter into this matter or not; that so I may know how to act both with him and the king. For it will be in vain for me in such an affair as this, to treat with the latter unless I can be sure that I shall be supported by the former. Monsr Bernstorff has taken time to consider of it; which I do not like. For indeed it is almost the same thing to me as if he had desired not to be concerned in it. I have offered to wait upon him, and to meet Monsr Bonet at his house about this affair, who has orders from his master to use his best endeavours to forward it.[1]

Events proved the impossibility of divorcing the ecclesiastical question from political issues; and the latter, both at home and abroad, were sufficiently complex to provide the maximum hindrance to the desires of Wake and Jablonski. In the first place Bernstorff, the chief Hanoverian adviser of George I and therefore the necessary consultant on all matters, including ecclesiastical, affecting the king's continental possessions, was less than lukewarm in his attitude. Bonet reported to the Archbishop that he had found the minister at first indisposed to meddle in the matter at all; and even his final reply, asking for time to consider it carefully, was interpreted unfavourably. 'Cette réponse dilatoire me parut équivoque', Bonet commented; and added that even the suggestion of an interview, made by the Archbishop, was coolly received when Bernstorff realised that it was intended as a prelude to action on the lines of Jablonski's proposal.[2] A further difficulty lay in the open quarrel between George I and the Prince of Wales, which had repercussions no less in Europe than at home.

Were our affairs abroad a little more settled, and could we be so happy as to enjoy a better union at home, much more might be done to the glory of God, the peace of his church, and the interest of true Christianity everywhere [observed Wake to Turrettini in February 1718/19]. But we have a misfortune in our royal family that breaks all our measures, and particularly puts me under such difficulties as I scarce know how either to overcome or avoid. God in his good time will, I hope, open a way to a better understanding between the king and the prince; and then, if I live, I may be in a condition to do that which I can only wish for at the present.[3]

Furthermore relations between George I and his son-in-law and nephew Frederick William of Prussia were strained; and the complex conflicts of

[1] Geneva MSS. Inventaire 1569, f. 49.
[2] Arch. W. Epist. 31, f. 270. F. Bonet to Wake, 20 Juin 1718.
[3] Geneva MSS. Inventaire 1569, f. 47.

interest which developed between the two countries, and also between the English and Hanoverian ministers of George, in the course of the northern war, created further obstacles to co-operation in the field of religious unity. Although it is not possible here to trace the tortuous diplomatic relations of Great Britain and Prussia during these years, nevertheless it is against the background of an unstable international and political situation that the attempts of churchmen to set forward the union of Protestants must be viewed.

Nor were all the difficulties on one side. Whitworth, writing from the Hague on 7/18 October 1718 warned the Archbishop that 'the success of these proposals depends in a great measure on the sincerity and good intentions of the court of Prussia. There is no doubt but Monsr Bonnet, Dr Jablonski and several others of that court are very well inclined; but it is a misfortune that contrary counsels have prevailed there of late.'[1] In support of this warning Whitworth enclosed a letter from M. de Wrisberg, the representative of George I as elector of Brunswick at the diet of Ratisbon, in which he emphasised the umbrage caused to the king of Prussia by the events of the northern war, and his consequent insistence on monopolising the proposed joint-directory for ecclesiastical affairs to the exclusion of the English king.[2] With such obstacles there may be little surprise that the union project made heavy weather; though Whitworth encouraged the primate to persevere in his efforts.

> Perhaps the most likely way of proceeding would be to have a scheme first digested and settled between one or two of the chief Protestant princes before it be proposed for the general consideration, to prevent the intrigues and cavils which in all numerous assemblies are never to be avoided, and might overthrow the design before it is once well laid. As the territories of His Majesty and the King of Prussia are the most considerable of all the Protestants in Germany, whenever a plan of reunion can be introduced there, it is scarce to be doubted but the neighbouring princes of the Reformed religion will readily conform to it, for their own advantage and security. The committing the direction of affairs in the college of Protestants at Ratisbon to the joint administration of His Majesty and the King of Prussia, as has been proposed since the electoral prince of Saxony owned the change of his religion, might have been a very good step and foundation for this work; but hitherto it has been unhappily disappointed by private views and jealousies.[3]

Since the prospects of ecclesiastical union depended on the realisation of political concord, little could be done so long as the sovereigns of Great Britain and Prussia continued to be divided in policy and alienated in person. Jablonski might write to the Archbishop on 28 March 1719, urging that George I should take the lead—'O, si Deus ille pacis det, ut magnus Georgius

[1] Arch. W. Epist. 31, f. 271. (This item is continued on f. 325.)
[2] *Ibid.* f. 326.
[3] *Ibid.* f. 271; and continued on f. 325

ubi orbem pacaverit, ecclesiam quoque pacare aggrediatur'—[1] and Wake might reply on 22 May affirming his own fervent zeal for union and exhorting his correspondent to consult with Whitworth—'animus unionis illius cupidissimus, summa cum praecipuis utriusque partis hominibus authoritas ...quid de tali viro non sperare debemus?'[2] But only a week earlier the primate had confided to the anxious Turrettini his conviction that the matter must remain at a standstill for the present.

At present the political state of our affairs is such, that to push the affair of a union just at this time, would in my opinion be to hazard the losing of it. If we can be so happy as to see a sincere peace in the north; if our king comes to a clear understanding with the Prussian court, and that prince with ours; if we could be so happy as to be at peace among ourselves within our royal family (the divisions of which have so broken our best friends to pieces that there is no uniting them in any affair); and could we trust our Germans here (Mr Bernstorff and the rest) to act sincerely and heartily in this matter, which I still much doubt of, at the present; we might then be able to push on a union of the Lutherans and Calvinists with great hope of success. In the meantime we must be content to keep the matter on foot, that it may not seem to be utterly laid aside; and try what can be done gradually to dispose the minds of those to it, who may be most likely either to promote or hinder it.[3]

In a further letter of 17 June 1719 Wake confirmed this pessimistic forecast.

I am sorry to end with an indifferent account as to my present hopes of a union, concerning which I lately wrote in a more sanguine manner to Mr Jablonski. But the unhappy difference between our court and that of Berlin, which I reasonably hoped Mr Whitworth would have been able to make up, and which I fear there is but little hopes of doing at this time, will for a while retard this affair; which nevertheless we ought to have still in view, and to be ready on the first fair opportunity that shall be offered, to push as far as it will go.[4]

For a time even Jablonski's favour with his sovereign declined and he was under a cloud; but with the signing on 14 August 1719 of treaties between Prussia, Hanover and Great Britain (though attended by Frederick William's outspoken expression of hostility to Hanover), the Archbishop's hopes of a step forward in church unity revived. 'Our last letters from Mr Whitworth', he wrote on 22 July to Turrettini, 'encourage us to hope that a new treaty of peace and friendship will be signed in a few days between our king and the king of Prussia, which may probably be followed with a peace in the north, and give a fresh opportunity to press on the project of union, which these unhappy troubles have hitherto chiefly prevented'.[5]

[1] Arch. W. Epist. 25, f. 129.
[2] *Ibid.* f. 130.
[3] Geneva MSS. Inventaire 1569, f. 65. 13 May 1719.
[4] *Ibid.* f. 67.
[5] *Ibid.* f. 69. The King of Prussia's opinions were: 'Lieber mit Hannover mit grossem Plaisir Krieg anfangen; würde mich gleich gesund machen, wen ich in Hannövrischen etliche hundert Dörfer brennen sähe!'

Even these modest hopes were tardy of realisation. Not until 2 May 1720 was Wake able to report to Turrettini some progress.

I have...more than once discoursed with Mons Bernstorff about it. The old gentleman expressed a great readiness to join his interest and endeavour for the carrying on of so good a work....He has promised to speak to the king about it, and to prepare him to discourse with me upon this subject; so that I hope in time to make some progress in this matter. But all things in our court go so slowly on, whether by the methods of doing business there, or by the temper and usage of His Majesty and those about him, that no dispatch can be made in any thing.

One happy circumstance, however, the reconciliation of the King and Prince of Wales, promised to make the Archbishop's position easier and his influence greater, especially if followed by a reunion of the hitherto divided Whig ministers.

This will much strengthen my interest, if it should happen; and may enable me to do more with the king than I have been able, since that unhappy division, to do. For as I never meddled in those matters, but paid my duty to both courts, I lessened my interest with those about the king, but kept it more strongly with those who stuck to the prince and, I have reason to hope, will now be restored with him to favour.[1]

Accordingly on 15 July Wake reported to Jablonski that he had talked with Bernstorff, who had entered readily into the project of union and had promised to do his utmost to forward it; and that, encouraged by this, he had mentioned the matter to George I, 'sed paucis et caute', leaving Bernstorff to follow up the initiative and to dispose the king to support it. Jablonski should therefore seize this favourable opportunity ('si hanc occasionem dilabi e manibus patiamini vix aliam tam favorabilem deinceps invenietis') to secure agreement between the principal Lutheran and Reformed divines, so that the churchmen should not lag behind the laity.[2] For a time therefore the primate's correspondence glowed with optimism. On 29 June he wrote to Turrettini:

Mons. Bernstorff is hearty in it, and will do all he can to promote it. I have had some talk directly with the king himself concerning it; and I cannot but hope that if your friends abroad will now follow the matter as they ought to do, the two kings (I mean ours and Prussia) will come seriously into any overtures that may seem likely to procure so great a blessing....The business now to be done is, to keep up this good disposition on all sides as much as we can; to do nothing on our parts to shake it by unreasonable disputes or writings about these matters; to exhort our friends in Germany, especially those at Ratisbon and Hanover to push on as well a union among ourselves as a security against our enemies; which we shall take care to do here; and I hope you will not be wanting to excite your friends abroad to do likewise.[3]

[1] Geneva MSS. Inventaire 1569, f. 79.
[2] Arch. W. Epist. 25, f. 175.
[3] Geneva MSS. *ibid.* f. 73.

In a further letter of 12 July 1720, he affirmed:

I cannot but flatter myself that there is some prospect also of accomplishing the union so often in vain attempted between the Lutherans and the Reformed, but never so likely to be attained as at this juncture. The Lutheran ministers come much more readily into the proposal than they would ever do before. And as the King of Prussia is very desirous of it on the one hand, I am in good hopes our King will be no less forward for it on the other. His Majesty was pleased to receive the proposal very graciously from me, the last time I had the honour to speak with him; and Monsr Bernstorff, whose credit is at present very great with His Majesty, has promised to assist with all his interest in the promotion of it. I shall write both to him and Mr Jablonski about it very suddenly. If those abroad will but now push on this affair, I durst almost promise good success to it.[1]

True to his promise and zeal, Wake on 8 August sent to Bernstorff a reminder and an exhortation to ensure the support of George I for the proposal of Prussia; particularly recalling the suggestion of Jablonski that Lutheran and Reformed theologians should be appointed to confer on the projected union, together with leading laymen. 'Si on voulait faire assembler quelques ministres modérés d'une part et de l'autre, avec quelques commissionnaires laïcs bien disposés àfaire réussir une telle concorde, je suis persuadé que par l'autorité des deux rois l'affaire serait bientôt fini.'[2] But in the primate's opinion, Bernstorff needed continual prodding; for 'as his age and temper incline him to move very slowly in all kind of business, so he will need to be pushed on, or he will do nothing'.[3] When therefore Bernstorff reached Hanover, his zeal cooled and he adopted the more cautious views prevalent there: to the effect that until the negotiations between the Protestant princes of the Empire and the Roman Catholic states concerning the oppression suffered by Protestants in the territories of the latter, and especially in the Palatinate, had been settled, it would be imprudent to embark on any discussion of questions of Protestant union which might create division where a common front was essential!

Je n'ai eu garde de perdre de vue les sentiments salutaires pour la réunion des Protestants que vous m'avez fait connaître, my lord, avant ma départ de Londres [wrote Bernstorff to the Archbishop on 10 October]. J'ai consulté là-dessus ceux de notre Église, et les Reformés qui sont en ce pays ici. Les plus sages sont d'opinion qu'il ne faut pas commencer à faire traiter cette matière par les ecclésiastiques, lesquels pourraient tomber en des disputes, mais faire régler certains principes par les conseils des princes, à quoi on mettra la main dès que les différends avec les Catholiques Romains seront en quelque train d'accommodement; ce que j'espère sera bientôt. On n'ose pas y toucher plus tôt, crainte que les difficultés qui pourront survenir entre nous ne donneraient occasion de troubler la bonne harmonie qui nous est si nécessaire pour résister aux adversaires communs.[4]

[1] *Ibid.* f. 77.
[2] Arch. W. Epist. 25, f. 187.
[3] Geneva MSS. Inventaire 1569, f. 85. 5 December 1720.
[4] *Ibid.* f. 84. 'Extrait d'une lettre de M. Bernstorff du 10 Octobre'; Arch. W. Epist. 25, f. 203.

Jablonski was justified therefore in lamenting to Wake on 3 October the little progress which had been achieved: 'illud vero perquam mihi dolet, quod eventus tantae spei nondum respondeat'; a mischance which he ascribed largely to the absence of Whitworth, who was the only person with sufficient influence at Berlin and Hanover to bring the scheme to fulfilment. Meantime Jablonski had communicated the Archbishop's letters to Baron de Printz, now 88 years of age, who had advised the sending of a copy to Abbot Molanus so that he might urge George I to nominate some theologians within his dominions to correspond with Jablonski on the matter. Accordingly this had been done on 20 August, but no reply had been received yet. Jablonski therefore now favoured a *démarche* at Ratisbon among the representatives of the Protestant princes there; but it was essential that Great Britain and Prussia should afford a joint lead if the lesser powers were to respond; and as a preliminary step he suggested a joint declaration of these two kings that they considered that a sufficient basis of fundamental agreement between Lutheran and Reformed existed in their dominions for further action to be considered.[1] To this letter Wake did not reply for seven months, until 30 May 1721; when he affirmed his own zeal and efforts in the cause of union, reported the opinion of Bernstorff of the previous October, and urged that the matter could only be hastened from Berlin and Hanover, where Jablonski and Whitworth should concert measures to this end. For his part the primate approved the idea of a joint declaration of George I and Frederick William, to which the lesser Protestant princes should be invited to adhere; 'sed haec ego tuo et Whitworthii judicio omnino relinquenda censeo'.[2] With Bernstorff still tarrying abroad, and such slender signs of progress to report, there was as little encouragement as enthusiasm therefore in the Archbishop's cautious statement to Turrettini on 20 February 1720/1:

Monsr Bernstorff's secretary is already come hither. The good old man will follow himself in two months' time; and I am persuaded, will enter with very good earnest upon the best measures to engage our king, with the king of Prussia, to set our great design on foot. I must ingenuously own that I expect more from the ministers of state in this case, than from those of the gospel; and do hope that they will bring the others to reason, and to agree to what is both in itself desirable, and so necessary at this time for our common preservation.[3]

The complaint against the ministers of the gospel was perhaps a natural impatience at the slow rate of advance, and was shared indeed by some of Wake's co-partners in the enterprise. Both Jablonski and Turrettini had been anxious to celebrate the bicentenary of the German Reformation in 1719 by inaugurating the project for healing the divisions amongst Protestants. In

[1] Arch. W. Epist. 25, f. 219.
[2] *Ibid.* f. 221.
[3] Geneva MSS. Inventaire 1569, f. 89.

particular Turrettini had published in that year at Geneva his *Nubes Testium pro moderato et pacifico de rebus theologicis judicio et instituenda inter Protestantes concordia*, with a dedicatory epistle to Wake. In a prefatory essay of fifty-six pages the author contributed his own plea for the recognition by Lutherans and Reformed of the distinction between fundamental and non-essential articles of faith, and the toleration of differences of opinion concerning the latter within the same ecclesiastical communion. This was followed by a further fifty pages of testimonies to this principle from scripture, from patristic writings, and from Protestant divines from Luther to Turrettini's contemporaries. A further hundred pages assembled citations from both Lutheran and Reformed divines in favour of union between the two traditions, and the volume concluded with a collection of Acts of synods and conferences recommending this desired end. The publication was of considerable importance as an argument to Protestants who followed Luther and Calvin to consider the volume and weight of testimony in support of schemes of unity; and, like all catenae of opinions, it was designed to further the aims of its compiler. Its provenance from the city and church of Calvin himself lent authority to its contents, and inspired the hope of a correspondingly eirenic reply from the Lutheran side. From Tübingen there came the desired response; for that university, under the chancellorship of Christopher Matthew Pfaff supported by Professor John Christian Klemm, was a protagonist in the cause of union, and both these theologians were regular and frequent correspondents of Wake. In 1720 Pfaff published his *Dissertatio Polemica de Successione Apostolica*, with a dedication to the primate; and justly so, for in this short pamphlet of thirty-three pages the author argued that the apostolic succession had been best preserved in the Church of England, next in the Eastern Orthodox Churches, and least satisfactorily in the Church of Rome. With Pfaff and Klemm, as also with another of their colleagues at Tübingen, Daniel Michael, the Archbishop maintained a regular correspondence, repeating his standpoint about the difference between fundamentals and non-essentials, urging them to perseverance, and promising the support of his counsel, his prayers, and his influence. The university of Helmstedt likewise continued its traditional sympathy for toleration; and Halle, the academic stronghold of Pietism, where moreover August Hermann Francke was busily employed in training Lutheran missionaries for work in India under the auspices of S.P.C.K., was also enthusiastic in support. But there were many adversaries to union amongst both Lutherans and Reformed. To the former a great stumbling-block was the acceptance by the latter of the decrees of the Synod of Dort; whilst the contemporary disputes in the Swiss Protestant cantons concerning the abstruse doctrines of predestination and election, as reflected in the controversy about the *Formula Consensus*, emphasised the continuing prominence of these issues, and increased the apprehensions of Lutherans. Wake indeed was fully aware that the Swiss *débâcle* provided almost irrefutable arguments to the Lutheran opponents of union. In similar manner the opponents of Pietism within the Lutheran states became enemies also to the project of Protestant union. Dr Solomon Cyprian, ecclesiastical counsellor of the Duke of Saxe-Gotha, was active with both pen and voice against union; and when at Hamburg pulpit polemics were added to inflame opinion against the Reformed, the hopes of agreement amongst divines seemed vain. On the Reformed side also there were fears of heterodoxy in respect of the Lutheran doctrine of consubstantiation, and mistrust of Lutheran ceremonies and vestments. Unless therefore the godly princes and their ministers could overrule the quarrels of their theologians, the prospect for unity was dark.

Pessimism indeed was the theme of the correspondence between the triumvirate of apostles of unity, Jablonski, Turrettini, and the English archbishop in the early months of 1722. Jablonski lamented to Wake on 16 February the new wounds received by the friends of reunion in the house of their fellow-churchmen: 'tantum abest ut antiquis vulneribus sanandis studeant theologi, ut potius infanda illa et plus quam civilia fratres inter Protestantes bella recrudescant'. His only hope lay in the political necessities of the German Protestants and in the reaction of the princes to the encroachments of Rome by affirming the necessity for union amongst themselves.[1] In point of fact before the end of that very month a new light shone from the most unexpected quarter, that of the Corpus Evangelicorum at Ratisbon. This association of Protestant states had indeed as its *raison d'être* since its foundation in 1653 the defence of Protestant interests against the aggrandisement of Rome as represented by the Corpus Catholicorum. But the mutual suspicions and jealousies of its thirty-nine members were so acute and its consequent lassitude so disabling, that the elector of Saxony had continued to hold the chairmanship of the body for some years after his apostasy to Rome! In 1720, however, Chancellor Pfaff published, both in Latin and German, a project for Protestant union (*Näherer Entwurf von der Vereinigung der Protestierenden Kirchen*), which Count Metternich, the Prussian representative at Ratisbon, made the basis of fifteen articles which he submitted to the Diet. On 28 February 1722 the Corpus Evangelicorum, to the equal surprise of its own members and of the states which they represented, responded to the lead of Prussia, Hanover and Cassel by adopting the *Conclusum* 'that they would live together in unity, abstain from all invectives, accusations of heresy, and sectarian names; use on both sides the name "Evangelical"; or if the need for differentiation was felt, use the names "Evangelical" and

[1] Arch. W. Epist. 26, f. 57.

"Evangelical Reformed"; and that henceforth all calumnious expressions both from the pulpit and in writing should be strictly prohibited'.[1]

This was indeed a very modest (albeit necessary) first step towards union; far from the organic unity desired by Jablonski, Wake, and Turrettini, but welcomed as a vantage ground from which further advance could be made. Nevertheless, despite its comparatively colourless and mild content, its publication aroused a storm of controversy. In May 1722 Metternich reprinted and circulated widely the famous letter of Calvin to Luther in 1545, which had arrived after Luther's death and had been found by Melanchthon with the seal unbroken, with a view to convincing the so-called champions of orthodoxy of his own day that both Calvin and Luther had more pacific sentiments than was generally supposed. On both sides of the dispute, ink flowed freely; and a list of publications on the subject in 1723 covered fifty-six pages! At Hamburg the troubles were intensified when the pastor of St James church, Erdmann Neumeister, not only continued his pulpit polemic, but also published a warning to Lutherans that the proposed union with the Reformed was contrary to the Decalogue, to the Apostles' Creed, and to Lutheran doctrines of Baptism, the power of the keys, the Lord's Supper and the catechism! So great was the furore aroused in the city that joint representations of the kings of Great Britain and Prussia were necessary to restore civic order. Moreover the *Conclusum* was but a recommendation, which needed ratification and enforcement by the civil authority in each of the several and separate thirty-nine states of the Corpus Evangelicorum before it could take effect; and the delays in securing this next step were protracted for several years.

In England the recrudescence of Jacobite plots, the consequent postponement of George I's intended journey to Hanover and the arrest of Bishop Atterbury in August 1722 turned attention to domestic instead of to foreign issues; and not only frustrated Wake's hopes of progress as a consequence of the King's visit to Germany, but made it impossible to press Protestant union on the ministers of state. Accordingly when Jablonski in September urged the Archbishop to approach Bernstorff in order to persuade George I to concert measures with the King of Prussia in respect of the *Conclusum*, he received the reply that not until the dangers of conspiracy at home had been dissipated, would it be possible to devote time to such extraneous matters. 'Nescio an ad res exteras animos eorum adhuc abstrahere licebit.'[2] Wake

[1] Hermann Dalton, *Daniel Ernst Jablonski*, p. 292. 'Man wolle mit einander in Einigkeit leben, aller Schmähungen, Verketzerungen, und Sektennamen sich enthalten, und sich gemeinsam Evangelisch nennen; sobald man aber sich unterscheiden wolle, Evangelische und Evangelische-Reformierte sagen; auch sollten fernerhin alle kalumniösen Äusserungen nicht nur auf der Kanzel, sondern auch in Schriften streng verboten werden.'

[2] Arch. W. Epist. 26, f. 72. 'xii Kal. Oct. 1722'; and f. 73. 5 November.

indeed was convinced that the key to the solution lay not in England but abroad; and in an interchange of correspondence during the early months of 1723 with Baron de Wrisberg, the Hanoverian representative at Ratisbon, pressed upon him the importance of using his influence there in order to secure the enforcement of the *Conclusum*.[1] At the moment the primate still had more confidence in ministers of state than in ministers of the gospel.

Si la paix de nos Églises et l'Union si nécessaire à tous les Protestans sera jamais accomplie, j'ose dire qu'elle doit être faite par les laïques; et que les ministres et professeurs ne doivent être trop entendus dans cette affaire. C'est une honte à notre caractère d'avouer cela, mais l'expérience montre fort clairement que l'observation n'est que trop juste.[2]

With the conclusion in October 1723 of the treaty of Charlottenburg between Great Britain and Prussia, designed to settle outstanding differences and to cement the political agreement by a double-marriage alliance between the two houses, the way seemed once more open for an accord on the religious question.

J'espère que par l'authorité des deux rois [wrote Wake to Wrisberg on 12 November] une paix ecclésiastique sera en fin établie entre les Protestans et les Évangéliques.... C'est à votre éminence et les autres ministres Protestans à Ratisbonne de concerter les mesures propres à fair réussir un entreprise si charitable et en même temps si nécessaire à la santé de tous qui aiment et qui ont embrassés la vérité de l'Évangile.[3]

To this exhortation Wrisberg returned the amiable reply, in terms appropriate to a New Year's greeting: 'J'espère que l'année nouvelle nous sera aussi favorable pour avancer les intérêts de notre sainte religion que l'année passée a été fertile en adversités et revers.'[4]

But the old year had brought changes in England which deprived the Archbishop of much of his former political influence. When Townshend and Walpole came into office in 1723 it soon became evident that the new bishop of London, Edmund Gibson, would be their ecclesiastical adviser; and the evidence of 1723 was confirmed and emphasised in 1724. On 28 July 1724 Wake observed to Professor Iselius of Basle that he did not know whether the reply of the Swiss cantons to George I had reached the English ministers of the Crown; for official papers were not shown to him since the change of ministry, and he would not ask to see them.

For indeed our affairs are in such a situation that with the change in the king's ministers, the familiarity which I had with their predecessors has been very much diminished, without however any, even the slightest, loss of the favour with which His Majesty has always honoured me. And although I am in a position easily to

[1] *Ibid.* ff. 101, 108, 109, 110.
[2] *Ibid.* f. 121. 24 June 1723.
[3] *Ibid.* Epist. 31, f. 311 (2).
[4] *Ibid.* f. 312.

get to know all these things, if I were to ask in but one word for them, yet so cautiously do we conduct our life that we all prefer rather to be ignorant of many things than to ascertain them by enquiring with over-much anxiety.[1]

At the same time there came curious reports from Ratisbon that Wrisberg had stated that his efforts for Protestant union were entirely personal and that he had no instructions formally from his sovereign to support it, with the inevitably unfortunate impression produced thereby.

I am surprised to hear of an incident at Ratisbon [wrote Wake to Turrettini], that seems to speak all hopes of a union to be vain and ineffectual. It is the declaration made by our king's minister there, that what he had done in that affair was all of his own private motion; but that as a public minister he had no instructions to favour it, but rather the contrary. If this account be true, which I have just received from a good hand, I cannot guess the meaning of it. I am sure Mons Wrisberg in his last letter to me, was very zealous in the pursuit of this union, and our king's letters to your country both turned upon the supposition of his hearty concern for it.[2]

The explanation offered by Wrisberg was that his instructions did not come directly from England, but indirectly via Hanover, and that the primate should therefore bring pressure to bear on George I's Hanoverian ministers. But the effect was undeniable; 'que le zèle pour cette Union est fort refroidi ici'.[3] At home, moreover, Wake's influence was further diminished by the absence from England of Bernstorff, who had been his intermediary with the King in these matters; 'ex quo enim illustrissimus Bernsdorfius a nobis discessit, neminem hic habeo cum quo de his rebus aut libere conferre audeam, aut eas serenissimo regi nostro efficaciter commendare'.[4] Notwithstanding, the matter was of such importance that the primate made a formal approach to George I through the Hanoverian minister Count Bothmer; and as a result of a long conversation severally with each of them hoped that both were well disposed in forwarding union.[5]

At the beginning of 1725 indeed Wake's hopes seemed somewhat to have revived. In a postscript to a letter to Turrettini of 2 January 1724/5, written two days later, he added:

I ought not to forget to tell you, that for some time past I have had a new intercourse by letters with two of our friends in Germany upon the old and almost

[1] *Ibid.* Epist. 26, f. 184. 'Ita quippe se habent res nostrae, ut mutatis ministris regiis, familiaritas illa quam cum eorum antecessoribus habui, plurimum imminuta sit, absque tamen ulla vel minima jactura illius favoris quo me semper honoravit ipsa regia Majestas. Et quamvis eo in statu sim, ut haec omnia facile cognoscere possim, si vel uno verbo ea exquirerem, adeo tamen caute inter nos vivitur, ut multa potius nescire omnes velimus, quam anxie nimis inquirendo ea cognoscere.'

[2] Geneva MSS. Inventaire 1569, f. 117. Cf. Arch. W. Epist. 26, ff. 184, 185, 187.

[3] Arch. W. Epist. 26, f. 216. Wrisberg to Wake. '3 Août 1724.'

[4] *Ibid.* f. 209. Wake to Klemm. 2 October 1724.

[5] *Ibid.* f. 220. Wake to Wrisberg. 22 October 1724.

forgotten affair of union: Monsr Klemm, professor at Tübingen, and Monsr de Wrisberg, His Majesty's commissioner at Ratisbon and the life of the congress there in what concerns the Protestant interest. The former much complains of the coldness and backwardness of our friends to obtain such a union. The latter professes his zeal for it, though he agrees at the same time that it rather seems to go backward than forward. To find out the cause of this, I have purposely entered into some conversations with the Count de Bothmer about it, who a little before Christmas took the pains to come over the water to me on purpose upon this subject....It is now said that they again begin to think of such a union. I have done my utmost to revive it both at home and abroad.[1]

In the following March, Jablonski broke a long silence by sending an estimate of the friends and opponents of union in Germany, and affirming the need of action in regard to the *Conclusum*. It had been enforced by the Reformed landgrave of Hesse and by the Lutheran margrave of Baireuth and refused by the elector of Saxony, whilst the electors of Brandenburg and Brunswick had deferred their decision. Jablonski believed that if George I would take the lead, Prussia and its satellites would follow.[2] In his reply the primate concurred in the desire but was doubtful of the practical prospects; not only because he had to work through Bothmer alone, but also because the minor matter of a royal brief for a collection in behalf of the persecuted Protestants of the Palatinate, which had been urged by the Corpus at Ratisbon, had remained undecided for two years! His conclusion was that the initiative must come from the Hanoverian counsellors of George I; 'id non a nostris hic ministris regiae majestatis proponi debuerit, sed ab iis quibus electoratus sui cura Hannoverae committitur'. This meant that Bernstorff and Wrisberg must take the lead, and Wake was convinced that if the King of Prussia could reach agreement with them on the matter and send one word of this to England, then the issue would be as Jablonski wished. 'Quod si serenissimus rex vester in eandem cum illis sententiam conveniret, et vel verbo hoc unico regi nostro significaret, nullus dubito quin tota haec res juxta vota tua protinus absolveretur.'[3] As evidence of his good will the Archbishop promised again to communicate with Bernstorff at Hanover and to use his good offices with Bothmer at home.

In what concerns the union so much desired among the Protestants especially in Germany [he wrote to Turrettini on 8 April], since the departure of Mr Wrisberg there is hardly anybody that makes it his business to support it. I have at the request of Mr Jablonski and Professor Klemm done what I could to engage the Count de Bothmer in pressing the regency at Hanover to come into the measures agreed upon two years ago at Ratisbon, which would induce the King of Prussia to do the same. That gentleman is very obliging to me, and seems ready to assist in

[1] Geneva MSS. Inventaire 1569, f. 121.
[2] Arch. W. Epist. 26, f. 269. 10 March 1725.
[3] *Ibid.* f. 270. 'xii Kal. Maii 1725'.

whatever I desire of this kind from him. But how far he enters upon principle into these measures, I cannot tell. I doubt he is not very zealous in pursuing of them. When the King goes to Hanover, if I have a messenger whom I can depend on, I will earnestly recommend this affair to Mons Bernstorff, who is truly desirous of promoting a union among the different parties of the Reformed.[1]

Accordingly in June he wrote to Bernstorff urging him to propose to George I during the King's visit to Hanover the publication of the *Conclusum* in his German territories.

Vous m'excuserez, monsieur, si l'amour que j'ai pour l'union de nos frères et le soutien de notre religion si violemment attaquée par nos ennemis, me fasse un peu plus zélé qu'à l'ordinaire pour cette concorde, par laquelle seulement nous pouvons vraisemblablement nous défendre contre leurs attentats. J'espère que par votre entremise le projet de Ratisbonne peut être mis en exécution, et d'un si bon commencement une union plus étroite être en fin accomplie.[2]

This missive was carried by Dr John Gilbert, the Anglican chaplain attending George I to Hanover; and hopes were even entertained that the diplomatic negotiations during the King's visit might result in an ecclesiastical no less than a political accord. These hopes were dashed by the terms of the treaty of Hanover of 3 September 1725 between Great Britain, France and Prussia. 'The treaty of alliance has, I believe, shewn Your Grace how much help our religion has to expect from it', commented M. Thorn; and Wake was further discouraged by the failure of Bernstorff to reply to two letters which he had sent, and by reports that Lord Townshend, who had accompanied the King to Germany, was firmly opposed to the execution of the proposal for a collection in Great Britain in behalf of both Lutheran and Reformed in the Palatinate.[3] With the fading of these hopes the primate began to express the same sentiments of disappointment with ministers of state as he had avowed in regard to ecclesiastics. For statesmen regarded religious affairs only from the standpoint of public tranquillity; 'caetera omnia, nisi quatenus in illis salus publica versatur, parum ad se pertinere putant'.[4] When Wrisberg informed him on 5 December that he had been ordered to stay at Ratisbon instead of proceeding to Hanover, Wake resigned himself to the consolation of having done all he could and of leaving the issue to Providence. 'C'est toujours une satisfaction de considérer que nous avons faits notre devoir; et que du reste il faut nous soumettre à la volonté de Dieu, qui ne manquera pas de soutenir son Église par des autres voies que nous dans le peu de lumière

[1] Geneva MSS. Inventaire 1569, f. 131.

[2] Arch. W. Epist. 26, f. 289. June 1725; cf. f. 286. 9 June.

[3] *Ibid.* Epist. 31, f. 320. 17–28 August 1725; f. 322. 10–21 November, from F. Thorn; Epist. 26, f. 317. Wake to Wrisberg. 18 October 1725; f. 322. 5 December 1725. Wrisberg to Wake.

[4] *Ibid.* Epist. 26, f. 301. Wake to Iselius. 6 October 1725.

que nous avons, n'avons pas attendues.'[1] The course of events, however, had made it clear that the failure of the plan was the fault not of Prussia but of George I; for on the one hand Jablonski had won over the Prussian delegate at Ratisbon, M. Ilgen, and therewith had persuaded the King of Prussia to offer another olive branch, and on the other hand the Hanoverian counsellors of the King of Great Britain had made no reply. To Klemm on 28 January 1725/6 the Archbishop confessed his frustration. 'Some reasons or other still hold back the Hanoverian counsellors of His Majesty from acceding to these our wishes, although the most illustrious King of Prussia had shown himself once more ready to put into effect these matters; nor can it be doubted that the other princes would follow their examples.'[2] In a letter of a week earlier to his most faithful friend in these matters, Turrettini, Wake confided his despair in very similar terms.

I have endeavoured all I could this last summer to push on the business of a union; at least to get what was concluded at Ratisbon in order thereunto, put into execution. My several letters coming at last to the knowledge of the King of Prussia, and Dr Jablonski having the good fortune to persuade Mr Ilgen (who before stood off) to come into it, letters were sent by that King's order to let the court of Hanover know that his majesty was ready to join with our King in ordering that conclusion to be executed in both their dominions. Mr Bernstorff, to whom I wrote two letters but without answer to either, was of opinion that things were not yet ready for it. So the matter stays with the Hanoverian ministers; and I cannot tell whether anything will come of all our pains in this point at the last.[3]

Thus the affair of Protestant union petered out; for there could be little surprise that the Prussian king lost heart and interest in face of the rebuffs which greeted his advances. Even the joint execution of the *Conclusum* was beyond the capacity of the sovereigns of Great Britain and Prussia to agree upon. Such a joint declaration, indeed, would have had only symbolic value; for in practice Prussia had long adopted this attitude in regard to both the Lutherans and Reformed within its dominions. The joint pronouncement therefore would not so much have altered the existing state of affairs in religion as provided an earnest of the intention of the two powers to advance towards the organic unity desired by Jablonski and seconded by Wake. With the failure to take the initial, symbolic step, the wider hopes naturally disappeared. *Nolite confidere in principibus* might well have been the conclusion of the two churchmen in face of the personal rivalries and jealousies of their

[1] Arch. W. Epist. 26, f. 323. Wake to Wrisberg. '14 Janvier 1725/6.'

[2] *Ibid.* f. 328. 'Sed nescio quae rationes adhuc retinent Majestatis suae consiliarios Hannoveranos, quo minus ad haec vota nostra accedant; quamvis ad ea pariter statuenda paratum se denuo ostendit illustrissimus rex Prussiae; nec dubitandum sit quin ceteri principes eorum exempla sequerentur.'

[3] Geneva MSS. Inventaire 1569, f. 125. 20 January 1725/6

respective kings, which prevented them from agreeing on measures for the common defence and unity of Protestants despite the need and urgency of such concord.

But it would be unjust to blame the sovereigns and their statesmen overmuch. Even if Protestant union could not be accomplished without their active support and initiative, they could hardly be expected to risk the possible ill effects of such a policy if it were opposed by many of their churchmen. In point of fact Wake had despaired of the divines more than of the ministers of state; and the plain fact was that opinion, particularly amongst the Lutherans, was not sufficiently agreed to make the venture possible. In addition to the vehement pamphlet controversy which had followed the issue of the *Conclusum* in 1722, other signs of theological division had been added. Even in the Palatinate, where Protestants were subjected to various acts of oppression by Karl Philipp, quarrels between Lutheran and Reformed (in which the former were accused by the latter of demanding such a share of their property and revenues as would drive them to insolvency) broke out, to the evident delight of the common enemy. Likewise during the course of Wake's negotiations for union, there came from the Lutheran side a proposal, emanating from Saxony and forwarded by Wrisberg in October 1724, for a union of Lutherans with the Church of England on terms exclusive of the Reformed. The summary of this project was that union between Lutherans and Anglicans was possible because both were Arminian in theology and closely approximating in liturgy and government, whereas no union could be contemplated by either church with the Reformed unless they formally disavowed the decrees of the Synod of Dort. In forwarding this memorandum indeed Wrisberg observed that

on pourrait soupçonner que cela vient de la part des ennemis des Réformés pour traverser l'union projetée ici entre les Protestans de l'Empire par un tel projet nouveau. Cependant il se pourrait aussi que l'union préalable avec l'Église Anglicane et les Évangeliques attirait aussi les Universalistes parmis les Réformés, comme il y en a beaucoup à Berlin, Genève et ailleurs, ce qui produirait à la fin une accession générale.[1]

Naturally, when this counter-move became known to the Reformed, it evoked a protest in which the authors had an easy task to demonstrate that many leaders of the Church of England in the sixteenth and seventeenth centuries had agreed with the Calvinist interpretation of the doctrines of predestination and grace; and that James I had appointed official delegates from the Churches of England and Scotland to attend the Synod of Dort who had subscribed its doctrinal decrees.[2] The episode had no direct effect or

[1] Arch. W. Epist. 26, ff. 218 and 219. 16 October 1724.
[2] *Ibid.* ff. 282 and 283. '5 Avril 1725.'

influence on the failure of the project for Protestant union; for Wake rejected it out of hand, observing to Wrisberg that it seemed to have been written 'pour empêcher l'union désirée' rather than to advance it. Notwithstanding, it drew from him rejoinders emphasising once again the Anglican position of toleration of differences of opinion on such points of theology, and repudiating the Lutheran suggestion of compelling the Reformed to disavow the Synod of Dort. Rather should both parties realise that only by adopting the Anglican attitude was union either possible or to be desired.

Nos Articles de la Grace et de la Justification sont composés avec une telle latitude qu'ils ne determinent rien précisément d'un côté ou de l'autre. Et nous sommes défendus de prêcher sur ces sujets dans la chaire; et depuis plusieurs années nous n'avons eu presque aucunc controversie sur ces points. Ainsi nous gardons la paix sans gêner les consciences. Pourquoi, monsieur, ce qui a été fait dans notre Église depuis près de cent années passées, ne peut-on faire dans les autres communions? Et laissant à tous leurs opinions particuliers, convenir dans des Articles généraux comme les nôtres pour la souscription publique et défendre aux ministres de prêcher les uns contre les autres sur des matières si difficiles à expliquer et si peu nécessaires au salut? Si on est résolu de n'avoir aucune concorde que par l'entière soumission d'une partie à l'autre il est en vain de poursuivre aucun projet de paix. On ferait mieux de dire franchement, nous n'aurons aucune communion avec ceux qui diffèrent le moindre de nos opinions, s'ils ne changent leurs sentiments et se soumettent absolument à notres déterminations.[1]

On the other hand the Reformed should not suppose that the presence of Anglican delegates at the Synod of Dort and their signature of its doctrinal decrees implied that the Church of England officially accepted them. 'Nous n'avons rien à faire avec la Synode de Dordrecht; nous ni approuvons ni condamnons la doctrine de cette assemblée.'[2]

The intervention of Wake both in the Swiss controversies concerning the *Formula Consensus* and in the negotiations for the union of Lutheran and Reformed in Germany, had sprung from the initiative made at the beginning of his primacy for a wider unity of all Protestant churches and specifically for the restoration of a reformed episcopacy amongst those churches of the continent which lacked it. It is important therefore to consider what rejoinders were made to this plea. The Antistes of Zürich, Peter Zeller, replied to the primate's overture by the expression of a pious wish for unity; and particularly exhorted those who found the innocent name of bishop odious and distasteful ('innocens episcoporum nomen tam invisum ac exosum') to consider how many and great benefits had proceeded from the episcopate since the Reformation both in England and elsewhere, and to reflect that, where agreement existed in doctrine, contention should not be stirred up

[1] Arch. W. Epist. 26, f. 220. Wake to Wrisberg. 22 October 1724.
[2] *Ibid.* f. 286. Wake to Wrisberg. 9 June 1725.

concerning differences in church government ('ubi consensus in doctrina, propter regiminis ecclesiastici aliquod discrimen nullas esse turbas').[1] The pastors, professors and doctors of the church and university of Basle sent a formal reply by the hand of Jerome Burchard, professor and antistes; in which, after recording their agreement in doctrine with the Church of England, they affirmed in respect of church-order that, if names and other externals in which religion was agreed not to consist were laid aside, there would be no difference between their churches as to principles. ('Denique quod ad Ecclesiae quoque regimen atque gubernationem attinet, si modo nomina et alia quaedam externa, in quibus religionem sitam esse nemo unquam affirmavit, seponantur, nequaquam vestras rationes dissidere a nostris, id quod etiam quamplurimi vestrae hujus florentissimae ecclesiae theologi atque eximii sacrorum antistites existimarunt ac ultro praedicarunt, plane persuasi sumus.'[2]) From Geneva likewise the pastors and professors of the church and university sent a formal response, signed by Turrettini as president and Le Fort as scribe, in which they assured the primate that, far from condemning the Anglican church-order, the theologians of their city reckoned it a particular felicity of the Church of England and accorded recognition of its ordinations. ('Nam ut de Ecclesia Anglicana primum dicamus, tantum abfuerant a damnando ejus regimine, a nostro quantumvis discrepante, theologi nostri, ut eam contra felicitatem vobis perpetuam esse optaverint; quo fit ut vestris ordinationibus suus semper nostra in Ecclesia steterit honos.'[3]) However, beyond the individual ordinations according to the Anglican rite of Swiss students and divines during their residence in England, no steps were taken to restore episcopacy and episcopal ordination in the Reformed churches of that country. The Archbishop's wish remained therefore unrealised. From the side of the Lutherans, Pfaff had contributed his pamphlet on the episcopal succession in the Church of England, in the hope of winning his fellow-churchmen to the recovery of episcopacy, of which they had preserved an analogous office in their Superintendents. ('Etenim fieri sic posset ut et nostros homines ardor quidem et cupido sic invaderet, ad ejusmodi successionem episcopalem ordinemque aspirandi, qui in Ecclesia Anglicana floret, maxime cum in Ecclesiis nostris analogi quid in Superintendentibus nostris habeamus.'[4]) From Berlin Jablonski welcomed the suggestion for a general restoration of episcopacy, since already during the primacy of Tenison and the reign of Queen Anne he had entered into discussions with Archbishop Sharp, at the authorisation of the King of Prussia, for the adoption both of episcopacy and of the Anglican Book of Common Prayer within that sovereign's territories. Indeed Jablonski was as warmly

[1] *Ibid.* Epist. 25, f. 36. 22 April 1717.
[2] *Ibid.* f. 145. 12 July 1719.
[3] *Ibid.* f. 140. 26 May 1719.
[4] *Ibid.* f. 225. 'Non: April: 1721.'

attached to episcopacy as Wake himself, and as persuaded of the necessity of its restoration as a condition of organic unity; but his hopes like those of the primate were frustrated by the combination of political and ecclesiastical obstacles which they encountered. No result was attained therefore in the unification of the Protestant churches by a general adoption of episcopacy.

In face of this discouragement, Wake fell back on his second line of approximation by the adoption of a common confession of faith and liturgy. In a letter of 5 December 1720 to Geneva he observed:

> As we shall never become a compact body nor make any great figure in the world, while we continue a disjointed people, and have every one his separate confession and form of worship, so I could wish that there might be an agreement in some common form of both; which would make us all appear one reformed church in the several countries in which we are dispersed. I add nothing as to government, because I take it at present to be impracticable. But as that is less observed, so it would not hinder us from being in all outward appearance one body, one church, were we united in one confession of faith and in one common manner of public worship in our congregations....I believe the Church of Geneva has no exceptions against either our liturgy or our Thirty-nine Articles, even the Thirty-sixth not excepted which only asserts the validity of our Book of Ordinations but does not affirm the necessity of the three orders which we retain in our Church. Could we by degrees bring ourselves to such a happy estate, that wherever we went, we should find the same method of public devotion used in our churches, as there is in the Romish church, we should soon wear off all our prejudices against one another, and begin to think ourselves as well as to convince others, that we are all together one communion, one body, one church under the same one head and saviour the Lord Christ Jesus.[1]

Even this reduced starting-point for unity proved too utopian. Turrettini, than whom the Archbishop had no more zealous seconder and supporter in his work for Protestant union, pointed out the strength of conservative opinion especially in matters of divine worship, the difficulties of introducing liturgical changes (with a sly but effective reminder of the fate of the Scottish Prayer Book of 1637!), the fact that the Reformed churches in the various countries of Europe had not yet agreed on a revised version of the metrical psalms, and the very partial success which had attended the attempt to introduce new habits of public worship at Geneva after the model of Ostervald's new liturgy at Neuchâtel.

> Je fais ce détail à votre grâce, afin qu'elle voie combien peu on a lieu de se flatter de faire recevoir partout une même confession et une même liturgie....Ainsi bien loin que ce dessein-là fût un acheminement à la réunion, au contraire ce serait un nouvel obstacle, plus fort et plus insurmontable que la plupart des autres. Il semble donc qu'à l'égard des Confessions, il faut se contenter de faire voir comment elles s'accordent toutes sur les articles essentiels et nécessaires au salut....Et à

[1] Geneva MSS. Inventaire 1569, f. 85.

l'égard de la liturgie (en attendant qu'on puisse disposer les esprits à recevoir celle d'Angleterre ou du moins à l'imiter comme un excellent modèle) je croirais qu'on pourrait s'en tenir à une maxime très sage et très pieuse, qui est dans toutes nos confessions de foi: c'est que les diverses cérémonies et les divers rites ne doivent pas empêcher la communion des églises, ni autoriser leur séparation.[1]

With this discouraging reply even Wake's second line of advance could not be exploited. In Berlin indeed Jablonski had already published a German translation of the Book of Common Prayer in 1704 which was reissued in 1717; but the hope of its adoption, first in the king's chapel and thence gradually throughout his territories, was frustrated by the failure to make any progress in the negotiations between the sovereigns of Great Britain and Prussia both before and after 1716. On all counts therefore Wake had to recognise that his efforts for Protestant union were premature, and that, as in his Gallican correspondence, so with his Protestant correspondents, all that could be hoped for was the preparation of the ground for some future harvest and the sowing of the seed from which future generations might reap.

The reasons for this failure were many and diverse. On the one hand the very political calamities which seemed to make Protestant union an urgent immediate necessity, such as the persecution of Protestants in the Palatinate or at Thorn in Poland, the aggression of the Roman Catholic powers abroad and the menace of Jacobite plots at home and the defection of former Protestant princes to Rome, served also to alienate ministers of state from adding to their difficulties by the disputes and controversies incident to the attempt to persuade churchmen to agree in matters of faith, worship, and order. In addition there were personal difficulties, such as the ineradicable mistrust and suspicion between the kings of Great Britain and Prussia, and the multiplicity of agents both in England and at Hanover through whom Wake had to work. On the other side lay the divisions and disunity of divines, alike Lutheran and Reformed, which were too obvious and powerful to be ignored or overridden. At home also the primate was conscious that his episcopal brethren were singularly insular in outlook and sympathies, so that he had to bear alone the burden of foreign correspondence and negotiation. 'I have nobody to help me', he lamented to Turrettini in a letter of 29 June 1724, 'in my application either to the king or the court. Our bishops hold no correspondence abroad, nor seem at all to trouble themselves about anything beyond our four seas.'[2] The Archbishop indeed had lost a friend (as well as finding a rival) in this respect by the translation of Edmund Gibson to the see of London in succession to John Robinson. For whereas Robinson's diplomatic and ecclesiastical experience at the northern courts had given him both knowledge of and insight into the circumstances of the Protestant

[1] Arch. W. Epist. 31, f. 109b. '4 Janvier 1721.'

[2] Geneva MSS. Inventaire 1569, f. 117.

churches abroad, and had also made him a ready partner in Jablonski's correspondence with Archbishop Sharp during the reign of Anne, Gibson had as little communication as sympathy with foreign churches. So Wake had no helper to hold up his hands when the battle went unfavourably for his projects of union and the children of Amalek prevailed.

During the course of the theological controversies which marked his correspondence, the Archbishop generally contented himself with emphasising the latitude of opinion allowed in the Church of England on matters not fundamental to salvation, without interpreting the Anglican position in particular points at issue between Lutheran and Reformed. It is therefore of interest to observe that on the question of consubstantiation, always a stumbling-block to the Reformed, he held that the Anglican doctrine of the Real Presence did not differ much from the Lutheran, and that in regard also to Predestination the Church of England inclined towards the Lutheran rather than to the Reformed position. In reply to a letter of Abbot Christopher of Lokkum (the successor of Molanus), urging the practicability of closer *rapprochement* between Lutherans and the Ecclesia Anglicana, he wrote on 20 May 1726:

> Indeed you judge very rightly concerning our Church of England that it differs in only a very few articles from your tenets; only a little in the question of the Eucharist and in other matters I do not know if we differ even a little from you. Certainly in those matters which concern divine grace, and in which you deservedly blame the rigidity of the Synod of Dort, the greater part of our theologians seem to hold the like positions with you. And although concerning the mode of the presence of the body of Christ in the holy sacrament of the Eucharist we differ from you to some extent, we hold firmly with you the Real Presence of the Saviour in its reception; and we say with the apostle: the bread which we break is the communion of the body of Christ, and the cup which we drink is the communion of the blood of Christ.[1]

In this connection also it is important to notice that, as in his correspondence with the Gallican divines of the Sorbonne, so in his commendation to Lutherans of the Book of Common Prayer, Wake was ready to meet their scruples in one point by omitting the Black Rubric, which had been before omitted in 1559 and replaced in altered form in 1662.[2]

If Wake passed hard judgments on the godly princes and their political ministers for refusing to take the lead amid so many and great dangers to the

[1] Arch. W. Epist. 26, f. 338. 'Ac tu quidem...de Ecclesia Anglicana nostra rectissime judicas, eam in paucissimis articulis a vestris placitis dissidere. In re quippe Eucharistica parum, in caeteris nescio an vel parum a vobis recedimus. Sane in iis quae Dei gratiam concernunt, et in quibus merito Synodi Dordracenae duritiem perstringis, major pars theologorum nostrorum paria vobiscum tenere videntur. Et quamvis de modo praesentiae Corporis Christi in sacro Eucharistiae sacramento a vobis aliquantum dissentiamus, realem tamen Salvatoris in illius perceptione praesentiam firmiter vobiscum tenemus; ac cum Apostolo dicimus: panem quem frangimus, communionem esse corporis Christi, calicem quem bibimus, communionem esse sanguinis Christi.'

[2] *Ibid.* Epist. 28, n.f. James Caesar to Wake. The Hague, 6/17 August 1717.

Protestant cause, his most severe censures were reserved (and repeated throughout his correspondence) for the churchmen who hindered unity by insisting on non-essential points of doctrine. Perhaps the strongest expression of his repudiation of the attitude of these rigid theologians occurred in his letter to Osiander of 28 November 1723, in which after cataloguing the obstacles to unity, he gave full rein to his scorn for their opposition.

To these efforts are opposed the malice of the devil, the interests and counsels of the world, the passions and concupiscences of our most corrupt nature, envy, hatred, emulation, pride: all these fight strenuously against an agreement of this kind. Each of us believes that the prestige of his own Church turns upon this, that it should attract all the others into its own following, recognising its authority and, as it were, law over all others. Few are willing seriously to consider or honestly to admit in how many and great issues we are all agreed; that in fact there is no article in fundamental matters of faith in which we do not think alike; and therefore none in which we ought not mutually to tolerate each other. The greatest part, and especially of those of us who are called to the sacred ministry of the church lay the greatest stress on those points on which we still differ; whether moved by zeal for the faith or led astray by the allurement of self-esteem I leave to the judgment of God, the searcher of hearts. Nor do I desire to stigmatise in this matter any one party more than the rest; rather I think that all are equally to be blamed. For it is plain that we all favour too much ourselves and our own opinions; and that whilst we demand to be granted liberty to defend our own opinions, we are willing to extend this to others only with difficulty, if indeed at all. This has been the beginning of evil. This too is the greatest obstacle to our peace and concord at present, and, unless God gives us a better mind, will always be so.[1]

Two centuries have elapsed since Wake penned this melancholy verdict on the causes of failure of his eirenic projects; and the problem of Christian disunity is still unsolved. Many superficial barriers to union amongst Protestant churches have fallen during the intervening period, a greater mutual understanding and sympathy have undoubtedly come to pass; and the emergence of the oecumenical movement and the constitution of the World Council of Churches have far outspread the tentative, timorous and negative

[1] *Ibid.* Epist. 26, f. 156. 'Opponunt se hisce conatibus, diaboli malitia, mundi studia atque consilia; corruptissimae nostrae naturae passiones ac concupiscentiae, invidia, odium, aemulatio, superbia; strenue contra hujusmodi concordiam militant. Unusquisque nostrorum honorem suae ecclesiae in eo versari credit, ut omnes alias in ipsius sese consortium tradat; illius authoritatem, et quasi jus in caeteras agnoscat. Pauci aut serio considerare volunt, aut ingenue fateri, in quibus quantisque conveniamus omnes; nullum esse revera articulum in rebus fidei fundamentalibus, in quo non idem sentiamus; ideoque nec ullum esse in quo nos mutuo tolerare non debeamus. Maxima pars ac praecipue nostrorum qui ad sacrum Ecclesiae ministerium appellamur, ea plurimi facimus in quibus adhuc dissidemus; fideine causa excitati an φιλαυτίας lenocinio seducti, Deo cordium scrutatori judicandum relinquo. Nec ego hic partem aliquam prae caeteris sinistra hujusmodi censura notandam cupio; omnes ex aequo culpandos sentio. Adeo nos omnes nobis nostrisque opinionibus nimium favere constat; et quum nobis in sententiis nostris tuendis libertatem concedi postulamus, aliis non nisi aegre largiri, si tamen omnino largiri, volumus. Hoc mali initium fuit. Hoc pacis et concordiae nostrae praecipuum et nunc est obstaculum, et nisi Deus meliorem mentem nobis indiderit, semper est futurum.'

measures of the Ratisbon *Conclusum.* Notwithstanding, the hard core of differences concerning church-order, confessions of faith and forms of worship remains intractable and unresolved. Nor does there seem any likelihood of its resolution save on the basis of Wake's principle of the sufficiency of agreement on articles necessary to salvation and of the toleration of differences in non-essentials. It seems difficult indeed to challenge either the legitimacy or the necessity of this principle. But perhaps the chief problems arise in the attempt to delimit the boundary between fundamentals and non-essentials. In Wake's own time questions concerning the doctrine of the Eucharist, Predestination and Reprobation, loomed large as obstacles to agreement. To later generations problems of episcopacy and the consequent validity of the sacraments have been prominent subjects of discussion and difference. In respect of these matters also Wake made plain his position in the course of his voluminous correspondence. On the one hand he defended episcopacy as the form of government universal in the church from the apostolic age to the Reformation, and as the indispensable foundation therefore of organic union amongst the Protestant churches; and to this end he was ready to offer such practical help as the Church of England could proffer towards the restoration of episcopacy in the continental churches. On the other hand he recognised the validity of the presbyterian ministry and sacraments of the foreign Reformed churches; and as an interim measure authorised inter-communion in regard to members of the Lutheran and Reformed churches sojourning in England and Anglican churchmen resident abroad. In so doing he was convinced of his adherence to the main stream of Anglican tradition, as moulded by leading representatives of Caroline high-churchmanship; though going farther in some respects and prepared to make greater temporary concessions in face of the urgent necessity of unity amongst Protestants. The failure of his protracted negotiations was evidence of the volume and gravity of difficulties encountered; but none will withhold an unstinted appreciation of the spirit and zeal of his efforts, nor refuse to echo his own epitaph on his individual part in the work of union.

> And when the day shall come, which cannot be far distant for me, in which I shall stand to be judged before the judgment seat of Jesus Christ, this will be not the least part of my confidence, or rather of my hope; that howsoever I have otherwise been an unprofitable servant of His, at any rate I have sought and consulted, and with all my labour and zeal have followed, those things that belong to the peace of Jerusalem.[1]

[1] Arch. W. Epist. 26, f. 61. Wake to Osiander. August 1722. 'Et cum dies ille advenerit, qui a me procul abesse nequit, quo coram tribunali Jesu Christi consistar judicandus, haec erit pars non minima fiduciae, seu potius spei meae: quod utcunque alias inutilis Ipsius servus fuerim, ea tamen quaesiverim, ae consuluerim, ea omni opera studioque prosecutus sim, quae ad pacem Hierosolymae spectant.'

CHAPTER VII

THE THINGS THAT ARE CAESAR'S

This day will be like unto a parliament. Ye know, when things are amiss in a realm, or out of order, all they that be good-hearted, that love godliness, they wish for a parliament; these would fain have that all the rulers of the realm should come together and bring all things in good order again. For ye know that parliaments are kept only for this purpose, that things which be amiss, may be amended. And so it will be at this last day, at this general parliament, where God himself with all his heavenly power will be present and oversee all things, and hear all causes, so that nothing shall escape him.

BISHOP HUGH LATIMER, *8th Sermon: On the Gospel for the Second Sunday in Advent*

'How so, Sir?' enquired Dr Johnson when Sir Adam Ferguson suggested a doubt of the propriety of bishops having seats in the House of Lords. 'Who is more proper for having the dignity of a peer, than a bishop, provided a bishop be what he ought to be; and if improper bishops be made, that is not the fault of the bishops, but of those who make them.' To the same effect Lemuel Gulliver in describing to the king of Brobdingnag the English house of peers, expatiated on the circumstance that to the temporal lords

were joined several holy persons, as part of that assembly, under the title of bishops, whose peculiar business it is to take care of religion, and of those who instruct the people therein. These were searched and sought out through the whole nation, by the prince and his wisest counsellors, among such of the priesthood as were most deservedly distinguished by the sanctity of their lives and the depth of their erudition; who were indeed the spiritual fathers of the clergy and the people.

His Majesty indeed shrewdly asked

whether those holy lords...were always promoted to that rank upon account of their knowledge in religious matters and the sanctity of their lives, had never been compliers with the times while they were common priests, or slavish prostitute chaplains to some nobleman, whose opinions they continued servilely to follow after they were admitted into that assembly?[1]

The episcopate of Queen Anne's reign has been generally accounted an honourable exception to the obloquy cast upon the prelates of William III's creation before her and those of Hanoverian, and especially Walpolean, nomination after. Nor can it be denied that the bench during her rule was

[1] Boswell, *Life of Johnson*, 31 March 1772. Swift, *Gulliver's Travels*, ch. VI.

distinguished by outstanding examples of learning and piety. But statecraft may not be excepted from the qualities requisite for the office and work of a bishop; and the circumstances of Wake's nomination to the see of Lincoln emphasised the importance attached by Her Majesty's administration to the presence on the bench of prelates of approved political moderation and prudence.

During the first three years of Anne's reign episcopal promotions had been confined to Tory divines, the queen having allowed to lapse the commission issued by William III in 1700 to the two archbishops and four bishops to advise him in the distribution of ecclesiastical patronage, and having added to the bench Bishops Nicolson of Carlisle, Hooper of St Asaph and of Bath and Wells, Beveridge of St Asaph and Bull of St David's. Meantime the Tory administration had found increasing difficulty in controlling its wilder supporters in the House of Commons; and upon the rebellion of the 'tackers' against ministerial discipline by their attempt to tack the Occasional Conformity Bill to the Land Tax Bill in 1704, the leading ministers resolved at the ensuing general election to excommunicate these unruly extremists, with a view to the formation of a mixed administration of moderate Tories and Whigs for the successful prosecution of the war of the Spanish Succession. The concurrence of the vacancy of the see of Lincoln by the death of Bishop Gardiner on 1 March 1704/5 with the dissolution of parliament on 5 April following, invested the conflict for nomination to this important bishopric with an unusual piquancy and prominence. For the ecclesiastical adviser of the Queen, Archbishop Sharp of York, was strongly pressing Sir William Dawes, whom he had in mind already as his own successor at York and for whom it was necessary therefore at the earliest opportunity to procure an influential diocesan bishopric; whilst Archbishop Tenison of Canterbury, supported by Godolphin, was equally determined to secure the see for Wake. Indeed, Tenison had already approached the Queen before the end of March, and 'had expectation given that something would be said to him in a few days'. But the delicacy of the position was reflected by the circumstance that Her Majesty did not sign the warrant for the *congé d'élire* until 16 July; and the eventual nomination of Wake was at once a result of the success of the tactics of the administration in the general election and a presage of a breach in the Tory monopoly of ecclesiastical preferments. The political campaign had been waged with peculiar fervour in the south-western counties, where the leading protagonists in both the parliamentary and ecclesiastical conflict had been engaged. In the county of Cornwall Mr Hugh Boscawen, brother-in-law of Godolphin, was returned head of the poll with 1405 votes against 858 for Sir Richard Vyvyan and 806 for James Buller, both of whom had been 'tackers'; so that the administration had unseated one of the rebels. For the city of Exeter, however, the former members, Sir Edward Seymour and Mr Snell, were returned unopposed; but in the election of proctors for convocation the ecclesiastical victory of the Bishop of Exeter's candidates, Dr John Hickes with 171 votes and Mr Robert Hoblyn, with 147 votes, over their two rivals Mr John Newte, with forty-two votes, and Mr Peter Fisher with only thirty-eight, partly redressed the balance; and the overall result was eminently satisfactory to party managers.[1]

When Wake took his seat in the House of Lords on 5 November 1705 (and proceeded straightway to preach the sermon in commemoration of the dual deliverance of the kingdom on that day from popery and absolutism by the discovery of the gunpowder treason and by the landing of William of Orange at Torbay), his presence was a symbol of the new policy of Her Majesty's administration in state and church. He was accordingly diligent in attendance and in service on committees, but appears to have limited his support of the ministry for some years to the service of silent suffrage. Cobbett's *Parliamentary History* contains no record of his having spoken in the debate on 'The Church in Danger' on 6 December 1705, nor in the debates on the Act of Union with Scotland in 1707. His first recorded speech indeed was upon the occasion of the impeachment of Dr Sacheverell in 1710. Meantime, however, he had not been neglectful of his duty to support the administration within his diocese of Lincoln at general elections. In 1707 the Duke of Bedford approached him to canvass the clergy of Bedfordshire in favour of his grace's son, Lord Edward Russell, who intended to offer himself for election as a knight of the shire in the forthcoming election of 1708. Wake thereupon sounded his archdeacon of Bedford, Thomas Frank, who replied with equal candour and wisdom that both his lordship and himself would do well to exercise their influence privately rather than to appear publicly in behalf of a particular party.

To your lordship's demands of my thoughts on the subject matter of the duke's letter, I am bold to answer that it is a general observation concerning clergymen even of the greatest integrity, that they very rarely step out of the way of their profession especially as to political matters, but they come off with scratcht faces.... My great concern is to keep the clergy quiet, that during the election they may not run into any extravagant heats and that when it is over we may meet together as friends and unanimously pursue the great ends of our holy calling. Therefore it is that I think it necessary to vote on both sides, or in effect to sit still. I have already assured his grace that I would serve him, if he would accept of what I can do without noise, and I will faithfully endeavour it among such friends as I can trust; but should I appear at the head of any one party, I should throw the body of the clergy

[1] N. Sykes, 'The Cathedral Chapter of Exeter and the General Election of 1705'. *English Historical Review*, XLV, pp. 260–72. April 1930.

into convulsions, and make myself uneasy ever after. If your lordship should ask, what measures can the bishop of the diocese safely take on application made to him, I humbly answer that if he shall publicly interpose his authority, or, what is tantamount, send his recommendations to his clergy, he runs the extreme hazard of prostrating his authority, and breaking off that happy correspondence and respect which he seems to have obtained among his clergy beyond any of his predecessors.[1]

In reply to a further letter from Wake, the archdeacon restated his position; that he would concur in the ends proposed by the bishop and the duke, but that he must be left to choose his own means. 'If they will be pleased to dispense with me as to the means, I do sincerely promise that I will faithfully pursue the end.' Accordingly he set forth his own ideas of how to accomplish the desired object.

What determined the last election in favour of Sir Pyncent Chernocke was the multitude of single votes; and if that game can be prevented now, my lord must in all probability obtain in this. On this principle I have already, I think, secured a great part of my own parish for Lord Edward, who before voted singly for Sir Pyncent, and shall make it my endeavour to confirm them. To take them off wholly is impossible, Sir Pyncent being a Justice of the Peace, living in the next parish, and having an estate in this. The like method I shall observe with such of my friends among the clergy as I can trust, so far as I can do it without noise and public controversy; and I do verily think that I shall be hereby enabled to serve Lord Edward more effectually than if I should make a public work of it. The clergy are now in good humour with me, and nothing that I do by way of jurisdiction is taken otherwise than kindly by them; but should I once set up to prescribe in matters of elections, I should only stir a nest of hornets, and render myself uncapable of serving my friends or doing any other good. I humbly lay before your lordship this sketch of my measures; and if it shall happen to concur with your lordship's sense, I beg your lordship to become my advocate with his grace and my lord chamberlain that I may have their good leave to proceed accordingly.

Wake appears to have been content with this method of canvassing; which indeed served so well that the archdeacon sent him a list of twenty-one votes promised for Lord Edward, thirty-one 'votes hopefull', twenty-eight 'votes which appear to be desperate', and thirty-two 'concerning the inclination of those underwritten I can say but little'.[2] At the election on 19 May 1708 Lord Edward Russell and Sir William Gastwick were returned, to the exclusion of Sir Pyncent Chernocke.

Even more remarkable, however, was the success attending the archdeacon's efforts in 1710, when, amid the general excitement prevailing after the fiasco of the Sacheverell trial, the Tories swept their rivals out of office

[1] Archdeacon Frank to Wake, 22 December 1707; cited in N. Sykes, *Church and State in England in the Eighteenth Century*, pp. 79–80; from Arch. W. Epist. 1, Lincoln I, f. 132.

[2] Sykes, *op. cit.* pp. 79–80; Arch. W. Epist. 3, Lincoln III, n.f.

and countenance; but when the county of Bedford remained true to its allegiance.

On Thursday last [reported Frank to his diocesan on 6 October] the election was made for the county of Bedford, and Mr Harvey lost it by only thirty-nine voices. I pursued your lordship's commands to Mr Leith, who notwithstanding voted singly for Mr Harvey, as did about twenty more of my brethren in a body triumphant, headed by Mr Dean of Gloucester....But notwithstanding this show, which was over before I got to Bedford, by the best information I can get, near forty of our brethren voted for my lord or Sir William or both; which must needs be a terrible mortification to Mr St John, who sometime ago by way of advertisement in the Post Boy, told the world with equal truth and modesty, that 'Mr Harvey would offer himself to the service of his country at the request of the whole body of the clergy of Bedfordshire'; when, by what I can learn, the generality of the clergy knew nothing of the matter. I'm sure I and my few friends were entirely strangers to the request till we were told it in print. Some men have a strange knack of fibbing for the truth.[1]

Nor did Mr Frank's zeal cool with frequent experience of triennial elections; for in the last general election which concerned Wake as bishop of Lincoln, he reported a further limited success for the county of Bedford in 1715.

The election for this county being made [he related on 18 February 1714/15] I beg leave to tell your lordship how it fares with us. It began on Wednesday the 16th inst, when was the greatest appearance ever known in Bedford. The Lords Bruce and St John headed the clergy, who out of a singular zeal for the church generally appeared for Chernocke and Harvey; and Mr Leith, the most zealous that way, was for his reward, honoured with the company of those two lords, who lay at his house that night. We who were for Cater and Hillesdon, in number about twenty, are loaded with all the opprobrious names to represent us as enemies of the Church of England and friends to the Dissenters. One man was discovered in attempting to vote the sixth time for Chernocke and Harvey, and another the third time. In the evening the mob began to be troublesome, and so by consent the poll was closed and sealed up, but not numbered. The next day about noon the election was declared for Harvey and Hillesdon: Harvey 1263, Hillesdon 1254, Cater 1246, Chernocke 1229. Thus we are rid however of our most dangerous man. Cater lost it by his good nature and concern to secure Hillesdon, who had above one hundred of his votes, he thinking himself secure beyond dispute.[2]

But although the archdeacon of Bedford was the most diligent of Wake's election agents and correspondents, in other parts of the diocese the episcopal influence was also exercised unobtrusively. On 11 October 1710 Laurence Eachard, the ecclesiastical historian, prebendary of Louth and subsequently archdeacon of Stow, reported to his diocesan: 'I am just now going to Lincoln to the election of knights of the shire, where I shall carefully observe your lordship's directions'; and the success of the Bishop's efforts was related by

[1] *Ibid.* p. 80.
[2] Arch. W. Epist. 5, Lincoln v, n.f.

another of his clergy, Mr Humfrey Hyde, writing from Lincoln on 13 October, that, 'as I acquainted your lordship with my intentions, I was at our county election on Wednesday; my Lord Willoughby and Champion Dymoke were chose by a great majority. There was a great body of the clergy.'[1] But notwithstanding the reality of Wake's influence in these cases, he acted with sufficient discretion to avoid the censure inflicted by the House of Commons in 1710 upon his friend Bishop Nicolson of Carlisle for interference in general elections.

In his speech in the House of Lords upon the trial of Sacherevell, Wake confined himself to the second article of the impeachment, dealing with the preacher's reflections upon the Toleration Act; but before embarking on the particular issue of toleration, he turned aside to declare that the origins of the comprehension scheme of 1689 were to be found in the project of Archbishop Sancroft in 1688, which was not only conceived in outline but committed in several details by that primate to various of his brethren and friends for their consideration and proposals. The object of this excursus was to remove the aspersion that comprehension was an invention of Whig and latitudinarian churchmen by revealing the sponsorship of the non-juring archbishop; and to justify the abortive attempt at the Revolution to carry such a measure, concerning which he avowed his conviction that it 'would have been for the interest and peace of our church and state, had it been accomplished'. In dealing with the question of the Toleration Act, he had little difficulty in stripping the veil of sophistries with which Sacheverell in his defence had endeavoured to conceal the meaning of his observations on the indulgence granted to the Dissenters. Wake showed that the preacher's references were undoubtedly to those orthodox Protestant Dissenters to whom toleration had been granted, and whom he had aspersed as 'occasional loyalists to the state as well as occasional conformists to the church', and not to the anti-Trinitarians who had been expressly excluded from the benefits of the Act. Furthermore he interpreted the doctor's pointed reflections on Archbishop Grindal's conciliatory policy towards the Puritans of his day in contrast with the repressive measures taken after his death, as a plain hint to Queen Anne to follow the example of her predecessor Queen Elizabeth I, by using the utmost force of the law against dissenters from the established church, and by abridging the toleration granted in 1689.[2] The speech was a powerful and logical criticism of Sacheverell's sermon on this point; and did not fail to make due impression. Hearne indeed related that an anonymous non-juror, 'an ingenious, honest gentleman, one who has suffered and is like to be a

[1] Arch. W. Epist. 1, Lincoln 1, ff. 258, 259. Eachard to Wake; and Hyde to Wake.

[2] *The Bishop of Lincoln's Speech in the House of Lords March 17th at the opening of the second Article of the Impeachment against Dr Sacheverell* (London, 1710).

sufferer still for his firm adhesion to James II and his lawful issue', had admitted to him 'that Dr Wake, bishop of Lincoln's speech delivered lately in the House of Lords against Dr Sacheverell is excellent, very close, and rational; and that neither Dr Sacheverell nor any of those of his principles, if his may be called principles, will be able to get over and fully to answer it'.[1] In the division in the House of Lords upon the question of the preacher's guilt, Wake of course voted him guilty.

But, although the Whig administration succeeded in obtaining a verdict against Sacheverell, followed by the infliction of ludicrously slight penalties, their impeachment of him proved a boomerang which brought down themselves and their party. In the general election of 1710 the country returned a large Tory majority to the House of Commons, and the Queen, delighted to be delivered from the uncongenial counsel of Whig ministers, constituted her new administration entirely of Tories; with a consequent sharpening of the ecclesiastical conflict between churchmen and dissenters and of the division on the episcopal bench between moderate and extreme prelates. Wake accordingly was drawn more deeply into party politics in the House of Lords. In regard to the two chief ecclesiastical measures passed during the last four years of Anne's reign, the Occasional Conformity Act was the result of a corrupt bargain between the Whigs who desired the support of Tory malcontents in their opposition to the terms of the Peace of Utrecht, and the Earl of Nottingham who was willing to join his rivals on this point if they would allow the passage of his favourite bill. Accordingly, as Burnet observed, 'no opposition was made to this in the House of Lords; so it passed in three days and it had the same fate in the House of Commons'; though much comment was aroused by the contrast between the long debates which had attended the appearance of similar bills in the early years of the reign, and the strange circumstance that in 1711 it 'went through both houses in so silent a manner without the least opposition'. The Schism Act of 1714, however, was hotly contested; and though Wake did not speak in debate, he signed a protest against its passing together with the Bishops of Ely, St Asaph, Bangor, and Llandaff. In view of his opposition in 1718 to the repeal of these two acts, his signing of this protest is of particular interest.

Nor could he avoid participation in party divisions of a more definitely political character. On 11 January 1710/11 he was one of the signatories of a protest against the refusal of the House of Lords to hear the Earl of Galway and Lord Tyrawly in their own defence in respect of the conduct of the war in Spain; and on the following day he signed a further protest against the Lords' censure of the recent offensive campaign in Spain, both matters being the occasion of acute controversy between Whigs and Tories. On 3 February

[1] T. Hearne, *Collections*, vol. III, p. 35. 7 August 1710.

he was similarly drawn into political and military matters when he signed a protest against the censure of the house 'that the two regiments upon the Spanish establishment, twice demanded and provided for by parliament, were not supplied as they ought to have been'; and against the consequent resolution 'that by not supplying the deficiencies of the men given by parliament for the war in Spain, the ministers have greatly neglected that service'. These were issues upon which the episcopal bench was not particularly qualified to pronounce, but being points of party quarrels, he supported the Whig lords; and in the former protest nine other bishops joined, whilst ten others signed the latter.[1]

The dominating question of the last year of the Queen's reign, however, was the security of the Protestant succession in the House of Hanover as provided for by the Act of Settlement of 1701. Widespread uncertainty prevailed about the intentions of the Tory administration on this vital matter, which overshadowed all other issues of domestic policy in gravity. The veteran hero of the Seven Bishops' trial, Sir Jonathan Trelawny, bishop of Winchester, whom none could accuse of Whig sympathies, raised the alarm as he saw the spectre of popery and Jacobitism again threatening the land. 'We addressed in defence of our laws which King James had broke in upon to make the quicker way for popery, which he was (and God be thanked that he was) in haste to establish', Trelawny wrote to Wake on 2 February 1712/13; earnestly begging that the bishops would not allow themselves to be side-tracked into addressing the Crown against the proposed peace terms, but would concentrate on the defeat of any attempt to restore the Stuart dynasty. On the following day he wrote again, emphasising the need of episcopal unity on this crucial problem in order to avoid the suspicion of a partisan move, 'dressed only by a parcel of Whiggish bishops to make the queen uneasy and her ministers odious'. Yet he avowed that 'I have hardly had a quiet night or a cheerful day since the advance of the peace to a certain people's liking. I can't but fear the Pretender is next oars; if so the coffin is bespoke for the queen, for popery is always in haste to kill when they are sure of taking possession.'[2] In face of this menace Hanoverian Tories and Whigs drew together, leaving their differences on lesser points for future settlement. Perhaps the most signal demonstration of this alliance was afforded by a debate in the House of Lords on 5 April 1714, when the house voted the Protestant succession not to be in danger by 76 to 64; but 'the most remarkable circumstance of the debate was that the Archbishop of York and the Earl of Anglesea spoke and voted with the Whig lords, the Archbishop drawing after him the whole bench of bishops, three courtiers only excepted'.

[1] Cobbett, *Parliamentary History*, vol. VI, pp. 983, 985, 990–5, 1358.
[2] Arch. W. Epist. 17. Miscellaneous I, n.f.

Similarly on 13 April the lords considered the reply of the Queen to an address from their house concerning the danger from the Pretender and the necessity of his expulsion from Lorraine. Some Whigs desired a further address to be presented; but the court party, by means of two proxies, carried a resolution in favour of an address in purely general terms. In the actual division there voted in person sixty-one peers on each side; and again it was noted as 'remarkable that of sixteen bishops then in the house, two only, Rochester and Durham, voted with the court, and that the new Bishops of London and Bristol, who were thought blindly devoted to the ministry, joined with the Whigs'. On the first of these occasions Wake was absent from the house, and present on the second.[1]

Notwithstanding these votes of confidence in the intentions of the administration, the general disquiet persisted. Wake's own fears and suspicions were set down in a private memorandum, written when the crisis had been overpast and when the impeachment of some of the Tory leaders was before the House of Lords during the first parliament of George I.

> I cannot deny but that in my judgment I do think (as I always did while those affairs were transacting) that the late ministry many ways acted against the interest of the nation and the religion and liberties of it. That they exposed us to the utmost dangers; and that, had they continued but a little longer in power, the Pretender would have infallibly come in upon us; and what might have been the consequence of that, as I have often with horror thought heretofore, so it even amazes me now to think. I cannot but hope that as far as her late majesty was concerned in these measures, she was misled, if not betrayed, by those about her.[2]

Fortunately the rapid sequence of events during the last week of Anne's life prevented the anticipated danger from realisation. With her death and the unpreparedness of the extremists for action, the Protestant succession was safely accomplished, and 'when George in pudding-time came o'er', it was a signal that 'moderate men looked big, sir'.

But the moderate men to whom, it was hoped, the new sovereign would give his confidence, were faced with a situation of equal difficulty and delicacy. It was assumed that George I would know who had been his friends in the recent dark days and would support the party which had remained constant to the House of Hanover; but the Whigs had one fatal weakness, they had never aspired nor pretended to become the 'church party'. The Achilles' heel of their political strategy lay in their disregard of the interest of the clergy of the established church. Nor were their enemies slow to point the moral of this attitude. In a political tract for the times,

[1] Cobbett, *Parliamentary History*, vol. VI, pp. 1335, 1343.
[2] Arch. W. Epist. 19, [f. 1].

published before the general election at the end of 1714 and probably from the pen of Bishop Atterbury, the author warned his fellow-countrymen:

> We say the Whigs resolve, if they can procure a House of Commons to their mind, to destroy the Church of England; whereby I do not mean that they have set up gibbets in their minds, and desire to hang, draw, and quarter every member of the Church, nor that all Whigs will come into the scheme. But we are persuaded that the generality of the Whigs are averse to the present hierarchy and government of the Church; that they neither like our doctrines nor our clergy; but would abolish bishops, priests, and deacons, assume the church lands to themselves, appoint a small allowance to the parsons, and prescribe them what doctrines to preach from the pulpit; that they would introduce a general comprehension, and blend up an ecclesiastical Babel of all the sects and heresies upon the face of the earth; and lastly deprive the bishops of their votes in the House of Lords; which particular they have contrived to render less odious by furnishing the reverend bench, as far as was in their power, with such members as few churchmen will pity or regret when they shall be unlorded.[1]

The picture was admittedly over-drawn; but it was a sound stroke of electioneering policy to raise in a new form the old, turbulent cry of 'The Church in danger'. As a prudent clerical politician, Canon Stratford of Christ Church, Oxford, observed: 'It is certainly the interest of the late cabal to make an open breach between the King and the Church party, and I have some reason to think it is their design too'.[2]

It was therefore an equal disappointment and surprise to Whig and Tory clergy respectively to find that the Earl of Nottingham was included in the administration of the new régime as lord president of the council. For although his appointment was the sole sop to the Tory Cerberus, he was the prime author of the Occasional Conformity Act and a zealot for the ecclesiastical interests of the 'church-party'. Nor were the first-fruits of his share in ecclesiastical promotions reassuring to the cohort of aspiring Whig divines who had looked confidently for the end of their long exclusion from royal favour. The sees of Ely and Gloucester were vacant by the end of August 1714; and it was intimated in a *News Letter* of 4 September that 'it was thought Dr Finch, dean of York, brother to the Earl of Nottingham, would be made bishop of Ely'.[3] The Whig candidate for this see was the redoubtable Bishop Fleetwood of St Asaph, who had enjoyed the easy martyrdom of having the preface to a recently published volume of his sermons burned in June 1712 by the common hangman at the order of the House of Commons. From the vantage-point of his situation in the household of Archbishop Tenison at Lambeth, Edmund Gibson voiced to his friend Bishop Nicolson of Carlisle the authentic apprehensions of the Whig churchmen. 'Now of

[1] H. C. Beeching, *Francis Atterbury*, pp. 259–61.

[2] Portland MSS. VII. 199 (Hist. MSS. Comm.).

[3] *Ibid.* V, 493.

late my Lord Nottingham has renewed his application with great vigour for his brother; by what I have learnt there is a good probability that he will not carry Ely, but I am afraid if he lets go that hold, and promises to be good-humoured with Gloucester or St Asaph, the court will be inclinable to oblige him.'[1] On 19 November the compromise foretold by Gibson was effected; Bishop Fleetwood was translated to Ely, the see of Gloucester was filled by the promotion of Dean Willis of Lincoln (whose name had been canvassed so often and in vain by the Whigs during the reign of Anne as to move Gibson to a ribald comparison of their tactics with those of a gentleman 'who had five or six daughters and, being bent upon marrying them in order, would suffer none of the rest to appear or be shown until the oldest could be disposed of'); and that of St Asaph by the nomination of Dr John Wynne, principal of Jesus College, Oxford and Lady Margaret professor of divinity, and prebendary of Brecon in St David's Cathedral, who had been pressed by Nottingham's son-in-law, Sir Roger Mostyn.

It was upon this last appointment that the interest of Tory and Whig was concentrated. 'The promotion was the greatest chance in the world', chuckled Dr Stratford, 'and owing solely to Mostyn. I little thought Sir Roger would have made bishops; but he has secured a good interest to himself in Flintshire by this.'[2] From the other side came the mordant comment of Gibson to Nicolson on the advancement of a divine,

> who, as far as I can learn, was not thought of till Friday, and was writ to by the Secretary of State on the Tuesday night following. It has been said that my Lord Pembroke had a hand in promoting him, but I cannot find that any other hand was concerned but my Lord Nottingham, moved to it by his son-in-law, Sir Roger Mostyn (who by this means will govern the diocese), and supported in his application by my Lord Townshend who seems not yet to have given over his experiment for a mixed ministry.

Another sign of the inclination towards a mixed administration had been the strong opposition offered to the translation of Fleetwood; and the leading Whig bishops were at a loss to account for the conduct of Townshend. 'While the business of St Asaph was going on for Dr Wynne, our good old patriarch', reported Gibson of the aged Tenison, 'plainly told them, they might do what they would, but for his part he knew not what to make of a motley bench and a motley synod.' Similarly, Wake was believed to be discontented with the turn of affairs, having gone to Dorset 'by no means satisfied with the conduct of Lord Townshend'; whereas Trimnell of Norwich,

> who is always on the charitable side, will by no means allow that Lord Townshend can mean anything but what is right upon the whole; and as to the difficulties that

[1] Bodleian MSS. Add. A. 269, f. 35. Gibson to Nicolson. 30 October 1714.
[2] Portland MSS. VII, 207.

occur, he thinks they are no more than what might be expected in the establishment of measures wholly new; and that they will mend day by day if we will be patient, and at the same time take advantage of the impatience of the Tories.[1]

Similar counsels were given by Trimnell in a New Year's letter to Wake, in which he expressed the hope that on his return to London, Wake would find 'that the government is likely to go on as steadily as our present circumstances will bear.... *Fair and softly goes far* is a proverb that will, I hope, be verified in His Majesty's conduct.'[2]

This confidence, however, was not shared at Lambeth; whence Gibson reported to Nicolson on 15 January that

His Grace does not like the posture of affairs at court for many reasons; our friends do not agree among themselves, the ministry is as yet a motley one;...add to this that all our church matters are at sixes and sevens, being obstructed with great diligence by N[ottingha]m and S[hrewsbur]y. We are told to have patience and things will be better in time; but I see no great signs of amendment, nor do I think it possible so long as those two men are supported.[3]

Much anxiety therefore was occasioned among the Church-Whigs when the see of Salisbury was vacant by the death of the faithful Gilbert Burnet on 17 March 1714/15. Rumour was busy everywhere with the name of Wake. Archdeacon Frank and others of his correspondents found that 'the prints are so full of his lordship's translation to Sarum' that there could be little doubt of the issue; and Gibson conjectured that the administration might 'sweeten Lincoln with Sarum', since it was generally believed to be the see 'which he desired above all others'.[4] But Lord Chancellor Cowper caught the King's ear on the very day of Burnet's death in behalf of his friend Bishop Talbot of Oxford, whose translation was announced on 19 March.

Hearing by accident [he related apologetically to Wake] yesterday very early the death of the late Bishop of Sarum, and not knowing your lordship's thoughts concerning that bishopric, I immediately did what I could to help the Bishop of Oxford to it, knowing he had lately been under some disappointment; and yesterday about one o'clock in the House of Lords, I was told by a good hand that the King had given it to the Bishop of Oxford and the bishopric of Oxford to Dr Potter. This pleased me till I had the honour of your lordship's, which hath made me dissatisfied that my little endeavours were not turned the way most agreeable to you. I yet hope for an opportunity of retrieving this misfortune.[5]

It is interesting to speculate on the difference to the personal fortunes of Wake and to the history of the Church of England which might have ensued

[1] Bodleian MSS. Add. A. 269, f. 36. 27 November. Hist. MSS. Comm. 13th Report, part VII, pp. 248–9. Bishop Nicolson to James Lowther. 4 December 1714.

[2] Arch. W. Epist. 5. Lincoln V, n.f.

[3] Bodleian MSS. Add. A. 269, f. 38.

[4] *Ibid.* f. 40; Arch. W. Epist. 5. Lincoln V, n.f.

[5] Arch. W. Epist. 20. Miscellaneous IV, f. 1. 18 March 1714/15.

from his translation to Sarum! But at least the influence of Nottingham, which Cowper believed to have been 'very pressing', had not prevailed on this occasion; and the alarm aroused by the appointment in the following November of Dr Thomas Sherlock, master of St Catharine's College, Cambridge, to the deanery of Chichester was undoubtedly excessive, though a portent of the exacerbated temper of clerical politicians. Gibson gloomily saw in it the forerunner of 'more instances of the same kind as there is opportunity, nothing being more evident than an unusual diligence in courting and caressing some of the heads of the Tory clergy'; whilst his observations on Sherlock himself were almost too splenetic even for his day.

This good man they have sent to Chichester had credit enough with the late ministry to obtain a prebend of Norwich to himself and his successors, heads of Catharine Hall, and thought fit before the queen's death to ridicule the fears of popery in a sermon which was made public. Might it not be expected that he should do somewhat by way of penance or retraction, before he became a fit subject for King George's favour, and that he should be taken reeking hot out of the midst of the Tories (of which body he is still most assuredly a member) to be cast immediately into a nest of Whigs?[1]

The mordancy of Gibson's language reflected the fears of the Whig entourage at Lambeth as to what might happen if their master, whose infirmities were a cause of growing concern, should die at this juncture in affairs, after having cheated the Tories of the coveted prize during the late reign. The chances of Wake's succession were thought by no means rosy.

I have sometimes suspected [Gibson confided to Nicolson] that when that vacancy should happen, distinguished abilities would be a secret objection in the mind of the courtiers against our friend in Dean's Yard, who if he were here, would be archbishop or nobody; and I could not but take notice of what a member of the court dropped lately: *that Lincoln was too knowing*....I know not how it comes to pass, but in fact it is true, that within these few months His Grace never mentions the Bishop of Lincoln, and frequently speaks of Norwich with great respect and concern as to his health.[2]

A fortnight later, reflecting on the growing weakness of Tenison, he could only console himself with the anticipation that if upon the occurrence of a vacancy,

the Junto should not be able to carry it for Sarum or Norwich, I hope our friend in Dean's Yard will not bear any ecclesiastical agent but himself, however willing the Junto may be to govern the church in the present method. They who do all are T[ownshen]d, St[anho]p, W[alpo]l, B[othme]r, and Ber[ns]dorf. I am very willing to hope the succession here is out of their reach; but it is a sweet bit, and they will not easily part with it.[3]

[1] Bodleian MSS. Add. A. 269, f. 44. 5 November 1715.
[2] *Ibid.* f. 40. 6 October.
[3] *Ibid.* f. 43. 20 October.

Behind these personal rivalries for place and power, however, there lay the dark shadow of public events of ill omen for the success of the policy of *fair and softly goes far*. Party passions seemed to be rising to almost unprecedented heights; and on each side events appeared to have taken charge of men. The triumphant administration could not forgo the opportunity of humiliating their former rivals; and impeachments were launched by the House of Commons against Bolingbroke, Oxford, Ormond and Strafford for their respective parts in the conclusion of the Peace of Utrecht. On the other side, the clergy and the universities were up in arms in defence of the church. Ormond was chancellor of Oxford, where his birthday was celebrated with demonstrations too obvious to be ignored by the government; and rumours soon circulated of the preparation of a Jacobite invasion of the kingdom. Each of these events was fraught with dangerous possibilities for the new dynasty and its administration; and the perils seemed of sufficient magnitude to justify the desires of many ministers for that mixed government of Whigs and Hanover Tories, which was so misliked by Tenison and his entourage.

I could really smile at such an invasion as is now designed [confided Wake to the Archbishop of Dublin on 25 August 1715] of forty or fifty persons, with arms and ammunition, depending upon men and horses here, but that I hear from all parts such accounts of the disaffection of the people as even affright me to think what will become of us. Our universities and clergy have almost undone us. They have raised such a ferment in the nation as I know not who can allay; and I pray God the end be not their own ruin, and ours and our religion for company.[1]

Meantime the impeachments were pressed by the commons and received by the lords, to the great anxiety of Wake who gave expression to his conscientious scruples and apprehensions in a long memorandum in justification of his personal conduct. On Sunday, 10 July, he set down his impressions of events in the House of Lords the previous day, 'being resolved by God's assistance to review every step I take with relation to the impeachments now going on against several of the great lords of the House of Peers'. He had remained in his place until midnight; and now, on the Sunday,

I am alone, and by God's blessing in a condition to recollect what was done in the House; and though I hope and am resolved, through the divine assistance, not to do anything in which I am not well satisfied that I ought to do it; yet lest I should be mistaken and on a sudden take any wrong measures, I will make the review so soon as I can; that so I may lose no time to set my conscience right with God, if in anything I shall chance to vote amiss.

Notwithstanding his severe censure of the conduct of the late ministry, he wished at first that the Whigs had been content *quieta non movere* in this respect.

[1] King Correspondence (Trinity College library, Dublin).

It having pleased almighty God of his great goodness to deliver us once more out of our dangers, by taking away the Queen at such a critical juncture and in such a manner as left it not in their power to bring in the Pretender upon us; I could have been content to let their faults die with their interest, and to have seen them as much despised and hated by all true lovers of their country, their constitution and their religion, as they deserved, and as one might have hoped they should have been.

Unfortunately their conduct since the arrival of George I, by stirring up the people to suspect the good intentions of king and ministry towards the Church, had convinced Wake that this leniency could not be continued.

At last I became convinced myself that it was necessary that some notice should be taken of their proceedings. But here again my good nature recurred, and perhaps too far biassed my judgment; whether I was right or not, I cannot tell; but so it is, that I could never think it either for His Majesty's or the kingdom's service, to impeach them of high treason. To high crimes and misdemeanours I could readily agree; and I hoped and therefore wished that their prosecution might have stopped there. The House of Commons have gone farther. Whether in this they have judged aright, time must shew. But as His Majesty is a most merciful prince, and the English nation not very much either used or inclined to cruelty; so I still continue to think that had they not obliged the King to begin his reign with such a heinous impeachment against persons of such great quality, it would have been more for his honour and the public good; and I could almost wish that they might be disappointed in this part of their prosecution.

With these general considerations he approached the particular proceedings in the House of Lords, expressing surprise at the outset that the Commons had reversed their first intention to begin with Bolingbroke and had substituted Oxford, 'unless it were that the Earl of Oxford is to stand his trial, while the other is gone away'. On Friday, 8 July the articles were determined by the Commons, and sent up to the Lords on Saturday about 5 o'clock, when a debate ensued as to whether they should be read forthwith; and not until nearly 9 o'clock was this point determined in the affirmative. After a further two hours' discussion a resolution proposing to defer debate until the following Monday was defeated by 86 votes to 52, Wake being of the majority; 'and that for this reason, that this had always been the practice; and in an impeachment of such great moment no delay ought to be made in the first step to justice, namely the securing of the person in order to his appearing and answering to the crimes of which he was accused'. Despite the lateness of the hour, a further discussion arose as to whether the judges should be forthwith summoned to give their opinion on the question whether the two articles alleging high treason were sufficient for this charge; and upon a division whether the judges should be heard previously to the trial, this was defeated by 84 to 52, Wake again being of the majority:

as thinking that the judges should not be called to deliver their opinion suddenly in a matter of this moment; and that in the trial they would not only be informed by the pleadings on both sides, but be directed by the particular proofs that would be brought of the facts upon which this heinous charge is founded; and would also have leisure in the meantime, duly to consider of those articles, and so be able with the better judgment to deliver their opinions upon them.

When the question arose as to what should be done with the accused, Wake had left the house.

It was now 12 o'clock. I was quite tired and faint; and to say the truth, was afraid the question would be for committing the earl to the Tower; which I had no mind to have done in a hurry, at that time of the night, though I could not have blamed those who should have voted for it. My desire was that he should only be taken into the custody of the Black Rod till these articles might be fully and clearly discerned....However, here I resolved to leave the house; and whilst I had but any scruple about his lordship's commitment to the Tower, not to vote for it.

The Bishop of Lincoln indeed had other and deeper scruples; 'For myself, by the help of God, I will do nothing but with a clear conviction; and I heartily bless God that even upon such a conviction, my vote can never be given to deprive any person of his life, though I should think him never so much worthy to lose it'.

On the Monday morning, he learned that the house had decided as he hoped, only to commit Oxford to Black Rod; and on Tuesday, before the accused was called to the bar of the house, a debate arose and upon a division it was carried by 81 to 55 that the house should agree to commit him to the Tower, but upon his request, and in consideration of his present ill state of health, should respite his being carried thither for such reasonable time as might be thought proper by the house. Oxford was then called in, and was granted one month during which to present his answer to the articles; and his committal to the Tower was respited until the following Saturday. Thus far Wake's conscience was untroubled, save by the tactics of the supporters of the accused, whom he suspected of wishing to drive the house to extreme action in order to raise a popular clamour equally against parliament, the administration, and the dynasty.

And now, what could be more fair, more honourable, and indulgent than the proceedings of the house in all this? I bless God, hitherto I have not the least scruple upon my mind; I think mercy and favour have rather prevailed than strict justice, much less than rigour, though I must own that those who appeared on this unfortunate lord's side did all they could to provoke the house even to an undue severity. What shall I say to this; what must I think of it?...I am not able to judge here. God the searcher of hearts, knows what they mean, and to him I leave the judgment of it. To the same God I humbly commit it to judge of my own integrity. O Lord, if I have unwittingly done anything amiss by frailty, or prejudice which I am not sensible of, nor do believe, I beseech Thee to forgive me; and so direct and guide me in what more is to be done in this or any other of these impeachments, that I may have nothing to reproach me, when I come to examine myself concerning my proceedings upon them, nor anything for which to incur thy displeasure, either now or in the day of thy judgment.[1]

More than a month elapsed before the proceedings against the other accused persons reached the House of Lords; and on 18 August the Lords gave a third reading to a bill of attainder against Bolingbroke, and a second reading to a similar bill against Ormond, which then went to a committee of the whole house and was read a third time the same day. The former bill was adopted without a division; but in the case of Ormond a division took place, the bill being carried by 59 to 23; Wake being amongst the majority, 'not out of any ill-will to the duke, God is my witness; but because I thought it my duty so to vote'. On 1 September the articles of impeachment for high crimes and misdemeanours against the Earl of Strafford were brought into the lords. Wake entered the house during the course of the debate, but the matter was agreed without a division. Five days later the Earl of Mar's proclamation of the Old Pretender at Braemar marked the beginning of the Jacobite rebellion of 1715, and diverted attention from these impeachments. Not until 1 July 1717, after nearly two years languishing in prison without trial, was Oxford unanimously acquitted of the charge of high treason by the House of Lords, Wake being present on that day. The Bishop's careful diary of the initial stages in these proceedings is of greater interest because on the motion for the committal of Oxford to Black Rod, 'it was observed that of twenty bishops who were that day in the house, six only were for the earl, viz. York [Dawes], London [Robinson], Rochester [Atterbury], Bristol [Smalridge], Chester [Gastrell], and Durham [Crewe]'; on the resolution to commit him to the Tower, these same six bishops were joined by their brethren of Bath and Wells (Hooper) and St David's (Ottley) in voting against it; whilst protests against the attainder of Bolingbroke and Ormond were signed respectively by the Bishops of Chester and Rochester, and by these same two bishops together with those of Bristol and Bath and Wells.[2] It is, therefore, of particular importance that Wake should have set forth in such fullness and detail the grounds of his action. The extreme scrupulosity of his conscience was further illustrated by his action in June 1719 when, as one of the Lords Justices, he desired to be excused from signing a warrant for the establishment of courts martial, whilst at the same time convinced of the necessity of this step.

The establishment of courts martial is a matter so disagreeable to my character as well as to my temper, that though I am fully satisfied of the necessity of it, and,

[1] Arch. W. Epist. 19, ff. 1–11.
[2] Cobbett, *Parliamentary History*, vol. VII, col. 106, 108, 144.

did His Majesty's service require it, would readily concur in giving authority to it, yet there being no occasion for my appearing in this affair, I am rather desirous to leave it to the other Justices to sign the warrant for it. I desire the favour of you, when the warrant is prepared, to send it to the rest of their lordships, and so pass me by.[1]

The Jacobite rebellion which had called a halt to the political proceedings against the Tory ministers of the late reign, unfortunately also gave further evidence of divided counsels amongst the episcopate. For, though the bench could do little to suppress the rebellion, even the attempt of Tenison to secure a unanimous condemnation of the rising by all his brethren failed of success. A draft of a declaration of loyalty to the throne and abhorrence of the rebellion was made by Bishop Willis of Gloucester and approved by Tenison. Bishop Smalridge of Bristol produced a variant version; and finally he, together with Gastrell of Chester and Atterbury of Rochester, refused to sign the original form. Accordingly the declaration appeared over the names of 'the Archbishop of Canterbury and Bishops in or near London', a veil which hardly concealed the division on the bench. Such a spectacle could hardly be consoling to the administration, or welcome to the aged primate, whose days in fact were drawing to a close. During the autumn Gibson took new courage from the circumstance that Wake was appointed lord almoner, by which step, he declared, 'a good deal of my infidelity as to the main point is cured'; and accordingly when on 14 December 1715 'old Totius', as Tenison had been affectionately known to his friends, died, Gibson had become convinced of the correctness of the town talk which 'divides the succession between Lincoln and Norwich, but I think the first is most talked of'.[2] Actually the matter was despatched with unexpected promptitude; for Wake kissed hands for the primacy on 16 December. 'The Bishop of Lincoln has kissed the King's hand for the archbishopric yesterday', reported Gibson triumphantly to Nicolson, 'he would have persuaded the court to delay it for some days till his predecessor should be laid in his grave; but they would not hear of any delay, being in haste I suppose on account of the nearness of the parliament.'[3]

Thus the prize of the primacy, of which Tenison's tenacious hold upon life had cheated the Tory administration of the late queen, had devolved upon the new dynasty and its ministers, and had been bestowed on Wake. It is of especial interest therefore to observe that the new primate was convinced that the hand of the Princess of Wales, the future Queen Caroline, had been seen in his promotion.

[1] State Papers, Domestic 35, George I. Vol. 16, f. 89. 4 June 1719.
[2] Bodleian MSS. Add A. 269, ff. 46, 49. 13 November, 10 December 1715.
[3] *Ibid.* f. 51. 17 December.

I am told [he wrote to Bishop Smalridge] the debate lay between the Bishop of Norwich and myself. Who determined it in my favour, I cannot tell; but do believe I chiefly owe my preferment to my most gracious mistress, the Princess of Wales, who, I have reason to think, was principally concerned in it.... Though I am now probably like to be better known to His Majesty, yet hitherto I have never spoke to him but on some public occasion and in a way of form, as when I kissed his hand for this promotion, so that as yet I have no manner of interest at court.

Smalridge's reply confirmed this opinion. 'I have good reason to be assured that your lordship is not mistaken in thinking her royal highness the Princess of Wales chiefly concerned in your promotion; and I hope it will sit the easier on your lordship as coming from so good and acceptable a hand.'[1] Further confirmation is forthcoming from a letter of the Princess Caroline to the philosopher-theologian Leibnitz, who had engaged her to approach Wake when bishop of Lincoln with a view to an English translation of his *Théodicée*; and to whom she announced the elevation of the bishop to the primacy. 'Vous sauriez que mon bon ami l'Évêque de Lincolne e[s]t Archevêque de Canterbury, ce qui ma estté un sensible plaisir, non seulement par raport aluy, mais davoir un home de son merite à la t'ette de nos Eglise Protestante.' The news was welcomed with delight by Leibnitz, who replied urging the princess to profit by the occasion to urge the new archbishop to take up the threads of the Anglo-Prussian ecclesiastical negotiations, begun during the late queen's reign by Jablonski on the one side and Archbishop Sharp on the other.[2] Thus not only was the promotion of Wake due to the prescience of Caroline of Anspach (whose influence in matters ecclesiastical hereby appears at a much earlier date than usually has been supposed), but it was associated with his reputation amongst continental Protestants as a vigorous friend and champion of Protestant union. With his appointment to Canterbury, all seemed set fair for the Church-Whigs; and the temporary clouding of the horizon since the arrival of George I had been dissipated.

The new Archbishop has wonderful respect paid to him by our friends at court [wrote Gibson delightedly to Nicolson] which I verily believe will make him easy in all church affairs; and his entire interest in the prince and princess, with his free access to the king, and the benefit of speaking French fluently, seem to bid fair for a speedy establishment of all things upon a right foot.[3]

In acknowledging the congratulations of the Dean of Christ Church upon his being the first son of the House to attain to the primacy, Wake wrote with becoming modesty and diffidence of his hopes and fears.

[1] Arch. W. Epist. 15, n.f. Wake to Smalridge. 24 December 1715; reply, 29 December 1715.

[2] J. M. Kemble, *State Papers and Correspondence* (London, 1857), pp. 535, no. 206, 10–30 December 1715, and 541, no. 209.

[3] Bodleian MSS. Add. A. 269, f. 52. 20 December 1715.

I most heartily thank you for your very kind expressions of your approbation of what His Majesty has been pleased to do in my translation. How it will prove to the Church of Christ, God, whose providence brought it to pass, alone can tell. For myself, as I never did, nor yet do think myself in any wise worthy of such a promotion, so I can truly say I neither directly nor indirectly, by myself or any other, aspired to it....Now that it is thus settled, I can only say, I will do my utmost to promote the honour and welfare of our established church; and whatever other defects shall appear in me (as I am sensible there will appear many), yet truth and integrity and a hearty zeal for the peace and prosperity of our Sion, shall by God's grace never be wanting in me. How far it may be in my power to be serviceable to Christ Church, the place of my education, I cannot foresee. This you may be assured; that as I always with pleasure remember my beloved college, and heartily bless God that I was bred in it, so I will never be wanting in my true endeavours for its servicc, as far as my other obligations of duty elsewhere will permit me to use them.[1]

With such fair promise of a happy inauguration of his rule, Wake might well have been taken by surprise when with disconcerting and surprising swiftness the calm was succeeded by a series of storms.

The first of these upheavals came not from the side of the Archbishop but from that of the court, in the person of Benjamin Hoadly. It was inevitable that some promotion should be given to Hoadly, for the House of Commons so long ago as December 1709 had requested the queen 'to bestow some dignity in the church' upon him 'for his eminent services both to church and state'. The fulfilment of this promise had tarried long, but was now to be discharged with full measure. Hoadly was made a royal chaplain on 16 February 1715; and further rewards were expected as a matter of course. Gibson believed that the administration 'want a good deanery for Mr Hoadly'; but that divine aspired to come upon the bench, even coveting the large and exacting diocese of Lincoln. 'Endeavours were used to obtain it for Mr Hoadly', reported Gibson of the succession to Wake's see;

but the Archbishop would not recede from his request in my favour, into which my Lord Townshend also very readily came. Mr Hoadly is to have the bishopric of Bangor. His friends thought a good deanery or residentiaryship of St Paul's more proper for him, but it seems he preferred a bishopric; and since it is so, I hope he will be able to attend at Westminster, though at first crutches will look a little ungainly there.[2]

Accordingly on 21 December 1715 Hoadly was nominated to the see of Bangor. Since he was instrumental in raising one of the most furious controversies of his (and almost of any) age, and therewith in provoking the suspension of sitting convocations, his polemical writings will demand fuller

[1] Arch. W. Epist. 15, n.f. Wake to Smalridge, 24 December 1715.
[2] Bodleian MSS. Add. A. 269, ff. 51, 52. 17 and 20 December 1715.

consideration in another context. Here it must suffice to observe that his rash and imprudent course of action rendered the greatest possible disservice to his brethren of the Church-Whigs, and particularly to Wake and Gibson, who were endeavouring to convince the clergy of the good will and intentions of the administration towards them. For he first published in 1716 his *Preservative against the Principles and Practices of the Non-Jurors both in Church and State*, and next followed this by his more famous sermon on 31 March 1717 on *The Nature of the Kingdom or Church of Christ*, which unleashed all the furies of clerical tempers. In the former treatise he adumbrated those peculiar notions of the authority of the church, which he set forth at length in his sermon. In reply to the non-jurors, he affirmed that God could not possibly require all men as a condition of salvation to belong to 'one external communion', nor apply any religious tests save those of private judgment and inner sincerity. 'Every one may find it in his own conduct to be true, that his title to God's favour cannot depend upon his actual being or continuing in any particular method; but upon his real sincerity in the conduct of his conscience and of his own actions under it.' Accordingly he concluded that 'the favour of God therefore follows sincerity considered as such; and consequently equally follows every equal degree of sincerity'. What was implicit in this treatise became explicit in his sermon; which dissolved the idea of any authority of the church, substituted the principles of private judgment and sincerity of conscience, and formally repudiated the idea of an established church. Such was the doctrine proclaimed by a favourite bishop of the Whig administration, in a sermon printed by royal command.

During the course of the Jacobite rebellion, Wake had confessed to the Archbishop of Dublin his concern at the distrust of the Whig administration sedulously fostered by many of the clergy in the minds of their flocks.

> Many worthy promises the king has made of securing our constitution to us, both in church and state. Some considerable instances he has given us of his good inclinations towards us. Not one thing has been done that looks otherwise. Yet when you argue thus to some men, all you get is, that they are not safe in the present ministry. They have yet done us no harm; very true; but they will destroy us when they have an opportunity. And to this I know no answer that can be given.[1]

What better confirmation of this suspicion could be afforded than the sentiments of Hoadly, and the evident favour which he enjoyed with the court and ministry? Was his sermon the prelude not only to further concessions to the Dissenters, but even to their admission to complete equality with the established church? Was Hoadly flying a kite to show the Whig ministers whether a new scheme of 'comprehension' might be well received?

[1] King Correspondence. Wake to King. 25 August 1715.

The primate at any rate was not long left in doubt of the reactions of his principal brethren towards this incursion into the field of ecclesiastical polity.

God deliver us from all such damnable and anti-Christian heresies [burst forth the impetuous and outraged Nicolson]; should these miscreants prevail amongst us, there's an end of our consecration and orders; both our bishops and priests being henceforth to derive their authority by commissions out of the chancery or the war office.[1]

Gibson had a cooler head than Nicolson, but his alarm was equally real.

I very much doubt whether some persons by venting their own private notions of the original of church government on this occasion, will not do us far greater mischief than all the charges of schism from the Jacobite quarter. In my humble opinion nothing can more dispose the clergy to think that charge right than the telling them that either that or Erastianism must be right.[2]

Similar sentiments were expressed by Potter of Oxford and Smalridge of Bristol.

Worse, however, was to follow in the subsequent actions of the administration. The dismissal from their office as royal chaplains of divines who entered the lists against Hoadly, the prorogation of convocation in order to forestall an attempted synodical censure of his opinions, and the widespread reports of an intention to elevate the bishop of Bangor to the civil dignity of a privy counsellor and to the ecclesiastical office of dean of the chapels royal, threatened the whole basis of the Church-Whig alliance as Wake and Gibson understood it.

Can the ministry find no way to content my brother Hoadly and his friends [Gibson enquired anxiously], but by affronting the whole bench of bishops at once? Do they think that the Bishop of S[aru]m will not think himself as well qualified to be dean of the chapel, and the Bishop of G[louceste]r to be privy councillor as his lordship? Is it to be supposed that others of the bench who have no views, will be easy to see a young brother advanced over all their heads, to sit in state at Your Grace's right hand? In a word is it possible for men that think, to hazard the loss of nine parts in ten of the Whig clergy by an unaccountable fondness for one man? I ask Your Grace's pardon for this sally, which my indignation at the thought of such a wild and provoking step forced from me. If they give him a bishopric better in revenue than his own and not attended with those collateral honours, they will use him kindly, and it may pass off without shocking their friends, as being no more than what is expected; but such a step as Your Grace mentions will be amazing, and therefore till I see it done, I cannot think that the ministry (whatever they may be inclined to) are mad enough to venture it.[3]

[1] Arch. W. Epist. 20, n.f. 5 November 1716.
[2] *Ibid.* n.f. 15 October 1716.
[3] *Ibid.* n.f. 25 July 1717.

A month later, Gibson, disturbed by reports that 'a certain bishop is very much at court', further urged the Archbishop to be equally diligent in attendance.

If any new mischief is brewing, I am satisfied well that Your Grace has or may have strength and credit enough to prevent it. This was what his late grace often said in times that were far worse than these: 'that though he could do no great good at court, yet he could hinder mischief', which he always gave as a reason for keeping in with those who were not perfectly in his way of thinking.[1]

These further indiscretions of the ministry were happily prevented; but the change in tone from Gibson's earlier confidence of Wake's influence at court to his modified hope of preventing worse mischief, was eloquent of the difficulties confronting the Church-Whig alliance.

In another field, that of ecclesiastical preferment, signs were also multiplying that the Archbishop did not enjoy the unchallenged confidence of the administration. During the autumn following Wake's accession to the primacy, Gibson had seen disquieting symptoms of opposition.

By what I can observe [he related to Nicolson] the Bishop of N[orwich] is still to be archbishop under the protection of the lay administration, who seem in no disposition to give up the management of the church to the proper hand; and if that usurpation go on, I hope there will not want those upon the bench who think it unjust and unworthy, and accordingly will give their testimonies against it as occasion shall serve.

Even more alarming was the observation made to Gibson by Trimnell of Norwich himself that 'a general opinion had obtained that there was a great intimacy and correspondence' between Wake and Atterbury; which Gibson believed to be a deliberate invention, 'so as to make His Grace suspected everywhere by the King's friends; and the good things which the Bishop of Bristol has said of him in his visitation charge at Blandford, where His Grace was born, will much strengthen the suggestion'.[2] Bishop Smalridge indeed, in holding his visitation at Blandford had made a purely complimentary and wholly innocent reference to the distinction enjoyed by that town in the promotion of one of its natives to the primacy; but the supposition that this indicated a Tory policy on the part of Wake was ludicrous. During the absence of George I in Hanover that same autumn, the see of Exeter became vacant by the death of Bishop Blackhall on 29 November 1716, and Wake was anxious to ensure the succession of the dean of Exeter, Lancelot Blackburne. But he warned his friend of the uncertainty as to 'who would have the influence in church affairs on the king's return'; and it was interesting to observe that Blackburne accordingly paid court to Trimnell to solicit his

[1] *Ibid.* n.f. 24 August. [2] Bodleian MSS. A. 269, f. 62. 16 October 1716.

assistance. Upon His Majesty's return, however, on 23 January 1716/17, the Archbishop waited upon him with a written memorandum in French relating to the vacant ecclesiastical preferments; and since Blackburne had attended the king as chaplain during the first part of his Hanover visit, the nomination was duly made, as Wake desired, on 28 January. But Trimnell's own description of the position as 'the embarrassing, pretty great jog, as it was styled', was not far from the truth.

Meantime the primate had been compelled openly to oppose a government measure for the reform of close vestries, introduced into the House of Commons, and brought up to the House of Lords on 25 May 1716. The bill, to cite its full title, 'for better regulating Select Vestries within the Cities of London and Westminster, the Borough of Southwark and the Bills of Mortality, and for preventing any misapplication of such sums as shall be raised or given by charitable persons at the sacrament or otherwise for the maintenance of the poor', began by referring to the 'frequent and great abuses' in the diversion of such money by churchwardens and parish officers to 'riotous feasts and other unnecessary expenses'; and proceeded at one blow to dissolve 'all and every the vestries' in question from Easter Day 1717, except so far as particular exemptions were made 'by some especial act of parliament'. Instead of the old vestries, the justices of the peace at their quarter sessions next after Epiphany 1716 and henceforth triennially, were to appoint a day in the Easter week following for the several parishes to meet and elect a new vestry for a period of three years. At such elections the said justices were to preside, electors were to be qualified by residence within the parish and the possession of an estate of £300, and the vestries were not to exceed forty in number nor to be less than sixteen, according to the size of the parishes. The persons chosen as vestrymen were to be inhabitants of the parish, with an estate of £1000; and no churchwarden or overseer of the poor was to be eligible for election within the space of three years from his holding either of these offices. Furthermore, to the newly elected vestries extensive powers were given: to meet monthly, choose their own president, doing 'all such acts as are proper to be done by a vestry'; and particularly to appoint all teachers and children in charity schools, and all collectors of money for charities; whilst all money so raised was to be devoted 'to the maintenance of the poor' and not otherwise; and even the sacrament offertory was to be counted forthwith in the church-vestry, the amount entered in the church register, and to be applied to poor-relief in accordance with the direction of the vestry.[1]

The most revolutionary features of the bill, as Mr and Mrs Sidney Webb observed, were that it 'sought virtually to disestablish the clergyman from

[1] Arch. W. Epist. 15, n.f. Text of the Close Vestries' Bill.

his immemorial participation in local government [and] to place in a completely subordinate position the churchwardens, who were the most ancient officers of the parish'.[1] The parish priest indeed disappeared from the scene; and instead of the former vestry a new body with extensive powers including matters relating to charity schools, was substituted. It was little surprising therefore that protests poured in upon the Archbishop and the Bishop of London. Petitions from the clergy of London and Westminster and from the trustees of charity schools against the bill were presented to the House of Lords on 5 June, on which day the second reading was taken and Wake made a set speech for its rejection. He began by emphasising the gravity of the bill and its allegation of abuses 'of a very high nature, and such as, if true, ought certainly to be redressed'. Indeed 'had the bill taken a proper method to redress these, nobody could have excepted against it; but the connection between the preamble and enacting part seems very remote'. Granted the existence of abuses, the correct procedure would have been to provide for their remedy, not to abolish the old vestries altogether. Why were some vestries to be exempted from the bill? Were they free from abuses? and if so, why not retain the other vestries in being, with similar provisions to prevent abuses? The primate argued that in fact the powers of the present vestries were so limited as to give them little authority to control or prevent abuses. 'It were therefore to be wished that somewhat might be found out to redress the abuses without making such a total change in the vestry.' He made great play with the monetary qualification for electors and vestrymen; observing that provided this condition were fulfilled, the person might be a Dissenter, Jew, Papist, Quaker, or Non-Juror; and he pointed out that the exclusion of the churchwardens from the vestry removed the only officers who were liable to compulsion by the ecclesiastical courts to levy church rates. In the new scheme all appeals were to go to the J.P.s at their quarter sessions; 'so here is an end of the ecclesiastical power and church repairs'. Indeed the new vestries were to be endowed with unprecedented powers: 'to spoil the churchwardens of their lawful powers and the ecclesiastical courts of their authority'; in contradiction of the Act of Uniformity 'to appoint collectors of the sacrament money and to order the disposal of it'; to control the charity schools; and in effect to exercise control over lecturers and preachers. In conclusion Wake averred that

the vestries have by law, little or nothing to do with the overseers or their accounts; nothing to do with the sacrament money, with beadles, constables; only the church rates are properly before them. Let but these be regulated, as they may easily be,

[1] S. and B. Webb, *English Local Government from the Revolution to the Municipal Corporation Act: The Parish and the Country*, p. 255.

in a way consistent with the ecclesiastical laws of the church and realm; and all the rest may be put in order, and yet the vestries never be altered, nor anything done inconsistent with our present constitution.[1]

The effect of this speech was seen in the fact that after the primate had ended, no further defence of the measure was offered; but the motion for its committal was defeated. Moreover the lord chancellor, speaking a few days later on another measure, 'confessed that what was said against the Vestry Bill' by the Archbishop, 'convinced him that there was not one sound part in its whole composition, and that therefore he was still of opinion that it was justly denied a commitment'.[2] The compliment was hardly exaggerated; for Wake had subjected the bill to detailed and destructive criticism. The episode was important further as a warning to the administration that he was a churchman first and a Whig second; and it would have been well if they had understood its significance from this standpoint.

Worse troubles, however, were to follow shortly; for during the spring of 1717 the smouldering quarrels between George I and the Prince of Wales burst into open flames; and the differences latent in the administration likewise proved impossible of further concealment or compromise. Accordingly Townshend, Walpole, Pulteney, Devonshire, Orford and Methuen left the ministry, which passed under the control of Sunderland and Stanhope. At first Wake was allowed 'to attend the princess about once a week, as a divine'; but soon the prince's household became a cave of Adullam for the discontented Whigs, and in December 1717 the king forbade any person attending his levées also to wait upon his son. Such a prohibition was not unnatural as applied to political ministers; but if extended to prelates could hardly be justified. Upon enquiring whether it was designed to restrict his freedom of access, the primate received a reply, surely astonishing alike in its discourtesy and rigidity.

His Majesty, having considered what you represented to him in relation to your attending the Princess, has commanded me to acquaint Your Grace: that he can by no means dispense with the late order signifying his royal pleasure, that any person who shall go to the Prince or Princess of Wales, do forbear coming into His Majesty's presence. But whenever Her Royal Highness shall desire to speak with Your Grace, if you will inform His Majesty of it yourself, or signify it by letter to one of his Secretaries of State, to be laid before His Majesty, you shall thereupon receive his further pleasure.[3]

It was entirely to his credit as a Christian bishop that Wake refused to cease attendance on the prince and princess, but continued instead to do his utmost

[1] Arch. W. Epist. 15, n.f. Notes of Wake's speech; also Epist. 7. Canterbury II, n.f. Gibson to Wake. 4 May.

[2] Arch. W. Epist. 7. Canterbury II, n.f. Nicolson to Wake. 18 June 1716.

[3] State Papers, Domestic 35. George I. Vol. 10, f. 80. 29 December 1717. Portland MSS. V, 550–2.

to dispose affairs to a reconciliation. Notwithstanding, his action was interpreted unfavourably by the king and reacted adversely on his relations with the sovereign and his ministers. This lack of confidence indeed was to be particularly unfortunate in view of the domestic policy of the administration, and its measures in relation to the universities, the church, and the Protestant Dissenters.

It was undeniable that the ministry owed the Dissenters some relief of their disabilities arising from the passing of the Occasional Conformity and Schism Acts during the reign of Anne, and some return for their loyal support of the Hanoverian dynasty during the Jacobite rebellion. The Schism Act indeed had never been enforced; but its removal from the statute book seemed to the Dissenters a simple and tardy act of justice. In regard to the Occasional Conformity Act, they had been assured at the time of its passing 'of earnest endeavours for relief as to this and other hardships whenever the Protestant succession should come to take place'.[1] Yet George I had been king for more than two and a half years, without any attempt being made to redeem the promise. Both the king and Stanhope, however, were convinced of the justice as well as prudence of such an endeavour; and Stanhope particularly was a firm advocate of religious toleration and equality, whose record was unsmirched by any backsliding. But it was evident also that the success of such a venture would depend to no small degree upon the support forthcoming from the episcopal bench; and it was to the primate therefore that a first overture was made in the early spring of 1717 to sound his opinion. On 14 March 1716/17, Cowper warned Wake of this approach.

I believe Your Grace has received before this time, notice of a visit from the Earl of Sunderland and Mr Stanhope, and hope this will come soon enough to let you know beforehand the business of it. 'Tis in the King's name to sound Your Grace's opinion on a repeal of the Act against Occasional Conformity. I dined yesterday with them and Mr Bernsdorf. The same matter was then the subject. I truly owned I never liked the Act and joined in passing it as it is, lest it should have passed, as it would have done if opposed, in a worse manner. But to my great surprise I was so fortunate as to convince them both that it was not fit to have that Bill of Repeal and that about the Universities going at the same time. Upon this they took a sudden turn and became resolved to have this of the Repeal first, and postpone that concerning the Universities, which, Your Grace knows, how lately and how much the King, as they said, had set his heart upon.[2]

The outcome of the interview was distinctly chilling; and Bishop Nicolson of Carlisle (who enjoyed the facility of being able to speak to the king in German) informed His Majesty on 18 March 'that eighteen or nineteen of

[1] E. Calamy, *An Historical Account of my own Life* (2 vols.), vol. II, p. 246.
[2] Arch. W. Epist. 20. Miscellaneous IV, n.f.

the bishops would be against repealing the Act against Occasional Conformity' on the ground that it had been 'so lately and unanimously agreed to'. Five days later, on the 23rd, Nicolson and six other bishops dined with Cowper, who asked 'how their sentiments stood' on this matter, and was assured 'that eighteen in twenty-five (as the king had been told) would be against the repeal'.[1] This same month the grievances of the Dissenters were discussed in the House of Commons and at a private meeting of two hundred members at the Rose Tavern near Temple Bar, at which Stanhope was present. In face of the divisions in every quarter, however, on the bench, amongst the Whigs and in the royal family, nothing could be attempted forthwith.

I think this session of parliament will go off without any attempts in favour of the Dissenters [reported Wake to the Archbishop of Dublin on 1 June]. If our ministry keep their words, our interval will not be long: four months at the most. Yet in that time I flatter myself we shall either see such changes as will prevent the threatened attempt; or have so settled the church's interest as to render any such attempt ineffectual. For I am still of the opinion I have openly professed here, that no men who bid such a free defiance to the established church will long be able to stand against the interest of it. And I never yet saw our friends, high and low (Jacobites only excepted, and even they will join with us on this occasion) more entirely united than in opposing the court projects in favour of those who make us so ill a requital for the toleration that has been so kindly indulged to them, and so inviolably been preserved on our part.[2]

Accordingly in the King's Speech at the opening of parliament on 21 November following, His Majesty said that he

could heartily wish that at a time when the common enemies of our religion were by all manner of artifices endeavouring to undermine and weaken it, both at home and abroad, all those who were friends to our happy establishment might unanimously concur in some proper method for the greater strengthening of the Protestant interest, of which as the Church of England was unquestionably the main bulwark and support, so she would reap the principal benefit of every advantage accruing by the union and mutual charity of all Protestants.

The two houses concurred in this pious aspiration; and once more therefore soundings were made amongst members of the episcopal bench, and amongst the Dissenters. But the administration, faced now by the factious opposition of its own Whig dissidents, was in a weaker position, and its ambitions were more modestly conceived in consequence. During the earlier approaches Nicolson had reckoned Gibson of Lincoln and Blackburne of Exeter amongst opponents of the repeals; but now they, with others of their brethren, were

[1] N. Sykes, *Edmund Gibson*, p. 72.
[2] King Correspondence. Wake to King. 1 June 1717.

disposed to compromise on the limited objective of admitting Dissenters to office in Corporations in order to prevent the Tories from controlling them at elections.

Yesterday [reported Gibson to Wake on 22 November 1717], the bishops of Worcester [Hough], Gloucester [Willis], and myself were desired to be at the bishop of Norwich's [Trimnell], this morning at 11 o'clock; and we found there the bishops of Sarum [Talbot], and Lichfield [Chandler]. The occasion of the meeting was, which way it would be best to proceed in, with regard to the Bill for Corporations; and though that of *offering* to receive the Sacrament and admitting such offer as a full qualification, was mentioned; yet it appeared to be the sense of the whole company that the more desirable method would be to abolish the Sacramental test so far as it concerns corporations. The bishops of Worcester and Exeter are privy to my writing this; and direct me to acquaint Your Grace that they hope (as I do) that Your Grace will speedily command our attendance upon you on this subject.[1]

Bishop Trelawny, however, though rejoicing that 'the phanatigs' would not be 'so high in their demands this season as they were in the last for the repeal of the Schism and Occasional Bills, since their eyes are now turned towards regulating the corporations', nevertheless assured the primate on 1 December that 'the corporations must be kept as they are, or the phanatigs by their own money and the government's will have a parliament which will do our business at once'; and he insisted 'that all attempts of this nature are to be opposed with the utmost vigour'.[2] Nicolson for his part thought that if some concession were imperative, 'it were better that the late Act against Occasional Conformity should be repealed, than that the Test Act be suspended in cities and great towns, which (upon such a suspension) will immediately be filled with Quakers, Anabaptists and other heretics and schismatics from all parts of the neighbouring counties'.[3]

Accordingly the episcopal deputation found the Archbishop in no mood to listen to compromise; but instead were met with an unequivocal negative.

His Grace as far as I can find, will not come into anything with regard to the Dissenters [related Gibson to Nicolson on 23 November], though his four friends here (Worcester, Exeter, Lichfield and myself) are unanimous in our opinion that there is a necessity of something to be done in order to prevent a Tory parliament, and to keep a good understanding among the friends of the present establishment. The consequence will be that His Grace will be caressed to the last degree by the Tory bishops, lords, and commons; and his levée and table will be filled with such company as we shall not care to mix with; which will render his old friends in a great measure incapable of serving him, however entire we may remain in our duty and respects to him, which I hope no circumstances will ever alter.... This is the sad state which things are running into; which might be prevented if His Grace

[1] Arch. W. Epist. 20. Miscellaneous IV, n.f.
[2] *Ibid.* 1 December 1717. n.f.
[3] *Ibid.* 28 November. n.f.

would go upon the bottom of his predecessor, and make this one step in conjunction with his suffragans, and thereby keep the whole Whig interest together, and establish such an entire credit with the king and his ministers, as would enable him to do what he would in church matters. The loss of all these advantages and a gradual disunion from his old friends will be the unavoidable consequences of his standing out; and yet stand out he will, as we greatly fear, having no hope that any who are attached to the prince's family will do otherwise.[1]

The prospect of acute division on the bench, although as yet rather latent than patent, was disconcerting both to churchmen and statesmen; and on each side of the gulf it was making strange bedfellows, Wake finding himself the subject of Tory encomiums and Gibson being in the same camp as Hoadly. The Bishop of Lincoln indeed insisted to his brother of Carlisle that the point at issue was of a purely political character, namely the best way to prevent the return of a Tory parliament, with all the ominous consequences this might involve for church and state; and from this overriding standpoint he lamented the rigidity of the Archbishop.

You will be sorry to hear [he wrote on 28 November], that there is too great probability of your three friends differing with His Grace on this occasion; we (as your lordship knows) having declared ourselves very freely the last year, and His Grace this year seeming to be against any expedient as much as we all were, and still are, against occasional conformity. However others may stand suspected for acting in obedience to Bishop Hoadly's doctrine, we three must stand clear in your lordship's opinion of that charge, since you know our judgments were formed long before his doctrine was preached; and the ground of that judgment, the apprehension of a Tory parliament and Tory administration if something was not done in that way to prevent them. The argument for it is far stronger in my opinion since the Tories have gained such a considerable accession of strength and spirits since that time, by the defection of the disgusted Whigs, who, you may depend upon it, are in common measures with the Tories to perplex the king's affairs and to unhinge the present ministry; and whether the next is to be a Tory administration, or, if Tory (as it certainly can be nothing else), whether the Archbishop or Bishop of R[ocheste]r is to be at the head of church affairs, judge you. In a word, there is now an opportunity of defeating the Tories and establishing the Archbishop's credit with the king and court once for all; if this be lost (as I plainly see it will) all hopes of compassing the desirable ends are gone, and His Grace must of course set himself at the head of the Tories, till they have gotten strength enough to make a church-head of their own. He can never go their lengths; and we may depend upon it, they will not value him longer than they need him, unless he will go their lengths; and whether he may be permitted to remain their head, even on that supposition, when they have gotten strength, is a question, or rather (with me) no question.[2]

To such a pass had the schisms within the royal family and the Whig party, combined with the stratagems of the Tories, driven Church-Whigs of

[1] Bodleian MSS. Add. A. 269, f. 70.

[2] *Ibid.* f. 71.

the calibre of Gibson; who was convinced that, the choice being between two evils, by far the lesser was the admission of Dissenters to Corporations by some relaxation of the sacramental test.

For my own part [he confided again to Nicolson on 3 December], all my political reasonings proceed upon these two positions; that there is no way to preserve the Church but by preserving the present establishment in the state; and that there is far greater probability that the Tories will be able to destroy our present establishment in the state than that the Dissenters will be able to destroy our establishment in the Church. This I always understood to be the reasoning of my old master; upon which he acted in the whole course of his administration, and from which he could never be driven by the continued clamours of the Tories about the danger of the Church. If he and the bench had regarded that noise, where had we been at this day?

Gibson indeed was already beginning to draw the contrast between Tenison and his successor, which was to be the justification of his own later displacement of Wake as the ecclesiastical adviser of the Whig administration under Townshend and Walpole.

Your lordship observes that old Totius was the centre of unity; and that young Totius is not likely to be so, is not owing to his friends who (out of duty and affection to him) have used all ways possible to persuade him to embark upon the same bottom that carried his predecessor through all difficulties with so much honour, and to resolve once for all to set himself at the head of fourteen bishops. If that is not done now (as I verily believe it will not) it is the fixed opinion of his friends here that nothing can follow but a union with the Tories. This is what he would not choose, especially attended, as it must be, with a separation from his old friends; but at the same time, if I guess aright, he will not choose to be a cypher.[1]

If on the one side the Bishop of Lincoln was preparing the ground of his own ultimate supplanting of the Archbishop, on the other hand Wake was giving anticipations of his later severe censure of his dissentient brethren.

If you think I have any credit at Lambeth especially at this time and on this occasion, you are much mistaken [Gibson informed Nicolson a week later]; assure yourself that we are already looked upon as betrayers of the church; and yet we are no otherwise betraying it now than his two predecessors were betraying it for about thirty years together, that is, in our language, supporting it in the most effectual manner, by supporting the Protestant establishment. If the step that is intended to be taken do not answer that end, we cannot help it; our superiors in the state are best able to judge of that; and if they be mistaken, it is not our fault who mean honestly, but theirs who judge foolishly. But when all is done, I believe it has always been a rule and always must be, to leave the laity to judge of the most proper methods of promoting elections and securing good returns; and if the clergy in the country shall think (as His Grace does and pretty plainly speaks it) that our concurrence is a betraying the church, I beg leave to return to my old maxim, the maxim

[1] *Ibid.* f. 72. 'Totius' signifies '*Totius* Angliae Primas'.

that made our old master's administration so full of honour, 'that the most necessary step towards preserving the church is to preserve the state; and that they truly and really desert the church who desert the measures which have hitherto put it out of the power of the Tories to destroy our establishment in the state'. In a word, we have not the least hopes of bringing His Grace into any scheme of any kind. What a union of the two courts might do, we cannot tell; but there seem little hopes of that. The confidences between him and his old friends wear off and cool apace; and I cannot see how it will be possible in the nature of things to avoid a separation from us and a union with the Tories, in which opinion I do not stand alone.[1]

Meantime the wildest rumours as to the intentions of the administration were current; and members of both houses gathered in London in early January in expectation of a government bill to deal with the question. The most extreme report had it that the Bishops of Salisbury, Norwich, Worcester, and Bangor in a conference with the Dissenters had 'offered them to have the Occasional and Schism Bill and Test Act to be repealed; and as to ecclesiasticals that they should come into livings not exceeding £50 a year'.[2] So seriously were such exaggerations received that Gibson was at pains expressly to deny their veracity to Nicolson.

Your lordship in your last letter takes two things for granted, which I verily believe are groundless [he observed on Christmas Eve], the first that more is now meant for the Dissenters than was intended them last year. For my own part I talked without reserve of some power in corporations and of places of meer profit in other parts; the first as necessary to the king's affairs, and the second as what could no way affect the safety and well-being of the Church. The second, that the Test Act is to be totally taken away; and it is true that a proposal has been afoot to take away the *Sacramental* test, as sacramental, but at the same time to substitute a *Declaratory* test in the room of it; which was couched in the strongest terms, and against which the Dissenters opened most liberally, to such a degree indeed that I am of opinion nothing at all will be done this session.[3]

The prophecy was true; for the divisions on the bench and the hostile attitude of the Dissenters led to the abandonment of the attempt to offer relief to the latter. But postponement was not the equivalent of solution; and during the ensuing summer fortune smiled abundantly on the administration. Stanhope secured the signature of the Quadruple Alliance, the Spanish fleet was annihilated off Cape Passaro, and at home the resignation of Cowper relieved the government of the chief lay opponent of a thoroughgoing relief to the Dissenters. The strength accruing to the ministry from these events was generally interpreted as an indication that bolder measures would be introduced in the next parliamentary session.

I am more and more confirmed in the expediency of keeping close to our established church [wrote Bishop Manningham of Chichester to the primate on

[1] Bodleian MSS. Add. A. 269, f. 73.
[2] Portland MSS. v, 554.
[3] Bodleian MSS. *Ibid.* f. 75.

30 August 1718], and I hope many of our bench are of the same opinion. There are four, who, I believe, will keep as close to the court as Mercury to the sun; but as to the rest, they will be pretty well united in their votes as to the real good of the Church, though upon different views and reasons as to matters in the state. I expect the design of gratifying the Dissenters will be put under different shapes, till they can fix upon one that they think will pass; but you who are at the top of affairs, will, I hope, be at the bottom too and discover the artifice.... Our late flush of success in the Mediterranean will make the Whig party push boldly for their ends this ensuing session; for they have grumbled of late that the court has been too remiss in serving them, and will be ready now to quicken all their friends to make good their promises to them, in so favourable a juncture.[1]

In anticipation of some emphatic move on the part of the ministry, attempts were made to bring together Wake and Gibson, whose lead would be followed by Worcester and Exeter if agreement could be reached.

What your lordship says concerning our quitting the *centre of peace* [replied the Bishop of Lincoln to his brother of Carlisle on 23 August], would concern me the more if I did not walk in such good company as your lordship knows, and were not very sure that the centre has quitted us, who reckon ourselves to be in exactly the same way of thinking and acting that our late master was for twenty years together.... In short what I have often told your lordship, continues to be my firm belief; that the differences on the bench are wholly grounded upon our master's attachment to one branch of the divided interest at court; and if that be the case, it is vain to think of union in parliament among the bishops till there is union at court. In ecclesiastical matters I hope we shall always behave ourselves as dutiful suffragans ought to do, and for the civil part your lordship knows well how great a grief it was to us to observe his grace's partiality to one court as diminishing and destroying his credit at the other; a grief which carried in it a most hearty concern for his honour and an earnest desire to see him sole head under the king in the administration of church affairs.[2]

The desired *rapprochement* seemed less unpromising since, as Gibson reminded Nicolson on 13 September, when the Schism Act was passed 'among the Protesters I well remember our present master's name as one; and His Grace has made no scruple to declare that he would readily come into a repeal of that act'.[3] Nicolson therefore assured the primate of his hopes that unity would be restored on the bench.

I heartily rejoiced at the news of my brother of Lincoln's being admitted to such a fresh share of trust by Your Grace in preparing a proper form of royal injunctions to the clergy [he observed on 29 November]. I would gladly hope that these will be thought sufficient in the affair of religion for this winter; and that no other step will be made in favour of Dissenters.... I am verily persuaded that my old friend means no more harm to the episcopal constitution than I do; and that therefore, now the fright of his metropolitan's turning Tory is over, he'll keep very staunch in Your

[1] Arch. W. Epist. 21, f. 32. [2] Bodleian MSS. Add. A. 269, f. 78. [3] *Ibid.* f. 80.

Grace's measures for the future. I could never observe that he inclined to oblige the Dissenters further than by admitting them into corporation offices, to prevent undue returns of members disaffected to the present government.[1]

To the general surprise the King's Speech at the opening of parliament on 11 November 1718 contained no mention of this question; nor is it easy to trace the course of events leading to the introduction by Stanhope, without previous notice, into the House of Lords on 13 December of a bill 'for strengthening the Protestant interest in these kingdoms'. The correspondence between Gibson and Nicolson, from which valuable information might have been expected, ceased during this difficult period owing to divergence of view. 'I have not troubled you with anything that has been doing at Westminster of late', reported the former on 30 December, when the issue had been determined; 'because I knew the attempt was contrary to your lordship's judgment; and having succeeded so far as the House of Lords goes, I did not care to be the messenger of ill news.'[2] By this time also Nicolson had been nominated to the Irish see of Derry and therefore bore no part in the debate in the Westminster parliament. On 23 November Sunderland wrote to ask if Wake could receive at dinner on the morrow at Lambeth, Stanhope, Parker, Craggs and himself;[3] but there is no evidence of what passed on that occasion, nor of any further communication until 12 December, when Sunderland intimated by letter the text of the bill to be introduced into the House of Lords on the morrow.

I had several things to have talked to Your Grace upon if I had waited upon you this morning; and in particular by the King's order to have shewn Your Grace the enclosed copy of the bill about the Occasional Conformity, which Lord Stanhope is to bring tomorrow into the house. Your Grace will see by it that, though it be absolutely necessary for the king's affairs to have this matter brought on, yet there is in the framing and shaping of it all the regard to the dignity of the Church and the ease of the clergy as was possibly consistent with making it effectual for the public service of the government; and indeed I think it is truly so framed as not to leave a real, conscientious, and religious objection to it. The king therefore hopes it will not meet with Your Grace's disapprobation. I am sure there never was a king who was more sincerely and more strongly determined to support the established church and to consult its honour, nor who has a greater desire to shew the utmost regard to yourself as the head of that Church under him; and this you will find more and more every day both in great and little things; for indeed all those that are concerned in the king's administration are out of principle determined to pursue in this the king's intentions, and are out of inclination and true esteem Your Grace's faithful servants.[4]

The abundance of honeyed compliments and assurances with which the pill was coated, could not succeed, however, in making its contents palatable

[1] Arch. W. Epist. 21, f. 63.
[2] Bodleian MSS. Add. A. 269, f. 81.
[3] Arch. W. Epist. 21, f. 61.
[4] *Ibid.* Epist. 8. Canterbury III, f. 84.

to Wake. For the bill was indeed bolder than had been conceived or anticipated; since it amounted in effect to a combination of the two projects of relief, proposed separately in the spring and autumn of 1717. The first clause repealed both the Occasional Conformity and Schism Acts; the second protected any parochial clergyman who refused to administer the Sacrament to a Dissenter for purpose of qualification for office, from liability to any censure, suit, or legal action in relation thereto; and the third clause proceeded boldly to enact that any person desirous to receive the Sacrament for purpose of qualification for office should give notice in writing of his intention to present himself at the holy table on a given day; and if the minister should refuse, or should not expressly promise to administer, at the time of his receiving this notice, 'in every such case such notice and refusal shall be accepted and taken in place of receiving the Sacrament of the Lord's Supper'. A fourth clause provided that within three months of admission to office the person concerned should present at the Quarter Sessions or at the Courts of Record at Westminster evidence of his notice and refusal, attested by two credible witnesses upon oath; and a final clause prohibited any magistrate from carrying the insignia of his office to any place of public worship other than the established church.[1] The audacity and comprehensiveness of the bill were indeed consonant with the liberal and tolerant outlook of Stanhope; for in addition to repealing the two obnoxious acts of Anne's reign, it provided in effect a way of escape from the requirements of the Test and Corporation Acts without a frontal repeal in their case.

But if no further approach had been made to the primate before the preparation of the measure, consultation had been held with some of his brethren. In a memorandum in his own hand, appended to the notes of his speech in the House of Lords, Wake wrote:

> In order to the settling of this worthy bill, a meeting was had the Sunday night (or not long before, on a Sunday evening), to which I was not invited, between the ministry and the bishops (proper for such a work). One, not in the secret, asked simply whether the Archbishop would be there. It was answered that being late and a stormy night, they believed not. Such was their sincerity. The lay lords came prepared to limit the bill to some offices only; a Right Reverend prelate was for all; and the great minister replied, they had nothing more to desire; they had offered more than was expected of them; or to that effect. I had my account of this meeting from my Lord Chancellor Cowper, and in part from the good Bishop of Lichfield and Coventry, who was not one of the cabal, but to be drawn into the design.[2]

Accompanying this memorandum was a printed copy of the division list in the House of Lords on the bill, with the names of those bishops who had attended the secret meeting marked with a cross. According to this identi-

[1] *Ibid.* f. 85. Also in the House of Lords MSS.

[2] *Ibid.* f. 88 verso.

fication mark, the Bishops of Lichfield, Worcester, Sarum, Gloucester and Lincoln had been present on that Sunday evening, and plainly had acted without previous concert with the Archbishop.

The episcopal speeches in the House of Lords therefore followed the lines anticipated. Both Archbishops spoke against the bill on principle and not simply on points of detail, as did also the Bishops of Bristol, London, Rochester, and Chester; whilst speeches in its favour were made by the Bishops of Lincoln, Gloucester, Sarum, Norwich, Bangor and the new Bishop of Peterborough, White Kennett.[1] Wake's full notes of his speech are extant, headed 'The heads of my speech in the House of Lords against repealing the Occasional Conformity Bill'; and they are of particular interest in view of his change of attitude since the reign of Anne. He began by admitting that the repeal of the Sacramental Test would be more acceptable to the clergy than that of the Occasional Conformity Act, 'because they will not be required to administer the Holy Communion to hypocrites and schismatics'; but it would be worse for the Church, 'because it will let in all sorts of schismatics into places, which the other would not have done; for which reason it was guarded against even in the Act of Indulgence upon the Revolution and has stood so ever since'. The real ground of Wake's opposition, however, lay in his conviction that the Dissenters were 'at present decreasing both in number and interest; no persons of quality left amongst them: but few gentlemen. Even in corporations the richer merchants would rather leave the conventicle than be shut out of the corporation.' If the repeal were carried, 'all these will be sent back again to their conventicles; and so 5 or 6000 men who were come off to the church, be driven again from it; so much will this bill tend to the union of Protestants.' Moreover, the steadfast friends of the church would be disquieted by this bill, fearing that it portended further concessions; 'for indeed nobody can think that this will satisfy either the hopes or expectations of the Dissenters; rather it will make them more importunate and encourage them to expect more'. It was a moot point also whether the administration would not lose more supporters by this measure than it would gain. Furthermore, the primate contended that outworks ought not to be given up; 'when we are attacked by an enemy, we ought to dispute every inch with them; it is a greater weakening to the church's interest than we are aware of that we are now giving away'. Nor could any credit be given to the assurance that no further concessions would be sought.

Promises or resolutions to stop here cannot be depended upon; we thought we should have stopped at the Act of Indulgence; that will not do. Now we are to stop

[1] *Episcopal Opinions on the Test and Corporation Acts, delivered in the House of Peers in December 1718* (London, J. Pridden, 1790).

here; how long? till other circumstances arise to persuade the ministry that they ought to go farther. We all know the Dissenters demand more; and we know their temper that they will never be quiet till they get more.

Wake even reverted to the period of the Interregnum to rebuke them: 'This, had they any modesty, should keep them from complaining of the hardship of the church towards them. I am sure it ought to make us cautious how we fall into their hands.' If Papists and Non-Jurors were disqualified as disloyal to the constitution, so might Dissenters be; 'our Church is as much a part of our legal constitution as the state; Dissenters by principles dangerous to the episcopal church (monarchy too); and for that reason the Test Act was made equally to keep them and Papists from the government'. The fate of the episcopal church in Scotland and the increase in the number of Dissenters in Ireland should give pause before granting further concessions in England.

The Archbishop turned also to examine the chief arguments for the bill; namely, the merits of the Dissenters themselves; the strengthening of the Church itself by its union with other Protestants abroad and at home; and the common rights of all subjects who give security of their fidelity and affection to the government. The merits of the Dissenters at the Revolution, at the death of Anne and since, he allowed; but held that they had been sufficiently rewarded by the Toleration Act, any breaches of which by mob-violence had been speedily corrected and redress offered. But members of the established church had been equally loyal to the Revolution and the Protestant succession in the House of Hanover (except the Non-Jurors who had suffered for their obstinacy); and the number of loyal churchmen far exceeded that of Dissenters. 'Should so many be disobliged for them?' In speaking of foreign Protestants, Wake was on stronger ground, for his zeal for their union with the Church of England was unquestioned. 'With the Protestant churches abroad we have as strict an union already as we can ever expect to have; this bill will neither make it more nor less.' Nor would it unite the Dissenters with the established church in England.

With the Dissenters at home, this bill will be so far from uniting us, that it will more divide us. Thousands will go off to the conventicles upon it, who now come to the established church. Nor will this make them ever the more our friends. The Toleration has not done it; they have never written more bitterly against us than since that. When men own they can with a good conscience communicate with us; that there is nothing materially unlawful in lay conformity; that occasional conformity is their duty; and yet no considerations of peace, unity, or charity will prevail with them so to do, what can we hope from such men?

As for the third reason, the common rights of subjects, the bill did not go far enough to satisfy its implications: 'Why is this bill so defective in restoring them?' But in point of fact, 'our laws go upon a contrary supposition;

Socinians, Arians, Deists not so much as tolerated'. Also the argument was repeated that Dissenters were 'not true to our constitution; that consists of the king as head and the estates of the spiritualty and temporalty. The Dissenters known enemies to the spiritualty, as part of our constitution, as lords of parliament, once turned them out.' Finally, Wake summarised his objections to the bill and restated his grounds for rejection; emphasising that it would relieve only occasional conformists, 'who the least of all deserve it, because they can communicate with us and do'; that the position of the clergy would be prejudiced in corporate towns by this relief to Dissenters; and that it would thereby be the parent not of unity but of further strife. Fundamentally the question was that

> if there must be a national church, that church must be in the first place supported by our governors and the laws. It must be supported against one sort of enemies as well as another. The least support is by negative discouragements. It would be folly to entrust enemies with the power to subvert the national church, when they please to use it to its prejudice. What law of Christ requires all his followers to be made equally capable of honours and trust by the civil magistrate? or forbids the civil magistrate to make a difference if the public good requires it?

Actually experience had told against the supporters of the measure. 'For five years past things have continued quiet and well under this law. Why should we now hazard the making them otherwise by repealing it? It is for the interest of the state to bring men as far to an union in the church established as may be. This the present act has in good measure done.'[1]

From other episcopal speeches, it was plain that the bill in its initial form would hardly survive the committee stage. 'I do not doubt', commented Nicolson to Wake, 'but that there are several excrescences in this bill, which are now plastered upon it on purpose to be pared off, in order to its passing the more glibly into law.' It secured a second reading in the Lords on 19 December by 86 votes to 68; the two Archbishops with the Bishops of London, Durham, Winchester, Bath and Wells, Chichester, Hereford, St David's, Rochester, Bristol, Chester, St Asaph, Oxford, and Lichfield voting against; and the Bishops of Worcester, Salisbury, Llandaff, Norwich, Ely, Gloucester, Lincoln, Bangor, Exeter, Carlisle, and Peterborough being in its favour. It was significant that the Prince of Wales headed the peers voting 'for the Church', that is, against the bill. In committee the lords deleted the clause dispensing with the Sacramental Test, Sunderland being reported as having stated that it 'had never been part of the bill unless the Bishops of Gloucester, Lincoln and Bangor had declared they would not appear for the bill without it'.[2] An attempt by Lord Nottingham at the third reading to add a clause to prevent the growth of Socinianism by requiring,

[1] Arch. W. Epist. 8. Canterbury III, f. 87.

[2] Portland MSS. V, 574.

as a condition of office-holding, subscription to the Articles of Religion relating to the Trinity and the divinity of Christ, was defeated. In the House of Commons, the Whig malcontents opposed the bill, and it was carried by a majority of only 41. In its final form therefore it restored the ecclesiastical compromise of the Revolution settlement by repealing the two restrictive acts of Anne's reign. In regard to corporations however an Act for Quieting and Establishing Corporations was passed during the same session, by which all office-holders in corporations who had not complied with the law in regard to the sacramental test but whose tenure of office was not questioned for six months, were confirmed in their offices.

It is interesting to compare the grounds upon which Wake had signed the protest against the passing of the Schism Act in 1714 with those upon which he opposed its repeal and that of the Occasional Conformity Act in 1718. The first reason averred by the protesters was that they could not apprehend 'that great danger may ensue from the Dissenters to the church and state, because (i) by law no Dissenter is capable of any station which can be supposed to render him dangerous; and (ii) since the several sects of Dissenters differ from each other as much as they do from the established church, they can never form of themselves a national church'. Secondly, the protest affirmed that 'if nevertheless the Dissenters were dangerous, severity is not so proper and effectual a method to reduce them to the Church as a charitable indulgence, as is manifest by experience'; for indeed 'severity may make them hypocrites, but not converts'. Thirdly, even if severity were a proper means, its use would be imprudent at a time 'when we are threatened with such great dangers to our Church and nation'. Fourthly, 'this must be the more grievous to the Dissenters, because it was little expected from the members of the established church after so favourable an indulgence as the Act of Toleration'; and fifthly, in previous similar instances of laws against the Dissenters, 'it is very remarkable that the design was to weaken the Church and drive them into one common interest with the Papists'. Substantially these arguments were repeated in the various episcopal speeches in favour of the repeals; and it was therefore surprising that Wake, particularly in view of his speech at the Sacheverell trial, should have opposed a return to the 1689 position.

Fundamentally, his argument appeared to rest on the facts that the operation of the Occasional Conformity Act had brought back many Dissenters to outward conformity to the Church, whereas its repeal would make a present of them to the conventicle; and that a national church has a right to protection against dissidents of all kinds, whether Papist or Protestant. The former ground ignored the circumstances that penal sanctions can produce only outward conformity, not inner conviction; and that the established church would draw little strength from such formal adherents. The latter position was indeed that of the Tories; but came strangely from one who had been reckoned hitherto a Whig in politics. Above all, Wake's speech made no attempt to meet the contention that the Occasional Conformity and Schism Acts were in themselves a breach of the ecclesiastical provisions of the Revolution Settlement, and that the Toleration Act was not intended to proscribe either the accepted custom and practice of occasional conformity or the creation of dissenting academies. Nor can there be any doubt that Wake had been to some measure affected by the court-rivalries, and had thereby been driven into closer, if perhaps involuntary, association with the Tory prelates. It was significant that of the fifteen episcopal votes against the repeals, nine (exclusive of Wake himself) were cast by bishops of Queen Anne's creation and only four by those of George I's nomination; whilst the supporters of the measure numbered six bishops of George I's creation, two of William III's nomination, and three of Anne's elevation during the brief period of Whig ascendancy in her reign. But these considerations alone would seem insufficient to explain the primate's change of mind. It may be conjectured that he had been shaken severely, on the one hand by the Trinitarian and Arian controversies and on the other by the Bangorian controversy; and had been driven in consequence to repressive measures as a means of defending both the credal orthodoxy and the political position of the established church. It is further probable that he feared lest his negotiations with the foreign Protestants, in which he was endeavouring to bring them to union with the Church of England, might be prejudiced if acts were passed which might be interpreted by foreign divines as bringing non-episcopal churches in England nearer to an equality with the establishment. For he was insistent that members of the foreign Reformed churches sojourning in England must join in communion with the Church of England, and not with any dissenting sect; and to this end he plied their leaders with various arguments to prove that the grounds on which Dissenters separated from that Church were insufficient to justify schism. From this standpoint he may well have thought that his position would be strengthened by the maintenance of the Occasional Conformity Act.

Whatever may be the truth of this matter, it was plain that the division in the episcopal bench had been deep and acute, and that Wake had found himself in the company of a solid phalanx of Tory bishops, with the majority of his friends and former associates on the other side. Attempts indeed were made to heal the breach once the repeal had been carried. White Kennett, although a friend of the primate and by his influence recently made bishop of Peterborough, had spoken and voted for the repeals; yet he made a valiant endeavour to restore the broken front.

Honest intentions were on both sides [he averred to the Master of University College]. They who opposed the bill, meant for the most part the honour and interest of the Church; and they who espoused it, as far as I know, meant nothing worse. They thought it would really strengthen the Protestant interest and quiet the minds of a great number of people; and that it would not at all affect the Act of Uniformity, nor the Test Act, nor the Union, nor any other security of the Church of England; but would only restore to the Dissenters the same indulgence they had given to them by law upon the foot of the Revolution, by taking off from them two subsequent penal laws which they verily believe, were brought upon them not merely as Dissenters, but rather as disaffected to the measures of the ministry at the latter end of the queen's reign; and when taken off will bring them nearer to the Church, or at least carry us further from the cry of persecution.[1]

It would be difficult to contest the charity or cogency of this plea; but from the two opposing protagonists in point of influence in the Church, Wake and Gibson, the response was not encouraging. The primate indeed had suffered the iron to enter into his soul; and the depth and bitterness of his chagrin were revealed in his scribbled comment upon the notes of his speech. 'Here I was both deserted and betrayed by my brethren, some of whom had encouraged me in my opposition. I pray God forgive them.'[2] Forgiveness certainly did not come easily to himself. On the other side, Gibson, in a memorandum written indeed at a later date when he had supplanted his metropolitan in the confidence of the Whig administration as ecclesiastical adviser, alleged Wake's fraternisation with the Tory prelates as the occasion of an irreparable breach.

Upon the death of the late archbishop, it quickly appeared that his successor did not intend to go on in the same path, but to strike out a new one of his own; and in order to that he fell into confidences with Bishop Smalridge, setting up for a better churchman than his predecessor had been. This had two effects: the first a coldness and distrust between him and the ministry; the second a no less coldness and distrust between his grace and those bishops and clergy who had acted under his predecessor upon a clear Whig bottom, and had not any concern with the Tory bishops beyond common civility. Upon this the ministry made choice of the Bishop of Norwich, a person much regarded and trusted by the Lords Sunderland and Townshend, to be their adviser in church matters.[3]

The most serious immediate outcome of the breach between primate and ministry lay in the former's loss of authority as ecclesiastical adviser. Gibson indeed had always considered it essential that Wake should be sole head in church matters, and had regarded with dislike the tendency, as he had earlier described it, for Trimnell of Norwich 'still to be archbishop under the protection of the lay administration'. The intimacy existing between

[1] Ballard MSS. VII, f. 144. 24 January 1718/19. Kennett to Charlett.
[2] Arch. W. Epist. 8. Canterbury III, f. 87. [3] N. Sykes, *Edmund Gibson*, p. 408.

Sunderland and the Bishop of Norwich, combined with the ambition of the former to control ecclesiastical appointments, had already been evident, and was shortly to be strengthened by the split amongst the bench. During the winter of 1716/17 in anticipation of the death of the nonagenarian Bishop Lloyd of Worcester, the Archbishop had intended the translation thither of Bishop Hough of Lichfield, and the promotion of his protégé Dr Edward Chandler to Lichfield. It was believed, however, that Dr Francis Hare, chaplain to the Duke of Marlborough during the Spanish Succession war, was ambitious of that preferment; and accordingly, when the news of the fatal illness of Lloyd reached him, Chandler by advice of the primate paid his court to the influential bishops and minister of state.

I went directly from Your Grace's house [he reported on 5 March 1716/17] to the Bishop of Sarum's; and hearing that he was gone to the Bishop of Norwich's, I followed him thither, and addressed them both together. The former was very frank and promised to give me a character and use his interest with Lord S[underlan]d tomorrow. The latter, after a civil reception, took me aside and gave this answer—'Upon the expectation of the Bishop of Worcester's death and the Bishop of Lichfield's removal, another was mentioned for Lichfield, who is without any exception. I was employed to speak to him of it, and in this situation I can't be against him and for you, unless some change of circumstances should make room for it. Were I at liberty, I should be glad to serve you (of whom I have a very good opinion) as far as I should be consulted. But pray take me aright, I shall avoid all occasion of opposing my lord of Canterbury in what he desires.'[1]

When the vacancy became actual by the death of Lloyd on 30 August, Chandler 'immediately left the news at Lord Sunderland's (he himself being abroad), who sent for me this morning, though I perceived he had not yet acquainted the king with the bishop's death....The obliging reception I found with him makes me hope there will be no change of measures.'[2] But this success on the Archbishop's part did not mean that his influence was secure. In the following January, the Archbishop of Dublin condoled with him on his lack of authority at court, observing that 'I am afraid Your Grace is only Bishop of Canterbury'.[3] Nevertheless, upon the vacancy of the see of Peterborough in October 1718, the support of Sunderland was successfully enlisted by Wake in behalf of White Kennett.[4] But the effects of the primate's attitude on the question of the repeals were soon evident. Reports reached his Irish friend, the Bishop of Meath, that 'his grace had not been at court since the bill passed'; and accordingly the Bishops of Kilmore and Killala had written strongly to the Bishops of Sarum and Norwich in relation

[1] Arch. W. Epist. 20. Miscellaneous IV, n.f. [2] *Ibid.* 'Sunday 12 o'clock.'
[3] Arch. W. Epist. 13. Ireland, f. 4. 11 January 1717/18.
[4] Arch. W. Epist. 8. Canterbury III, f. 32.

to a vacant Irish see.[1] But worse was to follow in England. The death of Bishop Smalridge on 27 September 1719 vacated both the see of Bristol and the deanery of Christ Church, Oxford, held *in commendam* with it. Wake was particularly anxious that the deanery should be given to Bishop Potter to be held *in commendam* with the see of Oxford, thereby enabling the bishop to resign the regius professorship of divinity; and he pressed this upon Sunderland, then away at Hanover with George I. Before his wishes could even be considered, however, the matter had been otherwise determined.

I have the honour of Your Grace's letter [replied Sunderland on 27 October (N.S.)], which I laid before the king, who has ordered me to acquaint Your Grace that, having received the post before the account of the Bishop of Bristol's death, he had already declared his intention of making Dr Boulter bishop and, considering the smallness of the bishopric, of making him also Dean of Christ Church, which post requires a man of integrity and courage. The Bishop of Oxford is certainly very honest and very well qualified; but the king thought it not so proper to have the same person bishop and dean of the same church.[2]

The interpretation placed upon this appointment in Oxford was expressed with pungency, if also with some exaggeration, by Dr Stratford of Christ Church in his report that

our new governor was recommended by the present ecclesiastical junto, whose recommendations only are regarded as to preferment, viz. Norwich, Sarum, Gloucester, and Lincoln. We are told he received express orders to wait on those four bishops and to thank them, and that he was expressly forbidden to take any notice of the Archbishop of Canterbury. Accordingly, he never waited on the Archbishop till the day before he came hither, when he could not avoid it, in order to know the date of his consecration. It is said that the Archbishop by way of rebuke, told him that he was surprised to see him, for that the public news had given him reason to think that he had gone to Oxford. His grace is said to be more affected with this slight, in relation to the preferment of his own college and the manner of putting it on him—such was the grossest that could be—than any other affront he has had.[3]

Other delicate measures were contemplated by the Whig administration, flushed with foreign success and the safe carrying of the repeals, which would place a further strain upon episcopal loyalty, particularly a bill to regulate the universities, always the nerve centre of clerical politics and Tory allegiance. Of the two academies, Oxford was the more vehement and ebullient in its Jacobite sentiments, though Cambridge was not exempt from suspicion. When Ormond's flight to France made necessary the choice of a new chancellor at Oxford, his brother Arran was elected. During the Jacobite rebellion, indeed, a garrison was sent there to preserve order; but

[1] Arch. W. Epist. 13. Ireland, f. 45. [2] Arch. W. Epist. 21, f. 168. 27 October 1719.
[3] Portland MSS. VII, 264. 11 November 1719.

matters finally came to a head after grave riots on the Prince of Wales' birthday in 1717. A more mollifying gesture had been made to Cambridge in 1715 by the royal gift to the university of the valuable library of the late Bishop John Moore of Ely, who had died in July 1714. Wake, however, professed to entertain only slight hopes of the good effects of even such a conciliatory act. Perhaps piqued by the implied slight upon Oxford, he grumbled to the Archbishop of Dublin that, though

His Majesty has certainly agreed to give 6000 guineas for the late Bishop of Ely's books and designs them for the University of Cambridge, I do not so much rejoice as might be expected, at it. They will neither make use of them, nor be obliged by the gift of them. You might have done more good with them; and books are greater rarities in Ireland than England.[1]

The general position in both universities, however, seemed too serious to be ignored by the administration; and in a letter to the Dean of Christ Church on 31 December 1715, Wake had averred that his correspondent could not 'be ignorant under how unhappy a character our university lies in this respect, and what a grief it must be to all who truly value its honour and welfare that there should be any occasions for it'.[2]

In the early spring of 1716, accordingly, Townshend, in consultation with Wake, Dean Prideaux of Norwich, Lord Chancellor Cowper and Lord Chief Justice Parker, considered the principles of a bill for regulating the universities, but nothing came of it at the moment. During the following spring, and after the Oxford riots, which were the occasion of a debate in the House of Lords, the matter was revived; and soundings of episcopal opinion were taken. Bishop Fleetwood of Ely wrote in some consternation to Wake about leakages from a meeting of bishops.

As secret as we resolved to have been in the affair of this morning, it was quickly told at court that fifteen bishops had thought it reasonable that the king should have the disposal of all offices, headships, and scholarships within the two universities for seven years; and a lord of the council was asked by another councillor: whether the king would deny his assistance to so many bishops? Your grace sees what a wrong turn is already put upon what was agreed on by us; and I doubt not but your grace will take care to set this matter right, since whatever odium may (as indeed much may) arise on this occasion, it must all be laid upon us, if we are represented as the makers and advisers to this proceeding originally.[3]

The bill was thereupon drawn up and sent to the primate by Parker. It was indeed a short and easy way of dealing with academic dissenters, singularly prophetic of some contemporary endeavours to control academic opinion. Its preamble began with the impeccable sentiment that

[1] King Correspondence, 7 July 1715.
[2] Arch. Epist. 15, n.f. 31 December 1715.
[3] *Ibid.* n.f. n.d.

in all well-ordered governments, it has been thought necessary for the preservation of the body politic that care should be taken of the education of youth not only in piety, virtue, and good learning, but also in principles agreeable to the constitution under which they live; [and proceeded to lament that] many in those nurseries dedicated to religion, learning, loyalty, and peace have been infected with principles of sedition.

More particularly, there could be 'no reasonable expectation of enjoying peace and tranquillity for any long time, if the youth of the nobility and gentry, and especially such as are designed for holy orders, are infected with false principles utterly inconsistent with our happy establishment in church and state'. The bill therefore proposed that the nomination and appointment of all the officers of the universities, heads of houses, fellows, students, chaplains, scholars, exhibitioners, and all members of every college and hall, should be vested in the Crown for a period of years, not specified in the extant draft of the measure, but according to Bishop Fleetwood's account, to last for seven years.[1]

It was surprising that so staunch a churchman as Wake and one so jealous of encroachment on ecclesiastical and academic rights, should have approved the principles of this radical bill. Nevertheless he defended it in a letter of 21 March 1716/17 to the Warden of All Souls (Dr Bernard Gardiner).

As I doubt, both the king and his ministers and the chiefest members of parliament do think there is great need to take some care of the nurseries of learning and religion, in which the minds of the whole youth of the realm are to be formed either to good or bad principles and dispositions, probably for their whole lives; so I am satisfied that there have been very serious thoughts and debates how this may be done in the best manner, for the true honour and interests of the universities themselves, as well as to the public good of the whole realm.... I am sorry there has been any occasion given to the government to think anything needful to be done for the better ordering of those illustrious corporations. I wish I could say I was myself of another mind.[2]

When the Warden replied that the university was 'not sensible how we have offended', the primate gave him chapter and verse.

My regard to the honour and welfare of our universities, as it has always led me to do them all the service I could, so will it still dispose me to serve them as far as is consistent with the other obligations which are incumbent upon me, to his majesty, the church and the realm. And even at this present time I have not been wanting in my endeavours to prevent that storm which has lately seemed to threaten them; and I shall be glad if I may be able yet to prevent it. But if the case be so as you represent it; if there be no disaffection in the universities to the present government; nothing either encouraged or done there to disturb the peace of it; or

[1] The text of the Bill is printed in Basil Williams, *Stanhope*, pp. 456–8, from the draft in Arch. W. Epist. 15, n.f.

[2] Arch. W. Epist. 15, n.f.

to send men away from thence with any ill impressions upon their minds towards it; I may truly say that you are very unfortunate in the reports which are everywhere spread abroad of your conduct; and the prejudice which I fear those reports have raised against you in many who are most heartily concerned for our public peace and security. It will, I believe, be no news to tell you that the business of the riot at Oxford upon the prince's birthday is to come before the House of Lords upon Wednesday next; and the letters and affidavits on both sides to be considered. What that enquiry and the debates thereupon may produce, I cannot foresee; but do heartily wish they may turn to the honour and justification of a place I have so true a value for.[1]

Actually the storm blew over for the present; for Cowper succeeded in persuading the principal ministers

that it was not fit to have that bill of repeal and that about the universities going at the same time. Upon this they took a sudden turn and became resolved to have this of the repeal first, and postpone that concerning the universities, which, your grace knows, how lately and how much the king, as they said, had set his heart upon.[2]

In December 1718 there were rumours that the universities' bill was again on the anvil; but once more it was deferred until the fate of the repeals was evident. In the spring of 1719 it gave place again to the Peerage Bill, which was introduced into the House of Lords on 14 March and, after considerable debate, withdrawn on 14 April. Despite this initial miscarriage the administration contemplated an ambitious programme of legislation for the autumn session of 1719, according to Sunderland: 'The King is more determined than ever to persist with vigour in the measures you and your friends wish; he is resolved to push the Peerage Bill, the University Bill, and the Repeal of the Septennial Bill; if this won't unite the Whigs, nothing will.'[3] The Peerage Bill enjoyed priority of place, and its rejection in the House of Commons carried the consequential disappearance of the University Bill. Oxford and Cambridge were therefore saved from a serious threat to their academic autonomy, which, though justifiable perhaps in the circumstances of the moment, might have been fraught with grave dangers on a longer view. The episode, however, was significant as evidence of the alarm created in episcopal and political circles by the disloyalty of the universities; and it stands in striking contrast with the measures later to be carried into effect by Bishop Gibson for winning over those seats of learning. Perhaps a contributory factor and a revealing cause of the political failure of Wake as leader of the Church-Whig alliance may be seen in the pregnant differences between the stillborn University Bill of 1717 and the Whitehall Preacherships and Regius Professorships of Modern History of 1724.

[1] Arch. W. Epist. 15, n.f.

[2] *Ibid.* Epist. 20, n.f. 14 March 1716/17.

[3] B. Williams, *Stanhope*, p. 410.

For the moment, however, the defeat of the Peerage Bill had a sobering effect on the administration, and led to the healing of the schism in the ranks of the Whigs. Indeed reunion all round became the order of the day. On 23 April 1720 Sunderland joyfully announced to Wake the reconciliation of the King and the Prince of Wales, 'the immediate consequence of which', he prophesied, 'would be the entire reunion of the Whig party in both houses, which would be attended with all other consequences honest men could desire'.[1] On that very day indeed 'Lord Townshend and Lord Cowper were at court, and they and Lord Sunderland caressed one another; and now the old interest being restored, friends look cheerfully upon one another, and public affairs are likely to go upon the old bottom with greater ease'.[2] The political *rapprochement* was consummated by the readmission to the ministry of Walpole as paymaster of the forces on 4 June and of Townshend as president of the council on the 11th. Among the differences due for composition were those between Wake and both lay and Church-Whigs, for which the reunion of the royal family gave opportunity by removing the stigma attaching to the primate for his attendance on the prince. It was doubly unfortunate therefore that his next venture into the field of ecclesiastical politics should be such as to bring him again into variance with the ministers of state and also with some of his episcopal brethren, and should thereby nullify the good effects and bright hopes of the recent reconciliation.

The problem of the suppression of profaneness and blasphemy which was vexing Wake at this time, was neither of recent origin nor of easy solution. Periodically attention had been drawn to the prevalent laxity of morals and opinions; but recently the rumour of the foundation of the Hell-Fire club and the association therewith of some prominent persons of quality, had revived concern for the protection of public morality. Moreover the Archbishop was much alarmed by the propagation of Arianising opinions. The age was one of theological heterodoxy, and the Arian movement of that century had this in common with its prototype of the fourth century, that its popular expressions were scandalising to devout and orthodox minds. Accordingly on 27 March 1721 Wake conferred with Lords Nottingham and Trevor concerning a bill on this issue, the draft of which was drawn by Nottingham and sent to Lambeth with the expressed hope that the primate would move for leave to introduce it into the House of Lords at the first opportunity. Considerable discussion ensued about the terms of the draft, after which Wake, 'communicating the substance of it to two of his brethren, and conferring with some of the other lords about it, had so little

[1] Arch. W. Epist. 21, f. 216.
[2] Bodleian MSS. Add. A. 269, f. 88. Gibson to Nicolson. 23 April 1720.

encouragement to proceed with it, that he thought it more advisable to defer the present motion for leave to bring in such a bill'.[1]

Notwithstanding, Nottingham initiated a discussion in the House of Lords on the subject on 20 April; and his speech was followed by the introduction of a bill to suppress atheism, profaneness, and blasphemy by Dr George Verney, dean of Windsor, in his temporal capacity as Lord Willoughby de Broke. His measure was substantially that considered by Wake, Nottingham, and Trevor. Its preamble referred to the recent publication of books denying the existence of God, the divinity of Christ, the doctrine of the Trinity, and the truth of the Christian revelation; and its several clauses proceeded to set forth measures for the correction of such enormities. The principal clause provided that any person speaking or writing against these doctrines as they were set forth in the Thirty-nine Articles or denying the divine inspiration of the holy scriptures, should be liable upon conviction to imprisonment for three months, unless he made a public recantation and profession of his orthodox belief according to a form of words provided. Subsidiary clauses provided that dissenting preachers should be deprived of the benefits of the Toleration Act if they denied any of the fundamental articles of the Christian religion; and that justices of the peace at their quarter sessions should have authority to summon before them any dissenting preacher in order to require him to subscribe the declaration of orthodox belief, upon penalty, in case of refusal, of deprivation of the protection of the Toleration Act. In the case of clerks in holy orders a like power was vested in the archbishops and bishops, and with the penalty of the delinquent being rendered incapable of holding any ecclesiastical benefice.[2]

The Archbishop admitted his dissatisfaction with the several drafts of the bill as exchanged between Nottingham and himself and as introduced into the House of Lords. 'The bill, as it was drawn, was very imperfect; nor did I like it as it was brought into the house. I was for amending many things in it, particularly that part which concerned the archbishop.' It seems probable also that he was somewhat taken aback by the introduction of the bill at a moment when he himself had decided to defer action. Notwithstanding when the second reading was taken on 2 May, he moved for its committal. His general sentiments may be sufficiently gathered from his notes for two intended speeches, the first 'upon moving for a bill' and the second 'after the second reading'. He had no doubt of the propriety of introducing such a measure into the legislature, the writ of summons to which explicitly mentioned ecclesiastical matters as subjects for deliberation.

[1] Arch. W. Epist. 9. Canterbury IV, ff. 39 and 46. 27 March and 22 April 1721.
[2] *Ibid.* ff. 43, 44, 47. *Parliamentary History*, vol. VII, pp. 893–5.

> Can it consist with the honour of such a body as this to refuse to see and consider of what is offered to restrain blasphemy and profaneness? A Christian legislature to be unwilling to stop the reviling and exposing the Christian religion? Were it only an establishment, yet it ought even as such to be supported; all nations have ever done so.... But 'tis not only a constitution we are here to maintain; 'tis a religion in which the glory of God and the salvation of souls is concerned. No man, no Christian can here be silent, especially no bishop.

Nor could it be fairly said that the bill involved persecution for religious opinions. 'The controversy here is not with the weakness, but wickedness of men. I am willing to allow as much to men's errors, innocent errors, as any; hate persecution; but am not to be frightened with the cry of persecution where there is no ground for it. Here is none, unless it be persecution to bring malefactors to judgment.' Similarly neither the measure nor his support of it implied any restriction of the Toleration Act.

> I would be far from offering or desiring anything that might affect the indulgence granted to the Dissenters, which I desire to preserve. But in the very foundation of this indulgence, care was taken that no Dissenters (no, not the Quakers) should be tolerated to the prejudice of these fundamental doctrines of the Trinity, divinity of the scriptures. And yet if men be so unhappy as to err even in these points, I desire not to enquire into any man's private opinions; but let them not disturb nor infect others with them which was never thought fit to be allowed in any state.... All I propose is to strengthen the laws already in force; not to look back but forward; not to restrain men's opinions, but their open attempts and actions; to support the religion established against the bold attempts that are made against it; to strengthen the Act of King William and preserve the peace of religion.

In the course of his speech, Wake traced briefly the introduction of Socinian opinions into England during the Interregnum, especially by John Bidle ('for which, though otherwise a valuable man, he suffered imprisonment'), and by the publication of the Racovian catechism; the spread of unorthodoxy after the Revolution, and the Trinitarian controversy within the Church of England as exemplified by William Whiston and Samuel Clarke; and he gave extracts from recently published books on the question. Finally he maintained that it was worth while to seek the desired end even though the present means should prove inadequate.

> How far this bill, or any other, can prevent these monstrous attempts, I know not. I am sure we ought to try what may be done towards it. 'Tis confessed, it cannot be denied, that the laws already in being have not restrained this impiety.... We need therefore some further provision. If this bill brings it, let us thankfully embrace it. If it does not, let us take the opportunity of it, however, to try if something may not arise upon our debates that will do so.[1]

[1] Arch. W. Epist. 9, Canterbury IV, ff. 49, 50.

The primate was supported by the bishops of London, Winchester (Trelawny having come especially to town 'to be at the bill'), and Lichfield, and by Nottingham, Trevor, and some other lay peers. On the other side however, were ranged Townshend, Sunderland, Wharton, Onslow, Cowper and the bishop of Peterborough. On a division the house decided by 60 votes to 31 to defer the bill 'to a long day'; only five prelates voting with the minority, namely Wake, and his brethren of London, Winchester, Lichfield, and Chester, whilst eight episcopal votes were cast with the majority, including Gibson of Lincoln. Once again the iron entered into the Archbishop's soul:

This was a new cause of offence [ran his comment, scribbled on the back of the notes of his speech] given to the ministers, though I had a meeting with them about this bill, and their consent to appear for it. And here I was again deserted by my brethren, as in the other bill for repealing the Act against Occasional Conformity.[1]

The administration sought indeed to make amends by the issue on 28 April of a royal proclamation for the suppression of blasphemous clubs and societies, followed by royal letters of direction to the archbishops and bishops on 7 May for the enforcement of the existing laws for the preservation of the orthodox faith in the doctrine of the Trinity.

Feelings, however, had been hurt on both sides; and Wake entered into correspondence with Sunderland in the hope of removing an unfortunate misapprehension concerning his speech in the house, as implying a reflection upon the administration.

I was exceedingly surprised [he wrote on 11 May] at the report my Lord Bishop of Lichfield made me this afternoon of your lordship's discourse to him concerning me. In answer whereunto I can only say that either your lordship must have very much mistaken somewhat that fell from me in discourse in behalf of the late bill to restrain blasphemy and profaneness, or I must have said somewhat utterly contrary to what I intended to speak, or can with my utmost endeavours recollect I did say. My lord, your lordship cannot but remember how often I have had the honour to hear you declare your dislike of the wicked, undue liberties that have been taken by some among us in opposing the great and fundamental doctrines of the Christian religion as professed in our Church by law established....Perhaps your lordship did not observe it; but I well remember that I both designed and did (as far as was fitting) intimate this much in my discourse to the house. It must surely have been very strange for me after this, to charge the spreading of these wicked doctrines upon the ministry of which your lordship is the chief....My lord, when I consider all these circumstances, and am sure that I had not the least thought of speaking one word that might reflect upon or justly offend your lordship, nor can possibly recollect that I did, I still flatter myself that however I had the misfortune not to be rightly understood by your lordship, yet I really did not let fall anything that was indecent towards your lordship or any others in the king's service. If I did, I am

[1] Arch. W. Epist. 9, Cantebury IV, f. 50.

not ashamed to say I am sorry for it. I did not intend it. But this is not the first instance in which I have been either mistaken or misrepresented. However, I have now done what became me in my own justification; and to satisfy your lordship that as I have had many obligations to you, which however you may treat me, I will always thankfully acknowledge, and were I able, would no less gladly repay; so I was far from thinking or designing to do or say anything that might bespeak me to be unmindful of them....I have my complaints which I might justly make in my turn. But as I am not moved by such trifles, so I will not trouble you with them. Your lordship may have me as you please. If you think fit, a friend such as I have professed myself and am still willing to be. But if I may not have that honour, I will, however, in a due sense of the favour I have received of you, whatever be the result of this transaction, always profess myself, my lord, your lordship's most obliged, humble servant.

The tone of injured innocence mingled with hints of ill-usage from the minister of state indicated the extent to which Wake's feelings had been wounded. In reply Sunderland expressed his preference for oral discussion to formal correspondence as a means of settling their differences, and offered to meet the Archbishop in the House of Lords 'for a friendly conversation'.[1] From another side, however, the breach between the primate and Gibson had been widened by the latter's circulation amongst his diocesan clergy of a letter justifying his vote against the bill.

These squabbles were the more serious when set against the background of the financial crisis resulting from the collapse of the South Sea Company, which threatened the stability of both the Hanoverian dynasty and its Whig administration. For the Jacobites naturally were not unwilling to profit from this opportunity to foment discord and discontent. Into the causes and results of the South Sea Bubble it is not germane to the present study to penetrate; beyond perhaps to echo the quaintly pertinent observation of Bishop White Kennett that 'enthusiasm in different shapes returns often on this poor nation; we have had religious enthusiasm, political enthusiasm, and this was mere secular enthusiasm'.[2] The wildest rumours gained credit, such as that the Archbishop had made great gains by speculation; and notwithstanding the return of the king from Hanover and the protracted enquiries and debates in both houses of parliament, the crown and its ministry weathered the storm only with much difficulty. Moreover the personnel of the chief actors in state and church was changing in a direction unfavourable to the influence of Wake. The deaths of Stanhope on 5 February 1720/1 and of Craggs on the 16th made way for the reconstruction of the administration under the leadership of Walpole as First Lord of the Treasury and Chancellor of the Exchequer, and Townshend as Secretary of State for the Northern

[1] *Ibid.* ff. 52, 53. 11 and 12 May 1721.

[2] Ballard MSS. VII, f. 83. White Kennett to Charlett. 20 October 1720.

Department. Similarly the deaths in the same year of Bishops Trelawny of Winchester and Crewe of Durham enabled the translation respectively of Trimnell from Norwich, a close friend of Townshend and always a potential rival to Wake, and of Talbot from Sarum, to two of the principal sees next to the primacies. The continuing favour enjoyed by Hoadly was signalised by his translation to Hereford; whilst perhaps the most ominous threat to the primate's authority was offered by the nomination of Gibson to be Dean of the Chapels Royal. Although White Kennett as a good Whig might express his satisfaction with these and other consequential appointments 'so far as they were within the political line of good affection to the government',[1] there were not lacking signs that among both statesmen and churchmen, one generation was passing and another coming. There needed only the death of Sunderland on 18 April 1722 to leave the Archbishop without a close friend in the king's administration.

From this standpoint it was a further misfortune that Wake should be at loggerheads with the ministry on the matter of relief to the Quakers in regard to the substitution of an affirmation by them in place of an oath in legal and judicial affairs. By the Toleration Act they had been accorded this privilege in one particular regard; and by the Affirmation Act of 1696 the right had been extended for a period of seven years to all other occasions when the law required an oath. In 1715 this Act was made perpetual; and henceforth the Quakers directed their efforts towards a modification of the actual terms of the affirmation required of them. The form prescribed by the Act of 1696 had been: 'I, A.B. do declare in the presence of almighty God, the witness of the truth of what I say'; which seemed to many Friends too closely akin to an oath, and for which they wished to substitute: 'I, A.B. do sincerely declare and affirm.' In 1721 they secured the promise of help from the administration for some modification; but it was insisted as a condition of this support that the form should be: 'I, A.B. do solemnly, sincerely, and truly affirm, testify and declare.' Accordingly a bill to this effect was introduced into the Commons, where it had an easy passage, and was sent up to the Lords on 9 January 1722. Wake was not present on that day, when the measure was given a second reading despite the opposition of Bishop Atterbury of Rochester; nor again on the 15th when its committal was carried by 65 to 14, despite the opposition of the Archbishop of York and the Bishop of Rochester, but with the support of White Kennett of Peterborough. The Archbishop of Canterbury, however, attended on the 17th, when his brother of York presented a petition of the London clergy against the bill which, however, the house declined to receive by 60 votes to 24; and when 'all the bishops present, except the two Archbishops, the Bishops of Oxford, Lichfield,

[1] Arch. W. Epist. 9, Canterbury IV, f. 124. White Kennett to Wake. 30 September 1721.

and Rochester', were against the petition. On the morrow the house went into committee; when, after the reading of the first clause, Wake moved 'that the Quakers' Affirmation might not be admitted in courts of judicature, but amongst themselves', an amendment which would of course have defeated the object of the bill; whilst the Archbishop of York moved for the insertion of a clause 'that the Quakers' Affirmation should not go in any suit at law for tithes'. The question was carried in the negative by 52 to 21; and after the defeat of a final amendment to require Friends desirous of enjoying the benefits of the bill first to subscribe to the orthodox profession of belief required by the Toleration Act, the measure secured its third reading. Wake and Potter of Oxford formally entered their dissent against its passing; whilst their lordships of York, Rochester, and Chester subscribed a protest with their reasons.[1]

It seems difficult at first sight to understand the degree of episcopal indignation evoked by this measure, which did not introduce any new principle, but merely modified the form of affirmation demanded of the Quakers. There can be no doubt, however, that they were the most unpopular of Protestant Dissenters in orthodox ecclesiastical circles; where indeed they were regarded as barely Christian since they possessed neither creed, nor ministry, nor sacraments. Furthermore, the Archbishop of York laid his finger on the sorest point of grievance in his amendment relating to suits for tithes, always a contentious matter between the clergy and Quakers. There was a widespread repugnance amongst many churchmen to the granting of particular favours to the Friends above other Protestants. Unfortunately for Wake, both Sunderland and Walpole were well disposed towards this bill; and he found himself once more unequally yoked with Tory high-church prelates in opposition to a measure sponsored by the administration. His chagrin was shown by the number of accounts which he sent to his Irish correspondents; one of whom, the Bishop of Kilmore, gently exhorted him not to be hyper-sensitive, but to accommodate himself more easily to the give-and-take of political affairs.

I am sorry anything should pass in parliament contrary to your liking. Most people here think the Quakers have too much favour shown to them.... Your Grace being in the highest station in the Church, makes you more affected by whatever happens to the disservice of it; but after you have done what you can to prevent anything of that kind, does not the monkish rule take place, *sinere mundum vadere sicut vult*? For my part, the more I see of the world, the more I see the necessity of that rule.[2]

A much greater *cause célèbre*, however, was to follow shortly in the proceedings against Bishop Atterbury for treasonable correspondence with the

[1] *Parliamentary History*, vol. VII, pp. 938–46; *Journals of the House of Lords* XXI.
[2] Arch. W. Epist. 13, f. 323.

exiled Stuart dynasty. The hopes of the Jacobites had been raised by the melancholy misfortunes of the Hanoverian house and its ministry, culminating in the economic crash of the South Sea Bubble. The birth of the Young Pretender on 31 December 1720 had further stimulated loyalty to the Stuart cause; and in the resultant correspondence with the court of 'James III', the Bishop of Rochester had become deeply involved. During the course of 1721 indeed the conduct of that enigmatic prelate presented a perplexing amalgam of apparent contradictions. On the one hand the frequent visits paid to him at the deanery house at Westminster by Sunderland, Trevor, Carteret, and even Walpole on one occasion, had aroused suspicions at least of a projected mixed ministry to enable the kingdom to ride the financial storm. On the other hand Atterbury had written a letter in April 1721 to the Old Pretender, expressing an unusually optimistic view of the prospects of his cause, which proved the beginning of a sustained correspondence. Plans for an invasion of Great Britain were mooted for January 1722; and with the growing volume of evidence accumulated by government agents and spies of communication between the Bishop and the Pretender, some kind of action could not be avoided. Walpole indeed essayed first the expedient of judicious offers of further preferment in return for a pledge of loyalty; but after the proferred terms were declined, the matter became public property when the conspirator was arrested on 24 August 1722 and imprisoned in the Tower.

This was a bold step for the Whig ministry to take; for it involved the danger of a second Sacheverell episode with a far more able and creditable defendant in the person of Atterbury. But Walpole, who had protested against the unwisdom of the prosecution of 1710, was resolved to avoid a repetition of its blunders. During the interval between the arrest of the Bishop and the parliamentary session, two circular letters were published to the clergy, assuring them of the respect and zeal of the government for the Church but containing emphatic warnings of the dangers and consequences of a Jacobite restoration. Beyond prayers offered for the bishop in some London churches, however, and the publication of pictures portraying his fortitude under the distressing conditions of his duress, no ecclesiastical repercussions ensued. Upon the meeting of parliament, a secret committee was appointed to examine the evidence of the alleged conspiracy; and after its report, the administration wisely resolved to substitute for the hazards of a public judicial trial the safer procedure of a Bill of Pains and Penalties. The complicity of Atterbury in Jacobite intrigue has been convincingly established by evidence published since the event; but contemporaries were justly apprehensive of the dangers even of the more summary method of procedure. Atterbury could not be denied the right to make his own defence in the House of Lords, and the temper of this house was less reliable than that of the Commons. His speech was indeed worthy of his talents, lasting only five minutes short of two hours and effectively criticising the evidence against him. But in the debate only Bishop Gastrell of his episcopal brethren spoke in his behalf and voted against the bill; whilst Bishops Willis, Gibson, and Wynne spoke against him and were joined in the division (when the bill was carried by 83 votes to 43 on its third reading) by their brethren of Carlisle and Gloucester. In the forum of public discussion outside parliament Hoadly under the pseudonym of *Britannicus* wrote thirteen articles in the *London Journal*, in which he tore to pieces the bishop's defence.[1] It was indeed a singular irony of fortune which made the author of *English Advice to the Freeholders of England* the one spiritual peer to be unlorded by the Whigs.

The silence of Wake throughout these debates in the House of Lords was significant and remarked. He was present on 16 March 1723 when the house appointed a committee of nine to examine the question; on 24 April when the report of the committee was received; and again on 6 and 7 May when the bill against Atterbury was read a second time and the accused summoned to make his defence. But he was absent throughout the crucial debates which followed on 9, 10, 11, 13, and 15 May, and from the division on the third reading. On 13 January Atterbury had written from the Tower to the Archbishop, protesting against the refusal to allow him to attend public worship in the Tower chapel; to which Wake had replied promising to support his protest with the administration: 'your lordship may be assured I will not be wanting in my sincere endeavours to procure this liberty you desire, and which, unless by the folly of other people, can, I think, give no offence to the government'. Accordingly Wake waited upon Townshend by appointment, and discussed the matter with him and Carteret.

> I did what I could for the Bishop of Rochester, but was told this affair had before been settled by His Majesty. He was not allowed to go to the chapel, but was allowed to have prayers in his lodgings as often as he pleased, and a congregation to join with him there on Sundays by the lieutenant's order.[2]

Apart from this fruitless and private intervention, the Archbishop played no part in the Atterbury affair. To the Duke of Newcastle indeed it seemed that 'the Archbishop did exceedingly well, and was very zealously with us'.[3] But this opinion was probably an expression of the profound relief felt by the administration that so delicate a matter had been safely negotiated without the anticipated clerical tempest, rather than definite testimony to any positive part played by Wake. Far different was his own account confided to the Archbishop of Dublin on 16 April.

[1] H. C. Beeching, *Francis Atterbury*, ch. IX–X.
[2] Arch. W. Epist. 22, f. 187 (1–3).
[3] B.M. Add. MSS. 32686, f. 236.

We have three bills sent us up from the Commons against three of the persons chiefly concerned in the late dangerous conspiracy. One relates to the Bishop of Rochester. I do not think I shall be so much as present when these bills are read, or trouble myself at all about them. I am a discarded minister; and have the satisfaction to see other bishops employed to do my business for me. This gives me that quiet which my age and infirmities require; and which I could not otherwise pretend to: and is more than an equivalent for the imaginary privilege and blessing of interest at court. I shall leave them to do with my lord of Rochester as they please; I do not desire to give my advice where it is neither asked, nor would be well received or followed.[1]

The truth lay with the Archbishop. He was in fact 'a discarded minister'. Among the personnel of the Lords' committee appointed to enquire into the case against Atterbury on 16 March was Gibson. On 10 April Gibson was nominated to the see of London, vacant by the death of Bishop Robinson, and in his new dignity spoke and voted against the Bishop of Rochester. When Wake wrote to Townsend to offer suggestions for filling the see of Lincoln, he received a discouraging reply on 14 April.

I have received the favour of Your Grace's letter concerning the vacant bishoprics, and your sentiments upon that subject would have been of the greatest weight with me if there had been room to move His Majesty upon it; but Your Grace will perceive that His Majesty had already fixed his resolution in this respect when I acquaint you that he has declared his intention that the Bishop of Bangor shall be translated to the see of Lincoln and that Dr Baker (who was to have attended His Majesty to Hanover if he had gone last year) shall be promoted to that of Bangor. So that it is not in my power to make use of the intimation I have received from Your Grace.[2]

No fewer than nine sees fell vacant during 1723, and all were filled in accordance with Gibson's recommendations. The hand which wrote thus to the primate was that of Townshend but the voice was that of Walpole, whose keen perception soon fixed upon the Bishop of London as the man for his measures. On 22 August Walpole reported to Newcastle the result of an interview with Gibson. 'His lordship seemed in a very good humour; and so long as we continue such good boys and obey our orders so punctually, I should hope our spiritual governors will not be much dissatisfied. But this is certainly the man among them whom I think we ought to manage and cultivate.'[3] The duke echoed his master's sentiments dutifully: 'Our man must be the Bishop of London. He has more sense, and I really think more party zeal than any of them.'[4] At a second interview Walpole clinched the matter.

At first it was all *nolo episcopari*; before we parted, I perceived upon second thoughts he began to relish it; and the next morning *ex mero motu* he came to me,

[1] King Correspondence. 16 April 1723.
[2] Arch. W. Epist. 22, f. 207.
[3] B.M. Add. MSS. 32686, f. 312. 22 August 1723.
[4] *Ibid.* f. 316. 25 August.

talked comically, is a moral man, wants to be ravished, and desired me expressly to write to my Lord Townshend to prevent the King's coming to any resolution about the disposal of the Clerk of the Closet's and Lord Almoner's places. We grow well acquainted. He must be pope, and would as willingly be *our* pope as anybody's.[1]

Thus Wake became a discarded minister, displaced by his junior and former confidant, Gibson. When the primacy of Ireland was vacant during the same year and Bishop Chandler of Lichfield was a possible candidate, the Duke of Newcastle disposed of his chances by observing to Townshend that 'he is by no means proper; he has parts, but a very odd understanding, and will be governed by nobody except the Archbishop; and sure that is not for the King's service'.[2] Accordingly, in the following January, Wake thus described his position as wholly sequestered from affairs. 'The public business is wholly taken out of my hands, and put into others, much more able than I am to discharge it; so that I have little more to do than to keep up a little living acquaintance with my friends, which I shall do while I am able; and when I am not, that must drop too.'[3]

The circumstance of 'two archbishops not in measures with the ministry and the bishop of London in measures, is a new case', as Gibson observed to his new political friends. Notwithstanding, having decided to accept the responsibility, he was not slow to prove that a new and much more vigorous hand was at the helm. In the *London Gazette* of 17–21 March 1723 there appeared the announcement of the institution of Whitehall preacherships; the holders of which were to be twenty-four fellows of colleges in Oxford and Cambridge, 'the best scholars and best preachers that could be found among the king's friends there', who were to take duty in the royal chapel for one month each, one Oxford and one Cambridge divine being appointed for each calendar month; and the first of whom were to begin their office on Easter Day, 5 April. For this service each preacher was to receive the salary of £30 per annum. By this means Gibson hoped both to offer tangible inducements and rewards for political loyalty to the university dons, and to raise the standard of preaching in the royal chapel. In the following year a further and greater benefaction was to follow by the foundation at Oxford and Cambridge of Regius Professorships of Modern History and Languages. A professor was to be appointed in each university with a salary of £400 per annum, out of which he was to maintain two assistants at a salary of £25 per annum, and these teachers were to instruct in modern languages and history twenty scholars to be nominated by the Crown.[4] By this benefaction, as by the preacherships, Gibson had in view a dual purpose; first to convince the

[1] *Ibid.* f. 326, 6 September.

[2] *Ibid.* f. 383. 1 November.

[3] Bodleian Browne Willis MSS. 36, f. 248. Wake to Browne Willis. 16 January 1723/4.

[4] N. Sykes, *Edmund Gibson*, chap. IV.

universities of the good will and bounty of the Hanoverian dynasty and its administration; and secondly, to provide for the needs of the state by ensuring a succession of persons qualified for the diplomatic service. These two foundations were evidence not only of the vigour but also of the constructive character of the new ecclesiastical minister. The contrast is marked between the negative and restrictive proposals of the abortive University Bill of the Stanhope-Sunderland régime with the support of Wake, and the positive and flattering schemes of Townshend and Gibson. Nor, it must be confessed, is there any hint throughout Wake's extensive correspondence that his thoughts ever ran in such audacious channels.

Correspondent with these measures were the principles of Gibson's proposals for the judicious dispensation of crown patronage. The Bishop of London's diagnosis of the failure of the primate to unite and lead the Church-Whig alliance was that he had shown dangerous deviations towards Toryism, and had thereby set up 'for a better churchman than his predecessor had been'. Accordingly when he himself engaged to advise the ministry it was

> upon a clear Church-Whig bottom, the same that we had been upon in the late archbishop's time; as the true way to support the Protestant succession and to maintain a good understanding between the Church and the Dissenters; we defending them in the full enjoyment of their toleration, and they thankful to us and content with the state of things as settled between the Church and them at the Revolution.[1]

It was evident therefore that the watershed in Wake's relations with the ministers of state and with those bishops who considered themselves as upholding the tradition of 'old Totius' lay in their divergent attitude towards the repeal of the Occasional Conformity and Schism Acts. Gibson regarded the passing of these acts during the Tory administration of the last four years of Queen Anne's reign as a breach of the Toleration Act and an encroachment upon the rights thereby granted to the Dissenters; and their repeal as a simple act of justice. Such, moreover, had been the accepted view of the Revolution Settlement in its ecclesiastical aspect amongst the Whigs, as set forth for example with every circumstance of authority and publicity in the charges against Sacherevell on this point. The rigid and unyielding attitude of Wake, therefore, when the question of the repeals was discussed, was an equal surprise and shock to Gibson and his friends. It was upon this issue that there came the parting of friends. This interpretation is confirmed from the side of the Archbishop also. The earlier episode of his successful opposition to the Vestry Bill had caused no more than a ripple on the surface of his relations with the ministry.

[1] N. Sykes, *op. cit.* pp. 408–9.

I am very glad [he wrote to Charlett on 27 June 1716] if what I honestly endeavoured and God blessed with good success as to the Vestry Bill, be satisfactory to any good members of our Church. All I desire in return is that they will believe me to be truly fixed to support the interest of it; and I am sure, would more of our clergy shew that a hearty zeal for the church is by no means inconsistent with the most firm and steady adherence to the king, the Protestant succession, and what is called the Whig interest in the state, such an accommodation might thereby be made as would settle us all in peace and quiet, and abolish those unhappy distinctions which still keep up factions and divisions among us.[1]

A month before this letter, however, Bishop Smalridge had confided to the same correspondent that 'you may depend upon it that several of my brethren who are called and are pleased to be called Whigs, are very uneasy at being thought so far friends of the Dissenters as to be willing they should make any encroachment upon the Church'.[2] When the matter of the repeals was raised, Wake's tone became more pessimistic and his resolve fixed to allow no concession.

How far my life may be of use to the Church of England, I cannot tell [he averred to Browne Willis on 22 February 1717], but I see no prospect of my doing any good for it. If I can prevent any evil, or if my life may stop the gap to any who would be more complying to some measures than myself, God be blessed that I am still in the way of doing this negative service to my dear mother.[3]

It is difficult to account for his attitude on the repeals as revealed by his speech in the House of Lords; and as difficult to avoid placing the blame for the episcopal split on this issue fairly on his shoulders. What followed in the lesser, yet not unimportant, episodes of the Blasphemy Bill and the Quakers' Affirmation Act, helped further to widen the breach. But the unity of the Church-Whig alliance had made irrevocable shipwreck on the repeals; and for this the captain himself must bear the chief responsibility.

Yet if this were the occasion of the calamity, its ultimate causes must be sought more deeply in the character of Wake himself. Gibson had predicted before the death of Tenison that if Wake were to succeed, he would not 'bear any ecclesiastical agent but himself'. There was an element of the imperious in his composition, which could not easily accept contradiction, and which made him prone to identify honest difference of opinion with treachery and disloyalty to his official position as primate. No less than Gibson, he must be pope or nobody. Moreover he was hyper-sensitive, and inclined too readily, as his comments on the conduct of those bishops voting against him on the repeals and the Blasphemy Bill showed, to interpret divergence of policy as a personal affront. Fundamentally indeed he was unfitted by temperament for the rough-and-tumble of political life, for he lacked the suppleness

[1] Ballard MSS. III, f. 123. [2] *Ibid.* VII, f. 22. 17 May 1716. [3] Willis MSS. 36, f. 2d.

requisite to accept the compromises and give-and-take of relationship with the ministers of state. He confided to the Archbishop of Dublin at the beginning of the parliamentary session of 1719 that

it is a time of trouble to me beyond any other. I neither can well bear the attendance it requires; nor be easy at the many difficulties and controversies which almost unavoidably arise in the prosecution of the great affairs of it. I am old, and more infirm than most men are at my age. I love quiet above all things. And my duty is never so uneasy to me as when it obliges me to differ from, and perhaps have thereupon some kind of scuffle with my friends, whose affection I should be glad, on any other terms, to preserve without interruption.[1]

Here perhaps may be found the secret of his *malaise*: in the contradiction between the desire for the quiet life of a student and the ambition which had led him to accept high ecclesiastical office, and in the burden of continuing ill-health which unfitted him further for public reponsibilities. So long ago as 1690 he had averred to Charlett his desire to withdraw from London to his 'little house and garden' in Christ Church; professing that he would then 'endeavour not to know what passes abroad in the world, and much less to concern himself in it', and avowing himself utterly weary of the 'circle of follies', the 'parties, factions, and interests in the world'. He affirmed indeed that he had 'such motives to determine him to a contemplative life that he would be very unwilling to be diverted from it'.[2] Consonant with this sentiment was his repeated refusal of the offers of a bishopric before being induced to accept the see of Lincoln in 1705, at the third time of asking. On the other hand, he took no steps to realise his desire, but remained at St James' Westminster, to the neglect of Christ Church; and was by some at any rate suspected to have fingers itching to be at work in all the current controversies of the capital. Nor did he maintain his *nolo episcopari* in relation to Lincoln; nor renew it when offered the primacy. If it be true, as seems most probable, that he was more fitted by character for the vocation of a scholar, the decision to exchange this milieu for that of an ecclesiastical statesman was of his own taking, and upon his shoulders must rest the responsibility for, and the consequences of, this mistake.

It is more difficult to ascertain whether his temperamental unfitness for high ecclesiastical office and its attendant political duties was the result or the cause of his constant ill-health. It is clear, however, that he was a chronic valetudinarian. Throughout his correspondence there runs a swelling threnody on this theme. As early as his thirty-fourth year, in 1690, he assured Charlett that his chief reason for choosing Christ Church 'for his retirement' was the circumstance that 'my health grows daily worse; and I am sensible I cannot live always in this world, nor very long in the way I

[1] King Correspondence. 19 November 1719. [2] Ballard MSS. III, f. 57.

am now in. I have a great many reflections to make and a large account to review in order to my removing to a better state; and I have deferred it too long already.'[1] Thirty years later the Bishop of Kilmore reminded him with humour and veracity that 'valetudinarians are often at death's door; but the strongest men as often enter there, and leave their sickly brethren behind them for many years'.[2] Certainly he suffered from recurrent attacks of the stone, which disabled him from regular attendance in the House of Lords, and drove him into the country to seek relief from the waters of Bath and Bristol. Nor may the effects of illness on his temper be discounted. Shortly after his extrusion from the confidence of the administration, he wrote to Browne Willis: 'My own strength evidently decays, and makes me still more unfit for much business every day. I am now got to the end of my 66th year; and that in a constitution never very strong, is more than 76 in another man. I thank God my business in this world is pretty well at an end.'[3] But if the decline of his influence during the twelve remaining years of his life was undoubtedly exaggerated and emphasised by his progressive physical deterioration, culminating in his falling 'into the animal life' as Gibson indelicately expressed it, there can be no doubt that his loss of power was first political and then physical. From the advent of the firm of Walpole and Townshend in the state, Wake fell rapidly out of favour with the administration. The septennium of his primacy had indeed been disappointing in the extreme; and had resulted in division among the Church-Whig prelates and the collapse of the Church-Whig alliance. A new and more robust hand was needed at the helm, and this was supplied by Gibson, in whom Newcastle rightly discerned 'more party zeal' than in the rest of his brethren. Henceforth Wake's ecclesiastical and political influence suffered a rapid and progressive eclipse until his successful rival could indulge the grim, yet not unjustified, jest that 'an archbishop had nothing to do, but to make two dinners a week and to sign dispensations'.

[1] *Ibid.*
[2] Arch. W. Epist. 13, f. 190. 3 August 1720.
[3] Bodleian: Willis MSS. 36, f. 248. 16 January 1723/4.

CHAPTER VIII

FALSE DOCTRINE, HERESY AND SCHISM

He is Truth's champion to defend her against all adversaries, atheists, heretics, schismaticks and erroneous persons whatsoever. His sufficiency appears in opposing, answering, moderating and writing.

THOMAS FULLER, *The Holy State*, Book II, ch. IV. The Controversial Divine

'There is another event', wrote Wake to his Genevan correspondent, Professor Turrettini in February 1718 in relation to English affairs at that time,

that does great harm to all those who sincerely pursue peace without the prejudice of any necessary truth. It has fallen out that a set of Latitudinarian writers (who call themselves free-thinkers) have made it their business for some time past to write down all confessions of faith, all subscriptions of any articles of religion whatsoever, as contrary to that subjection we owe to Christ as our king. These men are some of them Deists; some Socinians; a better sort Arians; all of them enemies to the Catholic Faith, in more or less of the most fundamental articles of it. They are not content with an universal toleration, but would be admitted to offices and dignities in the established church without subscribing the Articles or so much as approving the liturgy of it. These men in their writings abuse all the great names they can in their own defence. Wherever they meet a man speaking a word against impositions in matters of religion, against church tyranny, for a due liberty, or the like, never trouble themselves to state the point or report the whole sense of an author; but make quotations from him and tell the world that he is of their side. Thus yourself, Mr Werensfels, Mr Ostervald, [and] others have been served by them; and I cannot but think it would be of great service to Christian liberty, as well as a justice to yourselves if one or other of you could find leisure to state the case and shew how far you think the church of every country has a right and authority to draw up a confession of its own faith, and to oblige all those who will take any public employs or minister in it, to subscribe such a confession.[1]

Even stronger words of reprobation were used in a letter to the Antistes of Zürich, J. L. Neuschler, of 13 September 1718; in which the Archbishop soundly berated those of his brethren who were most prominent in the several controversies of the age.

Amongst us indeed have arisen men who speak perverse things; even, as I must admit, pastors, bishops, who destroy with their own hands the Church in which they minister, to whose doctrine and discipline they have often subscribed, to whom the defence of the Church is committed, whose office it is to advance against

[1] Geneva MSS. Inventaire 1569, f. 48.

its enemies and according to their deserts to refute, repress and punish them; these men strive to destroy the authority of the Church, for which they ought not only to contend, but if circumstances require, to die.

In particular Wake denounced, as he had done to Turrettini, the demands for release from all subscription to articles and creeds, which would lead to the overthrow of even such fundamental doctrines of Christianity as that of the divinity of Christ.

Whom would it not distress that such grievous wolves are not only not kept far from the sheepfold, but indeed are received within the precincts of the Church, and are admitted to honours, offices and its government? But such is the state of affairs; if we regarded only the things of this world, we should entirely forget those of the next world; and so by the toleration and promotion of such men, some persons hope to gain popular favour; who have only one thing at heart, to secure themselves in their dignities and authority, caring little what may befall the Church, the Faith, religion, or even Jesus Christ and his truth.

The letter concluded with an apologia for such vehement language.

I should think myself guilty of treason to the faith, if when occasion offers, I should not pronounce anathema against these heretics. Would that I were able to pronounce it publicly, with the authority of the Church and in the assembly of the faithful, according to the apostle's commands. And I still hope that the day may come, so much to be desired, when to the glory of God and the establishing of religion, I may see such a sentence brought against these heretics.[1]

It may seem strange that an English primate should thus lay bare the distress of his own Church before the eyes of foreigners. But Wake's outburst to Neuschler was no expression of momentary irritation. In July of the previous year he had written with equal mordancy to Peter Zeller, then Antistes of Zürich, to the same effect, deploring the prevalence of such internal discords.

[1] Arch. W. Epist. 25. Epistolae Latinae, f. 87. 'Inter nos ipsos exsurrexerunt viri loquentes perversa; et quid dico viri imo pastores, episcopi, suis ipsis manibus ecclesiam diruerunt, in qua ministrant, ad cujus doctrinam et disciplinam pluries subscripsere; quibus defensio ecclesiae commissa; quorum munus est inceptare contra hostes ejus, eosque pro meritis redarguere, compescere, punire. Etiam hi illius ecclesiae auctoritatem labefactare nituntur, pro qua non tantum certari, verum si res ita postulant, etiam mori debuerint....Quem non doleret hujusmodi λύκους βαρεῖς non tantum ab ovili non longe arceri, verum intra ipsa ecclesiae pomeria, recipi; ad honores, ad officia, ad gubernacula ejus admitti? At vero sic se res habet; totum ad ea quae sunt hujus saeculi unice respiciamus, prorsus obliviscamur eorum quae ad alterum spectant; et quia horum hominum tolerantia et promotione, quidam se populi favorem conciliaturos sibi sperant; quibus id unice cordi ut in suis sese dignitatibus et potentia tueantur, parum curant quid de ecclesia, de fide, de religione, de ipso denique Jesu Christo ejusque veritate eveniat....Reum me putarem proditae fidei, si non his haereticis quavis occasione oblata anathema dixerim. Utinam id et publice, et cum ecclesiae authoritate, et in ipso fidelium coetu juxta apostoli mandata, pronuntiare possem! Atque equidem non despero venturam illam diem pro Dei gloria et religionis stabilimento, tantopere expetendam, cum hujusmodi sententiam in haereticos istos ferri videam.'

Some contend about the authority of the king, others about episcopal government. These men defame all ecclesiastical polity as tyrannical and almost papistical; and (to omit mention of old controversies) a new species of libertines has arisen in recent years, to whom all confessions of faith, all subscription to any articles whatsoever, are displeasing; who wish to reduce the whole creed of a Christian man to this sole proposition, that they believe the Scriptures of the New Testament to be divinely inspired; and therefrom each individual should collect for himself what he ought to believe; nor should any one be required to profess or admit any other confession of his belief. Under this pretext some of these men are Arians, others Socinians, more Macedonians; and these not only amongst the people but (as is to be feared) amongst the churches and their pastors. Hence treatises have been publicly set forth against the mystery of the Holy Trinity, against the divine nature and status of the Saviour, against the deity of the Holy Spirit; and against the (at all events natural) immortality of the soul itself.[1]

If this revelation of the confusions which followed from the vaunted comprehensiveness of the Church of England was hardly calculated to persuade the Swiss Reformed churches to sit loosely to their own requirement of ministerial subscription to the *Formula Consensus* (as Wake indeed was striving so to induce them), the effects of the publication by Neuschler of the Archbishop's express desire for anathemas against such of his clerical brethren as fell under his condemnation, were equally devastating in England. For such was the boomerang result of this action. In commending the discretion of his Genevan correspondent, Professor Turrettini, Wake remarked ruefully that

I wish I could say as much with relation to one of my letters to the Antistes of Zürich; in which I gave him a faithful, but melancholy, account of the present state of religion among us. In this not only many of our clergy, but several of their friends are concerned; and of these some are persons of good estate and dignity among us. The Antistes not only permitted Monsr Hoffmeister to quote the very words of my letter, and that as mine, in his speech at your congress, but to print it; and several copies of this being come hither, I need not tell you what a flame it has kindled among the persons complained of and their friends, nor how much trouble it has caused me. I cannot but think this was a very imprudent step, not to say worse of it; and the method of hurrying that leaf of the speech hither, by one of the

[1] Arch. W. Epist. 25, Epistolae Latinae, f. 38. Wake to Zeller. 5 July 1717. 'His de jure regio, illis de gubernatione episcopali decertantibus. His etiam omnem politiam ecclesiasticam velut tyrannicam, et tantum non Papisticam, proscindentibus; et ut veteres controversias omittam, nova libertinorum progenies his ultimis annis prognata est, quibus omnes fidei confessiones, omnes articulorum quorumque subscriptiones displicent; quique totum hominis Christiani symbolum in unica illa propositione includi volunt, credere se Scripturas Novi Foederis esse divinitus inspiratas; ac deinde unumquemque pro se ex iis colligere debere, quid sibi sit credendum; nec a quoquam postulandum ut aliam quamcumque fidei suae confessionem vel edat vel admittat. Sub hoc praetextu quidam horum hominum Ariani, alii Sociniani, plures Macedoniani; iique non tantum e populo, sed (ut par est timere) ex ipsis ecclesiis pastoribusque. Hinc tractatus publice emissi contra S. Trinitatis mysterium, contra divinam Salvatoris naturam et ἀξίαν; contra Spiritus S. deitatem; contra ipsius animae (naturalem saltem) immortalitatem.

warm friends of the *Consensus*, makes me apt to suspect there was somewhat more than mere imprudence in it. But, however, I have learnt thus much by it, that I shall hereafter write to those gentlemen with such a reserve as if every letter were to be sent back in print to me.[1]

Whatever the degree of innocent inadvertence on Wake's part in disclosing so completely his sentiments concerning the prevalence of false doctrine and heresy, or of calculated indiscretion on the part of those who gave them public currency, there can be no doubt of the grave anxiety with which he contemplated the theological controversies of his age, nor of his desire for the forcible suppression of their protagonists. The growth of Socinianism in England during the latter half of the seventeenth century, indeed, had been marked, thanks to the general religious latitude of the times and to the particular activities of John Bidle, supported by the rich London mercer Thomas Firmin. The consequent ferment of opinion infected the established church, and Stephen Nye, rector of Little Hormead, Hertfordshire began a furious Trinitarian controversy by the publication in 1687 of *A Brief History of the Unitarians, called also Socinians*. Dr William Sherlock, master of the Temple, embarked on *A Vindication of the doctrine of the Holy and Ever-blessed Trinity* in 1690, in which his zeal to combat Unitarian views led him to the verge of Tritheism; as Dr Robert South retorted in his *Tritheism charged upon Dr Sherlock's new Notion of the Trinity* in 1695, only to find himself accused in turn by Nye of falling into the opposite error of Sabellianism. It was difficult indeed to sail between Scylla and Charybdis in such an abstruse mystery of faith; and there is good ground for the conclusion that 'the doctrine of the Trinity undoubtedly suffered more from Sherlock's defence than from Nye's attack'.[2] So fast and furious became the interchange of tracts that in 1695 William III issued his 'Directions to the archbishops and bishops for the preserving of unity in the church and the purity of the Christian faith concerning the Holy Trinity'; in which he laid down four rules:

I: that no preacher whatsoever in his sermon or lecture, do presume to deliver any other doctrine concerning the blessed Trinity, than what is contained in the holy scriptures and is agreeable to the three creeds and the Thirty-nine Articles of Religion; II: that in the explication of the doctrine they carefully avoid all new

[1] Geneva MSS. Inventaire 1569, f. 63. 23 April 1719. (The reference to 'your congress' related to the celebration at Zürich, and elsewhere in Switzerland, of the bicentenary of the Reformation.) The speech of M. Hoffmeister was published under the title of *Oratio Historica de beneficiis in ecclesiam Tigurinam collectis*; cf. *A Short Vindication of the Lord Archbishop from the imputation of being the author of a letter lately printed at Zurich concerning the state of religion in England* (1719), and *A Letter to the Lord Archbishop proving that His Grace cannot be the author of the letter to an eminent Presbyterian clergyman in Switzerland.*

[2] R. N. Stromberg, *Religious Liberalism in Eighteenth-century England*, p. 36; cf. E. M. Wilbur, *A History of Unitarianism in Transylvania, England and America.*

terms and confine themselves to such ways of expression as have been commonly used in the Church; III: that care be taken in this matter especially to observe the fifty-third Canon of this Church, which forbids public opposition between preachers, and that above all things they abstain from bitter invectives and scurrilous language against all persons whatever; IV: that the foregoing directions be also observed by those who write anything concerning the said doctrine.

In addition the prelates were exhorted to 'make use of their authority according to law' for the suppression of pamphlets and books written by laymen on this theme.[1]

Into this first phase of theological disputation Wake, despite the whisper of unfriendly critics that 'his fingers did itch to be at work', had not suffered himself to be drawn beyond the line advocated by Swift as to what was 'most reasonable and safe to do', namely 'upon solemn days to deliver the doctrine as the Church holds it and confirm it by scripture'. In so acting he had been aware of the perils of attempting to define these mysteries.[2] But when the royal directions did not succeed in stilling the controversy, but only in diverting it from Socinianism to Arianism, he was compelled first as Bishop of Lincoln and later as Archbishop to play a more prominent part in its suppression. The chief result of the Trinitarian debate indeed had been to show that orthodox divines must needs appeal to ecclesiastical tradition as interpretative of scripture in order to confute the Socinians. Accordingly William Whiston, the successor of Newton in the Lucasian chair of mathematics at Cambridge, forsaking the safer symbols of his profession, betook himself to the study of the pre-Nicene fathers and reached the conclusion that their doctrine of the Trinity was not Athanasian but 'Eusebian' or Arian. He asserted his standpoint in a series of works and sought further to popularise it by founding a Society for the Restoration of Primitive Christianity. Unfortunately he fell foul both of the authorities of his university and of the convocation; and in 1710 was deprived of his professorship by the former, and then formally censured by the latter, giving rise in this connection to a *cause célèbre* concerning the power of convocation to try cases of heresy. But although Whiston may have been a dangerous critic of orthodoxy, his friend Dr Samuel Clarke was a formidable heresiarch, who next took up the enquiry as to the exact and precise doctrine of the Trinity deducible from the scriptures alone.

Undoubtedly Clarke was one of the ablest divines of his age, whose talents

[1] E. Cardwell, *Documentary Annals*, vol. II, pp. 389–91.

[2] *V. ante*, ch. I, pp. 57–8. Wake also was persuaded that Sherlock's repudiation of Tritheism was sincere, and that 'he had no heretical design nor is knowingly involved in any Tritheistical opinion'; and he rejoiced that there was no opportunity on this occasion for convocation, thanks to its prorogation, to engage in heresy-hunting. (Wake, *The Authority of Christian Princes over their Ecclesiastical Synods Asserted*, pp. 327–30.)

as a metaphysician had been employed hitherto in defence of orthodoxy against the Deists, notably in his Boyle Lectures of 1704–5, wherein he had stated the traditional arguments for 'The Being and Attributes of God' with singular force and clarity. Now, however, he was led to examine with the utmost care and diligence the scriptural evidence for and formulation of the doctrine of the Trinity. Herein lay at once the importance and the disquieting nature of *The Scripture-Doctrine of the Trinity*, which he published in 1712; for his endeavour had avowedly been to state and defend that vital dogma solely in relation to the Bible; and, having examined no fewer than 1251 relevant texts in the New Testament, he had reached conclusions satisfactory neither to Athanasians nor to Arians. For on the one hand he held that the Father only is the supreme God, to whom alone supreme worship is to be paid; and on the other hand that although Christ existed from eternity, He is nevertheless a subordinate being, who may be worshipped only as mediator; and that the Holy Spirit is also a subordinate being, for the worship of whom there is no clear scriptural warrant. 'They are both therefore worthy of censure; both they who on the one hand presume to affirm that the Son was made out of nothing, and they who, on the other hand, affirm that He is the self-existent substance.' In the heated temper of the times it was little surprising that the publication of his book should provoke violent controversy; nor that Convocation should take notice of the matter, and its Lower House determine to follow its censure of Whiston by the like condemnation of Clarke.

In dividing the hosts of heresy, whose name was legion, into their several categories, Wake seemed disposed to think less harshly of Arians, whom he designated 'a better sort', than of Socianians. Moreover he had a tender regard for Clarke himself; whom he described as being, save for this one transgression, 'a good man and one who had done very good service to the Church by his excellent books written in behalf of the truth of the Christian religion and in strenuous defence against all the endeavours of Deists and libertines'.[1] Accordingly he sought to shelter him from the attacks of the lower clergy in convocation, who on 2 June 1714 solemnly arraigned Clarke's book before the Upper House as containing

> assertions contrary to the Catholic faith as received and declared by this reformed Church of England concerning three persons of one substance, power and eternity in the unity of the Godhead, and tending moreover to perplex the minds of men in the solemn acts of worship as directed by our established liturgy, to the great grief and scandal of pious and sober-minded Christians.

[1] Arch. W. Epist. 25, f. 153. Wake to Pictet. December 1719. 'Dominus Clericus, quem nisi hac una in re, et vir bonus est et ecclesiae longe utilem navavit operam, libris pro veritate Religionis Christianae optime scriptis, ac contra omnes Deistarum atque libertinorum conatus strenue defensis.

The indictment further alleged that Clarke had 'wrested with such subtilty' sundry passages in the Book of Common Prayer and the Thirty-nine Articles, in themselves 'directly opposed' to his heretical assertions, as to introduce a method of subscription which led to a liberty notwithstanding 'to retain and propagate the very errors which are most inconsistent with such their declaration and subscription'. In reply to a request from the bishops for specification of particular passages in Clarke's writings deserving of censure, the Lower House on 23 June presented the desired catena of citations, with a rider affirming, however,

that the offence given...seems to us to arise not only from such particular parts and passages thereof...but from the general drift and design of the whole; the said books in our opinion tending to nothing less than to substitute the author's private conceits and arbitrary interpretations of scripture in the room of those catholic doctrines, which the church professes and maintains, as warranted both by holy scripture and antiquity.

Premonished by his episcopal friends to bow to the storm, Clarke on 2 July offered to the house of bishops a declaration, which Whiston ascribed in part at least to 'the sinister motives of human caution and fear', in the following terms:

1. My opinion is, that the Son of God was eternally begotten by the eternal incomprehensible power and will of the Father, and that the Holy Spirit was likewise eternally derived from the Father by or through the Son, according to the eternal incomprehensible power and will of the Father.

2. Before my book entitled *The Scripture Doctrine* was published, I did indeed preach two or three sermons upon this subject; but since the book was published, I have never preached upon this subject; and (because I think it not fair to propose particular opinions where there is not liberty of answering) I am willing to promise (as indeed I intended) not to preach any more upon this subject.

3. I do not intend to write any more concerning the doctrine of the Trinity; but if I shall fail herein and write anything hereafter upon that subject contrary to the doctrine of the Church of England, I do hereby willingly submit myself to any such censure, as my superiors shall think fit to pass upon me.

4. And whereas it hath been confidently reported that the Athanasian creed and the third and fourth petitions of the Litany have been omitted in my church by my direction: I do hereby declare, that the third and fourth petitions of the Litany have never been omitted at all, as far as I know; and that the Athanasian creed was never omitted at eleven o'clock prayers, but at early prayers only, for brevity sake, at the discretion of the curate, and not by my appointment.

5. As to my private conversation, I am not conscious to myself that I have given any just occasion for those reports which have been spread concerning me, with relation to this controversy.

I am sorry that what I sincerely intended for the honour and glory of God, and so to explain this great mystery as to avoid the heresies in both extremes, should have given any offence to this synod, and particularly to my lords the bishops. I hope my behaviour for the time to come with relation hereunto will be such, as to prevent any further complaint against me.[1]

Unfortunately Clarke upon second thoughts was dissatisfied with this statement, which indeed seemed equivalent to unconditional surrender; and accordingly on 3 July he sent to Wake an explanatory memorandum, to be laid before the Upper House. In this statement he affirmed

that whereas I declared in that paper my opinion to be 'That the Son was eternally begotten by the eternal, and incomprehensible power and will of the Father, and that the Holy Spirit, etc.', I did not mean thereby to retract anything I had written, but to declare that the opinion set forth at large in the book entitled *The Scripture Doctrine of the Trinity* and in the *Defence* of it, is, that the Son was eternally begotten by the eternal incomprehensible power and will, etc. Which words [the eternal incomprehensible power and will of the Father] I desire may be so understood as to signify, that God the Father alone is, and is to be honoured as being, ἀναίτιος and παναίτιος, the original of all, himself without original.

And whereas I declared I did not 'intend to write any more concerning the doctrine of the Trinity; but if I should fail herein, and write anything hereafter, etc.', I desire it may be so understood, as not to preclude myself in point of conscience from a liberty of making any inoffensive corrections in my former books, if they shall come to another edition; or from vindicating myself from any misrepresentations or aspersions which may possibly hereafter be cast upon me on the occasion of this controversy; but only to signify that I have no present intention of writing any new book; and that if hereafter I shall at any time write anything which your lordships shall judge worthy of censure, I shall readily submit to such censure.

On receiving this document Wake took counsel at once with Bishops Trelawny of Winchester, Smalridge of Bristol, and Fleetwood of St Asaph, and implored Clarke not to press his further interpretation.

According to my promise, I have this afternoon [4 July] communicated your paper with your reasons for it to my Lords of Winchester, St Asaph, and Bristol; who are all your very good friends and have appeared very hearty on your behalf. I cannot express the trouble they are under, both upon your account and their own. Upon yours who, they think, will hereby expose yourself to the censures and reproaches of your enemies and that without any need; for they are extremely clear that you have already expressed yourself so fully on the two heads you propose to explain, as not to need taking anything more upon you. Upon their own, that having done so much to bring this matter to a peaceable issue, and being come almost to the end of it with the general approbation of all good men, and particularly of the bishops on both sides, they must now break all in pieces, and begin anew; and then, where these matters will end or what may be the result of them, nobody can tell.

[1] E. Cardwell, *Synodalia*, vol. II, pp. 785–93; and *A Full Account of the Late Proceedings in Convocation relating to Dr Clarke's Writings about the Trinity* (London, 1714).

He enclosed also a letter from their lordships of Bristol and St Asaph, in which they acknowledged the receipt of the statement which Clarke had put into Wake's hands on the previous evening, and commented that

we are all of us clear in our opinions that you will be at liberty to act in the very same manner though this paper be not offered to the bishops, as if it were tendered to and received by them; but that it will rather cause reflections on you than prevent them, and occasion new disturbances which, we are sure, you would willingly avoid. We promise ourselves that having gone so far as you have done for the peace of the church, you will not insist upon anything which may endanger it.

To this missive Wake added his own personal persuasion.

I do confess these considerations have such weight with me that, being to send you the enclosed, I could not forbear writing thus much to you; and I do take the liberty to beseech you so far to weigh them, as if possible to comply with all our desires. I cannot ask anyone to act against his conscience or to do that which he thinks will prove a lasting uneasiness to him. But when you see how clear your friends are that you have not made any retraction in the first article; nor are under any promise by the second more than what you will still lie under after this paper is delivered to the bishops; perhaps you may be willing to withdraw it, and not run yourself into a certain censure, to avoid what we take to be merely an imaginary danger of reproach. When I know your resolution upon this report, I will after all act as you desire, though against my own judgment; but I would willingly hope we may both agree in letting all things rest as they are; which I am very confident would be no less for your honour and peace than to the satisfaction of your friends, and particularly of him who truly is, etc.[1]

It was only to be expected that so powerful an appeal would be heeded; nor was Clarke the first, or last, heresiarch to offer explanations or to withdraw interpretations under the persuasive pressure of episcopal counsel. On 5 July therefore the Upper House of Convocation resolved that

we, having received a paper subscribed by Dr Clarke, containing a declaration of his opinion concerning the eternity of the Son and the Holy Spirit, together with an account of his conduct for the time past and intentions for the time to come (which paper we have ordered to be entered in the Acts of this house and to be communicated to the Lower House) do think fit to proceed no further upon the extract laid before us by the Lower House.

The inferior clergy, indeed, were not so easily to be satisfied or pacified; and on 7 July in turn they

resolved that it is the opinion of this House that the paper subscribed by Dr Clarke and communicated by the bishops to the Lower House on the 5th inst., doth not contain in it any recantation of the heretical assertions and other offensive passages complained of by this House in their representation, and afterwards produced in their extract out of the books published by that author; nor doth give such satis-

[1] Arch. W. Epist. 18. Miscellaneous II. n.f. 4 July 1714.

faction for the great scandal occasioned by the said books, as ought to put a stop to any further examination and censure thereof.

In face of the bishops' resolution, however, the Lower House was powerless to carry the matter further.

Thus Clarke emerged unscathed from the fire (as Wake himself pleasingly expressed it—'quasi ex incendio tutus evasit'), and remained true to his promise not to write or preach further on the Trinity. That he had been fortunate to escape censure may be admitted, and it may be also allowed that he had been rash in seeking to define so great a mystery; but in his defence there may be pleaded the comparable difficulties encountered in his pre-episcopal days by a modern divine of impeccable, not to say implacable, orthodoxy.[1] *Quis idoneus?* But for Clarke this indiscretion effectively barred his enjoyment of that preferment to which his Boyle lectures had seemed securely to point the way. Archbishop Potter testified

that there was once a formed design to make Dr Clarke a bishop; and upon this Bishop Trimnell came over to Archbishop Wake in order to get his acquiescence in it. But the Archbishop expressed his utter dislike of the thing, and declared he would not consecrate Dr Clarke, whatever the consequences to himself. He would incur a *Praemunire* and the loss of everything rather than act thus far in it. And upon this resolution of the Archbishop, the design was dropped.[2]

On a later occasion Gibson likewise refused to act in the commission to consecrate, if Queen Caroline's desire for Clarke's nomination to the bench were effected.[3] Whether therefore elevation to the episcopate would have wrought in Clarke, as in some other divines of ancient and modern times, a sufficient degree of orthodoxy to satisfy authority must remain an unanswered riddle. It is evident that though Wake was anxious to save him from censure, he regarded his heterodoxy as a bar to further promotion.

Having rebuffed the Lower House in respect of its desire to censure Clarke, the bishops had recourse by way of compensation to a further royal direction on 11 December 1714, addressed to the archbishops and bishops, 'for the preserving of unity in the church, the purity of the Christian faith concerning the Holy Trinity, and also for preserving the peace and quiet of the state'. This document brought together the controversies concerning the doctrine of the Trinity and the 'unusual liberties...taken by several of the clergy in intermeddling with the affairs of state and government and the constitution of the realm'; and in regard to the theological issues it repeated the first three articles of the previous direction of William III of 1695 and

[1] Cf. K. E. Kirk, 'The Evolution of the Doctrine of the Trinity', in *Essays on the Incarnation and the Trinity*, ed. A. E. J. Rawlinson, p. 199.

[2] *The Christian Remembrancer*, vol. III, June 1821, p. 337a.

[3] N. Sykes, *Edmund Gibson*, pp. 134–5.

the injunction to the bishops to prevent the publication of books and pamphlets on this subject. In respect of civil government, the clergy were forbidden 'in their sermons or lectures...to intermeddle in any affairs of state or government or the constitution of the realm, save only on such special feasts and fasts, as are or shall be appointed by public authority', and except for sermons in defence of the royal supremacy.[1] But it was easier to silence Clarke than to stop the continuing controversy, which indeed showed no signs of exhausting itself, the more particularly since debate on the specific doctrine of the Trinity was expanded to embrace a general discussion of the ethics of subscription and the proper latitude which might be claimed and exercised in subscribing to the Articles of Religion and the Prayer Book. Bishop Potter of Oxford indeed held that because Clarke's

> book against the Christian Trinity is introduced with a prevaricating method of eluding subscription, it seems to me wholly in vain to endeavour to answer them by any other way than by confuting their false doctrines; for whatever opinion such men may have of the Church's authority to require subscriptions, they will never be easy whilst they look upon those doctrines to be false, to which their subscription is required. If Dr Clarke had not first disbelieved the doctrine of the Trinity or some others received in the Church, it seems probable to me that we should never have heard anything of his peculiar way of subscribing. I confess it seems to me no small disgrace to us that after the doctrine of the Trinity (to say nothing of others) hath been so publicly attacked for so many years together, though some replies have been made which perhaps neither Dr Clarke, Mr Whiston nor any other can fully answer, yet no just treatise hath been published on that subject.[2]

The learned bishop was writing, however, before the publication of Dr Daniel Waterland's successive and successful defences of orthodoxy in his *Vindication of Christ's Divinity* in 1719, followed by further works on the same theme in 1723–4; and in his *Case of Arian Subscription considered* in 1721, and a *Supplement* in 1722. It was therefore upon such defences that Wake relied as evidence to his foreign correspondents of the soundness of the Church of England in the fundamentals of faith, despite the aberrations of individual divines. Thus he referred Professor Pictet to the works of Waterland as convincing proof of the staunchness of Anglican theologians in defending the orthodox doctrine; and to Professor Pfaff of Tübingen he likewise urged them as sufficient testimony against the presumption that the Church of England and its leading divines had erred altogether or grievously in any article of the faith.[3] Nor was the Archbishop himself backward in fulfilling the royal directions to prevent the publication of heterodox books. Indeed

[1] E. Cardwell, *Documentary Annals*, vol. II, pp. 415–17.

[2] Arch. W. Epist. 7. Canterbury II, n.f. Potter to Wake. 18 September 1717.

[3] Arch. W. Epist. 25, f. 153. December 1719; *ibid.* Epist. 26, f. 133. August 1723. ('At Ecclesiam Anglicanam, ejusque genuinos pastores in aliquo fidei articulo aut graviter aut omnino errare.')

he related with evident satisfaction to Turrettini the success of his efforts to suppress an English edition of the works of Servetus.

I believe Mr Ott has informed you of the progress that was made by a Dutch bookseller in reprinting all the tracts of Servetus here. The edition was almost come to an end, when being informed of it, I got the Secretary's warrant to seize the whole impression, and the printer is now under a legal prosecution for his attempt. This would have effectively given occasion to your rigid professors to have published their invectives both against you and us; though so many public orders have been sent abroad by the civil and ecclesiastical authorities to suppress both the Arian and Socinian heresies and to support the faith of Christ's divinity, that one would think it impossible for any to lay such imputations to our charge.[1]

The importance which he attached to this preventive action was further illustrated by his account to Pfaff of how,

when the news was reported secretly to me, I acted thereupon with such good fortune with some of the chief ministers of the king that the whole impression, together with the original exemplar as it is called, were seized by an apparitor; and the artificer of this evil obliged to make a judicial defence as guilty of blasphemy against Christ. Thus it is that we favour either Arians, or Socinians, or Pelagians![2]

In his own diocese also Wake devoted the major part of his visitation charge in 1720 to a denunciation of English Arianisers. Certainly therefore, so far as his own endeavours were concerned, Wake could not be accused of lack of vigilance in suppressing heterodoxy, even if some doubt may be entertained of the appropriateness of some of his measures.

Accordingly it was a particular misfortune that at the very outset of his primacy he was faced by one of the most vehement and intractable of internal controversies, the Bangorian dispute, and that its author should have been a bishop and one of the earliest episcopal nominations of the new dynasty. Samuel Clarke indeed had been only a presbyter, albeit a learned theologian; but Benjamin Hoadly was a bishop and a notorious political controversialist, who in a sermon before the king on 31 March 1717 discoursed on *The Nature of the Kingdom or Church of Christ*, from the text 'My kingdom is not of this world'. He began by the trite observation that in course of time 'the signification of a word...is very insensibly varied...till it often comes to stand for a complication of notions, as distant from the original intention of it, nay as contradictory to it, as darkness is to light'; and concentrated his exemplification on the particular phrase of 'the Kingdom of Christ', which 'is the

[1] Geneva MSS. Inventaire 1569, f. 109. 1 October 1723.

[2] Arch. W. Epist. 26, f. 134. 'Re ad me secreto delata, adeo feliciter cum primariis quibusdam regiis ministris egi, ut tota impressio, cum exemplari quod vocant originali, ab apparitore occuparetur; ipseque mali artifex, tanquam blasphemiae in Christum reus, ad respondendum in judicio obligaretur; adeo nos scilicet Arianis, adeo Socinianis, atque Pelagianis favemus!'

same with the Church of Christ'. By appealing to the New Testament, he deduced two important propositions:

1. As the Church of Christ is the Kingdom of Christ, He himself is king; and in this it is implied, that he is himself the sole lawgiver to his subjects, and himself the sole judge of their behaviour in the affairs of conscience and eternal salvation. And in this sense therefore, his kingdom is not of this world; that he hath in those points, left behind him no visible, human authority; no vicegerents who can be said properly to supply his place; no interpreters, upon whom his subjects are absolutely to depend; no judges over the consciences or religion of his people. For if this were so, that any such absolute vicegerent authority, either for the making of new laws, or interpreting old ones, or judging his subjects in religious matters, were lodged in any men upon earth; the consequence would be, that what still retains the name of the Church of Christ, would not be the Kingdom of Christ, but the kingdom of those men, vested with such authority. For, whosoever hath such an authority of making laws, is so far a king; and whoever can add new laws to those of Christ, equally obligatory to those of Christ, is as truly a king as Christ himself is. Nay, whoever hath an absolute authority to interpret any written, or spoken laws, it is he, who is truly the law-giver to all intents and purposes; and not the person who first wrote, or spoke them....

But it is otherwise in the Kingdom of Christ. He himself never interposeth, since his first promulgation of his law, either to convey infallibility to such as pretend to handle it over again; or to assert the true interpretation of it, amidst the various and contradictory opinions of men about it. If he did certainly thus interpose, he himself would still be the legislator. But, as he doth not, if such an absolute authority be once lodged with men, under the notion of interpreters, they then become the legislators, and not Christ; and they rule in their own kingdom, and not in his.

It is the same thing, as to rewards and punishments to carry forward the great end of his kingdom. If any men upon earth have a right to add to the sanctions of his laws; that is, to increase the number, or alter the nature, of the rewards and punishments of his subjects, in matters of conscience or salvation; they are so far kings in his stead, and reign in their own kingdom, and not in his. So it is, whenever they erect tribunals and exercise a judgment over the consciences of men; and assume to themselves the determination of such points, as cannot be determined but by One who knows the hearts; or when they make any of their own declarations or decisions to concern and affect the state of Christ's subjects, with regard to the favour of God; this is so far, the taking Christ's kingdom out of his hands, and placing it in their own.

If therefore the Church of Christ be the Kingdom of Christ; it is essential to it, that Christ himself be the sole lawgiver and sole judge of his subjects, in all points relating to the favour or displeasure of almighty God; and that all his subjects, in what station soever they may be, are equally subjects to him; and that no one of them, any more than another, hath authority, either to make new laws for Christ's subjects, or to impose a sense upon the old ones, which is the same thing, or to judge, censure, or punish the servants of another master, in matters relating purely to conscience or salvation....

This enquiry will bring us back to the first, which is the only true account of the

Church of Christ, or the Kingdom of Christ, in the mouth of a Christian; that it is the number of men, whether small or great, whether dispersed or united, who truly and sincerely are subjects to Jesus Christ alone, as their lawgiver and judge, in matters relating to the favour of God, and their eternal salvation.[1]

The second fundamental point of the sermon related to the nature of the laws, rewards and punishments of Christ's kingdom; all of which, since that kingdom itself was not of this world, must relate 'to the favour of God in another state than this', that is, must be other-worldly. They

have nothing of this world in view, no tendency either to the exaltation of some in worldly pomp and dignity;...not the rewards of this world; not the offices or glories of this state; not the pains of prisons, banishments, fines or any lesser and more moderate penalties, nay, not the much lesser negative discouragements that belong to human society.

From these premises three conclusions were drawn; first

that the grossest mistakes in judgment about the nature of Christ's Kingdom or Church have arisen from hence, that men have argued from other visible societies and other visible kingdoms of this world to what ought to be visible and sensible in his kingdom;

secondly, that Christians should

trust no mortal with the absolute direction of their consciences, the pardon of their sins, or the determining of their interest in God's favour; [and should not] set up to themselves the idol of an unintelligible authority, both in belief and worship and practice, in words under Jesus Christ, but in deed and in truth over him;

and thirdly,

that it evidently destroys the rule and authority of Jesus Christ as king, to set up any other authority in his kingdom, to which his subjects are indispensably and absolutely obliged to submit their consciences or their conduct in what is properly called religion; [whether in the form of compulsion] to profess what they do not, what they cannot, believe to be true [or] to forbear the profession and publication of what they do believe.[2]

The sermon when published gave rise to furious controversy, into the labyrinthine mazes of which it is not necessary to penetrate. It was evident that by a judicious sprinkling of the epithets 'absolute' and 'indispensable', Hoadly had left open a way of retreat from the logic of his argument; and this irrespective of the circumstance, which in itself occasioned much dispute, as to whether he had uttered these words in the discourse as spoken, or inserted them before publication in order to evade the attacks of his critics. But the main tenor and purpose of the sermon were clear; and were succinctly stated

[1] B. Hoadly, *The Nature of the Kingdom or Church of Christ* (London, 1717), pp. 11–17.
[2] *Ibid.* pp. 18, 24–8.

by his most effective critic, William Law, who averred that the Bishop's objective plainly was 'to dissolve the church as a society'.

Wake indeed ridiculed the attempts of Hoadly when challenged by Dr Andrew Snape, master of Eton, to advance a minimising interpretation of his words.

> I doubt not but that Your Grace has seen the Bishop of Bangor's answer to Dr Snape [he wrote on 11 June 1717 to Archbishop King of Dublin]; and are very well satisfied that by his long preamble of clearing words and notions, he only intended at last to come to this mighty discovery: That no body has an absolute, authoritative, infallible right or power to make or declare articles of faith, which every Christian shall be bound to receive and submit to, right or wrong, without the liberty of private examination or private judgment. Which I dare say no one person in his congregation needed to be told by him. But 'tis a pretty way to clap in a few, seasonable terms for self-defence into a discourse; and then do the work proposed, as well as if no such restrictive words had been used at all.[1]

Here lay the gravamen of Hoadly's offence. His sermon had established the inability of any ecclesiastical authority to require subscription to any confession of orthodoxy, to set up judicial courts for the trial and punishment of heresy, or even to erect any hierarchy in which any one of Christ's subjects exercised authority over the others. Similarly his repudiation of all temporal rewards and honours attaching to religion appeared strangely inconsistent with the theory and practice of an established church, supported by a Test Act; whilst the entire tenor of the whole discourse was impossible to reconcile with the office and work of a bishop in such a church. 'In the meantime', observed Wake on 10 December 1719 to King, 'will posterity believe that a bishop of the Church of England should write against his own authority; and yet continue not only to exercise it, but to seek by these very means to become more considerable in the very church whose foundations he is so zealous to root up?'[2] Whether the sermon had been directed against proposals in convocation by Gibson for regulating proceedings in excommunications and against its procedure in the cases of Whiston and Clarke, or whether it represented a *ballon d'essai* of the new Whig ministry in regard to a projected repeal of the Test and Corporation Acts, its maxims were equally dangerous to upholders of the principles and prerogatives of the Church of England. Most ominous of all its possibilities perhaps was the reinforcement given to theories, already widespread and prevalent in connection with the Trinitarian and Arian controversies, of the unlawfulness of requiring subscription to any articles of religion or confessions of faith, save perhaps a general acknowledgement of the divine inspiration of the scriptures. 'The sum of all their aims',

[1] Correspondence of William King (library of Trinity College, Dublin). 11 June 1717.
[2] *Ibid.* 10 December 1719.

wrote Wake to King on 23 May 1717 of the several enemies to orthodoxy and the authority of the church,

is a general latitude and toleration of all opinions and religions in which the interest of the state is not immediately concerned; without any creeds, confessions, or subscriptions, and I think, without any communion but such as depends upon present fancy, and is to be broken whenever that fancy alters for any other, or for none at all; for so far I think their new hypothesis reaches. I confess this libertinism seems to me the most dangerous of anything to our established church. The clergy have so many of them run into it.[1]

The most alarming symptoms of the controversy evoked by the Bangorian sermon were its fusion of all other disputes around the question of church-authority and the divisions amongst bishops and clergy on this vital issue.

It is indeed [Wake further lamented to King some years later, on 24 March 1720, when the contentions showed no signs of ending] a most melancholy prospect we are under on all hands. Our morals have long been too much corrupted. Deism, if not atheism, or at best a great indifferency in matters of faith, has been a growing evil among us. And now, at last, our bishops and clergy come avowedly into the controversy, and tell us plainly that heresy is but an ecclesiastical scare-crow; that 'tis a matter of indifference what a man believes, so he does not dissemble but profess sincerely his belief, and takes care not to suffer his errors, if he has any, to lead him into anything that is sinful in practice.

But how, my lord, shall we put a stop to this evil? Subscriptions signify nothing. Injunctions from the king, could we obtain them, experience shows would be as little regarded. Our House of Lords has done justice upon one blasphemous book. The judges have declared that our law is very express both in the description and punishment of blasphemy; yet in despite of all this, men go on every day to oppose our Lord's divinity; and no prosecution is made of this crime, though confessed to be within the laws in force.[2]

But if the Archbishop was convinced that his lot was cast in an evil and adulterous generation, his efforts were not lacking to stem the tide of infidelity and unorthodoxy. In December 1718 Bishop Gibson after discussion with Wake made a draft of a Letter to be issued by the King to all the bishops, which he submitted to the primate for correction. The letter began with censures upon certain non-juror tracts (for example Dr Brett's pamphlets on

[1] *Ibid.* 23 May 1717.

[2] *Ibid.* 24 March 1719/20. Upon complaint made of a pamphlet, *A Sober Reply to Mr Higgs's Merry Arguments from the Light of Nature for the Tritheistick Doctrine of the Trinity, with a Postscript relating to the learned Dr Waterland*, the House of Lords appointed a committee to enquire after the author, printer and publisher, on 12 February 1719/20. On 15 February the House endorsed the committee's report 'that the whole book is a mixture of the most scandalous blasphemy, profaneness and obscenity, and does in a most daring, impious manner ridicule the doctrine of the Trinity and all revealed religion'; and ordered the arrest and prosecution of the author, Joseph Hall, gentleman and serjeant at arms to the king, printer, William Wilkin of Little Britain, and publisher, Thomas Warner of Paternoster Row. *Journals of the House of Lords*, XXI, 229b–232b, 242a (6 George I).

extreme unction, prayers for the dead, priestly absolution, lay baptism, and the necessity of tradition) 'maintaining and publishing several doctrines and superstitions of the Church of Rome', for which prosecution was threatened. It turned next upon writers who in opposing these tenets, advanced 'such principles and reasonings as do seem in their consequences to deny all kind of power within a Christian church and to subvert all order and discipline in the same'; and upon others who had treated the doctrine, worship and discipline of the Church of England 'in a reproachful and unworthy manner, contrary to that decency and regard which is owing to all establishments whether in church or state'. All these extremes were reprobated, and the king's intention to support and defend the established church and especially its clergy was reaffirmed. A further clause reinforced the earlier declaration concerning the Trinity; and a final paragraph, added by Wake, also announced the royal purpose to suppress the activities of papists.[1]

Before sending this draft to Wake on 2 December, Gibson had shown it to Bishop Trimnell of Norwich, who approved it as 'a foundation on which to prepare somewhat for a larger meeting of the bishops'; and a week later, after the primate had revised it, Gibson reported the opinion of his lordship of Norwich and himself that 'if it be conceived in stronger terms, Your Grace will find difficulty at the general meeting'.[2] On 27 December Sunderland intimated to the primate that the King 'approved of the draft in every part and was desirous that no time should be lost in the sending of it in form'; and further informed Trimnell that if a royal message to this effect would help towards securing the approval of the bishops, he would procure such a letter.[3] At this stage however episcopal opposition began to frustrate the design. For when the Bishop of Norwich showed the draft to his brother bishops Talbot of Salisbury and Willis of Gloucester, the former was filled with misgivings, saying that

> he was in judgment against having any such letter at all, and if there was to be one, he thought it should not fall upon the friends of the government who had deserved well of it, though he did not think they had been discreet. He concluded by saying he would obey the orders he should receive though he did not like them.

The Bishop of Gloucester indeed 'made less objection' and left Trimnell 'freely to pursue his commission'. But Sunderland, whom Trimnell was using as a mediator to persuade Talbot to acquiescence, found both him and Bishop Hough of Worcester 'much in the same mind' of opposition and criticism. Indeed Trimnell himself at first had been doubtful of the wisdom of the proposed step.

[1] Arch. W. Epist. 8. Canterbury III, f. 65.
[2] *Ibid.* ff. 63–4.
[3] *Ibid.* f. 68. 27 December 1718; f. 69. 28 December.

> I must freely own to Your Grace that when my Lord Sunderland first mentioned the matter to me, I thought of it as the bishops I beforementioned, do. But when I found that Your Grace and my lord thought it would be of service, and the king had been spoke to about it, I was desirous to have it go in the way that was likely to do most good and least hurt. And I do further in judgment agree with Your Grace in being willing that a gentle stop should be given to some of our friends who go greater lengths than I approve of in themselves or think good for the public. I have therefore acted very sincerely ever since I engaged at all in it, and...I have therefore put the draft...into my Lord Sunderland's hand who desires me to assure Your Grace it shall pass in the form he receives it. He does indeed think, and I confess I am of that opinion, that it will be better to keep it back to the rising of the parliament, or at least till the troublesome part is over. I think soon after the rising will be best, when the bishops are supposed to be going into the country;... and it seems more natural at the recess than to write to them about diocese work when they are attending other affairs. But be the delay more or less, my Lord Sunderland desires Your Grace to be assured it is not with any view of defeating the thing but only bringing it out to better advantage.[1]

The 'troublesome part' of the parliamentary session was occasioned by the bill for the repeal of the Occasional Conformity and Schism Acts, which bedevilled all hopes of cordial co-operation between the primate and the administration. Sunderland indeed, when sending Wake on 12 December a draft of this bill, added as evidence of the King's desire to support and defend the established church, that his majesty 'has ordered me to tell you that whenever you think it proper he will order' the letter concocted by the Archbishop and Gibson 'to be prepared for his signing, approving and liking every part of it, and to assure you that he will be ready to do everything towards making it effectual which Your Grace can suggest to him'.[2] Unfortunately this message only increased Wake's suspicions that the promise in the king's name was designed as a *douceur* to procure his acceptance of the repeals. Trimnell strove valiantly but vainly to remove the doubts.

> Nor can I be quite easy myself [he wrote on 7 January], while I do but imagine that there remains the least doubt with Your Grace of my Lord Sunderland's sincerely intending to pursue Your Grace's design in the method agreed on, or of my as sincerely concurring in it, and endeavouring to make those bishops who liked it least, easy in it.[3]

The divisions on the bench revealed and exaggerated by the debates on the bill for repeals, and the acrimony with which Wake reacted towards what he believed to be a betrayal of the interest of church as well as treason to himself by those of his brethren supporting the administration on this issue, destroyed, however, the hope of agreement on measures for the suppression of attacks on the faith and constitution of the church.

[1] *Ibid.* f. 70. Trimnell to Wake. 5 January 1718–19. [2] *Ibid.* f. 84. [3] *Ibid.* f. 71.

The next occasion for action on the primate's part came in relation to the Blasphemy Bill in 1721, which he had first intended to introduce in his own person into the House of Lords; but after conference with some of his brethren in March of that year, he had shelved his purpose. On 20 April, however, the measure was introduced by Dr George Verney, Lord Willoughby de Broke (who was also Dean of Windsor) after a speech on the question by Lord Nottingham. The bill provided the penalty of imprisonment for speaking or writing against the doctrines of the divinity of Christ and the Holy Trinity or denying the inspiration of the scriptures; and required the compulsory subscription on the part of divines suspected of heresy, both Anglican and Dissenting, to a declaration of orthodoxy. The Archbishop supported it in a strong speech, in which he traced the growth of Socinianism in England and the recent Trinitarian and Arian controversies. The bench was again divided in sentiment, five bishops voting for the bill and eight against; and Wake once more accused his brethren of desertion.[1] The only practical results therefore were the issue on 28 April of a royal proclamation for the suppression of blasphemous clubs and societies, and on 7 May of royal letters of direction to the archbishops and bishops for the enforcement of existing laws in defence of the orthodox doctrine of the Trinity.

Behind the specific attacks on the doctrines of the Trinity and of the divinity of Christ there lay the general movement conveniently, if not very accurately, known as Deism; which because of its elusive and multifarious manifestations, was more difficult alike of definition and suppression.[2] It was indeed part of the *Zeitgeist*; and was woven of many strands and composed of many elements. Perhaps the strongest single influence was that of the nascent scientific movement, which to its champions seemed to have established irrefragably the existence and attributes of the Creator and the ability of man to apprehend the nature of God through study of his works. Together with this scientific revolution there went the dethronement of the saecular authority in the universities of the philosophy of Aristotle in favour of Ramus and Descartes; whilst on a more popular level the vogue of natural religion as containing the essentials of a simple yet sufficient creed led to disparagement of revelation as clouding the simple tenets of the religion of nature with mysteries of dogma, priesthood, and sacraments. From these various roots there sprang an extensive proliferation of novel and strange theories, some of which percolated from the academy to the coffee-house and the forum. Of the general impact and importance of these changes in fashions of thought, especially as illustrated by the scientific movement and

[1] *V.* ch. VII, pp. 136-8.

[2] See G. R. Cragg, *From Puritanism to the Age of Reason, 1660–1700*; and R. N. Stromberg, *Religious Liberalism in Eighteenth-Century England.*

the modern philosophical tendencies, Wake was well aware. In a letter to Professor J. P. De Crousaz of Lausanne on 11 October 1725 (a decade after Joseph Butler's complaint against Oxford philosophy as consisting of 'frivolous lectures and unintelligible disputations'), he reflected on the dispossession of Aristotle from the dominance which his works and authority had enjoyed so long in the English universities.

In our universities, Aristotle has been dominant until today; nor are there lacking some who ascribe to him the highest praise for wisdom and erudition, with this error, that they recognise nothing beyond the limits which he established. Such are those professors who, never coming out of their schools, rule from their chairs, applaud themselves, and are applauded not less by their own disciples. Hence they hold almost all others in contempt; nor do they suffer those things to be brought into contempt or discredited which they can both turn to their profit and by which they can attain honours. But this weakness is almost confined to the universities.... Yet even there some enjoy a kinder disposition which gives them a mind more free to reflect; and they, wearied of scholastic trifles, pursue a more solid way of thought. But these men are neither many in number nor generally approved. In the city of London however a much better way of philosophy by far prevails; which, thanks to the renowned Royal Society's favour, has made and makes daily the greatest progress in the investigation of matters hitherto unknown even to the most learned men.[1]

The primate wished indeed that his Swiss correspondent (who had been in trouble with his own authorities) were living amongst this society of men, whom he characterised as 'saeculi sui ornamenta'.

It was one thing, however, to approve the deposition of Aristotle from his academic pedestal or to applaud the members of the Royal Society in the polite circles of the capital, and quite another to tolerate the rejection of Moses and the prophets by the advocates of Deism. For the rivalry between natural and revealed religion led the defenders of the former to scrutinise closely the credentials of the latter, in order both to test their authenticity and to achieve a critical appraisement of their contents. In particular the validity of prophecy and miracle as evidences of Christianity was subjected to detailed examination. Following the general argument of John Toland's

[1] Arch. W. Epist. 26, f. 307. 'Etiam in nostris Academiis, Aristoteles usque hodie dominatur; nec desunt qui summam sapientiae atque eruditionis laudem in eo ponunt, cum illo errore, certi nihil ultra terminos ab illo positos cognoscere. Hi sunt professores qui e scholis suis nunquam egredientes, in cathedris dominantur, sibi plaudunt et a suis discipulis non minus plauduntur; hinc alios fere omnes despectui habent; neque illa contemni aut explodi patiuntur, quibus simul et quaestum faciunt et honores adipiscuntur. Et quidem hoc vitium Academiis fere peculiare.... Sunt etiam illic aliqui cui benignior natura liberiorem cogitandi animum dedit; quique nugarum scholasticarum pertaesi solidam ineunt philosophandi viam. Sed hi nec numero multi nec pariter ab omnibus approbati. In urbe nostra Londiniensi longe melior obtinet philosophandi ratio; quae ab inclyta Societate Regia promota, maximos in rerum antea etiam doctissimis hominibus incognitarum disquisitione progressus fecit atque indies facit.'

Christianity not Mysterious of 1696 came Matthew Tindal's *Christianity as Old as the Creation* in 1730, Anthony Collins' *Discourse upon the Grounds and Reasons of the Christian Religion* in 1724, which criticised sharply the argument from prophecy, and Thomas Woolston's *Six Discourses on the Miracles of our Saviour* in 1727–9 which allegorised the supernatural events related in the gospels. It was not surprising that these attacks caused consternation in the orthodox camp; for if revelation lost the buttresses of prophecy and miracle, upon what could its apologists fall back for verification? Wake did not enter the lists openly against the Deists; though he dealt with their errors briefly in a visitation charge of 1728, as he had done with those of the Arian and Bangorian controversialists in 1720, without, however, publishing either of these manifestos.[1]

In private correspondence, however, he expressed his views of the controversy freely.

I do not esteem the niceties which the enemies of Christianity here throw out against our religion, of any moment [he confided to Professor Turrettini in a letter of 28 November 1728]. At this distance of time it is hard to answer all the difficulties that may be raised against the explication or application of some particular prophecies. But take the whole course of the predictions of the Old Testament and compare them with their accomplishment in the New, as Mr Bullock has done, and no one who is not wilfully blind will be able to doubt either of the interpretation or the fulfilling of them. This therefore I think is the true way of answering these men; let them cease to cavil upon points which neither of us understand, and take the whole view of the two Testaments (the Old and the New) together, and then judge whether the former does not speak of what was performed under the latter, and both together prove the divine revelation of one another. Our adversaries begin to be so sensible of this, that instead of continuing to reason with us, they have set up a man, that was awhile mad, and whose friends would persuade us he is so still, to cover him from the punishment his blasphemies deserve, to ridicule the miracles of our Saviour and treat them in so ludicrous or rather impious a manner, as none of our ancient enemies Porphyry, Celsus, or Julian himself did. This way of writing is exceedingly pleasing to the younger sort of Atheists, who have neither piety, nor judgment to restrain them, nor seem at all to care in how ridiculous a way the most serious and religious matters are treated. These pieces are published in small tracts of three or four sheets; vast numbers are printed, and read in an hour's time over a dish of coffee; and yet this man (under the shelter of madness) goes unpunished and even unrestrained, to the scandal of our country and of everything that is either sacred or serious. I wish these pieces, which no true Christian can with any patience read, may keep within our own country; but as many are sent abroad, I fear they will be translated into other languages and the poison infect other places. This is our misfortune; we are so afraid of the least tendency to persecution, that we cannot bear the least restraint. It is a sad case that we cannot keep in the middle

[1] *V.* ch. III, pp. 224–6.

way, and allow what is fit to be published, or may be read without reproach, but at the same time both restrain and punish what is openly blasphemous and tends to the ruin of all religion and indeed of all respect for every thing that is either pious or serious.

But I must not enlarge upon so melancholy a subject; nor yet leave it without assuring you that we have the government with us against these bold men, some of which are legally prosecuted, their books suppressed, and who privately disperse them in such a manner that it is hard to discover it, or make a legal proof against either the printers or sellers of them.

In the mean time we do what we can to prevent the mischief of these wicked aggressors of our holy religion; their arguments are answered; our preachers everywhere oppose their schemes; and at this time I am told the bishop of St David's [Richard Smalbroke] is preparing some observations against this mad man's blasphemies, and to show the falseness and malice of the author (Woolston) to be equal to his impiety. The bishop of London [Gibson], where these pieces are chiefly both printed and published, has lately himself written a pastoral letter to those of his diocese, to prevent in some measure the mischief of them.[1]

Bishop Gibson indeed was diligent in issuing pastoral letters and charges against infidels and deists alike; and also in setting in motion the law against authors and publishers.[2] Toland and Collins fled to avoid proceedings; and Woolston was actually prosecuted, though allegedly of unsound mind, and died in prison. But Wake himself was harsher in words than in deeds; and provided the tracts were suppressed, he inclined to mildness towards their authors. Thus in respect of a trivial pamphlet by Edward Elwell on *A True Testimony for God and for his sacred Law*, which ridiculed the divinity of Christ, the atonement and the sacraments, and all this 'not in a scholastic manner to convince men of learning but in a popular, light way', the Archbishop did not ask for penalties against the writer but only for confiscation of the work.

I am so far from desiring any such punishment [he wrote to Lord Townshend] to be inflicted upon the author of this book, that I rather wish he may not suffer at all for it. He seems willing to be made a confessor for his heretical opinions and I am as desirous he should not. For indeed I am by principle not only a hearty friend to the indulgence granted by law to our Protestant Dissenters, but an utter enemy to everything that looks like persecution upon the account of religion. But yet the book may be suppressed though the writer be not punished, and I think ought to be so.[3]

[1] Geneva MSS. Inventaire 1569, f. 163. Bishop Smalbroke published *A Vindication of the Miracles of our Blessed Saviour* (2 vols. 1729) and Thomas Bullock, *The Reasonings of Christ and his Apostles Vindicated* (1728).

[2] N. Sykes, *Edmund Gibson*, pp. 240–61.

[3] S.P. Domestic. George I. Vol. 52, f. 34. 14 September 1724. The pamphlet was printed for J. Nunn in the Poultry, Sam Billingsley at the Judge's Head in Chancery Lane and James Roberts in Warwick Lane, 1724.

Indeed the ministers of the crown testified that they had been more rigorous in carrying out the legal procedure than the primate had always approved.

You have never complained of any such writings but prosecutions have been immediately ordered against the offenders; and have in some instances been carried on with so much vigour that Your Grace has been pleased to express to those unhappy people themselves a charitable commiseration of their sufferings.[1]

It is in the light of this leniency therefore that Wake's laments to his foreign friends of the insufficiencies of the law, must be read.

It is a reproach to us [he avowed again to Turrettini on 7 April 1729] that so many advocates for Deism are suffered openly to appear in public on its behalf and to blaspheme our holy religion and the name by which we are called. But indeed, our ecclesiastical discipline is so weakened and even subjected to the civil authority, that we know not how to prevent it; nor can we do anything but employ our prayers and pens in the defence of Christianity; and I trust neither of these have been, or shall ever be, wanting in that case. And though the adversary makes a great noise and uses his utmost diligence to destroy not only all faith, but all practical religion and piety from among us; yet by the blessing of God, we have a very great number of excellent Christians among us who bewail their impiety, and both by their prayers and principles support the interests of true religion, and implore the blessings of heaven upon us.[2]

It may perhaps be wished that the Archbishop had developed in detail the line of argument adumbrated in his former letter to Turrettini, and had also extended its application from prophecy to miracle; for he might thereby have anticipated that modern apologetic which contends for the general reliability of prophecy and miracle in the Old and New Testaments without committing itself to acceptance of any particular and detailed example of prediction or miracle. At least credit must be accorded to the humane sentiments which moved him to rest content with the suppression of Deist works without demanding the infliction of penal sanctions upon their authors.

If heretics constituted the graver danger to the fundamentals of faith, schismatics were equally reprehensible from the standpoint of the unity of the Church; and where by a singular infelicity of fortune, dissent from the Church of England was combined with Arianising opinions, the crime seemed to Wake doubly to be deplored. His attitude towards the Dissenters indeed was a puzzle to contemporaries. At the time of the passing of the Occasional Conformity and Schism Acts, he was reckoned a Whig and an opponent of these measures; and he had even signed a protest against the latter act. But when the question of repeal was under consideration, he not only refused all

[1] S.P. Domestic. George II. Vol. 10, f. 129. 9 March 1728/9. Newcastle to Wake.

[2] Geneva MSS. Inventaire 1569, f. 165. Cf. Wake to Le Courayer, 7 December 1721, in *Biographia Britannica*, vol. VI, part 2, 40952b; footnote.

suggestions of relief for them, but split the Whig bishops on this very issue by his uncompromising opposition to the bill of December 1718. Whereas the protest against the Schism Act declared that the Church had no ground for fear of the Dissenters, that severity was less successful than charity in reconciling them to the Church, and that the Act was a violation of the toleration granted in 1689, in his speech against the repeals Wake represented the Dissenters as a dangerous and restless element in the nation and argued for no relaxation of the laws against them. That such was his firm judgment at this time was clear from his correspondence with the Archbishop of Dublin concerning the parallel ambitions of the Irish Dissenters for the repeal of the Test Act.

Your Grace I believe has heard [he wrote to King on 16 July 1719] that in our last session I opposed with all my little interest and ability, the repeal of the Occasional Conformity bill. I then did venture, upon the repeated assurances I had received of it from Ireland, to say that the presbyterians there did reprint their Solemn League and Covenant with their catechetical books; and bred up their people in an opinion that it was their duty to endeavour the alteration of the established church in Ireland, as they had effectually done it in Scotland; and should they ever get an establishment in both those kingdoms, one might without a spirit of prophecy foresee what would become of the Church of England....

I am glad the Test Act, which our house shewed so much resolution to defend the last winter, and some of the bishops were for giving up by a side wind, is like to stand as firm with you this summer....I am hearty for the Toleration (yet if that goes on, pray provide a little better than we have done against Arianism and Socinianism).[1]

He repeated these sentiments on 2 September following. 'The Dissenters are a busy, indefatigable generation; and our court seems to be very fond of favouring them';[2] and therefore he believed that whilst they should be reassured as to their legal toleration, they should be refused any further concession.

But as it is my principle to leave everybody at liberty in the business of religion, for which they are to answer at a higher tribunal than any upon earth; so while the Dissenters are kept out of power to do us harm, I envy them not any quiet or security in their own way. Self-preservation natural reason dictates to everybody; and as I doubt we should not be very safe in our own constitution, should it be in their power to destroy it, I am for that reason desirous to keep them out of a possibility of doing us harm by entrusting them with a capacity of doing it. But when that is provided for, I am not against making them easy in their toleration; wishing if it were possible, that they might be so well satisfied with that, as not to press for anything more.[3]

[1] King Correspondence (library of Trinity College, Dublin). Archbishop of Canterbury. 16 July 1719.

[2] *Ibid.* 2 September 1719.

[3] *Ibid.* 19 November 1719.

In addition to these political reasonings, however, the existence of so many and various dissenting churches was obnoxious to Wake by reason of his zeal for Christian, and especially Protestant, union. It seemed to his mind unreasonable to separate from a pure and reformed church because of dislike of things indifferent; and it was particularly afflicting in face of Roman hostility that Protestants should be at war amongst themselves. In his correspondence with the foreign churches, he gave forceful expression to these opinions. To Peter Zeller he wrote on 5 March 1717, that

> even those who fight for their country and faith together with us against the papists, differ amongst themselves and from us concerning ecclesiastical polity; they set up separatist assemblies from the Church of England, appoint their own pastors, are divided into parties against each other not less than against us; and administer their own affairs each according to their own rules. But you, who are impartial judges, should decide: whether an episcopal presidency (both moderate and truly primitive), or a liturgy seriously composed and devoutly used, or a few indifferent ceremonies, appointed solely for the preservation of order and decency in our public congregations, are of so great importance that for their sake the communion of the church should be broken, the church of Christ forsaken, and everything thrown into schism and faction. If these things are allowed, in vain shall we strive to establish peace, concord and union in the church; in vain pursue the apostolic rule, 'let all things be done decently and in order'. But all things must be permitted to everybody; and so many independent churches set up in every region, city, and village, and as many unbridled pastors, or more truly fanatical seducers, who under the pretext of a purer Christianity, seek to attract the miserable people to themselves and attach them to their parties. Such is our fate, such our danger. Besides the Papists, who are a common enemy to all, we have to contend with Presbyterians, Independents, Anabaptists, Quakers, and I know not what other monstrous names, almost unknown before these present times, nor even now known hardly anywhere else than amongst ourselves, and would that they were never to be known![1]

The Dissenters therefore constituted an obstacle to the Archbishop's desire for a strong and united Protestant church in England. Furthermore,

[1] Arch. W. Epist. 25, f. 29. 'Etiam illi qui pro patria, pro fide contra pontificios nobiscum contendunt, de disciplina ecclesiastica a nobis et inter se dissident; et ab Ecclesia Anglicana coetus suos separatim agunt; proprios sibi pastores constituunt; in partes a se invicem non minus quam a nobis scinduntur; et suis quique juribus res suas administrant. Vos interim, judices aequi, discernite; an episcopalis *προστασία* (moderata illa et vere primitiva); an liturgia graviter composita et devote usurpata; an caeremoniae, paucae et indifferentes, atque ad ordinem ac decorem in publicis coetibus conservandum unice institutae, tanti sunt momenti, ut propterea communio ecclesiastica sit violanda, ecclesia Christi delinquenda, omnia in scismata et factiones projicienda. Haec si liceant, frustra pacem, concordiam, unionem in ecclesia stabilire conabimur; frustra canonem illum Apostolicum prosequemur *πάντα δὲ εὐσχημόνως καὶ κατὰ τάξιν γινέσθω*. Omnia omnibus permittenda; et tot ecclesiae independentes in qualibet regione, urbe, pago instituendae, quot pastores effrenati, seu verius fanatici seductores fuerint, qui sub purioris Christianismi praetextu, miserum populum ad se alliare, suisque partibus addicere valeant. Haec nostra sors, hoc periculum. Praeter pontificios, communem omnibus hostem, cum presbyterianis, independentibus, anabaptistis, tremulis; et nescio quibus aliis nominum monstris nobis contendendum, ante haec tempora prorsus ignotis; nec alibi fere quam apud nos jam cognitis; utinam nunquam cognoscendis.'

they were apt to mislead and deceive those foreign churches with whom he was anxious to establish intercommunion and eventual union. For the English Dissenters sought to persuade the Reformed churches of the continent that their true affinities lay not with the Church of England but with the churches separating from it. Accordingly Wake was at pains to dispel this false opinion. In a letter of February 1717 to J. B. Ott of Zürich (father of the young divine whom he had taken into his household at Lambeth), he insisted on the error of such a supposition. 'These are our schismatics, who seek to obtain commendation and patronage for their conventicles from the foreign churches (which they boast to be like to their own). But let them know that none of these churches forsake our communion, or concede that their separation from the Church of England either was or is legitimate.' Wake continued to emphasise that his repudiation of the lawfulness of these schisms did not imply a denial of legal toleration. 'Let me add this one thing, that with us nobody is disquieted on account of religion. Freedom is granted to all the reformed, even to the worst fanatics who are called Quakers, whatsoever their religion. Their assemblies are held publicly, and not only are not forbidden by the laws, but are protected by them.'[1] The position of Wake towards orthodox Dissenters therefore was to allow them the legal indulgence granted by statute in 1689, but to resist all attempts towards its extension in any direction.

When, however, to schism there was added heterodoxy, his opposition became more determined and the tone of his criticism sharper. For the Arian controversy which had menaced the established church, spread to the Dissenters and wrought havoc amongst them, particularly amongst the Presbyterians who suffered a virtual landslide into what became later known by the name of Unitarianism.[2] The dispute began in Exeter, where four ministers, Joseph Hallett senr, John Withers, James Peirce and John Lavington, were suspected of unorthodox leanings. Peirce certainly had been much influenced by Samuel Clarke's book on the *Scripture Doctrine of the Trinity*; and the controversy spread to the capital, where in February and March 1719 meetings were held at Salters' Hall to consider the case of the Exeter ministers. A deep and almost equal division of opinion was revealed; and although endeavours were made to find a formula to which both parties to the dispute could subscribe, the issues were too serious to admit of com-

[1] Arch. W. Epist. 25, f. 31. 'Sunt nunc scismatici nostri, et suis conventiculis laudem et patrocinium ab ecclesiis transmarinis (suis—sic enim gloriantur—similibus) quaerere satagunt. At sciant nullas esse earum quae communionem nostram refugiant, aut eorum separationem ab ecclesia Anglicana legitimam fuisse aut esse, iis largiantur.... Id unicum adjicere liceat, neminem apud nos religionis causa vexari. Reformatis omnibus, etiam pessimis istis fanaticis quos Tremulos vocant, qualiscunque suae religionis libertas concessa. Coetus suos publice tenent; legibus adeo non prohibentibus, ut etiam tueantur.'

[2] See J. H. Colligan, *The Arian Movement in England* (1913).

promise. Henceforth the literary and theological contest waxed fast and furious, producing, as Wake calculated, between fifty and sixty works on one side and the other during its first year. The rapid penetration of Presbyterianism by Arianism produced an accentuation of the primate's antipathy towards Dissenters and a sharpening of his criticism of their policy. In replying to a letter from Archbishop King concerning the position of the Irish Dissenters, he commented:

We have the very same here; and I verily believe more than sixty tracts have been printed by them against one another, upon the great controversy of our Saviour's divinity. It is true they endeavour to palliate the matter, by stating the difference not concerning the truth of the doctrine, but the authority of men to impose upon their brethren human forms of subscription to the truth of it....New principles of wicked insincerity and prevarication have been openly advanced in the point of subscription, according to which an Arian may subscribe both to our Liturgy and Articles as well as the most orthodox Christian.[1]

To Professor Pictet at Geneva he pointed the contrast that, whilst heretical tendencies within the Church of England had always been confined to a very small number and had been vigorously and successfully combated by episcopal charges, sermons and more substantial works such as those of Waterland, amongst the Dissenters they had almost destroyed the being of an orthodox church. Indeed he insisted that the responsibility for the widespread vogue of Arianism rested fairly and squarely on the shoulders of the Dissenters. 'Illud constat, clamorem illum qui ad vos usque pertingit, quique animos vestros tantopere affligit, non a nostris sed ab iis Nonconformistis praecipue exoriri.'[2] In similar vein he averred to Turrettini that

this evil has already spread so far that the ministers of those who separate from our Church are utterly divided among themselves upon this point; and openly refuse to subscribe the divinity of our Saviour. The ministers that refuse this are many in number; some of their chief leaders and the people are entirely divided among them; so that if some stay be not put to this licentiousness, not only the established church, but Christianity itself will be in danger of being subverted by us. The single question therefore is, not what sort of confession nor of what points, should be required to be subscribed as the test of sound doctrine in its pastors; but whether an established church may either prepare any confession at all, or require anything to be declared, promised or subscribed by its pastors more than this: I believe the Scriptures to be the word of God? Now in this I dare say you have no difficulty. You may wish that curious and unnecessary points were not brought into general confessions of faith. But I am sure you would not have a gate opened to all sorts of heretics and enthusiasts to become the guides of Christ's flock and to keep sober, pious and orthodox pastors out of the ministry of it.[3]

[1] King Correspondence. Archbishop of Canterbury. 24 March 1719/20.
[2] Arch. W. Epist. 25, f. 153. December 1719.
[3] Geneva MSS. Inventaire 1569, f. 65. 13 May 1719.

Notwithstanding the acrimony of these references to Dissenters and his resolve to confine them strictly within the limits of the Toleration Act, Wake was sincere in his profession of aversion to persecution for conscience sake and of support of the principle of religious toleration. He even averred his desire, if it were possible, to place Papists on the same basis as Protestant Dissenters in this regard. In actual practice, he assured J. B. Ott, a considerable measure of indulgence was allowed to Roman Catholics. 'Nor are their sacred rites denied even to papists, who attend mass everywhere; nor are measures taken against their sacrificing-priests or their followers on account of religion; but when penalties are inflicted on them it is on account of their rebellion, not of their religion.'[1] In correspondence with Dr Martin of Louvain, who had sent him a copy of his defence of the bull *Unigenitus* and advocated a religious conference between Protestant and moderate Roman Catholic divines, he expressed his approval of such eirenic sentiments and justified the differentiation in the Toleration Act between Protestant and Popish Dissenters on the ground not of religion but of temporal allegiance. The former 'though they separate from our Church, yet live peaceably under our civil government, and for this cause they are protected by it and enjoy the full liberty of their religion in their own way'.[2] When Martin in reply pointed out that the Dissenters, not the Papists, had been responsible for the civil war and execution of Charles I, and protested against the abjuration oath which required a formal disavowal of 'the pretended Prince of Wales', the primate defended it as a necessary bulwark against the papal claim to a power of deposing heretical sovereigns.

I cannot but highly approve of your zeal both for catholic unity and civil obedience to those whom God hath set in authority over us. But if you will give me leave freely to speak my mind, I doubt it will be found no easy matter to compass either of them. You may expound the canon of the Lateran council as you please, the pope will not relinquish his pretensions of power not only to excommunicate the greatest heretical princes but to absolve their subjects from their allegiance to them; and you know what flagrant instances our history affords us of both these. I do agree with my good friend the archbishop of Tuam that were it possible to make as secure of the peaceableness, fidelity and true allegiance of his majesty's popish subjects as we are of our other Dissenters, they would then be no less worthy of the favour and protection of the government than the others are, and might justly expect the like liberty of their religion. But you speak a little too harshly of the oath of abjuration, when you not only call it *abominable* but say 'that no man of learning, honour and conscience can swallow it without remorse and horror'. I do not much pretend to learning, nor value myself upon being a man of honour. But I hope I

[1] Arch. W. Epist. 25, f. 31. 1717. 'Quin nec pontificiis sua sacra denegata; Missas passim adeunt; neque vel sacrificulis vel sequacibus eorum hujus rei causa vi aliqua intentata; quando in eos animadvertitur, non id religionis, sed rebellionis causa factum.'

[2] *Ibid.* 26, f. 28. 1 June 1722.

have a good conscience both towards God and man; and yet I do assure you I never felt either remorse or horror in the taking of it. For indeed, when all is said, but one can be the lawful and rightful king of this realm. He therefore who believes King George to be that rightful king (as I do in my conscience believe that he is) must in consequence of such his persuasion believe the Pretender not to be lawful or rightful king of it; which is the substance of that oath and that upon which all the rest of it depends.[1]

But within little more than a generation of the expulsion of James II and with much more recent memories of the 1715 rebellion, argument for equality between Protestant and Popish dissenters in respect of religious toleration was necessarily academic and theoretic; and Wake's generous sentiments towards the Roman Catholics were incapable of translation into legislation.

The last company of schismatics whose claims were refuted by the Archbishop came more directly and immediately from his own communion, in the persons of the Non-Jurors. The little company of bishops, clergy and laity who in 1689 had carried their conscientious objection to acceptance of the Revolution Settlement to the point of separation from the established church, had suffered a steady diminution both in numbers and influence during the succeeding interval. The continuation of the episcopal succession by the consecration as suffragan bishops in 1694 of George Hickes and Thomas Wagstaffe had been evidence of the determination of a party amongst the surviving Non-Jurors to perpetuate their schism; and the abjuration oath had undoubtedly militated against the healing of the breach. In 1713, moreover, a further important step was taken when Hickes with the assistance of two Scottish non-juring bishops consecrated Jeremy Collier, Nathanael Spinckes and Samuel Hawes to perform episcopal functions for the little city of Zoar to which their communion was now reduced. Accordingly they sought to remedy their ecclesiastical isolation and insignificance by approaches to the Eastern Orthodox Church for formal union. Thanks to the presence in England of Arsenius, the metropolitan of Thebais, an approach was made through him to the Tsar of Russia, in the form of 'A Proposal for a Concordat betwixt the Orthodox and Catholic remnant of the British Churches, and the Catholic and Apostolical Oriental Church'. What the authors of this project lacked in numbers they made up in confidence; for they proposed in their first article 'that the Church of Jerusalem be acknowledged as the true mother church and principle of ecclesiastical unity'; and they assumed that the negotiation between themselves and the Eastern Orthodox Church should be conducted as between equals; to which end they appended twelve articles of belief in which the two churches already were agreed, and five 'wherein

[1] Arch. W. Epist. 26, ff. 43–4. 1722.

they cannot at present so perfectly agree'.[1] Although this document was dated 18 August 1716, the reply to it did not reach England until 1722; and, after a detailed and thorough response to all the points raised by the Non-Jurors, it demanded an unqualified acceptance by them of Eastern Orthodox standards of belief and practice. A further 'Reply' was sent from the Non-Jurors, which in turn evoked an equally firm and uncompromising demand for submission. Meanwhile, however, the existence of the correspondence had become known to Wake, who took the occasion of a farewell call made upon him by Marcus Nomicus, an emissary of the Patriarch of Jerusalem, to send a letter on 2 September 1725 explaining the exact position of the Non-Juror church and episcopate in relation to the Church of England. After an expression of thanks for books sent to him by the patriarch and of compliments to the patriarch personally and to his church for their steadfast resistance to the claims of Rome, he continued to deal with the domestic issue of the Non-Juror correspondence.

And now, as I am writing these things to your illustrious Reverence, I ought by no means to pass over what I heard a year ago from one of my presbyters, who is still amongst our merchants at Constantinople: to wit, that certain schismatic priests of our own Church have written to you under the pretended titles of archbishop and bishops of the Church of England, and have sought your communion with them; who having neither place nor church in these realms, have bent their mind to deceive you, who are ignorant of their schism. As to the true status of these men and the occasion of their schism, you will learn more fully from my faithful presbyter, Thomas Payne.[2] He will relate to your Reverence, how unjustly they have separated from us; and how they have at once withdrawn their due allegiance from the king's majesty and their obedience from their bishops, and have violated the unity of the church for this only reason, that we have decided to obey the laws of the realm, and to recognise as king him whom our lords and commons and the princes and states of all Europe acknowledge to be king; and to whom the laws of the realm and the consent of all orders amongst us (to whom alone pertains the right of determination in these matters) have committed the imperial authority of Britain.

For this cause a few of the clergy, fewer still of the bishops, have seceded from us; have persuaded many of the people to their side; and have established congregations separating from the Church. Finally they have reached such a degree of madness that, upon the death of the first authors of this schism, they have consecrated for themselves new bishops to succeed to their places; and it is these who have presumed to write to you. These have tried to seduce you from the communion of our Church; one of whom, I hear, usurping my place and authority, though he has not ventured to call himself Archbishop of Canterbury, has styled himself by the new title of 'First Bishop'. Of these men, I pray and beseech your Reverence

[1] G. Williams, *The Orthodox Church of the East in the Eighteenth Century* (London, 1868). J. H. Overton, *The Non-Jurors* (1902).

[2] Thomas Payne: chaplain at Constantinople; rector of High Halden, Kent, 1713–59.

greatly to beware. Meanwhile we, the true bishops and clergy of the Church of England, who profess the same faith with you in every article of fundamental importance, shall also not cease to hold communion with you at least in spirit, for otherwise we cannot, owing to our great distance from you. And I, as I do profess myself most specially bounden to your Holiness, so do I most earnestly entreat you to remember me in your prayers and sacrifices at the holy altar of God.[1]

To this letter the Patriarch Chrysanthos replied on 19 January 1727, thanking Wake for his full statement of the non-juring position, and explaining that before receiving this missive, he had already answered the Non-Jurors' approach, an act of courtesy which no man of goodwill could censure. Notwithstanding the hope expressed in the conclusion of his reply that the primate would continue to favour him with his correspondence, there is no evidence that Wake included the Eastern Orthodox churches in his oecumenical projects; though it may seem somewhat surprising that he should not have done so. Apart from an occasional interchange of courtesies, however, his only important letter to an eastern patriarch was concerned thus with the domestic issue of the non-juring secession.

In his estimate of the political danger from the Protestant Dissenters Wake was evidently mistaken; for with the repeal of the Occasional Conformity and Schism Acts, they settled down to a period of ease in Sion. He himself indeed was to live long enough to see the failure of their attempt to secure the further repeal of the Test Act in 1736, a defeat to which Gibson, who had supported the former relief, contributed considerably. From the theological standpoint it seems clear that the Archbishop's laments concerning the Trinitarian and Arian controversies so far as they affected the Dissenters, were inspired chiefly by his passion for union with the foreign Protestant churches. From this point of view the rapid decline of the Presbyterians into formal heresy militated severely against his continuous endeavours to persuade the Swiss cantons of Berne and Zürich to relax their requirements of ministerial subscription to the *Formula Consensus*, just as the refusal of English Dissenters to accept the reformed episcopate of the Church of England weakened the effect of his repeated appeals to the Reformed churches of the continent to restore the episcopal polity to their communions. In both respects the dissidence of the Dissenters on the one hand and their infection by Arianism on the other were object-lessons to the foreign churches, of which they did not fail to take notice. Similarly the primate's plea for the

[1] Wake's letter, the draft of which is in Arch. W. Epist. 26, f. 298, is translated into English by G. Williams, *op. cit.* pp. lv–lviii. All the documents relating to the Non-Jurors' approach to the Eastern Orthodox Church, including Wake's letter and the reply of Chrysanthos, are printed in both Latin and Greek in full in *J. B. Martin et R. P. Ludovico Petit: Collectio Conciliorum Recentium*, Tomus I. Londinenses et Constantinopolitanae Synodi: pro ineunda concordia Anglicanos inter et Orthodoxos: 1716–25, pp. 370–623. Paris, 1905. I am indebted to Brother George Every, S.S.M. for drawing my attention to this collection.

Anglican expedient of meeting differences of theological opinion by comprehension proved distinctly less persuasive when his own bishops and clergy were a prey to heresies concerning the Trinity, the Person of Christ and the authority of the Church. Granted that Hoadly was as unrepresentative of the bench of bishops as Samuel Clarke was of the lower clergy in convocation, nevertheless the preferment which they enjoyed and the influence which their opinions gathered, offered an unimpressive picture to foreign theologians of a Church lacking unity within itself.

Notwithstanding, Wake did not waver from his acceptance of the Toleration Act and of the right of the Dissenters to maintain their separatist churches.

For what concerns the new controversies which have arisen these late years in our church [he wrote to Turrettini] I must observe that besides the established church, which is founded upon the episcopal constitution, and has for its doctrine the English confession in Thirty-nine Articles, for its worship our English liturgy; there are great numbers of Dissenters among us, who separate from our communion; though many of them join with us in the most solemn acts of religious worship. These, though of infinite variety among themselves, are all with respect to us reducible to four kinds, Presbyterians, Independents, Anabaptists and Quakers. They have all of them a full and free toleration of their religion; the two first on the condition of subscribing thirty-six of our Thirty-nine Articles, in which they agree with us; the third sort subscribe the same, except that part of our Articles which relates to infant baptism. The Quakers subscribe none; only profess their faith in the holy Trinity, in a form of confession drawn up on purpose for them. The late controversies do not concern anything of this. We leave all persons to the liberty the laws have given them, and do not so much as desire to restrain them in their indulgence.[1]

It was therefore only in so far as the heresies of the Dissenters touched the question of their legal subscription that the Archbishop considered himself justified in resisting any demand for relaxation of the existing provisions concerning them. But he was naturally and necessarily more concerned with the prevalence of heterodox opinions about the Trinity and the Person of Christ amongst the clergy of his own church; and most particularly with the Bangorian sermon which he interpreted as opening wide the door to all kinds of unorthodoxy, by its repudiation of the authority of the church to demand subscription to any confession of faith. This he regarded as the root of all the evils afflicting the Church. Hence his chief thunders were reserved for the Hoadleians.

The new disputes [he further explained to Turrettini] are these. Some of our divines have openly espoused the Arian notions; others are fallen into other gross heresies. Now to cover their particular sentiments, a new notion of libertinism is set up, that there ought to be no confession of faith, no subscription to anything but the truth of the holy scriptures, required to qualify any man to be a pastor, a

[1] Geneva MSS. Inventaire 1569, f. 65. 13 May 1719.

dignitary or even a bishop of the established church; and that 'tis usurpation upon the peculiar authority of Christ for any one to require such subscriptions to be made to any confessions of faith whatsoever. This is the doctrine and this the occasion of it.[1]

Against these tenets, which proceeded both amongst members of his own Church and amidst the Dissenters from 'the Bishop of Bangor's Independent principles', Wake waged unceasing war; for they cut at the root of his desire for catholic union and concord. As he had bewailed to foreign Protestants these internal divisions and heresies, so to his Gallican correspondent Du Pin he lamented the obstacles which they placed in the path of his hopes.

Indeed there are amongst ourselves and everywhere amongst many others, not a few persons to whom nothing of moderation, peace and of what appertains to the promotion of catholic unity, either pleases now or will ever be pleasing. These not only condemn inflexibly all authority in the church, but particularly believe that Christian liberty consists in this, that every one should take freedom to himself of thinking what he wishes and proclaiming what he thinks; and of communicating with whatever company of fanatics he wishes. They are a daring, restless and altogether heretical kind of men; who contend to such a degree for liberty of prophesying because they know well what monstrous things they nourish within and how far by their impious doctrines they have declined from the catholic faith. Therefore I do not concern myself with these common enemies to the catholic church; nor with those whom our church justly regards as schismatics, though they are tolerated by the civil laws of the kingdom, and who are comprehended under the names of Presbyterians, Independents, Anabaptists and Quakers. Far be it from me to compel these schismatics, who have separated themselves contumaciously from our communion, to return unwillingly to the fellowship of the Church of England.[2]

Compelled to essay the difficult task of navigating the barque of the Church amidst so many and conflicting cross-currents, Wake strove to repress heresy without stifling freedom of opinion and to discourage schism without denying toleration to Dissenters. Well might he have echoed fervently the traditional suffrage of the Litany: *Ab omni falso dogmate, haeresi et schismate, libera nos, Domine.*

[1] Geneva MSS. Inventaire 1569, f. 65.

[2] Arch. W. Epist. 25, f. 100. 18 January 1718/19. 'Sunt quidem inter nos, uti apud plerosque alios, non pauci quibus nihil moderatum, nihil pacificum, nihil quod ad unionem catholicam promovendam faciat, aut nunc arrideat aut unquam deinceps placere poterit. Hi non solum omnem ecclesiae potestatem praefracte contemnunt, sed et in eo praecipue collocari libertatem Christianam credunt, ut quilibet sibi licentiam sumat et quicquid libuit sentiendi, et quicquid senserit, proferendi; et cum quocumque sibi videbitur fanaticorum grege communicandi. Audax, inquietum et plerumque etiam haereticum hominum genus; qui ideo tantopere pro libertate prophetandi decertant, quod probe sciunt quae intus monstra alant et quam longe a catholica fide impiis suis dogmatibus abscesserint. Hosce igitur non moror communes ecclesiae catholicae hostes, sed nec quos ecclesia nostra, utcunque legibus municipalibus regni toleratos, pro schismaticis habet quocunque nomine Presbyterorum, Independentium, Anabaptistarum, Tremulorum habeantur. Absit ut ego hujusmodi schismaticos, qui sese a communione nostra contumaciter subduxerint, invitos in consortium Ecclesiae Anglicanae pertraham.

CHAPTER IX

GRATEFUL EVENING MILD

Sweet the coming-on
Of grateful evening mild; then silent night.

MILTON, *Paradise Lost*, Book IV, l. 646

Bishop of St Asaph: Your wish then, Sir, is γηράσκειν διδασκόμενος.
Dr Johnson: Yes, my Lord. BOSWELL, *Life of Johnson.* 9 April 1778

'For myself I live almost a monastic life', wrote Wake to Le Courayer on 7 December 1726.

I have a large and numerous family, and I keep it under the best regulation I can. We have the service of God within ourselves and that in public in my chapel four times a day. We live orderly and peaceably together. And though necessity of business draws a great number of persons to me, yet I reduce even that as much as possible to certain days in the week. To the Court I seldom go, save when obliged to attend my duty either in the public or cabinet councils. And when in parliament time I am rather faulty in not going so often as I should to it than in attending constantly upon it. So that I use my best endeavours to live clear of the world and die by degrees to it. My age and infirmities (being now ready to enter on my 70th year) admonish me to look upon myself as a citizen of another country and ready to go from hence to it.[1]

The legend of Wake's withdrawal so far as possible from all temporal concerns and of the ascetic strictness of his private way of life spread widely no less amongst his foreign friends than at home. Even Hearne related in (for him) muted and muffled tone how 'the present Archbishop of Canterbury, Dr Wake, is one of the most abstemious men living'.[2] Yet at the time of writing this letter to Le Courayer, there lay a decade more of life before the primate; so that for him it was truly a case of (slow as well as) 'sweet the coming on of grateful evening mild'. In great part this impression of a complete retirement from the world is accentuated by the sudden termination of his erstwhile voluminous correspondence. The continuance of letters to his friends abroad, however (the latest extant bearing the date of February 1731) suggests that his incapacitation was gradual and that his bodily weakness especially increased during the last six years of his life.

There can be no doubt that his eclipse in matters political by Gibson led to his resolve to accept relegation to the sphere of less public events. Formally

[1] *Biographia Britannica*, vol. VI, Part 2, 4095b. [2] Hearne, *Collections*, vol. IX, p. 395.

the two prelates remained on terms of correct communication. The Bishop of London sent to the Archbishop his schemes for reconciling the Whig churchmen and statesmen, no less than his projects for bishops in the plantations and his pastoral letters to his diocese. In reply Wake acknowledged them politely and courteously. 'Your lordship's papers I have read pretty carefully over', he wrote on 29 August 1728, in relation to Gibson's first pastoral letter 'occasioned by some late writings in favour of infidelity';

and I bless God for them. I hope they will do good, and put some stop to the endeavours of the wicked and unbelievers. You will think me very desirous to do somewhat when you see the little corrections I offer and observations I make upon your papers. But what should I do? I had nothing left me but these trifles to approve my sincerity in what your lordship was willing to commit to my view. I doubt Wollaston is an arrant knave. I have occasionally examined several of his quotations and find him a cunning and dissembling man. I have given you only one instance with respect to Origen, which you may please to take notice of or not, as you see cause. I pray God to bless your lordship's good endeavours; but while religion runs so low in the practice of some and revelation seems so little regarded by others among our own selves, who seem to think as lightly of our order as if there were no more in the consecration or office of a bishop than in that of a constable or churchwarden, what can we expect but ruin and confusion? From which God deliver us. I am with all esteem, My Lord, Your Lordship's very affectionate friend and brother.[1]

To Gibson's second pastoral letter, 'occasioned by some late writings in which it is asserted that reason is a sufficient guide in matters of religion without the help of revelation', the Archbishop replied with one sentence of thanks on 21 April 1730, together with the assurance that he had 'twice read [it] over in print' and was 'persuaded [it] will do a great deal of good'.[2] When the third letter was published in 1731, 'occasioned by the suggestions of infidels against the writings of the New Testament considered as a divine rule of faith and manners', Wake was much afflicted by the recent death of his wife and his own consequent ill-health.

In the midst of my trouble, I rejoice to receive the mark you send me of your remembrance of me. What your lordship published before was so well performed by your lordship and so well received by the world, that I make no doubt but that this will do as much good as I may without flattery say the others have done. It was merely your lordship's care and kindness to think of my perusal of it before it came abroad. My age and weakness have scarce left me with sufficient judgment to take care of my own most common performances, even that of writing to friends. I am sure you want no such assistance nor could I afford it if you did.[3]

Yet these were but a formal interchange of courtesies; and when the primate tried to secure a residentiary's place in St Paul's cathedral for his

[1] Gibson MSS. (now in the University library, St Andrews), III, 2002–2851, f. 1.
[2] *Ibid.* f. 25. [3] *Ibid.* f. 26.

son-in-law Dr Lynch, Gibson was not slow to point out to Townshend the implications of such a move.

I thank your lordship for communicating to me, in confidence, what you mentioned at the House today; and you may depend upon it that it shall remain an entire secret. But I beg leave to lay before you a true state of this case; that if you think my reasons for opposing anything of that kind to be fair and just, you may guard against giving any encouragement to such motion, and also prevent His Majesty's being surprised by any private application.

As to domestic affairs I do not blame His Grace for having a concern for his family; nor can he blame me for having some concern for mine, which is much larger than His Grace's. As to the church of St Paul's, His Grace is no further concerned in it than to obtain the favour of a profitable place for one of his own family; but besides the concern for my own family in common with His Grace, I have a very great concern in point of administration and the ease and quiet of my own life. I have already put myself at mercy as to the deanery in favour of one to whom I know the ministry wished well, but not without prospect of securing a balance in the chapter as vacancies should fall. And if any dispute should happen between the dean and me, I leave your lordship to judge which side the person is like to take who shall be under the direction of the archbishop.

Dr Lynch's estate is near Canterbury; and His Grace has not only three prebends of Canterbury and the archdeaconry in his own gift, but is also in actual possession of a promise of the very next prebend that shall fall there in the king's gift by way of exchange for the deanery of Bangor. For these reasons I hope your lordship will be of opinion that it is by no means a fair motion on the part of His Grace, and that so far as anything may depend upon my concurrence, it cannot be expected from me. You will lay what stress you think proper upon the good words that accompanied the motion that was made to you; but I beseech you to let the regard which you think they deserve, either to be confined to His Grace's own church, or at least be expressed with a *salvo* to mine.[1]

Lord Townshend assured Gibson of his agreement that both the Bishop's personal ease and quiet and also 'his power of doing service to His Majesty and the public' depended upon the personnel of his cathedral chapter; and so the Archbishop's initiative was unsuccessful. In matters of state there could be no doubt that Fulham carried affairs over Lambeth; and even in ecclesiastical issues Wake was the *roi fainéant* and Gibson the mayor of the palace.

Notwithstanding, the Archbishop continued to exercise himself with care and diligence in various points of business relating to church and state. Moreover there was one major occasion, that of a coronation, on which an archbishop of Canterbury could assert the rights of his office against even the most powerful and resolute bishop of London. Upon the accession of

[1] Gibson MSS. IV, 2086–2141, f. 19. N. Sykes, *Edmund Gibson*, pp. 129–30. Francis Hare had been made dean of St Paul's in 1726.

George II in 1727, therefore, Wake determined not to be ousted from the discharge of the duty of crowning His Majesty and his consort, Queen Caroline. On 15 August he reported that in preparation for the forthcoming coronation on 12 October, 'I propose God willing to return to Lambeth the next week, and have carefully read over so many and different offices for the coronation, and made such remarks upon them, that I hope in a very little time after my return to lay an Office, properly fitted for the approaching solemnity, before the Lords' Committees for their perusal and approbation.'[1] He consulted the forms for the coronation of Charles I, James II, Anne and George I;[2] and from them compiled that for the ensuing occasion, which was approved by the King in Council on 20 September.

At the outset Wake added a prefatory rubric concerning the provision of the necessary ornaments for the unction. 'In the morning of the day of the coronation early care is to be taken that the Ampulla, filled with oil, and the spoon with it, be laid ready and left upon the altar in the Abbey church.' At the entry of Their Majesties to the church, the choir and clergy were to sing Psalm 122, verses 1–7 as an anthem; but, unfortunately, eighteenth-century coronations were not ordered with the same diligence as present-day solemnities; so that Wake appended a note to his copy of the service to the effect that 'this was omitted and no anthem at all sung in the coronation of King George II, by the negligence of the choir of Westminster'. Nor did the singers improve much upon this when their next occasion came, after the Recognition, in the anthem Psalm 21, verses 1, 2, 5 and 6; for the archbishop again commented: 'The anthems in confusion; all irregular in the music.' Moreover another *contretemps* occurred in respect of the communion vessels; for Wake observed that 'neither paten nor cup carried at King George II's coronation, by the neglect of the officers; yet the bishops who should have borne them, walked in their places; the Bible carried'. The Litany was read, instead of being sung, by the Archbishop's direction in order 'to shorten the service'. In the Communion Service Wake restored the recital of the Decalogue, which had been omitted for the coronation of George I; whilst the sermon, 'which is to be short and suitable to the great occasion', was preached by Bishop Potter of Oxford. At the taking of the oaths, Wake inserted an epithet into the promise, relating to 'the *respective* laws and customs of the same'; and for the sake of precision changed the rubric requiring the Bible, for the swearing of the oath, to be 'brought from the altar by the archbishop', to 'by the Dean of Westminster'. At the solemnity of the unction, once more the choir showed their inefficiency; for whereas they should have sung both the *Veni, Creator Spiritus* before the

[1] S.P. Domestic. George II, vol. 2, f. 36.

[2] Lambeth Palace Library. 1079B; 1079A; 1081A from which the following account is drawn.

anointing and *Zadok the Priest* after the prayer for the blessing of the king, 'this hymn by mistake of the music not sung, but the next anthem instead of it'. At the actual unction, Wake added a note that 'the anointing was made with a white silk tuff dipped in the oil'; and he inserted a further rubric directing that 'then the Dean of Westminster layeth the ampulla and spoon upon the altar'. At the investiture with spurs and sword only slight alterations were made. But at the investiture *per Anulum et Baculum*, instead of the formula:

> Receive this ring, the ensign of kingly dignity and of defence of the catholic faith; that, as you are this day consecrated head of this kingdom and people, so being rich in faith and abounding in good works, you may reign with Him who is the King of kings; to Whom be glory and honour for ever and ever. Amen.

Wake wished to substitute the prayer which he had found amongst Sancroft's papers as follows:

> Receive this ring, a pledge of the marriage between the king and his people; And Thou, O Lord, who by thy good providence hast brought this our king and his people together, blast the wicked designs of all that would put them asunder. Bless, O Lord, and prosper Thy own handiwork, and keep His Majesty and his people together in love inviolable; and in a faithful performance of their several duties, to our comfort and the glory of thy holy name, through Jesus Christ our Lord.

To the Archbishop this latter form 'seemed much better; but His Majesty would have nothing changed'; for which most probably posterity owes him much thanks. The rest of the coronation of the king was substantially unchanged; but after the fivefold blessing of the king, his majesty 'vouchsafed to kiss the archbishops and bishops assisting at his coronation, they kneeling before him one after another'. There followed the inthronisation and homage, and then the crowning of the queen; and the communion of their majesties. Before this time the singers and musicians had recovered their poise; so that after the homage an anthem was sung 'with instrumental musick of all sorts as a solemn conclusion of the king's coronation'.

The long service was a considerable tax on Wake's strength; and he had accepted gratefully the kind offer of the king that 'by reason of his infirmity and the great business he is to perform in the abbey', he should be 'excused by His Majesty from walking in the procession' from Westminster Hall to the church. Their Majesties arrived there at 9 a.m. and did not leave, after the customary banquet, until 7.30 p.m. To his friend Turrettini, the Archbishop sent a full account of events and their purport.

> Since I returned from thence [Tunbridge Wells] my time has been almost wholly taken up in preparing for the ecclesiastical part of Their Majesties' coronation; a very solemn, as well as splendid office; and yet such as, I bless God, I went through

with almost beyond my hopes. I do indeed still labour under one very ill effect of that work, a violent defluxion and cold which my extreme heat in the performance of my duty exposed me to, though I took all possible care to prevent it. I am now managing myself in the best manner I can to get rid of it, and flatter myself that I shall in a little time, by God's blessing, overcome it....

Your condolence with me upon the loss of my late royal master and benefactor, our late most gracious king, was very kind and seasonable. It is to him I owe all I have either of honour or advantage in the Church; and I must be of all men the most ungrateful, if I should ever forget my obligations to him. His memory will ever be precious with me; as indeed it ought to be to all his subjects. His loss was such as nothing but our hopes in the experienced wisdom and goodness of their present majesties could have compensated; in whom we justly expect to find the same tender care of their subjects, concern for the common peace and welfare of Europe, and protection of the reformed religion in all parts of it.

The beginnings of His Majesty's reign are truly, as you observe, wise and encouraging. We see no change in our former measures, no persons disgraced or otherwise called to account for their proceedings, scarce any of the late king's servants dismissed from their offices. The same persons who were our chief ministers before, continue in their posts now; so that the court, excepting only in the person of the prince whom God has taken from us, has the very same look and appearance as it had before.[1]

All Wake's foreign friends were delighted that he had been able to perform the coronation without serious ill effects.

Je suis charmé, Monseigneur [wrote the faithful Abbé Girardin], que votre chère santé ne se soit point ressentie de votre dernière fatigue; je craignais fort que la longueur de cette cérémonie, dans une saison où les rigueurs du froid sont plus sensibles que dans le fort de l'hiver même, n'augmentât la maladie donc vous aviez eu quelques attaques par le passé. Mais grâces au Seigneur, vous voilà entièrement tiré de l'affaire.[2]

The coronation indeed had even awakened convocation from its passivity; for at its next session it presented a congratulatory address to the new sovereign on his accession. Moreover, the Archbishop continued to remind ministers of state of the next convocation-day and to ask their directions when and how to prorogue it further. On 15 August 1727 he informed them that his registrar,

not receiving the writ of summons for the convocation, had called upon the clerk of the crown and was told by him that no orders had yet been given about it. I beg leave to put your lordship in mind of it and to intreat your lordship to procure His Majesty's order for it the next council. I believe there cannot be a more proper day for its meeting than the Friday after the parliament, which I think will be the 1st of December.[3]

[1] Geneva MSS. Inventaire 1569, f. 153. Wake to Turrettini. 18 October 1727.
[2] Rawlinson MSS. A. 275, f. 85. Girardin to Wake. 20 October 1727.
[3] S.P. Domestic. George II, vol. 2, f. 63.

Accordingly the convocation met and was duly prorogued; and on 11 March 1728 Wake further reminded Townshend that

the time for the convocation's meeting after its last prorogation drawing on, I think it necessary to enquire after His Majesty's pleasure, whether he will be pleased to continue it by his royal writ till after Easter, or whether he will have me to go on to continue it. If nothing is intended to be done, as I suppose nothing is, I should think it would be as well at once to let the clergy know it, as to keep things in suspense, and in that case would propose a writ to be ordered for my continuing the convocation at their next meeting to Friday the 27th of April.[1]

Notwithstanding the refusal to allow the convocation to do business, the interest of the clergy in proctorial elections was sustained; and in 1722 Wake burned his fingers rather badly by a well-meant intervention in the choice of proctors both for the cathedral chapter and for the diocese. Being asked by several beneficed clergymen for his advice as to the election of proctors and being informed that the two former proctors, Dr Elias Sydall and Mr Charles Bean, 'would appear again if he approved of them', he gave the desired approbation. Similarly the name of Dr Bradshaw, vice-dean, was suggested as the representative of the chapter; in which also he concurred. Unfortunately jealousies were speedily aroused. Mr Edward Lunn announced his intention of standing for election at the repeated request of sundry amongst his brethren; and was much disturbed to learn that his action was 'by no means well pleasing to his grace'. Equally the dean of Canterbury was surprised and affronted to hear first of Bradshaw's candidature from the vice-dean himself, accompanied by the intimation that 'it was his grace's pleasure without my sollicitation that I should appear as a candidate to represent the chapter'. The dean dutifully assured the archbishop that 'his signification of it will meet with all due submission not from me only, but I dare say from the whole society'. He observed, however, that this was not the way in which such matters were usually transacted. Dr Blomer had just grounds for expecting to be chosen, 'as the very senior of our body who is either desirous or capable of it', and 'his application (to me at least) much earlier'. The whole affair seemed to Dean Stanhope to indicate 'a small neglect' of himself; and, moreover, the very phraseology was not seemly.

To the same reason I ascribe the expression *appearing candidate;* for really, my lord, with this, both name and thing, our chapter hath all my time continued unacquainted. Our method hath been to wait the determination of the senior; and then, if any other had more pressing occasion for this post, as kindly to give way upon request.

Several precedents to this effect were cited; and the dean concluded:

Thus, my lord, by freely conferring together, by preserving the customary regard to seniority, and by mutually kind indulgences where there was greatest need

[1] *Ibid.* vol. 5, f. 185.

of them, the order and amity of our body hath been not only constant but remarkable. And I hope we shall not now begin a different course, which may be of example and consequence hereafter, worse than any man at present can foresee. I speak this on supposition that your grace's authority do not interpose; for if it do, our choice is a submission (and a unanimous one, I presume it will be), which will not affect common cases.[1]

In the diocesan election Lunn assured the primate that he had only consented to stand because of doubts about Mr Bean's opinions, 'particularly with relation to the late bishop of Bangor's doctrine of sincerity'; since he himself had heard Bean defending Hoadly and especially asserting 'with his lordship that the favour of God followed sincerity and equally followed every equal degree of sincerity'.[2] Wake had evidently blundered by supporting a candidate involved in reverberations of the Bangorian controversy. Nor was the difficulty wholly removed by Bean's private assurance that not only was he innocent of 'the least tendency towards Arianism', but that he had simply maintained 'that when a man had taken what care he could to inform himself, his conscience must be the immediate rule of his moral actions'; since he 'still conceived that nothing under infallibility can claim an absolute authority over men's consciences'. He informed the Archbishop, however, that he would not offer any reassuring declaration to the clergy.[3]

In this situation therefore Wake wrote letters of explanation and apology to Dr Stanhope and Mr Lunn. To the former he recited how the anticipation of a forthcoming election had

led several of my friends both of the church and the diocese to offer me their thoughts of fitting persons to be chosen for the next convocation. I took it very kindly of them and readily went in with them to consult together of this matter, in which I am in many respects more than ordinarily concerned.

For the diocese they agreed upon the old members and I saw no reason to except against them; so I consented to their proposal and promised all the little countenance I could give to it. For the chapter a junior was mentioned, I believe out of respect to myself, but I refused the motion, and then Dr Bradshaw, as vice-dean, was named (perhaps by myself at first, though that I am not sure of), however not with his knowledge; and it being proposed to him, he acquiesced in what he was told I had approved, and his friends of the chapter had thought proper to offer to him. I think he was to blame in not writing to you immediately about it; I dare say he did not design any affront to you in the omission. As for any settled rules in these cases in your chapter, if there be any such, I may well be excused my ignorance of them, when those who have been long of the body either did not know them or did not inform me of them; for till this day I never heard of them. I conferred freely with all those who were so kind as to apply to me upon this occasion; and what was

[1] Arch. W. Epist. 9, Canterbury IV, f. 179. Stanhope to Wake. 30 March 1722.
[2] *Ibid.* f. 190. Lunn to Wake. 24 April 1722.
[3] *Ibid.* f. 191. Bean to Wake. 26 April 1722.

agreed, was done with the greatest unanimity; and long before any other person was known to offer himself to the chapter's choice; and I question whether but for this accident I should ever have been at all consulted about it. You have here the whole of this matter as near as I can remember it with the utmost exactness.[1]

To Lunn he gave the same account, so far as concerned the diocese; adding that 'as for yourself, you may be assured that I have a very true esteem for you; for though I am in great measure a stranger to your person, yet your good character is not unknown to me'.[2]

Being in the contest, however, the Archbishop did his best to win; offering to send his chaplain, Mr Ott, to help Bean if there should be occasion. Dr Sydall had already taken the precaution to issue a circular letter to the clergy, emphasising his opposition to heterodox opinions.

And lest any jealousy should arise in the minds of our reverend brethren, I do for my part here freely profess to you...that I do not approve of those wild notions and schemes which seem to me not only to strike at all human establishments of religion, but to be hardly consistent with the being of a visible church; and that if I have the honour to be concerned in any business done in convocation, I shall not give in to any measures to unsettle the present good constitution of the Church of England.[3]

When the matter came to an issue, the cathedral chapter proved submissive, but the diocesan clergy, as Wake had experienced previously at Lincoln, were less amenable to episcopal direction. The Archdeacon of Canterbury reported to the Archbishop on 2 May that

Dr Bradshaw was yesterday chosen proctor for our chapter by a great majority. This day came on the election for the diocese, where there was a greater appearance than ever there was upon the like occasion, at least of late. Dr Sydall had 110 votes, Mr Bean and Mr Lunn 59 each; which is one more than Mr Bean had when he carried it last time by 11. The Tories exerted themselves very much, both laity as well as clergy.

Since each candidate challenged some of the votes cast for his opponent, the archdeacon 'adjourned the determination of the case till Monday morning, 9 of the clock, that I may have in the meantime your grace's advice and opinion how to proceed. If in your opinion the votes are equal, I desire to know whether it be not in my power to return which of the two I like best.'[4] Instead Wake ordered a double return to be made; and the convocation would then have to determine the matter. Finally, however, Bean withdrew;

[1] *Ibid.* f. 180. Wake to Stanhope. The Archbishop had presented his kinsman, Edward Wake, to the sixth prebend in 1721.

[2] *Ibid.* f. 176 b. Wake to Lunn, 3 April.

[3] *Ibid.* f. 172. Cooke to Wake. 14 March.

[4] *Ibid.* f. 192. Archdeacon T. Bowers to Wake. 2 May.

and the Bishop of Chichester, as commendatory-archdeacon of Canterbury, reported to the Upper House on 2 November

that the Reverend Mr Charles Bean who was returned jointly with the Reverend Mr Edward Lunn one of the clerks of the convocation for the diocese of Canterbury, together with the Reverend Dr Elias Sydall whose election is not contested, doth not insist upon his return, but desires it may be withdrawn. His Grace the Lord Archbishop of Canterbury, President of the Convocation, with the consent of his brethren, agrees that it be accordingly withdrawn; and His Grace does order that his name be erased out of the list of members of the Lower House of Convocation.

On the same day this decision was reported by the Prolocutor in writing to the Lower House, which thereupon 'nomen Caroli Bean deleri decrevit et Edwardum Lunn membrum hujus Domus rite electum agnovit'.[1]

But there were still difficulties to be smoothed out; for Mr David Jones informed the primate that

at the late election of our proctors, an insinuation was publicly used in court, intimating that those who voted for Mr Lunn (of which number I confess myself to be) acted in opposition to your grace's will. A heavy charge against those who are ready with all cheerfulness to pay that obedience which they have solemnly professed, and whom it most nearly concerns to take effectual care that they become not the marks of their most reverend diocesan's displeasure, if they are not so fortunate as to be the objects of his favour.

Accordingly Jones on his own behalf 'and a great number of my brethren', wrote 'to acquaint your grace that no perverse desire of opposition, but a general dislike of one of the late proctors induced the clergy to attempt having another more agreeable representative in his stead'.[2] Once again, Wake had to pour oil on the troubled waters, assuring his correspondent that

I thought nobody could have raised any such story upon me, or have gained credit to it should anyone have ventured to suggest any such things as you mention in my name. I am sorry to see that even wise and good men (for such I hope most of our brethren are) cannot differ in their opinions in so small a matter with that calmness and charity that one would wish; that their disagreements in the choice of two proctors, both good men and equally qualified in the opinion of their several friends for the trust to be committed to them, should occasion any alteration in their love and esteem for one another; but especially that in consequence of what perhaps they may feel in themselves, they should suspect that all others must have the same impressions upon their minds; for in truth it must be this, if anything, that must have prompted some to suggest and disposed others to believe, what you write of me. Whereas indeed I have no manner of concern in it, nor am at all changed in my esteem of or love to anyone, for what has been done upon this occasion. Would to God my brethren were as heartily friends with one another, as

[1] Convocation Act Books. No. 21. Upper House, f. 24; No. 15. Lower House, f. 84.
[2] Arch. W. Epist. 9. Canterbury IV, f. 200. D. Jones to Wake. 4 May.

I shall still continue to be with all of them; that they would learn by my example not to be the less a friend to any for differing in his vote from him. This is what I signified to Mr Lunn to be my chief concern. This is what I most heartily repeat to you; and desire all my brethren to believe.[1]

Though the episode was indeed a very small storm in a minute teacup, it emphasised the dangers of episcopal intervention in proctorial elections, and suggested that clerical tempers were insufficiently cooled even after a quinquennium since the Bangorian sermon for a sitting convocation to be a risk worth the running.

Notwithstanding the failure of his attempts to secure the union of all the Protestant churches, Wake continued to be much occupied with the affairs of particular foreign churches. Amongst the favourite and most promising was Neuchâtel; the principality of which, after being ruled since 1529 by the ducal family of Orléans-Longueville, had passed to Marie, duchess of Nemours in 1691 on the failure of the male line of its former rulers; and again on her death to Frederick I, king of Prussia in 1707. This diplomatic coup had been achieved by the united efforts of Great Britain, Holland and Austria, then allies in the war of the Spanish Succession, with the support of Sweden, against the pretensions of the prince of Conti championed by France. The Tribunal of the Three Estates of Neuchâtel had declared for Prussia as being Protestant, distant and at that time comparatively insignificant; whereas Louis XIV was Catholic, very near and equally formidable. Furthermore Neuchâtel enjoyed co-citizenship with Berne, Lucerne, Fribourg and Solothurn; and, though passing under the political sway of Prussia, remained ecclesiastically and in sentiment part of the Swiss Protestant league. Accordingly when reports were bruited abroad in 1725 that the king of Prussia intended to dispose of Neuchâtel to the duc de Bourbon, Turrettini wrote in great alarm to Wake to beseech his intervention with George I to prevent such a calamity. He protested that the transaction of 1707, subsequently confirmed by further solemn Acts, had guaranteed 'que le Roi ne pourra jamais donner ce pays en fief ni en appanage à aucun prince de sa maison, mais qu'il sera toujours uni à la couronne et possédé dans toute sa souveraineté, inaliénabilité et indivisibilité'. If Neuchâtel should be alienated to a French prince, its religion would be gravely menaced; on which account more especially, he appealed to the Archbishop

de nous tirer, si cela se peut, de la cruelle inquiétude où nous nous trouvons.... Agissez, au nom de Dieu, dans votre cour et dans celle de Prusse, par tous les moyens que vous jugerez les plus convenables, pour détourner un coup si fâcheux, qui ne menace pas seulement cette ville-là, mais tout le Corps Évangélique de Suisse.[2]

[1] *Ibid.* f. 201. Wake to D. Jones. 7 May.

[2] Arch. W. Epist. 31, f. 200. 7 December 1725.

Wake on his part accordingly set to work with a will at once to secure information, if possible of a reassuring kind, on the matter.

> My desire to have given you full satisfaction concerning the affair of Neufchattel [he replied on 20 January 1725/6] has made me defer, somewhat longer than usual, my acknowledging the favour of yours dated 7 December. I could not learn by any of our great men to whom I discoursed of that affair, that they knew anything certainly of it. And although I have endeavoured it, yet my Lord Townshend has been so taken up in preparing matters for the parliament, which began this day, that I could not have any opportunity hitherto of discoursing with him. This ignorance of our great men here makes me hope there was not so much ground as I feared for the report you heard of the King of Prussia's intention in that particular. However, I will try what I can do to get to the bottom of it; though my seldom going to the court except when business necessarily calls me thither, denies me the opportunities I might otherwise have of knowing more of these matters.[1]

The Archbishop was as good as his word, and secured an interview with the Secretary of State for the Northern Department; of which he reported the result to Turrettini on 2 February.

> I can now with pleasure give you some better account of the several matters you had written to me about, than I have yet done. I have had an opportunity of discoursing fully about them with my Lord Townshend, and am allowed to write his thoughts to you, though I beg his name may not be used. Concerning the report of the King of Prussia's intention to alienate the principality of Neuf-chattell, his lordship knows nothing of it; and verily believes he never had any such design. As the canton of Berne have written to His Majesty concerning it, the king will do all he can to prevent any such alienation, if ever there should be (as he hopes there never will be) any occasion given for it.[2]

It was fortunate therefore, as Wake was assured, that the rumour proved unfounded; and a letter from Turrettini crossing his own, informed him that the King of Prussia had written to the Neuchâtel Council of State to reassure them as to his intentions; though Turrettini was not quite persuaded that there had been no fire to cause the smoke.[3] Moreover, there were other incidents to disturb the confidence of the Swiss; for Neuchâtel was very anxious to preserve all its civic and ecclesiastical rights in close association with other Swiss cities, and differences had arisen which had led the Prussian king to suspend from his office the mayor, M. Chambrier. When therefore a deputation from Neuchâtel was to visit Berlin to discuss the points at issue, Wake was again besought to use the utmost of his influence in their behalf. Not only did he recommend their mission to Jablonski, 'my principal, if not only, friend' in the Prussian capital;[4] but he also made an approach through Princess Caroline. 'I can now with pleasure account to you', he wrote to

[1] Geneva MSS. Inventaire 1569, f. 125. [2] *Ibid.* f. 129.
[3] Arch. W. Epist. 31, f. 203.
[4] Geneva MSS. Inventaire 1569, f. 143. Wake to Turrettini. 13 August.

Turrettini on 27 October 1726, 'one of the steps I took in favour of our friends of Neuff-chatel. I obtained the favour of the Princess of Wales to recommend their delegates and their affair to the Queen of Prussia, and by Her Majesty to the King. The request had its effect; what we desired was done, and by the answer I have reason to hope they may find the benefit of it.'[1] Unfortunately the difficulties were not so easily to be overcome. The deputation on its return home, met with criticism; so that Wake was asked to intervene again. 'I pursued my measures a second time, and so far prevailed, that the delegates were allowed to draw up their own form of what they desired His Majesty to order; and it was approved of and confirmed by the King as they drew it.' Therefore the Archbishop hoped not only that the Neuchâtelois 'are for the present at quiet', but 'will continue so, unless by the ill-management of their affairs they expose themselves to new troubles'.[2] He himself had been likewise handsomely treated by the Prussian sovereigns, having received both a letter of thanks from the Queen and a copy of the official settlement by order of the King. At the same time Jablonski assured him of the cordial and honourable reception accorded to the deputation at Potsdam; where they spoke to the sovereigns personally, received a present from the Queen and were entertained after a most friendly fashion. Moreover their business finally was despatched with expedition: 'hoc pacto evenit ut paucos intra dies res tota ex voto Neocomensium conficeretur'. Indeed even the Swiss divines were contented when they were invited to dine with their majesties; 'caeterum theologis illis Neocomensibus taedia priorum quos hic exegerant mensium, variis posteriorum solatiis, abunde compensata sunt'.[3] In particular Jablonski commended the pacificatory part played by Baron de Ilgen; and finally the dean and pastors of Neuchâtel themselves expressed their thanks formally to Wake on 5 February 1727/8, in a letter full of gratitude; 'et hoc in cumulum gaudii nobis accidit, quod non solum Ordinis et Disciplinae nostrae sed etiam Patriae et Urbis securitati et tranquillitati prospectum fuerit'.[4] It was indeed a case of all's well that ends well. The Archbishop, therefore, sent to Baron Ilgen 'a letter full of thanks on the behalf of our friends of Neuff-chatel as well as on my own account; hoping thereby to bring him to a better disposition to these good men, by imputing what was already done in great measure to his good offices on their behalf, and thanking him for them with a desire of the continuance of them'.[5] With proper modesty, Wake congratulated Turrettini on the outcome of the negotiation.

[1] *Ibid.* f. 145. 27 October. [2] *Ibid.* f. 149. 31 January 1726/7.
[3] Rawlinson MSS. A. 275, f. 90. Jablonski to Wake. 13 December 1727.
[4] *Ibid.* f. 100. The dean and pastors of Neuchâtel to Wake.
[5] Geneva MSS. Inventaire 1569, f. 149. Wake to Turrettini. 31 January 1726/7.

Colonel du Bourgay, our envoy at Berlin, assures me by a late letter that the court there has been very kind (the queen in particular) to the delegates of Neuffchattel, and that they are returned well satisfied both with their reception and success. It was very fortunate that I prevailed with Her Majesty to interest herself in their affair, which in part helped to bring it to so good an end.[1]

Much more intractable were the persecution and oppression suffered by Protestants in several parts of Europe, notably by the Vaudois in Savoy, the Huguenots in France and the Reformed in Poland and the Palatinate; in behalf of whom the primate's diplomatic influence no less than his financial aid were sought. The acrobatic diplomacy of the King of Sicily (for this royal title had been accorded to Victor Amadeus of Savoy by the allies for his services during the Spanish Succession war) brought little relief to the Piedmontese Protestants, to whichever side of the European balance of power his tortuous course inclined. On 6 January 1718 Turrettini appealed to Wake to ensure the continuance of the financial aid given during the reigns of William III and of Anne to the Vaudois pastors and schoolmasters, without which their very existence would be jeopardised. 'Cependant il serait bien triste que, faute de quelque petite subvention, on vît périr des Églises si vénérables par leur antiquité et par leur piété; et que nous opposons si utilement aux controversistes de l'Église Romaine, lorsqu'ils nous reprochent la nouveauté de nos Églises.'[2] The Archbishop thereupon busied himself to secure a renewal of the royal bounty; and together with the Bishop of Gloucester, the Lord Almoner, and Mr J. Chetwynd arranged for the distribution of the promised £500 per annum for the period of eighteen months ending at Michaelmas 1719. This aggregate sum of £750 was divided between thirteen ministers and thirteen schoolmasters in the Piedmontese valleys and seven ministers and seven schoolmasters living in exile in Germany.[3]

But the existence of these Protestant outposts depended not only upon foreign aid but also upon the benevolence of their royal master; and renewed complaints reached Wake again in 1724 of further oppressions inflicted upon them.

Our poor brethren of the Vallées have again renewed their complaints [he reported to Turrettini on 29 June] and intimated their fears to our ministers. I have just received a melancholy letter and memorial from them; which I shall make the best use of I can to their advantage. But, the truth is, we seem too much unconcerned in these matters; and I have nobody to help me in my application either to the king or court. Our bishops hold no correspondence abroad; nor seem to trouble themselves about anything beyond our four seas.[4]

The Vaudois alleged that the privileges granted to them by the intercession of Great Britain and the States General in 1694 were being now consistently

[1] Geneva MSS. Inventaire 1569, f. 155. 18 October 1727.
[2] Arch. W. Epist. 31, f. 54.
[3] *Ibid.* ff. 217–18.
[4] Geneva MSS. Inventaire 1569, f. 117.

violated; and that new oppression was being added in that they were being compelled to observe the principal festivals of the Roman Church.[1] Accordingly the Archbishop laid the matter before the Duke of Newcastle, Secretary of State for the Southern Department; who replied on 6 July, that

upon what Your Grace was pleased to mention to me concerning the Vaudois, I have ordered copies to be made of the letters and papers which have been transmitted hither from Mr Molesworth at Turin, as likewise of the answers which have been returned to him, in relation to that affair; and herewith send them enclosed for Your Grace's perusal, as containing the whole of what has passed upon that subject. You will please to observe that the Vaudois have not yet transmitted such a particular state of their grievances as they proposed to do, and which will be necessary in order to their obtaining such relief as His Majesty is desirous to procure for them. However I have in the meantime taken occasion to talk with the Marquis de Cortanzo, and have in His Majesty's name so strongly recommended to him the case of these poor people, that he has assured me he will write to his court in their behalf and use his best endeavours to get their grievances redressed.[2]

In addition to these representations by George I, the King of Sweden sent a formal letter on 3 August, protesting alike on the ground of right and of friendship that the Protestants should be justly treated.[3] To such powerful diplomatic pressure the King of Sardinia (for Victor Amadeus had exchanged Sicily for Sardinia in 1720) returned the soft answer designed to turn away wrath. On 2 January 1724/5, Wake reported the result of his endeavours to Turrettini.

Though I have not troubled you so frequently of late with my letters, yet I have not been unmindful of the affairs you have been pleased to recommend to me. As for that of the poor Vaudois I have followed it as much as I could with his grace the duke of Newcastle, in whose province they lie; and had the pleasure to receive from his grace the Marquis de Cortance's letter relating to their affairs, a copy of which I shall subjoin to you. I hope we shall get their rights in time secured against the new body of laws by which they were, I doubt designedly, infringed.

Certainly so far as words could carry conviction, the marquis' letter was wholly reassuring. He informed Newcastle on 26 November 1724

que l'intention du roi, mon maître, n'a jamais été d'ôter au Vaudois aucun des privilèges, ni retracter aucune grâce, qui leur ont été accordées par ses édits ou par ceux de ses prédécesseurs, pendant qu'ils continueront dans la fidelité et zèle qu'ils doivent à leur souverain. Qu'independement même des traités et de l'intercession de Sa Majesté Britannique, pour laquelle le Roi son maître se fera un plaisir d'avoir tous les égards possibles, il regarde les Vaudois avec un œil de bonté et de protection, et il les aime comme des fidèles sujets. Dans cette disposition il veut députer un ministre pour les écouter, et qu'il doive même se porter sur les lieux, s'il est nécessaire, pour reconnoitre les choses, en manière que leurs privilèges, et ce que

[1] Arch. W. Epist. 31, f. 216. [2] *Ibid.* f. 215. [3] *Ibid.* f. 184.

leur a été accordé par l'Édit du 1694 leur soit conservé, et pour qu'en même tems, ce qui de leur côté pourrait être abus soit corrigé, y ayant des choses, qui se sont glissés par des abus et non point par des usages legitimes, continuels, et paisibles.[1]

Notwithstanding these elaborate assurances, the Archbishop was too cautious to suppose that he had heard the last of the Vaudois' grievances; and even their formal letter of thanks for his intercession and financial help, on 16 June 1726, besought his continued protection and patronage since all their griefs still remained.[2]

I am sorry the King of Sardinia has formed a new design against his Protestant subjects of the valley of Pragela [he wrote again to Turrettini on 31 January 1726/7]. It is not yet known what party that prince will take. If he accedes to the treaty of Hanover and our court stands well with him, we may then be in a condition to do them some service. If otherwise, I doubt our interest will be but small with him. We shall soon see what turn his affairs will take. I believe our envoy at the court of Turin has general orders to do those poor people all the services he can.[3]

Once again, therefore, Wake approached Newcastle

to represent their case to the Marquis de Cortanzo, the Sardinian envoy here, and to desire him in the king's name to write to his court on their behalf; which he has promised to do. Mr Hedges our envoy at Turin has already presented a memorial to the king on their behalf, and done all he can for their service. He is ordered to continue his good offices and press their relief in the king's name. I have prayed Monsr Hop, the Dutch envoy, to write to his masters on the same account, and to desire the States to join with our king in demanding their relief at the court of Turin. I have gotten some men of great character and interest in Holland to be written to on the same account, and to engage the States to comply with what their envoy recommends to them. And by this post I have prayed the same thing of Monsr Dayrolles, who manages our affairs at the Hague. May God give a blessing to all our endeavours in so good a cause.[4]

But the condition of the Vaudois did not improve when in 1731 Victor Amadeus II gave place to his son Charles Emmanuel III. Instead, further persecutions were their lot; and Wake succeeded (as he reported to Turrettini) in persuading Queen Caroline to place to his credit

in the Bank of England a £1000 sterling to be paid by me into such proper hands as I should think convenient for their present assistance upon their coming cold and destitute among you. This charity of Her Majesty's she does not think fit to be made public; being rather desirous to do such acts of mercy than to make a noise of them, yet was willing to intrust the knowledge and management of it to you. I am therefore ready to answer such sums as you shall draw upon me for this purpose not exceeding one thousand pounds in the whole.[5]

[1] Geneva MSS. Inventaire 1569, f. 121.
[2] Arch. W. Epist. 31, f. 219.
[3] Geneva MSS. Inventaire 1569, f. 149.
[4] *Ibid.* f. 151. 13 April 1727.
[5] *Ibid.* f. 171. Wake to Turrettini. February 1731.

The generosity of the Queen was the more noteworthy since the Archbishop's health had not permitted him to solicit personally but only by letter. Furthermore she promised to urge George II to use his efforts 'for their deliverance either from the whole or at least from so much of their persecution as he can procure for them'.[1] It was regrettable therefore that upon occasion the beneficiaries did not appreciate the nature of the services done to them by their friends; and Wake complained bitterly to Turrettini of their ingratitude towards Mr Chetwynd. 'As for the Vaudois churches in Germany, if they do not hurt themselves they are in no danger here', he wrote on 3 February 1729/30.

Their allowances from the Crown are continued, and I may venture to promise will be duly paid....But their misfortune and the danger they are in is this. Mr Chetwynd who was our envoy at Turin and has in truth been a zealous friend to and advocate for those churches both in the Valleys and in Germany, has hitherto received their pensions and returned them to them without either charge or trouble, only upon the account of charity and the kindness he has had for them. This has saved them money for receipts and returns, besides the care he has had to get their money from the Exchequer. For what reason I know not, but they have desired to exchange their receiver and to employ some other person in their affairs. Mr Chetwynd I doubt takes this unkindly of them; though I have done all I could to make this matter easy with him. I know not where to find out another person to do their business either as carefully or charitably as he has done it. Their salaries are paid by my Lord Chetwynd, a relation of Mr Chetwynd, to their use. By this means they are sure duly to receive them by Mr Chetwynd's hands; but if he gives up their business, a new man will be perhaps at a loss how to get them paid. So that they will certainly put themselves under great difficulties by the change of their agent. My humble advice is that they should write a letter signed by all who are concerned, to pray Mr Chetwynd to continue to act for them, as he has done these many years past, and to go on in the same method they have been wont to do. I will do my part to dispose him to it, and hope I shall be able to prevail with him. If I cannot, I am afraid what the consequences may be. Their allowances are all paid up to Michaelmas last (excepting what was in arrears from the late king) so that they will have no cause to complain.[2]

The intractable nature of the Vaudois' situation was illustrated by the fact that the two latest extant letters from Wake to Turrettini, those of February 1731, were entirely devoted to their fresh persecutions and to the distribution of Queen Caroline's munificent bounty.

If the good will shown by archbishop, king and ministers in seeking the relief of persecuted Protestants was not matched by the success of their efforts, this was due to political circumstances beyond their control. 'I have your last letter with two enclosed from Monsr du Plan, one to myself, the other to His Majesty', Wake wrote to Turrettini on 2 January 1724/5.

[1] *Ibid.* f. 173. February 1731.

[2] Geneva MSS. Inventaire 1569, f. 168.

I immediately communicated both to my Lord Townshend, our Prime Minister of State; and got his lordship to read them both. His lordship assured me that the king needed no representations to put him in mind of the sufferings or dangers of the poor Protestants in all parts; that he had taken all the care he could to get some mitigation to those in France; but that he received little encouragement from their ministers to think he should prevail much on their behalf; that however Mr Walpole, his ambassador at Paris, had directions to watch all opportunities of doing them service, and that our ministers did the same with the French ambassador here. I am satisfied this is true, and that the king has a very deep sense of the persecutions abroad; and is exceedingly concerned for what has passed at Thorn before his letter could get to the King of Poland. Where he has, by treaties, a right to interpose, I am persuaded he will do it vigorously on the behalf of our brethren; where he has none (as I think in France he has none) he can only order his ministers at home and abroad, to do them all the service they are able, and this I am assured he has done; and you may give Monsr du Plan the like assurance. Yesterday, being New-year day, I waited on the king with the bishops of England, and at their head recommended the case and protection of our persecuted brethren in all our names to him. His Majesty seemed to receive what was said very well; so that you see we do all we can on their behalf.[1]

The sufferings of the Huguenots indeed, like the persecutions of the Vaudois, were ever with the Archbishop.

Concerning the Galerians whom you mention in your letter [he reported again to Turrettini on 20 January], I have had a long discourse with Mr Walpole, our envoy to the court of France, who is at present with us. He assures me he has concerted the best measures he could for their service with the Dutch envoy, and used his utmost endeavours with the French ministers, particularly with the Bishop of Fréjus. All he can yet get is an intimation that if a particular person were desired, such an one's liberty might be obtained; but that there could be no hope of a general release.[2]

Further endeavours to secure a promise of release for those Protestants sent to serve in the Mediterranean galleys produced no better assurances.

As to the freedom desired to be obtained for our brethren in the Gallies, I had a long conference with our ambassador, Mr Walpole, concerning them [he informed Turrettini on 3 February]. He assures me he has done all that in him lay with the Bishop of Fréjus on their behalf; that the bishop promised to try what could be done, but declared his opinion that though any one or two might be released that His Majesty should desire, yet he believed it impossible to get them all discharged. Nevertheless I am promised that he shall have the king's directions to solicit for them all upon his return to Paris, and do all he can to procure their liberty. It is the opinion of our ministers that though no liberty or indulgence will be granted to our brethren in France, yet the new edict against them will not be put any longer into strict execution; and that for that our minister will also use his best endeavours.[3]

[1] Geneva MSS. Inventaire 1569, f. 121. [2] *Ibid.* f. 125. [3] *Ibid.* f. 129.

In these hard circumstances Wake when appealed to directly in behalf of individual victims could only advise emigration as the price of release. To M. Marc Guitton, who had reported the arrest in a private house at Alais of seventeen Huguenots, who had been imprisoned at Nîmes and five of whom had been sentenced to perpetual slavery in the galleys, and also the compulsory education of the children of Huguenots in Roman Catholic schools, he wrote on 8 April 1725:

Monsieur, Le triste état de nos pauvres frères en France me donne beaucoup de douleur. Si on continue la persécution sur le pied qu'on semble vouloir poursuivre, je ne vois aucun remède contre les attentats de leurs ennemis que de sortir du royaume et de sauver leurs enfans, s'il est possible, de la perversion.... Je ne sais pas si on peut échapper de leurs mains par un tel exil volontaire; mais si un tel poursuit en perdant ses biens sauve la vie et l'âme, on choisirait plutôt d'abandonner tout ce qu'on possède dans un pays d'idolatrie et de persécution, que de vivre ou sans aucun exercice de la religion ou dans un tel exercice qu'est contraire à l'honneur de Dieu et à la conscience de celui qui fait semblance de se joindre à un cult au dehors, qu'il haisse dans son cœur et son esprit.[1]

One particular case, that of M. François Baumet, No. 3778, an actual galley-slave, condemned to several years of that service for his religion at Marseilles, was brought directly to the Archbishop's notice in a series of letters from the sufferer; to whom Wake could only reply by setting forth in full the difficulties of acceding to his request for the good offices of the English king to procure his release.

Monsieur, J'ai les deux lettres que vous m'avez addressées. La première n'est pas venue à mes mains avant que le Roi s'était allé à Hanover, où je crois qu'il continuera pour six mois à venir; de sorte que je n'aurai aucun moyen de lui en parler de votre affaire pour le présent. Mais s'il était ici, je n'oserais lui communiquer votre requête; sachant qu'il ne se mêlerait pas dans un tel affair. Vous êtes un particulier; inconnu au roi; il n'y a rien de singulier dans votre cas sur lequel on pourrait fonder un demand auprès la cour de France pour votre delivérance. Vous n'êtes pas un de ses sujets, ni establi ni naturalisé dans ce royaume. Enfin il n'y a rien de distinguer votre cas de cel d'aucun autre de vos compagnons dans l'esclavage où vous êtes misérablement tombé. Si le roi jugerait à propos, comme il a fait autrefois, d'intercéder pour la liberté de tous ceux qui sont dans les galères pour leur religion, ce serait une action digne de la clémence et la charité d'un prince Chrétien. Mais d'engager ses intérêts et d'emploier ses bons offices pour une seule personne—comme vous, c'est ce que le roi ne fera jamais, et que je n'ose même proposer à lui. Comme je suis fort sensible de ce que vous souffriez dans les galères, je voudrais de tout mon cœur vous rendre le service que vous désirez, s'il y avait la moindre espérance du monde d'obtenir la faveur du roi dans votre cas. À present je ne puis faire d'autre chose que de prier notre bon Dieu de vous donner de la

[1] Arch. W. Epist. 30, n.f.

patience de vous soumettre à sa volonté; et de vous recompenser mille fois dans l'autre monde ce que vous souffrez pour la vérité de son Évangile dans celui-ci.[1]

The unhappy victim acknowledged both the receipt of this letter and the justice of its contention; and replied by sending a petition for transmission to George I for the release of nineteen prisoners condemned to the galleys. But, as the Archbishop had explained to Turrettini, the prospect of securing liberty for a company was even less promising than intercession on behalf of an individual; and in the last resort he could do no more than offer the assurance of his prayers and counsel patience under affliction. For the relief of those who accepted exile and came to England, however, the King granted an annual sum of £15,000, of which £12,000 was earmarked for the laity and £3000 for ministers.[2]

Amongst the subjects of religious strife, the Protestants of Poland presented a problem of peculiar complexity. Russia, having evacuated Poland in 1713 under the terms of the treaty of Adrianople, found a pretext in the internal divisions of the country to return in 1716; and in the following year the settlement of differences between the contending parties included an article defining the position of the Dissenters, as the Protestant minority had come to be called. By Article IV of the treaty of Warsaw the restoration of old Protestant churches was forbidden, and the destruction of those erected between 1704–9 authorised. Persons continuing to use these churches for worship were liable to a fine for the first offence, imprisonment for the second and banishment for a further transgression. Moreover, other things being equal, civil and military offices were to be granted to Roman Catholics in preference to Protestants. The discriminatory nature of these conditions against the Dissenters was obvious; and Prussia, as a self-constituted protector, sought to enlist the support of Russia in a joint *démarche* to safeguard the position both of Protestant and Orthodox subjects of the Polish king. Jablonski was particularly anxious for this co-operation, but the Russian tsar steadily refused to accept a formal policy of joint intervention. Thus the position of the Protestants deteriorated as the provisions of the treaty were put into operation; and diplomatic efforts were made to enlist the support in their behalf of the chief Protestant powers, Prussia, Sweden, Great Britain and the United Provinces. But without Russia nothing practical could be done, as Bernsdorff insisted to Wake on 10 October 1720, since the Roman clergy were too powerful.[3] In these circumstances it was little surprising, though altogether deplorable, that at Thorn in July 1724, a Protestant mob should have broken into the grounds of the Jesuit college there and desecrated the chapel. This *émeute* provoked condign punishment; fifteen persons,

[1] Arch. W. Epist. 30, f. 246. [2] Arch. W. Epist. 27, f. 129. [3] Arch. W. Epist. 31, f. 291.

including the mayor of Thorn, being sentenced to death, and all save one executed. In view of Wake's regular correspondence with Jablonski, it was to be expected that long and sombre accounts of the persecution which followed the Thorn 'massacre' should reach Lambeth from Berlin, no less than from Turrettini and the Swiss Reformed.[1] A personal protest, indeed, was addressed by the Kings of Prussia and Denmark to the King of Poland; whilst George I had already written to Augustus before the episode.[2] In September 1725 an article was included in the treaty of Hanover between Great Britain, France and Prussia; by which the signatory powers, as guarantors of the treaty of Oliva,

> s'engagent d'employer leurs offices le plus efficacement qu'ils pourront, pour faire réparer ce qui aurait pu être fait de contraire au dit traité d'Oliva, et pour cet effet, les dites Majestés s'instruiront de concert par leurs ministres en Pologne des infractions qui auraient pu être faites au dit traité d'Oliva, et des moyens d'y remédier d'une manière qui assure entièrement la tranquillité publique contre les dangers auxquelles elle serait exposée, si un traité aussi solennel que celui d'Oliva souffrait quelque atteinte.

It needed little insight to perceive that this article was more magniloquent than practical; and the position of Great Britain was weakened by the circumstance that it had not been a signatory of the treaty of Oliva, of which together with the other powers it now constituted itself a guarantor. Accordingly Wake in the same month of September could only inform Turrettini that 'we are still uncertain what turn the affair of Thorn will take. Just before the King left England, I got all the bishops in a body with me, and by an unanimous consent, I in their names recommended the case of those poor Reformed to him. He took our addresses very kindly and seemed resolved to do all he could for their relief.'[3] Nor did the treaty itself do much to relieve them; for in 1727 when the Archbishop's chaplain, Mr Ott, visited Berlin, he sent a melancholy account of their continued oppression. Although the degree of persecution differed in various parts of Poland, the general picture was one of continuous pressure and discrimination.[4] Not until the treaty of 1730 between Prussia and Russia was agreement reached that the two sovereigns should pledge themselves 'to protect their co-religionists, i.e. the Greek Orthodox and Protestants living in Poland and in the Grand Duchy of Lithuania, to defend them and to ensure through good offices and representations made to the King and the Republic that the Dissenters shall enjoy the same privileges, liberties and rights as they had done of old, in

[1] Rawlinson MSS. A. 275, f. 90; Arch. W. Epist. 31, ff. 189, 192, 297.
[2] Arch. W. Epist. 31, f. 274.
[3] Geneva MSS. Inventaire 1569, f. 134. 15 September 1725.
[4] Rawlinson MSS. A. 275, f. 46.

matters secular as well as spiritual, and which were later curtailed and denied them'.[1] But these issues of *haute politique* lay beyond the province of an archbishop. All that Wake could do was to succour the Polish Protestants by financial aid so far as possible; whilst the English king provided a grant for the education of four of their candidates for the ministry, two at Berlin and two at Frankfort. The treaty of 1730 governed the co-protectorship of Prussia and Russia until the first partition of Poland.

A problem of almost equal difficulty and delicacy arose concerning the position and rights of the Reformed churches of the Palatinate, whose fortunes followed too faithfully the changing political and military balance of power in the Empire. The Reformed church had been introduced by the Elector Frederick III and had maintained an uneasy foothold until the outbreak of the Thirty Years War in 1618. By the Peace of Westphalia in 1648 its position had been restored, except that the Lutherans in the Palatinate had been granted the rights possessed by them in 1624. During the long wars against France after 1689, however, both the religious and political situation had undergone several vicissitudes. With the French invasion and occupation came the supremacy of the Roman Catholic faith; but the treaty of Ryswick in 1697 had once more restored the Reformed church to its former position, though with the provision that the Roman Catholic faith should continue in its present state, despite the protest of the Protestant princes of the empire against this clause. After the outbreak of the Spanish Succession war, the tide of French arms and influence again flowed into the Rhineland, until the King of Prussia in 1705 issued his Declaration of Religion which ensured to the Reformed entire freedom of religion and also five-sevenths of the ecclesiastical property and revenues. Thus the religious problem in the Palatinate as in Poland was tripartite; with Reformed, Lutheran and Roman Catholic in the west corresponding to Orthodox, Roman Catholic and Protestant in the east; and the Peace of Westphalia occupying a similar position as the safeguard of the Reformed to the treaty of Oliva in regard to the Dissenters. Moreover the balance of power within the Empire was uncertain; and the Emperor Charles VI had little occasion for gratitude to his Protestant allies, Great Britain, the United Provinces, Prussia and Hanover for their desertion of his cause in the Peace of Utrecht. When therefore Roman Catholicism once more assumed an aggressive policy in the Palatinate the Reformed churches were alarmed. They protested against such discriminatory actions as the diversion of part of their revenues to Roman Catholic congregations, the denial of their right to teach the Heidelberg catechism, and especially their exclusion from the nave of the Church of the Holy Ghost in Heidelberg,

[1] L. R. Lewitter, 'Peter the Great and the Polish Dissenters', in *The Slavonic Review*, XXXIII, no. 80, December 1954.

which they had enjoyed since 1618 and which was itself the symbol of their relationship with the Roman Catholics, who used the choir of the same church for their services. With such an inflammatory situation and in view of his close correspondence with the Swiss Reformed churches, Wake could not hope to avoid being drawn into the affairs of the Palatinate.

He realised that the chief means of helping these Reformed churches was by diplomatic agreement between the principal Protestant powers and the Empire. Accordingly when the King's Speech at the opening of parliament on 23 November 1719 affirmed that 'such a foundation is laid by our late treaties for an union amongst other great Protestant powers as will very much tend to the security of our holy religion', the Archbishop moved that a clause might be added to the address of thanks from the House of Lords 'to acknowledge His Majesty's seasonable interposition in favour of the Protestants abroad'. The house therefore agreed to an expression of 'the deep sense which we have of Your Majesty's seasonable interposition for the poor persecuted Protestants, and we humbly beseech Your Majesty that you would be pleased to continue your powerful protection and offices in favour of them'.[1]

Notwithstanding this action, adjurations continued to pour in upon Wake from the Swiss Reformed to engage the King and his administration further in the matter, as also from other Protestant quarters. In reply to M. Wassenaer at The Hague, who had written to Lord Sunderland also, pressing for joint representations of Great Britain and the United Provinces in February 1720, the primate observed:

J'ai communiqué à my lord Sunderland la lettre que vous m'avez fait l'honneur de m'écrire. J'avais tâché auparavant de convaincre ce seigneur qu'il serait pour l'intérêt de nos frères du Palatinat et même pour l'avantage de la Religion Réformée en général, de procurer une addresse du parlement au Roi pour le prier de soutenir les droits de ces pauvres gens sur le pied du Traité de Westphalie, et de l'assurer de leur assistance pour rendre ce traité efficace et inviolable. My lord Sunderland entra promptement dans les mêmes sentiments, et me promit de consulter avec des autres ministres là-dessus, et de me communiquer le résult de leurs délibérations. Enfin comme on attend bientôt une réponse favorable de l'Empereur et une résolution de l'Électeur Palatin conforme aux demandes des princes Protestants, on a resolu de procéder comme les circonstances des affaires requireront; et de faire en sorte que le parlement en fera une addresse au Roi pour obtenir effectuellement ce qu'il a demandé de l'Électeur en faveur de ses sujets Réformés, si cela sera nécessaire, ou de lui rendre leurs remerciements pour ce qu'il aura fait pour l'obtenir, si cette affaire sera fini à la satisfaction des princes intercesseurs.[2]

The ensuing parliamentary session of 1720, however, was fully occupied with the Peerage Bill; and the nation was thrown into confusion thereafter by

[1] Cobbett, *Parliamentary History*, vol. VII, cols. 603–4. [2] Arch. W. Epist. 31, f. 249 (2).

the South Sea Bubble scandal. Wake however was able to report in June to Turrettini concerning the Protestant cause that

great endeavours had been used, and much time fruitlessly spent to bring our ministry into a hearty resolution of engaging the parliament to appear on the king's behalf in the securing of it abroad. A friend of yours applied to Monsieur Bernsdorff and the other Germans of note, and first brought them to be hearty in it. The same person then, seeing the design drawn out in time, resolved to propose it himself to the king, and had the good fortune to engage His Majesty in it.... This has so strengthened the king's authority abroad that by the last letters and memorials from Vienna, my lord Cadogan does prepare us to expect that the emperor will do the Protestants justice; and that we shall see the treaty of Westphalia in this respect better enforced than it ever has been hitherto.[1]

But even when the emperor was amenable, the elector Palatine presented difficulties, being surrounded, as Wake affirmed, by a 'Jesuitical, or even popish, faction', which meant that 'the work of doing justice to our oppressed brethren goes very heavily with the Palatine ministers'.[2] So in the address of the House of Lords in reply to the King's Speech on 8 December 1720, hopes could rise no higher than to 'acknowledge with the greatest gratitude His Majesty's care and endeavours for the security and support of the Protestant religion'.[3] Furthermore, and even more distressingly, the Palatine Protestants were divided against each other; for the Lutherans laid claim to part of the revenues enjoyed by the Reformed; and in this matter George I, as a Lutheran, was antipathetic to the Reformed churches.

I cannot tell whether I had before informed you [Wake wrote to Turrettini on 8 January 1723/4] that I had discoursed with His Majesty about the demand made by the Lutherans of the Palatinate of the seventh part of the revenue of the Reformed. I found His Majesty prepossessed with an opinion that they ought to be allowed it. I endeavoured to satisfy him of their inability to part with it....Since that we have had several applications made to the King, by the ministers of the Protestant powers at Ratisbon, for a collection to be begun here and carried on through all the other reformed countries of Europe; and the sum which shall be gathered to be kept as a perpetual fund, not to be lessened; and that with the interest thereof a provision shall be made for the stipends of ministers and schoolmasters in the Palatinate and some other places where it shall be found necessary. I cannot yet discover how this comes to be so much opposed, as I find it is underhand. For though I recommended it as far as I thought proper to His Majesty at Baron Wrisberg's request, above a year ago, yet I found the King not ready to embrace the motion then, and none of our ministry seem willing yet to encourage it.[4]

[1] Geneva MSS. Inventaire 1569, f. 73. 29 June 1720.
[2] *Ibid.* f. 89. 20 February 1720/1.
[3] Cobbett, *Parliamentary History*, vol. VII, col. 678.
[4] Geneva MSS. Inventaire 1569, f. 113. 11 February 1723/4.

Indeed Wrisberg had been so incautious as to state that 'what he had done in that affair was all of his own private motion; but that as a public minister he had no instructions to favour it, but rather the contrary'.[1] The Archbishop therefore was compelled to avow on 31 January 1726/7 that

I have done what I can to promote the collection so long and greatly desired by the plenipotentiaries at Ratisbon and the ministers of the Palatinate. I cannot discover where it sticks; but I find the King no way disposed to it, and those who have the chief power in these matters, much against it; so that at present nothing can be done in it.[2]

In fairness to the reluctance of king and ministry to order royal briefs for such collections, it must be remembered that Great Britain was regarded by many foreign Protestants as an almost inexhaustible treasury of alms and charity. Between 1715 and 1717, for example, the Rev. Krystian Sitkoswki of Leszno collected in England about £5000 for the Bohemian Brethren and in 1717 also, £10,000 was given to the Protestants of Poland and Hungary; whilst the Reformed churches of Lithuania collected in Scotland by 1720 about £4000. There was justice in Wake's remonstrance to Turrettini that England was a milch cow which must not be overdrained.

The many public undertakings that have been set on foot among us, and the large subscriptions of our bishops and clergy to them, render us almost uncapable of coming into any collections for our friends abroad. The propagation of the gospel in foreign parts; the promotion of Christian knowledge and piety at home; our charity schools; our new scheme for a college to be erected and endowed at Bermudas; our proposal for the maintenance of four bishops in America, to settle and take care of the churches there; these, with some other the like establishments, are a large and standing tax upon us. Our charges to proselytes are heavy and yet do not answer their needs or expectations; so that indeed it is not an easy matter to persuade men, who are thus already burdened, to take any new load upon themselves. Many are the applications that are made to us for help to erect churches in Germany; one at this time for a church at Durkheim; all which considered, I doubt very little will be gotten here for that you mention; nothing being given on these occasions by the government; little, if anything, by the laity; and the bishops and clergy loaded beyond what they are well able to bear.[3]

In view of the difficulties of meeting the demands of persecuted foreign Protestants, it might seem indeed a work of supererogation to encourage proselytism from the Roman Church by offering rewards for conversion to Protestantism. Yet this, as the Archbishop observed, constituted another call on English generosity. In 1717 George I gave the sum of £400 per annum to support proselytes from Rome, and Commissioners for Relieving Poor

[1] *Ibid.* f. 117. 20 June 1724. [2] *Ibid.* f. 149.
[3] *Ibid.* f. 141. 21 June 1726. Arch. W. Epist. 25, f. 87. Wake to Antistes of Zürich. 13 September 1718.

Proselytes were established, of which the archbishop and the lord chamberlain were permanent members, together with other lords appointed by His Majesty. The difficulties of such a trust were evident: the examination of alleged converts to ascertain the genuineness of their change of faith; the problems of former priests whose conversion to Protestantism was followed by their marriage; the selection of suitable beneficiaries amongst so many applicants and the question of their continued supervision. In 1721 therefore Wake drew up rules for the guidance of the commission; providing for two examiners, one English and one French, of each candidate; for the naming of some commissioners whose presence should be necessary to constitute a quorum; for 'particular care [to] be had not to encourage any proselytes that were ecclesiastics (especially Regulars) who marry before they apply to the commissioners or without their consent afterwards'; and for ensuring 'that all allowances made to any proselytes be for a time limited, that so they may be obliged in that time to apply themselves to some business to keep themselves; the commissioners to judge of any exceptions to this rule but to be very cautious in departing from it'.[1] Despite these precautions and the compilation of a lengthy questionnaire for the interrogation of applicants, difficulties multiplied and the task was singularly unrewarding. A good many conversions proved transient; impostors too easily deceived the commissioners; and vagabond refugees of no religious conviction secured grants. In August 1722 Wake confessed to Henry Newman, secretary of the commission, that 'I am out of all hope of doing any good in the business of the proselytes; you may try on a little longer, but you will be forced to drop it in the end'.[2] The other commissioners declined to accept this advice; so the Archbishop counselled them to reduce the number of candidates receiving grants to between thirty and forty; to avoid absolutely the subvention of monks, who, 'except some of the order of the Benedictines, are looked upon abroad as the scum of the Church of Rome'; and to limit the meetings of the commissioners to three or four each year. The commission accordingly decided to reduce the total number of persons helped to fifty, and to institute a more searching enquiry into each case; but even so the Archbishop's prophecy was realised. In June 1728 the commissioners resigned their trust; and in the following September the primate, the bishop of London and the lord chancellor formally wound up the commission. Its good intentions had not been fulfilled in practice; and other needs pressed more urgently upon the bishops and clergy, as Wake had impressed upon Turrettini.

Foremost amongst the concerns of the church were the manifold good

[1] Arch. W. Epist. 27, f. 108.

[2] *Ibid.* f. 141; cf. Add. MSS. 47030, f. 22. Newman to Lord Perceval; L. W. Cowie, *Henry Newman*, chap. VI, for a fuller account of the Protestant proselytes (London, 1956).

works both at home and abroad undertaken by the twin societies, the Society for the Propagation of the Gospel and the Society for Promoting Christian Knowledge, with both of which Wake was intimately and continuously concerned. In his capacity as annually elected president of the S.P.G. he was much involved in the perennial problem of the provision of bishops for the plantations. Towards the end of Queen Anne's reign indeed this much-canvassed project had seemed at last on the verge of realisation; for in 1712 a committee of the S.P.G. drew up and the Society approved, a project for the settlement of four bishops, two on the mainland at Burlington, New Jersey, and Williamsburg, Virginia, respectively, and two for the islands, in Barbados and Jamaica, with salaries of £1000 per annum for the continental bishops and £1500 for those of the islands, and with detailed proposals for raising the total sum required of £5000 per annum. On 27 March 1713 the archbishop of York was deputed to present the scheme to Her Majesty; and just over a year later a second representation was laid before her, upon receiving which she assured the archbishop and the bishop of London (as they reported to the Society on 21 May 1714) that 'she would direct the same to be referred to the proper persons to consider and make report thereof'.[1] Unfortunately her death in that year put an end to the promising overture; but the Society's hopes received a fillip by the legacy of £1000 from Archbishop Tenison, to be applied as to one-half for the provision of bishops for the North American mainland and the other half to the islands of the West Indies. Armed with this bequest, the Society on 17 June 1715 requested Wake, Archbishop Dawes of York, the Earl of Clarendon and the Bishops of London, Norwich and Bristol to wait upon George I with the former representation of the need for, and suggested provision of, four bishops; and the deputation duly received from His Majesty an assurance that he 'would favour and encourage the pious designs and undertakings of the Society'.[2]

Nothing came of this move, however; but when Gibson was translated from Lincoln to London in 1723 and thereby found himself burdened with responsibility for oversight of the plantations, he lost no time in enquiring into the basis and nature of this charge and in projecting a means of relief by the despatch of suffragan bishops there. His scheme was more modest than that of the Society; for it embraced two bishops only, one for the mainland and one for the islands. The need was evident, both from the standpoint of the colonial churches, which lacked the means of confirmation of the laity and ordination and visitation of the clergy, and from that of Protestantism generally in view of the French establishment of a bishopric at Quebec. None of these considerations however moved the Whig administration,

[1] Arch. W. Epist. 15, n.f. Minutes of S.P.G. 1712–14.

[2] *Ibid.* 21 May and 17 June 1715.

which was better aware than its episcopal counsellors of the volume and intensity of opposition on the part of the colonists to the plan. Nor when two non-juring bishops appeared in North America to increase the confusion of Anglican congregations there by offering irregular episcopal ministrations, could Gibson prevail with ministers of state to send out orthodox and loyal bishops. Once more he approached Wake in 1725 to ascertain 'how far this incident might be improved to the forwarding the design of sending bishops of our own to the Plantations', as he did also the Duke of Newcastle.[1] About this time indeed the Archbishop seemed optimistic of success; for in writing to Turrettini of the missionary activities both of S.P.G. and of S.P.C.K. he observed on 21 October that

the new college in Barbados is almost finished; and that of William and Mary in Virginia, I hope, is now upon a better foot than it was. There is more care taken than has ever been, of what ministers, catechists and schoolmasters are sent abroad; and if we can but prevail for four bishops to be sent to look after the discipline of all, which is what we are again endeavouring, we may promise for all these a good increase of Christianity in the West Indies.[2]

His hopes were without foundation; for the administration would take no positive step towards the sending of bishops to America; and the unvarying reply to all episcopal pressure was that of the Duke of Newcastle to Gibson's successor in the see of London, Bishop Sherlock, that 'the appointing bishops in the West Indies was a great and national consideration, that had long been under the deliberation of great and wise men heretofore and had been by them laid aside'.[3]

In the other matters mentioned by Wake to Turrettini, better fortune attended his efforts. General Christopher Codrington, who had been born in Barbados and died there in 1710, left by will his estates in that island to the S.P.G. for the foundation of a college consisting of 'a convenient number of professors and scholars to study and practise physick and chirurgery as well as divinity, that by the apparent usefulness of the former to all mankind, they might both endear themselves to the people and have the better opportunity of doing good to men's souls while they are taking care of their bodies'. In accordance with this bequest the Society on 21 September 1716 designated Archbishop Wake and Bishop Robinson of London to wait upon George I, and to present to him 'the design of the Society for building a college in Barbados pursuant to the will of the late General Codrington, in order to procure a Licence or Letters Patent from His Majesty for building the said College'.[4] The desired authority being given, the Society's minutes

[1] N. Sykes, *Edmund Gibson*, p. 370.
[2] Geneva MSS. Inventaire 1569, f. 136. 21 October 1725.
[3] N. Sykes, *Edmund Gibson*, p. 372.
[4] Arch. W. Epist. 15. S.P.G. Minutes. 21 September 1716.

embraced many entries concerning details of the scheme, such as the provision and carriage of timber from Tobago to Barbados and the transportation of carpenters and other workmen from England to the West Indies; a process of much longer duration than Wake's over-confident forecast, so that the college was not completed until 1743. Notwithstanding, this project at least did not founder owing to the *vis inertiae* of the administration.

With regard to William and Mary College, the Archbishop likewise took a particular interest in its welfare. It had fallen on evil times, partly owing to local differences of opinion, towards the pacification of which he gave his mediatorial endeavours. As a result, he wrote to the Governors on 10 August 1724 to express his satisfaction with the better prospects of the college.

It is a great pleasure to me to hear that you are all so happily united amongst yourselves, and do so entirely agree in your desires and endeavours to advance the interest and prosperity of the college committed to your care. I cannot but repeat my hearty wishes that you would fill up the number of your masters as soon as you conveniently can; and prepare such a body of statutes as may be necessary for the future good order and government of the college; being well assured that none who shall succeed you, will be either better disposed or better qualified for such a work than you are. I hope you will not be wanting to improve the lands granted to the college to the best advantage; and to finish the building of it so far as may be needful for the reception and use of those who shall resort to it. The term of that relation in which, by your favour, I have the honour to stand to this royal foundation, is very short; and my age and infirmities may probably render it still shorter. It would be a singular satisfaction to me to see somewhat more done towards the settlement of it before my time expires; and if it be in my power to contribute anything towards it, I should think myself happy to be employed by you. Whensoever I can be of any use to the college or yourselves, I hope you will always account yourselves to have a right to command my best service.[1]

This gracious missive brought an equally grateful response from the president, James Blair; who announced on 6 April 1725 that the Archbishop's letter when read to the governors at their annual meeting on the Monday after Lady Day, had produced an instant resolution to put the revenues, building and administration of the college on a better foundation, to set about the preparation of statutes, and so far as possible to provide better salaries in order to remedy the inadequate staffing.[2] Moreover Blair himself, who was also commissary of the bishop of London for Virginia, was fully appreciative of Wake's diligence and zeal. The business of president of the S.P.G. involved a good deal of correspondence, much of which was unrewarding, thanks to the insuperable difficulties of overseeing the affairs of clergy, churches and congregations at such a distance and without episcopal governors to whom they could go for counsel and advice. It was particularly

[1] Arch. W. Epist. 24, f. 79.

[2] *Ibid.* f. 74.

gratifying therefore to receive the compliments of Blair in a letter of 16 February 1723/4 that

nothing encourages me more than the surprising kindness I meet with from Your Grace. I could not have expected that a person whose time and thoughts are employed in all the weighty affairs of church and state, would have remembered me or our poor concerns of this country. Instead of this, I find every letter answered, every opportunity embraced that the utmost friendship from persons of an inferior station could expect. My lord, I am perfectly astonished at this both kindness and humility; and shall take care to abuse neither of them.[1]

The work of the Societas pro promovendo Evangelio had its lighter sides and its less solemn occasions, however; and one of these occurred in the visit to England in 1734 of seven Indians, including King Tomachiki, from Georgia. Despite his age and infirmity Wake assured their sponsors of his readiness to receive them; and on 18 August they waited upon him,

and were extremely pleased with their visit. They had apprehensions that he was a conjuror, but the kind reception he gave them altered that imagination. The Archbishop would have put some questions to them concerning their notions of religion, but they have a superstition that it is unfortunate to disclose their thoughts of those matters and refused to answer....Nevertheless the King was so taken with the Archbishop that he said he must come again to talk with him. At coming away he said he now really believed they should have some good man sent them to instruct them and their children. He showed his politeness in that visit. The Archbishop refused (out of respect to them) to sit down, though so weak as to be supported on the arms of two servants all the time they were with him; whereupon the King, who saw him in pain, forbore to make him a speech he had prepared; and said he would speak it to his servants, meaning Dr Lynch, dean of Canterbury, the Archbishop's son-in-law, and other clergymen then present.

More than a year later memories of the occasion were revived when the trustees of the Georgia Society received a donation of 10 guineas from the Archbishop for converting the Indians in General Oglethorpe's colony.[2]

In his relationship to the Society for Promoting Christian Knowledge, however, Wake encountered a problem of equal difficulty and even greater delicacy than that of the provision of bishops for the American plantations, in regard to the Danish-German Lutheran mission in south India. The association of 'the Church Society' with these missions has been described by two of its historians as 'curious, unique, anomalous yet providential. By a chain of circumstances it became the patron and supporter of a Danish mission. By unexpected developments it had to employ Lutheran clergy. In default of English missionaries (to our shame be it spoken) it was driven to

[1] Arch. W. Epist. 24, f. 76.

[2] Diary of the first Earl of Egmont (Viscount Perceval) 19 August 1734, II, 121–2; 2 October 1735, p. 198. (Hist. MSS. Comm. Egmont MSS.)

look to a German university for its agents.'[1] The work originated in 1705 in the zeal of King Frederick IV of Denmark and Professor A. H. Francke of the university of Halle in Saxony, which led to the financial support by the former of two German-Lutheran clergymen trained by the latter and ordained by the Danish bishop of Zealand. Thanks to the marriage of Queen Anne to Prince George of Denmark, the interest and support of the S.P.G. were invited in 1709; but that society was prevented by the terms of its charter from undertaking work save in the English settlements, and so the request devolved upon the S.P.C.K., which espoused the project warmly and made the Tranquebar mission one of its principal interests. In 1712 one of the two original missionaries, Henry Plutschau, visited London and addressed a special meeting of the Society, a precedent followed in 1714 by his colleague Bartholomew Ziegenbalg. The anomaly of the support by an Anglican society of a mission conducted by Lutheran clergymen, most of whom were not episcopally ordained, was felt and voiced within the S.P.C.K., and was the subject of a formal discussion in 1713. When Wake succeeded to the primacy he supported the venture ardently. In January 1719 he addressed a printed letter to Ziegenbalg and Grundler, in which he referred to their work in flattering superlatives. After thanking them for their letters to the S.P.C.K. ('cujus vos ipsi praecipuum estis decus et ornamentum'), he praised their pioneer labours in a part of the Lord's vineyard which they had planted as well as cultivated, and as a result of which the name of Christ was now proclaimed where formerly it was unknown. In a particularly laudatory passage, he ascribed to them a character and reputation far greater than those of pontiffs, patriarchs and popes adorned with purple, scarlet or gold; and foretold their rewards in the world to come.[2] When Ziegenbalg died in the following month, Wake busied himself to secure a successor to carry on the work; and in 1725 he related to Turrettini that 'the little colony at Tranquebar flourishes very well; and Mr Schultz who is now at the head of it, supplies the place of Mr Ziegenbalg as well as one could have expected. I have used my utmost industry to have more labourers sent into that harvest, and I thank God I have at last succeeded in my endeavours.'[3] Indeed, in reply to urgent requests from Schultz, he had procured through Francke three missionaries, Messrs Bosse, Pressier and Walthar from Halle in 1724; who had gone to Copenhagen to receive the King's approval, and ordination there.[4]

In 1735 however the question of non-episcopal orders was raised afresh upon the ordination by the Lutheran missionaries at Tranquebar of a native convert and catechist, Pastor Aaron; whereupon the Society's secretary,

[1] W. O. B. Allen and F. McClure, *Two Hundred Years: The History of S.P.C.K., 1698–1898*, p. 258.

[2] Arch. W. Epist. 24, f. 119.

[3] Geneva MSS. Inventaire 1569, f. 136. 21 October.

[4] Arch. W. Epist. 24, f. 125.

Henry Newman, called for a formal report from Francke on the incident. On 6 June the secretary thanked the professor for his letter

in answer to the enquiry I was desired to make of the power vested in the missionaries at Tranquebar to confer orders on such persons among the Malabarian converts to Christianity as shall be found fitly qualified for divine offices, particularly the administration of the Holy Sacraments. A translation of your letter was read at the last General Meeting of the Society, which happened to be a full one, and they unanimously expressed their entire satisfaction at the account you gave of that affair, and have ordered me to put them in mind of giving their directions at the next return of their ships to India, for preventing any difficulties or misunderstandings that may hereafter grow in those parts upon a supposition of the holy orders conferred in India not being valid.

In a report of this decision which Newman sent on 6 February following to the two chaplains at Fort St George in India, he emphasised the approval given by Wake to the step. 'The sending over candidates for orders to Europe would be attended with insuperable difficulties. You have seen the Archbishop of Canterbury's opinion in favour of ordination in India.'[1] As with the S.P.G. missions in North America, so with the Lutheran missionaries at Tranquebar, Wake maintained a regular correspondence, until on 2 March 1730/1 Newman informed them that

if you have not a letter as usual from the Archbishop of Canterbury, you must impute it to His Grace's great age and infirmities; which have in a manner deprived him of any more taking a pen into his hand, who was formerly so ready and great a master of it. But in conversation His Grace always mentions you with honour, and was very much pleased with the sight of the last missionaries who went hence to join you.[2]

Actually the archives of the S.P.C.K. contain one letter later than this date from Wake to Schultz, written on 3 August 1731.

It was a far cry from the North American and Indian continents to the small island of Minorca in the Mediterranean, yet this outpost likewise claimed its share in the Archbishop's pastoral care. During the war of the Spanish Succession, the British in September 1708 had seized Port Mahon and had proceeded thence to the conquest of the island of Minorca, nominally in behalf of 'King Charles III of Spain', then the Archduke Charles of Austria, but actually with a shrewd view to its importance, together with Gibraltar which had been captured earlier in the war, to Great Britain's naval operations in the Mediterranean. When the Peace of Utrecht was

[1] N. Sykes, *Old Priest and New Presbyter*, pp. 156–7; citing S.P.C.K. *Society's Letters*; L. W. Cowie, *Henry Newman*, ch. v (London, 1956).

[2] S.P.C.K. *Society's Letters*. CS. 2/22, f. 37. Postscript added by Newman to his letter of 3 February 1730/1.

signed in 1713, the political situation had changed considerably by the accession of the Archduke to the imperial title as the Emperor Charles VI, by the failure of the allied arms to capture Spain itself for the House of Habsburg, and by the consequent coolness of diplomatic relations between Great Britain and the Empire. Accordingly Minorca was surrendered to the British Crown; and provision had to be made for the conversion of the temporary wartime occupation into a permanent administration, involving also the determination of the ecclesiastical settlement. The island hitherto had been subject to the bishop of Majorca, who was represented in Minorca by a vicar-general, whose duties included the presidency of the ecclesiastical court sitting in the capital Ciudadela, which heard all suits, civil and criminal, in which an ecclesiastic was defendant, though ecclesiastical prosecutions of laymen were held in the civil court. There was an appeal from the ecclesiastical court to the bishop of Majorca, and thence to Rome. There were six parishes in the island, two of which, Mahon and Ciudadela, had been in the gift of the King of Spain, and now became in the patronage of the British Crown. There were also several convents, exempt from the jurisdiction of the bishop. By Article XI of the Treaty of Utrecht the British sovereign promised to

> take care that all the inhabitants of the said island, both ecclesiastical and secular, shall safely and peaceably enjoy all their estates and honours; and the free use of the Roman Catholic religion shall be permitted; and measures shall be taken for preserving the aforesaid religion in the island, provided the same be consistent with the civil government and laws of Great Britain.[1]

In 1714 Lieutenant-Governor Richard Kane sent to England Dr Manuel Mercader the vicar-general and Dr Sanxo to advise concerning the drawing up of a new constitution for Minorca; and in 1716 himself paid a visit to forward the project. Accordingly on 21 June 1718 the King in Council issued a variety of instructions to this end; to the archbishop of Canterbury for ecclesiastical affairs; to the lord chancellor for laws and constitution; to the commissioners of the treasury for revenues; to the lords of the admiralty and to the duke of Marlborough for the fortifications; to the secretary at war; and to the lords commissioners of trade for the island's trading laws.[2] Wake therefore took steps in close consultation with Gibson to frame an ecclesiastical establishment; and the result of their deliberations, when completed,

[1] Article XI. 'Spondet insuper Regia Sua Majestas Magnae Britanniae se facturam; ut Incolae omnes Insulae Praefatae tam Ecclesiastici quam Seculares, Bonis suis universis et Honoribus tute, pacateque fruantur; atque Religionis Romano-Catholicae liber usus iis permittatur; utque etiam ejusmodi rationes ineantur ad tuendam Religionem praedictam in eadem Insula, quae a Gubernatione Civili atque a Legibus Magnae Britanniae penitus abhorrere non videantur.'

[2] I am greatly indebted to Mrs G. R. Elton of Cambridge for information about Minorca; and particularly for drawing my attention to Miss Ella Murdie's unpublished dissertation on 'Minorca under British Rule, 1713–1783', presented for the M.A. degree of the University of London in 1931.

was shown to 'such of the bishops of the province as were in or near the Town', and was then formally delivered to His Majesty.[1]

The document fell naturally into two parts; the first concerning the regulation of the Roman Catholic religion, and the second the establishment, for the benefit of the English garrison and civil servants, of a branch of the Church of England. The former section recommended:

1. That no clergyman whatever, regular or secular, be hereafter admitted as a member of the churches or convents of Minorca, or have any benefice there, but the natives of the island, who shall reside there, and own Your Majesty as their lawful sovereign.
2. That it will be for the peace and safety of the island, to be wholly discharged from the government of the bishop of Majorca and of the archbishop of Valencia, and from all manner of dependence upon either of them; and that the convents in like manner be discharged from all dependence upon and obedience to any foreign Generals or Provincials.
3. That no clergyman be admitted to preach but the natives of the island, who shall take an oath of allegiance to Your Majesty. And that no foreign clergyman be permitted to collect money in the island under pretence of charitable uses in foreign parts; but that all such collections be made by Your Majesty's subjects only with the licence of the Governor.
4. That if any missionary or other foreign clergyman, regular or secular, shall come into the island, the heads of the churches or convents to which they shall come, be required to acquaint the Governor with their names, business, etc.; and that in case such travellers be concealed, they be treated as spies, and those who conceal them to be punished with banishment.
5. That no Inquisition, or Officers belonging to it, be admitted on the island, nor any such Court held as that of *Santo Officio*.
6. That no sanctuary be given in churches, chapels or convents to any persons to screen them from the justice of the King's civil laws, nor to conceal any arms, ammunition, or contraband goods.
7. That the clergy be not permitted to tamper with the soldiers about religion; nor to marry, baptise, or visit the sick, nor bury any of Your Majesty's British subjects without leave from the Commander of the Garrison.
8. That for all civil crimes the clergy to be liable to be tried and punished as other subjects are.
9. That Your Majesty may please to give a general direction to the Governor that in case any person be delivered by any ecclesiastical judge whatsoever to the secular power, in order to be punished with death, he take care to prevent such execution.
10. That Your Majesty be pleased to secure such persons as shall embrace the Protestant religion from suffering any loss or detriment on that account.

[1] Arch. W. Epist. 24, ff. 143–6. The paper is in Gibson's hand with corrections by Wake; and there is a fair copy of the same, with a preface by Wake to the King.

The second part, relating to the Church of England, advised:

1. That there be two churches built in the said island, one at Mahon and another at Fort St Philip for the use of your Protestant subjects.
2. That there be a settled minister in each of those churches, constantly residing, to officiate duly in the same.
3. That to encourage men of learning and prudence to undertake the service of those churches, the salary of those ministers be not under £200 a year to each of them.
4. That there be another fixed minister at Ciudadela, and one other between Aleyor and Fournelles; and that the salary of these two last mentioned ministers be not under £150 a year each. All which several sums, we humbly conceive, will be in great measure answered by what is now allowed yearly to the Governor's chaplain and the chaplains of the four regiments to be quartered in that island.
5. That a school be settled at Fort St Philip to teach the children of the soldiers in garrison to read, write and cast accounts; and to instruct them in the principles of the Christian religion as professed in the Church of England; the salary of the said schoolmasters to be £40 a year.
6. That a collection of books be sent thither for the use of the ministers and garrison, the care of which to be under the direction of the Governor.
7. As to the ecclesiastical government of the island, we are of opinion that it should be committed to the care of some archbishop or bishop of England, whom Your Majesty shall be pleased to appoint.

These proposals had the enthusiastic support of Colonel Kane, whose imagination indeed conceived two English churches of such magnificence as to impress the Papists, one of which, at Fort St Philip, should be of cathedral proportions with two steeples, organs and other ornaments duly detailed, including even the suggestion that in the Book of Common Prayer to be used in the island 'the psalms in all those books are proposed to be in the version of Mr Brady and Mr Tate'.[1] Nobody indeed could have been more zealously qualified to exercise the royal supremacy in Minorca than its lieutenant-governor. He even thought that the English soldiers should be encouraged to marry young Spanish women of the island (but not widows); 'and there is no reason to doubt but that the mild and familiar temper of the English would be an inducement to the young women to marry them rather than the Spaniards'; and that the children of such marriages should be educated as English subjects and members of the Church of England. The gallant colonel's Irish extraction and his experience as an officer of the 18th Royal Irish Regiment should have reminded him of the different outcome of the similar Cromwellian experiment in Ireland! But in point of fact the second part of the recommendations of Wake and Gibson became a dead letter from

[1] *Ibid.* f. 140.

the outset. The Whig administration had enough problems at home and were to find sufficient difficulties with the Roman Catholic clergy in Minorca, to distract their attention thoroughly from the provision of a comprehensive establishment of schools and churches after the order of the Church of England.

It was therefore the problem of regulating the Roman Catholic clergy, alike secular and regular, which engaged the interest of governors on the spot and, somewhat languidly, of ministers of state at home. It was natural that these clergy should direct their attention to Spain and Rome rather than to England; and that they should do their utmost to deepen the division between the native Minorcans and the invading British garrison. So long as the secular clergy looked to the bishop of Majorca and the regulars to their superiors in Rome, little could be done beyond negative orders to prevent acute trouble. Kane was both a popular and a tolerant governor, anxious to do his best for the temporal welfare of the islanders and not to interfere with their exercise of the Roman Catholic religion. But from the first he set his face firmly against any clerical intervention in the administration of the island; and from this bone of contention there developed a series of difficulties. On 1 December 1721 he issued a code of seventeen articles, based on the recommendations of Wake and Gibson, modified according to the practical conditions prevailing, but faithful to their principles. In turn the vicar-general and his clergy complained to the pope; who in 1725 protested to the emperor and to the kings of Spain and France that the code violated the Treaty of Utrecht. In November 1727 Cardinal Fleury forwarded to the duke of Newcastle a copy of the papal protest; and the issue was brought up at the congress at Cambrai in 1728. Nothing effective was done, however; and in 1730 the governor of Minorca, Lord Carpenter (who never resided there) and his deputy, Kane, re-presented to the Whig administration the first eight points of Wake's memorandum with an urgent request for their execution; since 'until some rule be laid for the clergy by royal authority, they will never cease acting illegally and when obstructed they complain to foreign courts'. Difficulties arose continually in judicial processes, where the clergy claimed exemption for themselves from the ordinary civil law and asserted their own right to try laymen in the ecclesiastical court. Kane did his best, with lukewarm support from London, to carry out his own code; and not without some measure of success. But the problem of reorganising the administration, civil and ecclesiastical, was never taken in hand by the home government.

In particular the linchpin of Wake's scheme, the provision of a native bishop of Minorca and the abolition of the jurisdiction of the bishop of Majorca was never accomplished; and without this, the other rules were of little effect. So long as the clergy of the island were dependent on Majorca (and thereby on the archbishop of Valencia in Spain) for licences, nothing could be done to wean them from Spanish sympathies. Repeatedly Kane urged upon Wake and the king's ministers the imperative necessity of a native bishop; and in particular proposed the nomination to Rome of Dom Manuel Mercader; 'for his being so long in England, I am persuaded, has removed a good deal of his error and bigotry, and given him a better notion of the religion and government of England'. Nothing was done to carry out this project, even if Spain and Rome could have been persuaded to consent; and the reprisal of confiscating for the service of the British administration in Minorca all the ecclesiastical revenues formerly enjoyed by the bishop of Majorca only aggravated the situation. Minorca in point of fact did not receive a bishop until Spain had resumed possession of the island. Meantime Dr Mercader remained in London in receipt of a government pension of £300 per annum in lieu of the preferment he had forfeited; the bishop of Majorca was not allowed to visit Minorca; and for the administration of the rite of confirmation, the islanders were dependent upon such fortuitous occasions as the capture in May 1719 by a British warship of the bishop of Mazzara in Sicily and his temporary sojourn in Minorca, where he confirmed the islanders!

Notwithstanding these disappointments, the indefatigable Kane continued to send lengthy reports, memoranda and letters to Wake; to which the faithful Archbishop duly replied, though his replies are not extant. When Kane went to Gibraltar in 1720 as governor, he conceived a similar project for detaching that station from the jurisdiction of the bishop of Cadiz and establishing a joint bishopric of Minorca and Gibraltar, in order to rivet more firmly the British occupation of both outposts. Neither the zeal of Kane nor the pressure of Wake and Gibson, however, could avail to carry such ambitious schemes. Not only did the proposals of the memorandum of 1718 fail of realisation; but the very document itself disappeared and perished. For when, in 1765, after the cession of Canada to Great Britain at the end of the Seven Years War had presented a parallel problem of the religious administration of a French and Roman Catholic population, the privy council ordered search to be made in the Paper Office for Wake's memorandum concerning Minorca, as a potential precedent, it was nowhere to be found.[1] Thus ended ingloriously both the suggestions for a Roman Catholic bishop of Minorca and Gibraltar, and the possible anticipation also of the later Anglican suffragan episcopate on the continent of Europe.

At home Wake was much concerned in the Charity School movement,

[1] Arch. W. Epist. 24, ff. 138–98; E. Murdie, *op. cit.* for citations from MSS. in the British Museum and the Public Record Office.

which was one of the principal agents of the S.P.C.K. for the religious education of the children of the poor. If the eighteenth century 'was *par excellence* the age of benevolence', to the philanthropic men and women of the time 'the charity school was their favourite form of benevolence'.[1] Founded to combat the prevalent irreligion and licence, these schools sought to cultivate virtue and religion on the basis of literacy; but their curriculum was strictly utilitarian. Their object was to give the children of the poor sufficient education to earn their living by manual labour and to read the improving religious tracts issued by the S.P.C.K., without raising them above their station and producing an aversion to menial work. From 1699 when the 'Church Society' undertook the co-ordination of the movement, the number of schools multiplied rapidly, so that the enterprise became of national proportions and importance. Unfortunately for the schools, during the reign of Anne and especially after the Sacheverell episode in 1710 they became suspected of high-church and even of Jacobite influences and tendencies. Accordingly when Wake became primate, one of the chief questions engaging his attention was the general complaint that these schools, through the character of their masters and mistresses, especially in London, were seminaries of disaffection to the house of Hanover. Dr Thomas Bray, the founder of the S.P.C.K., was himself convinced of the truth of these accusations; and the Archbishop could not ignore such representations nor the dangers involved in the continuance of subversive influences. The Whig attack on the schools was preparing; and although Wake defeated its first assault in the shape of the Vestry Bill,[2] his success only increased the necessity of strong action to purge the charity schools from the taint of disloyalty.

To Edward Jennings, chairman of the committee of the trustees of the London schools, therefore, Wake wrote after the defeat of the bill,

> I can now with satisfaction acquaint you that I presented your petition in behalf of all our charity schools yesterday to the House, and that the effect was as happy as could have been wished. For the bill was rejected, and therefore the danger which threatened these pious nurseries for the present is no more. But indeed I can't tell you how soon it may return if some effectual care be not taken by you to purge them from all such masters and mistresses as instil any factious or seditious principles into their children, and rigorously to animadvert upon all, whether children or teachers, who either appear or suffer them to appear at any times further to affront the government, and bear a part in those tumults and riots which are so great scandal as well as a prejudice to the good order and peace of the realm.[3]

This was followed by a letter to the S.P.C.K. recommending a scrutiny of its own members and of the masters and mistresses of the schools in order to

[1] M. G. Jones, *The Charity School Movement*, p. 3 (Cambridge, 1938).
[2] For Wake and the Vestry Bill see above, chap. VII, pp. 112–14.
[3] M. G. Jones, *op. cit.* p. 116.

remove all persons suspected of disaffection. 'But the tempered exhortations of the Archbishop and the co-operation of the society produced little effect.' The minutes of the Society and the correspondence of the primate equally revealed the extent of the complaints made and the concern of the responsible authorities for their remedy. The S.P.C.K. proposed a royal charter, incorporating trustees and managers of the schools, to whom under the presidency of the Archbishop, full powers should be given in respect of the personnel, the finances and the rules of the schools.

But once again the Archbishop, who clearly disliked any scheme of reform which admitted even the thin end of the wedge of state interference in the schools, disappointed his party. The plan of incorporation failed to secure his support. He contented himself by demanding from the chairman of the committee of trustees a promise that henceforward all persons exercising control over the schools should testify their fidelity and loyalty by making the following declaration: 'I am fully satisfied of the just right of His Majesty King George to the Crown of these realms, and I will undertake by the grace of God to behave myself as it becomes a subject well-affected to his said majesty and his government.'[1]

When the trustees declined to submit this proposal to the Society, Wake accepted their decision with due humility.

I was indeed satisfied [he wrote to Newman on 2 June 1718] with the reasons Mr Jennings and Mr Hoare gave me for their not proposing to the Society what my reverend brother the bishop of Carlisle offered privately to Mr Jennings in my name. But I am still of opinion that as all possible care should be taken to see the charity schools furnished with masters and mistresses well affected to the present government, so in order thereunto every such master and mistress should be obliged not only to take the oaths to the government before their admission; but at the time of their admission should subscribe some such solemn promise and declaration as this: they do heartily acknowledge His Majesty King George to be the only lawful and rightful king of these realms; and will, to the utmost of their power, educate the children committed to their charge in a true sense of their duty to him as such; that they will not by any words or actions do anything whereby to lessen their esteem of or their obedience to the present government; that upon all public days, when their children may be likely to appear among any disorderly persons in public, they will do their best to keep them in, and severely punish them if they hear of their running into any tumults or public meetings, contrary to the good order of such schools and scholars; with any other engagements of the like kind that the Society shall think fit to add for the security of their schools with respect to the children's duty to God and the government. This I should be very glad your Society would consider of, and come to some resolution upon it. For I would fain have these schools not only be made truly nurseries of loyalty and religion, but to be so ordered that all may see that those who have the direction of them, do heartily desire they shall be so.[2]

[1] M. G. Jones, *op. cit.* p. 119.

[2] Arch. W. Epist. 15, n.f.

The Society recommended this letter to all trustees of charity schools for their direction; and Jennings 'readily promised to use his good offices with the trustees of the schools where he is chairman to recommend what Your Grace proposes in Your Grace's name, lest the name of the Society might give an umbrage that might hinder the good effect of Your Grace's advice'.[1] Notwithstanding, the attack on the alleged disloyal principles inculcated in charity schools continued, fortified by the popular excitement caused by the uncertainties of the foreign situation, the South Sea Bubble collapse in 1720, the Jacobite plot in England of 1722, and the attainder and banishment of Bishop Atterbury in 1723. Amidst such a ferment of public opinion *The Independent Whig* renewed its assaults, reinforced by Mandeville's essay *On Charity and Charity Schools* in 1723, together with a second edition of his earlier work, *The Fable of the Bees.* Supporters of the S.P.C.K. and the schools rallied to their defence, with such vigour that 'nothing is more remarkable in the vehement controversy of 1723 than the easy victory of the schools and their supporters against their redoubtable antagonists'. In that same year also Bishop Gibson was translated to London from Lincoln; and 'the man and the moment had arrived to root out sedition from the schools for ever'. Gibson at once began to concert measures to this end with Lord Townshend, Secretary of State for the Northern Department; and in this as in other branches of ecclesiastical administration, the Bishop of London eclipsed the Archbishop of Canterbury. If it is perhaps too strong a contrast to deduce that 'where Wake had failed, Gibson succeeded',[2] the evidence suggests that the latter took the lead both in the S.P.C.K. and in the capital, whilst the former accepted relegation once more to the background.

Amongst the recipients of, and contributors to, the extensive correspondence of Wake, none were more forward or expansive than leading prelates of the Church of Ireland, and more especially perhaps those who had been translated from English to Irish sees and had already formed an acquaintance with him before they crossed the sea to a far different ecclesiastical establishment. In particular this category embraced Bishop Evans of Meath, whose prolixity was equalled only by his execrable handwriting, and Bishop Nicolson of Derry, both translated from English sees, the former from Bangor in 1716 and the latter from Carlisle in 1718. Amongst the metropolitans of the Irish church too were such figures as the primate, Thomas Lindsay, a schoolfellow of Wake at Blandford, and William King of Dublin, a notable prelate in any age, whom John Evelyn described as 'a sharp, ready man in politics as well as very learned',[3] and who lost the succession to Armagh because of the inflexibility of his opposition to the Ulster presbyterians (whom he had

[1] Arch. W Epist. 15,. n.f. Newman to Wake. 13 June. [2] M. G. Jones, *op. cit.* pp. 122–9.
[3] E. S. de Beer, *Diary of John Evelyn*, vol. V, p. 597. 4 June 1705.

known formerly as Bishop of Derry). Nor were there lacking problems of mutual interest and concern on both sides of the Irish Sea to occupy the episcopal correspondents, particularly the relations of Protestant Dissenters to the established churches of Ireland and England, the convocations of the respective churches and the perennial source of friction in the rivalry and jealousy of the English- and Irish-born bishops of the Church of Ireland.

The most urgent and important of these issues was that of the Ulster presbyterians, who formed with the Irish churchmen the Protestant minority in the midst of the native Irish Roman Catholics. After the upheaval of the Interregnum, the Church of Ireland had found itself confronted by a powerful presbyterian church, conscious of its kinship with the Church of Scotland and well organised on a territorial basis. With the triumph of presbyterianism in Scotland at the Revolution, the Irish presbyterians hoped for a similar fortune in Ulster; but their hopes were destined to disappointment. Although enjoying a practical toleration, they did not receive a corresponding legal security to that granted to Dissenters in England in 1689. Nor would such a toleration at that date have seemed satisfactory to them; for they were not, as were their English counterparts, a comparatively small minority compared with the established church, but an active competitor with the Church of Ireland for the official recognition of the government. Archbishop King never tired of insisting to his English correspondents, as he wrote to Wake on 2 June 1719, that

> as to granting the Dissenters a toleration such as is granted them in England, it has been offered them again and again, and it has been refused by their leaders; by which I think it is evident that the ease of their conscience and the liberty of serving God in their own way, is not what they aim at; their design is plainly to get the whole power in their hands, and settle presbytery in Ireland, as it was in Scotland by the National Covenant in 1638 and the Solemn League and Covenant afterwards in Great Britain.[1]

Accordingly the Church of Ireland strove to maintain its privileged position as the only safeguard of its existence; whilst the Irish presbyterians had no option save to support the Revolution Settlement and the Protestant Succession, whether any concessions ensued from their support or not, since there was no other security for the Protestant minority in Ireland. During the reign of Anne, moreover, the Sacramental Test was extended to Ireland in 1704 by the English parliament, thereby worsening the position of the presbyterians. Henceforth therefore they sought to effect the repeal of this statute, or failing that, to barter for its continuance the enactment of a legal toleration. Furthermore in 1714 the payment of the *Regium Donum* to the

[1] R. Mant, *History of the Church of Ireland* (2 vols. London, 1840), vol. II, p. 333; W. A. Phillips (ed.), *History of the Church of Ireland* (3 vols. Oxford, 1933), vol. III, ch. v.

Irish presbyterians, which had been granted by William and Mary, was suspended as a further evidence of high-church and Tory hostility. With the accession of George I, however, the hopes of the Ulster presbyterians revived; and the *Regium Donum* was forthwith restored. But other expected measures of relief tarried, just as happened to the Dissenters in England. The truth of the matter indeed was that 'the Irish presbyterians had to deal directly and continuously with the Irish government, which allowed itself to be guided in its policy towards them by the views of the Irish Church, and consistently refused or postponed, concessions urged by the English ministry'.[1] It was this common bond of opposition to the demands of Protestant Dissenters in England and of Ulster presbyterians in Ireland, and therewith of lukewarmness, to say the least, towards the policies of the Whig administration of George I in both respects, which drew Wake and King together in sympathy and frequent interchange of letters.

It was natural that the Irish bishops should regard with particular anxiety the projects for relief of Dissenters in England by the repeal of the Occasional Conformity and Schism Acts, and still more by the proposal, favoured by some Whig bishops, of abolishing the Sacramental Test. For if such measures were carried in England, their effect would be felt much more powerfully in Ireland where the presbyterians were stronger in numbers and more closely organised.

> I think this session of our parliament will go off without any attempts in favour of the Dissenters [reported Wake to King on 1 June 1717]. Permit me to say that you must lose no time but do somewhat in yours, to prevent their being set over the Church of Ireland's head, by a general clause in the good bill the next session that is to hoist them over ours. Nothing but making it a national concern, can restrain such an attempt in them; and I hope you may bring both your houses into it. If our ministers keep their words, our interval will not be long: four months at the most. Yet in that time I flatter myself, we shall either see such changes as will prevent the threatened attempt, or have so settled the church's interest as to render any such attempt ineffectual.[2]

Ten days later the English primate renewed his warning. 'When Your Grace comes into Ireland, I hope you will consider how to prevent such applications from thence another session, as you will find were intended, had the bill to repeal the Occasional Conformity and Test Acts been proceeded upon in our parliament this session.'[3] It was with much relief therefore that Wake received from the Lord Lieutenant of Ireland, the Duke of Bolton, the assurance 'after all his instructions given him, that he had not one word signified to him about any liberty intended to be granted to the Dissenters'.[4]

[1] J. C. Beckett, *Protestant Dissent in Ireland, 1687–1780*, p. 18. (London, 1948.)
[2] King Correspondence. Wake to King. 1 June 1717.
[3] *Ibid.* 11 June.
[4] *Ibid.* 31 August.

Events in Ireland accordingly waited upon the outcome of the expected bill for relief of the Dissenters in the Westminster parliament; and during the course of his speech against the repeal of the Occasional Conformity and Schism Acts, Wake observed that the Irish presbyterians reprinted with their catechetical books the Solemn League and Covenant; a practice which he alleged as evidence of their intention 'to endeavour the alteration of the established church in Ireland, as they had effectually done it in Scotland; and should they ever get an establishment in both those kingdoms, one might without a spirit of prophecy foresee what would become of the Church of England'. The accuracy of his statement was challenged by a Scottish peer; but King provided abundant evidence in support of his brother-metropolitan.[1] After the carrying of the repeals in England, it was anticipated that the Whig administration would urge a parallel concession on the Irish parliament. The only doubt in Wake's mind was what form this might take.

I would willingly hope [he wrote to King on 12 June 1719] that the government does not intend to press the repealing of the Test Act with you; the very apprehension of which was, the last sessions, resented with such a warmth as I hardly ever saw in the House of Lords here. I cannot imagine that you need lesser securities against papists than we do; or, by consequence, that the reasons which first induced the making of the test, should be less strong with you than with us. Should the government desire the like toleration in favour of the Dissenters in Ireland, that is granted them in England (even with the allowance of occasional conformity) I cannot tell whether it would be advisable to refuse it. But surely if what Your Grace apprehends, shall be offered, it will become every man that has any regard to the security either of the church or state, to give the utmost opposition he can to it. I have no fear of the late bishops sent from hence to you; and what such an one as I am, can do here to prevent this evil, either by myself or friends, you may depend upon. I am glad I am so well prepared by Your Grace to answer what will very probably be offered in favour of such a bill; I will make the best use I can of it.[2]

A month later Wake rejoiced to learn that the abolition of the Sacramental Test in Ireland was not likely to be pressed.

I am glad the Test Act which our house shewed so much resolution to defend the last winter, and some of the bishops were for giving up by a side-wind, is like to stand as firm with you this summer.... I am hearty for the Toleration (yet if even that goes on, pray provide a little better than we have done against Arianism and Socinianism). Nay I would not scruple to let them into anything in the army, or militia, under the degree of a captain. But civil trusts are dangerous things; and I hope our friends will consider very well before they consent to go so far with them. I hope our English bishops have done their parts, and will always join heartily with you in the defence of our constitution both in church and state.[3]

[1] King Correspondence. Wake to King. 12 June and 16 July 1719; R. Mant, *op. cit.* vol. II, pp. 333–4.

[2] King Correspondence. 12 June.

[3] *Ibid.* 16 July.

Notwithstanding the retention of the Test Act, King was by no means satisfied with the concessions granted in the Toleration Bill as it passed the Irish parliament in 1719.

> The House of Commons were resolved to preserve the Test in its full latitude, as it stands at present [he reported on 1 August], nor had they any great mind, that I could perceive, for the toleration; but being so hardly pressed in the lord lieutenant's speech, they seemed under a necessity to do something which might be reckoned a compliance.

Accordingly a bill was agreed, which the Archbishop of Dublin found, when it came to the council, to lack

> the subscription to the Thirty-nine Articles, as it is ordered in the English bill; it wanted also the profession in the Trinity that is to be made by the Quakers, and the clause requiring a certificate that they are Dissenters....We laboured with the utmost diligence to have the clauses omitted, added there; I have hardly seen or heard a longer or warmer debate; when we came to a division, whether the clause relating to the subscription to the Articles should be added, it was ten for it and ten against; so the negatives carried it. On the Quakers' clauses it was the same.[1]

He hoped therefore that the measure would be amended at Westminster before being sent back to Dublin. When his letter reached Wake, it found the English primate drinking the Bath waters; where

> in this rambling state, I received Your Grace's letter, and do most heartily thank you for the account you are pleased to give me of what relates to your toleration bill since it passed the parliament. The stand you made against the designs of those men there, shews both what you are able and what you are willing to do in defence of the established church; and I hope when the bill returns from England, you will be very careful rather to reject it altogether than suffer any very dangerous clauses to remain in it. The only danger I can foresee in this procedure is, that if the present bill does not pass, it will be a handle for a new one to be brought in another session; and whether matters may not be so managed that such a new bill may be drawn more in their favour than this is, I cannot foresee; though upon the whole I fear it. The Dissenters are a busy, indefatigable generation; and our court seems to be very fond of favouring them; and how matters may change in two years' time with you, between both, I cannot tell. Your Grace will be much better able to judge what is safest to be done; whether to pass the present bill, or to drop it and get a better drawn another session. But it may be the council here will be influenced by my lord lieutenant, and mend all. I wish they may; but I fear we shall not make it less agreeable to the Dissenters than when it came out of your hands to us.[2]

In England only one clause was added to the bill, in favour of persons qualifying themselves under the terms of the act after prosecutions had been actually begun against them; and thus it was sent back to Ireland, sub-

[1] Mant, *op. cit.* vol. II, pp. 334–5.

[2] King Correspondence. Wake to King. 2 September 1719.

stantially unchanged as to its principal provisions. In this form it finally passed the Irish parliament, to the great dismay of King, who averred to Wake in respect of its concessions to the presbyterians, that

in truth we have granted them such a wide toleration, as I think is not precedented in the whole earth. The bill could not have passed, if our brethren that came to us from your side the water, had not deserted us and gone over to the adverse party. I fear we shall all feel the effects of it; and in truth, I can't see how our Church can stand here, if God do not by a peculiar and unforeseen providence, support it.... By my opposition to these bills, I have quite lost the favour of the government here and interest in it. But that doth very little concern me. I lost the favour of the former government by struggling for the succession; and I think the cause of the Church is of no less moment.[1]

On his side, too, Wake had had recent experience of desertion in the House of Lords by some of his episcopal brethren on the like issue of concessions to the Dissenters. Nevertheless, he thought King's fears to be exaggerated. During the consideration of the Irish Toleration bill by the privy council, he had been out of town in the west country; and so had not seen its text nor taken part in the deliberations. But he avowed to King that he favoured toleration of a purely religious character for the Dissenters;

wishing, if it were possible, that they might be so well satisfied with that, as not to press for anything more. In this point I am persuaded none of my lords the bishops will ever forsake Your Grace; and then they ought not to be much censured for the other; in which I doubt (though I have not yet seen your Toleration act) I should have fallen into the same sin.[2]

It would perhaps have been wiser, as Wake himself averred, if the Irish parliament 'had taken the very exact copy of our act' of toleration; but certainly King's forebodings were unjustified.

The bill did not contain what the Presbyterians really wanted—repeal of the Sacramental Test. Without this, the toleration gave them no more than they already possessed. It legalised but did not extend the existing indulgence....Such fears have little connection with the facts; the act did no more than give legal recognition to the position which the Irish Protestant dissenters had occupied since 1714. For the high churchmen it was the symbol rather than the substance of defeat.[3]

Indeed the original desire of the English administration had been for the repeal of the Sacramental Test; and instead they now had recourse, as in England, to the expedient of an indemnity act for Dissenters who had failed to take the test as required by law.

The Archbishop of Dublin's complaint of desertion by the English bishops

[1] Mant, *op. cit.* vol. II, pp. 337–8.
[2] King Correspondence. Wake to King. 19 November 1719.
[3] J. C. Beckett, *op. cit.* pp. 78–9.

on the Irish bench was always a sore point with His Grace, who had constituted himself the champion of the Irish party in the endemic rivalry between the two interests. The English administration at Westminster believed the maintenance of a solid phalanx of English-born bishops in the Irish church to be an indispensable condition of the preservation of English supremacy in the government of Ireland. Naturally therefore the Irish prelates (and on this point King had the support of his redoubtable dean of St Patrick's, Jonathan Swift) protested that although the majority of the clergy were Irish by birth and training, they could hope for little beyond the leavings when the English intruders had chosen the best sees and livings. Ubiquitously in Wake's correspondence with the Irish bishops there was this undercurrent of competition, not to say hostility, between the two elements. 'When I came over hither', related Bishop Godwin of Kilmore in January 1716/17, 'we were poor six to sixteen; and when the Bishop of Derry is gone, we shall be ten to twelve'.[1] The see of Londonderry indeed was the occasion of the sharpest encounter between King and Wake. For on the one hand it was the wealthiest see in Ireland, and on the other hand it was the diocese in which King himself had served his episcopal apprenticeship and for which he had an especial concern. When therefore it fell vacant in 1718 for the second time in five years, he despatched to Wake his ideas for a comprehensive shuffle of preferments. Observing that 'I left it about fifteen years ago without vanity in the best order of any diocese of Ireland and entirely in the interest of the government and Revolution', he lamented its decline during the interval, and urged the need of 'a diligent, active, popular bishop, that will reside among them, the two former not having been in the diocese two years during their time of being bishop'. His recommendations therefore were the translation of Bishop Stearne of Clogher, an Irishman, to Derry, of Bishop Downes of Killala, an Englishman, to Clogher, and the nomination of the dean of Derry, Dr Bolton, to Killala. 'Your Grace sees that this way of making as many removes on a vacancy as conveniently can be made, is a popular thing, gratifies a great many, and is much for His Majesty's interest.'[2]

Great was his indignation, therefore, when Derry was filled by the translation of Bishop Nicolson of Carlisle, whose name indeed had been canvassed at the previous vacancy in 1717.

Since the person nominated for the bishopric of Derry is so very useful to Your Grace [he wrote to Wake on 25 March 1718 in a letter of studied irony and insolence], I have been thinking of a way by which Your Grace may have the benefit of his assistance without hurting his wife and family. I do consider that a man may

[1] Arch. W. Epist. 12. Ireland 1, n.f. Bishop of Kilmore to Wake. 4 January 1716/17.

[2] *Ibid.* King to Wake. 26 February 1717/8.

govern in a country diocese in Ireland as well if he live in London as in Dublin... that he will have so many and strong precedents to justify him in the practice that he need not fear any condemnation from the world for his absence....As for the diocese of Derry, I see no reason why it may not do as well without a resident bishop for fifteen years to come as it did for the fifteen years last past. Your Grace will see by this how heartily I come into your measures and how solicitous I am to gratify you.[1]

Unfortunately the two replies sent by Wake on 1 and 2 April are not extant; but they provoked an equally vehement further letter from King on 12 April. In the former reply, as the Archbishop of Dublin acidly commented,

Your Grace doth most justly represent the inconveniences of passing by the persons that are the best judges and most proper to be consulted in the disposal of the preferments of the Church. I humbly conceive that the mischievous consequences of that practice are no less in Ireland than in England; and thought that I might have expected that one who saw and felt the evils both to the Church and His Majesty's interest arising from it, would not have given a precedent to justify those that are too apt of themselves to make many.

This was indeed the retort courteous to the English archbishop's frequent complaint of his loss of interest with the court and ministry! But worse was to follow. After remarking that Wake in his second letter seemed 'to be ill-pleased with mine of the 25th of March last and call it an extraordinary one', he observed that 'it was on an extraordinary occasion', since he himself had sent a list of recommendations, only to find them entirely ignored. 'Your Grace instead of coming into it or giving us your interest and assistance to make it effectual, has, as far as you could, effectually broke it, and given a precedent to make all such recommendations signify nothing for the future.' Furthermore, 'the only thing Your Grace allegeth as the reason for making this step is the extraordinary merit of the person you appeared for'. Surely, then, such outstanding merit should not be lost to England! 'Can he be as useful in Londonderry or in any part of Ireland?' Over against this consideration there should be set the murmuring and discontent of the Irish clergy, who 'by this breach upon them, are grievously out of humour'. Finally, King defended the outspokenness of his letter as essential both to the circumstances of the case and to the demands of friendship; and indeed he could say much more if Wake wished to hear it! For, he concluded, 'I am one of those whimsical men that will not always do or say or think what I am bid'.[2]

Such a stinging reproof in turn aroused the English primate to give a Roland for the Irish Oliver.

Had Your Grace given yourself the trouble to have enquired how the bishopric of Derry came to be disposed of as it is [he replied on 29 April], you would not, I

[1] *Ibid.* 25 March.

[2] *Ibid.* 12 April 1718.

dare say, have treated me as you have done about it. I am not much concerned to clear myself of any part I had in it; which everybody here knows was very little. Whether your schemes were right or wrong; or whether those who had the judging of them thought so, I cannot tell. I am sure I have lost a good friend, and a useful brother; and since you know not how to esteem him as he deserves, it is a pity but you had another English, or British, bishop in his place, who is said to take it very ill that he was not removed thither. My fault in this whole transaction is yet unknown to me; and Your Grace by the method of your former letter, took the worst way in the world with me to awaken my consideration of it. How far I may be hereafter consulted in any Irish promotions, I cannot tell. If I am, I beg leave once for all to undeceive Your Grace, that I shall consider nobody's schemes so far, as not upon the whole to give my own opinion agreeably to my own judgment; though it should chance to displease those who differ in their notions from me. Your Grace will have the goodness to excuse me in this; especially when I return it in your own words; That *I am*, also, *one of those—men that will not always do—as I am bid.* I never was so complaisant to my governors, and I hope my friends will not expect it from me. I beg Your Grace's excuses of this short, because unnecessary, apology for nothing.[1]

The Irish Church indeed had escaped the realisation of a very general expectation that Hoadly might be sent to Derry; both because his political principles were congenial to the policy of the Whig administration towards the Dissenters, and also because his exile would be welcome to the ecclesiastical authorities as a way out of the imbroglio in Convocation! Such hopes, and fears, were widespread on both sides of St George's Channel. 'That which occasioned the report of the Bishop of Bangor's coming among us, I suppose', wrote the Bishop of Kilmore to Wake on 12 April, 'was the expediency of removing him out of the Convocation in England. The fear of him has had this good effect that it has made the Bishop of Carlisle more welcome to some at least.'[2]

But the Archbishop of Dublin did not leave the last word to his English brother. In a further letter of 10 May, after emphasising that Derry was 'his first love', he insisted that Wake himself had informed him that his recommendation was put by through the English primate's own intervention; and accordingly 'instead of granting us this favour, Your Grace employed your interest to defeat our good intentions'. The Irish bishops and clergy were therefore 'apt to imagine that some reason should appear for such a conduct, if not an apology'. As for the peril which they had escaped,

Your Grace sees by this what a gap is opened to the oppression of this church and nation; and I pray God...that in time it do not come to the pass that every obnoxious bishop or worse, who is disliked or troublesome in England, be not sent

[1] King Correspondence. Wake to King. 29 April 1718.
[2] Arch. W. Epist. 12. Ireland. I. 12 April 1718.

into Ireland to our best bishoprics to be rid of him. Your Grace's predecessor never encouraged such a practice; it is begun in Your Grace's time and I wish you be not remembered for it.

King repeated his argument that the least he could have expected was an explanation of the reasons for the recent translation; and finally he promised to keep a close watch on the behaviour of the new bishop.

If the Bishop of Derry act otherwise than some of his brethren have done, I shall have the vanity to think my letters to Your Grace have had some influence towards that good effect. I will observe his conduct in his diocese and the Bishop of Clogher in his; and if he do more good in Derry than the other in Clogher, then everyone will justify those that placed him there; but if otherwise, every lover of the Church will have reason to see the choice was wrong.[1]

The irate Archbishop indeed had just ground of complaint in the passing over of all the Irish bishops when the richest see in the kingdom was vacant. But he was wrong in laying the responsibility solely at Wake's door. As for Nicolson, he had the initial shock of being told by George I himself that His Majesty expected him to reside on his new see; and on 10 May, he avowed to Wake that 'had I known a fortieth part of what I now hear and see, I would not have gone into that kingdom for the primacy. But—*jacta est alea*: go I must; and resolve I must (so the King tells me) to reside at Derry. God's will and the King's be done in righteousness.'[2] Whereupon he became a model diocesan for diligence, energy and devotion to his pastoral duty in Ireland, as well as constituting a formidable champion of the English interest.

The Archbishop of Dublin, moreover, paid the price of his opposition to the policy of the Whig administration in regard to the Dissenters and of his championship of the Irish interest on the bench, by being passed over for the primacy of Ireland when that dignity was vacant by the death of the archbishop of Armagh in 1724. By that date indeed the influence in Irish ecclesiastical preferments of Bishop Gibson at London was already being felt. Bishop Downes of Elphin assured Nicolson on 24 March 1724 that he was conscious that he owed his own recent translation to Meath to the Bishop of Derry's influence with Gibson.

I knew his power, yet, never having had any correspondence with him, I could not find out any way of coming at him to so good advantage as by your lordship. Your readiness to use your interest in him, and his to use his interest at court in my favour, lays strong obligations upon me to both.... I had a letter from our good friend the Lord of Canterbury by the last post.... He complained that he should be the last that would be consulted in these matters; and therefore did not trouble

[1] *Ibid.* 10 May. [2] *Ibid.* Nicolson to Wake. 10 May.

his head or concern himself about them. I really feared that so it continued with him; however, I thought not fit to suppose so much, or to seem to neglect him by omitting to write to his grace in this affair.[1]

If any lingering doubts needed to be dispelled, they were scattered shortly by the nomination to the primacy of Bishop Hugh Boulter of Bristol; who had preached the sermon at Gibson's consecration to the see of Lincoln and was one of his close friends. Now indeed Archbishop King was to find that if at times Wake had chastised him with whips, Boulter would chastise him continually with scorpions; for the new primate made no secret of his object 'to break the present Dublin faction on the bench', and in order to that end to ensure that no English bishop was translated to Ireland who might 'be tempted by Irish flattery to set himself at the head of the Archbishop of Dublin's party in opposition to me'. Boulter identified the English interest with his own person and policy; and whilst determined to maintain the number of English bishops on the Irish bench, insisted repeatedly that they must be firm in loyalty to himself and not such as were 'restless or good for nothing there, or not likely to agree with me'.[2]

In these circumstances the position of Wake was more delicate and difficult than when he had to deal with King alone. Boulter indeed wrote about ecclesiastical preferments in Ireland to Gibson only, and not to Wake; with the significant exception of the short period after the death of George I in 1727 when it was generally expected that the new sovereign would effect a change of men and measures both in church and state. At that juncture he assured the Archbishop of Canterbury that

I have in particular done my endeavours here to serve his late majesty with the greatest faithfulness and shall serve our present sovereign with the same fidelity; but the services I can do will be much lessened if I am not supported in my station; and as I am satisfied Your Grace will come in for a great share of power under the king, I must beg the favour of you to give me your support here upon proper occasions.[3]

At the same time he wrote to Gibson that

I remember when I was in England, it was thought other persons would come into play in the church upon the change which has now happened....By the change that your lordship thinks will happen in church affairs, I shall be greatly at a loss for your friendship; but hope still for your assistance as it shall lie in your way, and shall on all occasions hope for the continuance of your good advice.[4]

This skilful diplomacy was rewarded when after a short uncertainty Walpole was continued in office by the new king in the state, and with him his 'pope' resumed his authority in the church.

[1] R. Mant, *op. cit.* vol. II, pp. 398–9.

[2] *Letters written by Hugh Boulter, primate of All Ireland* (2 vols. Oxford, 1769), vol. I, pp. 14–15, 138–9.

[3] *Ibid.* vol. I, p. 175. 30 June 1727.

[4] *Ibid.* p. 178. 4 July.

On all other questions, however, Boulter was most correct and careful in informing Wake of his projects and problems. Despite his intense suspicion of the Anglo-Irish and his resolute championship of the English interest, he was zealously devoted to the good estate of the Irish Church. Moreover he represented to the Whig administration the universal hatred of Wood's halfpence, and was partly instrumental in procuring the withdrawal of the patent. On this occasion, when the Irish House of Lords moved a resolution of thanks to the King, 'and to express the grateful sense they have of His Majesty's royal favour and condescension', the Archbishop of Dublin proposed the insertion of the words 'great wisdom' before 'royal favour'. This was construed by the Irish primate as a reflection on the unwisdom of the King's ministers in recommending the patent, and as such he stoutly resisted it. The House, notwithstanding, carried the addition; and Boulter had much difficulty in securing its omission at the committee stage, though he finally succeeded by 21 to 12 votes. 'I was sensible of the advantage of having some strength of English on the bench', he reported to Wake, 'nine of the thirteen bishops that voted against that addition being English. I shall get my brethren to manage the intelligence they send you so as not to put you to the trouble of so many answers for the same news.'[1] The Irish primate also consulted his brother of Canterbury about a practice which he desired to stamp out, by which presbyters held livings in plurality not by faculty or dispensation but *in commendam*, thereby avoiding institution or induction;[2] about the challenge of the Archbishop of Dublin to his own right as primate of issuing licences for marriages at uncanonical hours and places;[3] about forms of prayer for a national fast day;[4] about various ecclesiastical bills sent by the Irish parliament to England for approval;[5] and about the revision on the accession of George II of some of the Occasional Offices.[6] Unfortunately none of Wake's replies appear to be extant; but it may be gathered from Boulter's correspondence that both the English Archbishop and Bishop Gibson counselled great caution in engaging in litigation with Archbishop King; and that Wake 'under so great weakness' recommended the several church bills to the oversight of Lord Trevor, the lord privy seal, whereupon Boulter thanked him 'for the services you did our church bills in England'.[7] The last mention of a letter from Canterbury to Armagh was on 21 November 1728; and the last letter from Boulter to Wake was of 5 May 1730, when he besought support for his petition to George II for the erection of a corporation to

[1] *Ibid.* pp. 43–5. 24 September 1725; Arch. W. Epist. 14. Ireland III, f. 298. 21 October.
[2] *Letters of Boulter*, vol. I, pp. 27–30. 22 May 1725.
[3] *Ibid.* pp. 75–80. 21 May 1726.
[4] *Ibid.* p. 126. 24 January 1726/7.
[5] *Ibid.* pp. 210–23. 13, 17, 24 February 1727/8.
[6] *Ibid.* pp. 258–9. 1 October, 9 November 1728.
[7] *Ibid.* p. 232. 2 April 1728, and p. 258.

establish Protestant charter schools for the education of children of Papists in the faith of the Church of Ireland.[1]

In view of Wake's preoccupation with the problems of convocation in England, it was natural that he should watch with peculiar vigilance the proceedings of that body in Ireland. Moreover the historical development of clerical representation in parliament differed in important respects between Ireland and England. In the former island clerical proctors had continued to sit in parliament until the Henrician Reformation; where, as the preamble to 28 Henry VIII cap. 21 stated, 'at every parliament two proctors of every diocese have been used and accustomed to be summoned and warned to be at the said parliament; and they are charged usurpishly to take on themselves to be parcel of the body, in manner claiming that without their assent nothing can be transacted at any parliament'. For which presumption on their part (though historically justified) and for their opposition to the reforming bills, they were henceforth excluded. But the representation of the lower clergy in Ireland was by two proctors from each diocese only, without the addition of deans, archdeacons and proctors for cathedral chapters. Accordingly ecclesiastical matters were transacted in provincial, diocesan or national synods; the last being summoned but rarely, whilst traditionally provincial synods were convoked triennially and diocesan annually. In the province of Dublin this tradition survived the Reformation changes, and continued to be observed. At the Archbishop's summons the diocesan bishops appeared, together with the deans, archdeacons and proctors for the cathedral chapters as well as of the other clergy. At the Reformation, however, the religious changes were imposed on the Irish Church by acts of parliament; and the first post-Reformation Convocation was summoned by James I in 1614, concurrently with a session of parliament. In so doing the King naturally followed English custom, by which royal writs were directed to the several metropolitans requiring them to summon their provincial synods. But the curious circumstance ensued that the clerical proctors were still elected by authority of the *Praemunientes* clause in the writs summoning the bishops to parliament. Furthermore each metropolitan was ordered to summon his convocation to meet in St Patrick's cathedral, Dublin, *vel alibi prout melius expediri videritis*; and the possibility of four provincial synods, each meeting in a different place, was avoided only by the restraint of the other archbishops in allowing their synods to assemble in Dublin. This Irish Convocation distinguished itself by adopting the Articles of Religion of 1615, of a decidedly Calvinist character; and no further Convocation was held for twenty years, until in 1635 the lord deputy, Wentworth, coerced the bishops and clergy into conformity with the Church of England by acceptance of the Thirty-nine

[1] *Letters of Boulter*, vol. II, p. 10.

Articles instead of the Irish Articles of 1615. The next Convocation met in 1640 on the eve of the civil war; and no further Convocation sat until the Restoration, when the English liturgy as revised in 1661 was adopted. Once more Convocation thereafter lapsed into quiescence; and it was noteworthy that after the Revolution, the parliaments in Ireland in 1692 and 1695 were unattended by meetings of convocation, and the *Praemunientes* clause was omitted from the writs of summons to the bishops.

When, therefore, the campaign was launched in England for the revival of sitting convocations, the Church of Ireland might be expected to share in the fruits of Atterbury's victory. Accordingly in 1703 Queen Anne restored the *Praemunientes* clause, and clerical proctors were elected in obedience to its mandate, including representatives of cathedral chapters and also deans and archdeacons. When the Convocation assembled, the lower clergy petitioned the bishops to ask from the Crown provincial writs addressed to the several metropolitans, in order to convert a parliamentary assembly into a provincial synod. Hurried recourse was had to Gibson's *Synodus Anglicana* for the correct forms of such writs and for other matters of procedure; and in January 1703/4 the Convocation was fully authorised. The lower clergy drew up a statement of reforms needful for the church, both general and specific; but the Upper House showed little haste in dealing with them, so that the sessions produced small results. The next Convocation in 1705 was fruitless, owing to a controversy between its Lower House and the Irish House of Commons. The Prolocutor and another member of the Lower House then crossed to England to testify to their brethren of Canterbury Convocation concerning the rights of the Irish lower clergy in relation to the Upper House, and brought back a due portion of the Atterburian spirit to Ireland. Notwithstanding these *contretemps*, sitting convocations were allowed in 1709, 1711 and 1713; but the death of the Queen put an end to their proceedings in 1714.

With the accession of the House of Hanover and the succession of Wake to the archbishopric of Canterbury, the question was raised afresh by the Archbishops of Armagh and Dublin and sundry Irish bishops of the prudence of resuming the experiment of a sitting convocation in Dublin. Wake accordingly was led to a closer inspection of the history of the Irish Convocation. The bishop of Kilmore explained to him the procedure hitherto adopted.

I communicated your thoughts to the archbishop of Dublin about the *Praemunientes* clause, but his grace notwithstanding thinks it necessary to execute it. He saith the provincial writ in use here doth not order that proctors should be chosen, but only that they should meet. They are therefore to be chosen by the *Praemunientes* and turned into a Convocation by the provincial writ....His grace acknowledges they cannot meet when they are chosen upon the *Praemunientes* and therefore we are to order them to stay at home till the provincial writ comes.[1]

Archbishop King, remembering the stormy scenes in Convocation during the last reign, was not disposed to risk a repetition of the experience. Indeed the bishop of Kilmore believed that he would 'never be for our Convocation sitting till we can get a party to throw out Dean Percival from being Prolocutor'.[2] Accordingly the provincial writs were not issued; and no convocation sat with the first parliament of George I. Moreover King inclined to the opinion expressed by Wake in his *Authority of Christian Princes* concerning the inadvisability of withdrawing the clergy from their parochial cures to attend convocation.

Our Lower House of Convocation consists of about one hundred and fifty members; and the number of beneficed clergy in Ireland do not much exceed six hundred. Now if a convocation should always sit during the parliament, it would call one-fourth of the beneficed clergy from their cures and exempt them from the jurisdiction of their Ordinaries.[3]

The Irish primate, Archbishop Lindsay of Armagh, however, thought otherwise and desired convocation to sit with the next parliament.

I look upon it to be a right for the convocation to meet and sit concurrent with every parliament that is holden in this kingdom [he wrote to Wake in 1717]. Now upon calling this last parliament, the *Praemunientes* clause being inserted in the bishops' writs, the proctors for the clergy were chosen and returned, but for want of the provincial writs by which they have usually been embodied, they did not proceed to choose their Prolocutor.

Therefore he appealed to his brother of Canterbury 'to procure the provincial writs against the next meeting of the parliament'.[4] The enunciation of such Atterburian doctrines was well calculated to make Wake wince; and to Archbishop King he confessed that he could make nothing of this 'new phrase of embodying your clergy to sit in convocation'.[5] His reply to Lindsay delicately concealed dissent under a becoming cloak of diplomacy.

Though Your Grace knows my private opinion to be entirely different from what your lordship mentions, both as to the choosing proctors and as to the obligation of the king to assemble a convocation with every parliament, for the which I beg to refer to my books published upon that very subject; yet have I duly represented Your Grace's desire to such of our great men as I thought the most proper to speak about it, and must leave it to them to advise His Majesty what they think fit to be done as to this matter.[6]

[1] Arch. W. Epist. 12, n.f. 22 October 1715.
[2] *Ibid.* n.f. 12 October 1717.
[3] Arch. W. Epist. 12, n.f. 12 September 1717.
[4] *Ibid.* 22 June 1717.
[5] King Correspondence. 31 August 1717.
[6] Arch. W. Epist. 12, n.d.

With the suspension of sitting convocations in England thanks to the Bangorian controversy, however, there was naturally little disposition on the part of the administration to continue the risky experiment in Ireland. Indeed, instead of the issue of the provincial writs to constitute the lower clergy into a house of convocation, even the *Praemunientes* clause was quietly dropped from the bishops' writs after 1716.[1] Nor when Boulter succeeded to the primacy of Ireland, did he show any great zeal to disturb this position.

I find by my Lord Lieutenant [he reported to Wake on 13 January 1727] the ministry are not desirous that a convocation should sit here; nor do I desire it, except they had some useful business to do, and I was thoroughly certain they would confine themselves to that.

I have had no great occasion or leisure to enquire into the nature of our convocation here, but as it is made up of the clergy of four provinces, I find some of our bench question whether they have ever been settled in such a regular method of being called as to make a truly legal assembly.[2]

The pressure of other and more urgent problems appears to have prevented him from pursuing the question further; since his correspondence betrays no wish to change the policy *quieta non movere*.

Among the ill consequences of the suspension of convocation was the lack of official authorisation of such additional offices to the Book of Common Prayer as those debated by the Canterbury Convocation during the reign of Anne for the consecration of churches and churchyards and for the reception of converts to the Church of England. At the beginning of his primacy Wake's attention was drawn to an edition of the Irish Book of Common Prayer, printed by the King's printer at Dublin, which contained a form for receiving lapsed Protestants or reconciling converted Papists to the Church, a form of consecration or dedication of churches and chapels according to the use of the Church of Ireland, an office to be used in the restoration of a church, and a short office for expiation and re-lustration of a church desecrated or profaned; together with the form of a public instrument to be made and publicly read at the end of the consecration and afterwards laid up in the bishop's registry. Accordingly he enquired of the archbishops and bishops of Ireland by what authority these offices had been included in the Prayer Book since the edition printed in 1700. In reply the Irish prelates reported that the form for receiving lapsed Protestants and reconciling converted Papists had been drawn up by Bishop Anthony Dopping, bishop of Meath from 1682 to 1697, whilst the rest were the work of Bishop Jeremy Taylor. They had been 'added to a Common Prayer Book but not put into the Contents, nor intimated that they belonged to it' in 1700, by order, as

[1] W. A. Phillips, *History of the Church of Ireland*, vol. III, p. 195.

[2] *Letters of Boulter*, vol. I, p. 206.

Mr Crook, the King's printer, affirmed (though without producing evidence) of Archbishop Marsh of Dublin, Bishop Moreton of Kildare, Bishop Tennison of Meath 'and some others'. The deprecatory testimony was further added that

> the bishops never looked upon these forms as obligatory and in several particulars do not approve of them. Yet they have suffered them these seventeen years to be printed with the Common Prayer Book, and the rubrics to stand, which plainly imply an authority in them. They disclaim any appointment of them to be used, and believe there never was any such.

Notwithstanding, Wake procured a royal warrant declaring that

> for the making, publishing, printing and annexing of the same to the said Book of Common Prayer and appointing of them to be used, it does not appear that any licence or authority was granted either by His Majesty himself (since whose happy accession to the throne of these realms the Book of Common Prayer beforementioned, with all these several forms annexed thereunto was printed and published) or by any of his Royal predecessors;

and calling the Irish hierarchy to account for the irregularity.[1] From the legal and constitutional standpoint Wake's action was impeccably correct; but the problems of providing such necessary offices and their authorisation were not solved by minatory letters, any more than they have been by the insertion of the uninterpretable formula 'except so far as shall be ordered by lawful authority' in the Clerical Subscription Act of 1865.

During the first septennium of his primacy Wake did his best to support his friends on the Irish bench by championing their interests and measures, both judicial and legislative, at court, in the privy council and in parliament. But his efforts were hampered by his own recurrent bouts of illness and by the uncertain character of his relations with the Whig administration. With the advent of Gibson to the see of London and his admission to the confidence of the Townshend-Walpole circle in 1723 and with the translation in the following year of Boulter to the Irish primacy, however, the Archbishop's influence in Ireland virtually ceased. In this as in other spheres, alike ecclesiastical and political, the rise of Gibson meant his own eclipse. In general Wake shared the standpoint of Englishmen of his day, both churchmen and statesmen, concerning the necessity of maintaining the English supremacy in Ireland. Nevertheless, his conception of this supremacy did not involve the exploitation of Ireland solely for the benefit of England; and he desired the relationship to be one of subordination, not servitude.

> I do not hear of anything that has been done this session [he wrote to Archbishop King on 7 March 1722] to put any load upon your manufactures; and our hands are

[1] Arch. W. Epist. 13, ff. 258–9.

at present so full of other business that I believe we shall think of little else. I cannot tell whether I judge aright; but I was always of opinion that the King's interest and our own require us to make the best improvement we can of every part of His Majesty's dominions; and that it must be a great mistake to hinder the commerce or manufactures of one country, only to raise the riches or trade of another. But self-interest, which is the same on your side the channel that it is on ours, will, I fear, always be too apt to prompt men to sacrifice the public interest to their own; and how to prevent this I cannot tell. I wish none would complain of this temper, but such as stand clear of it themselves. I am sure I heartily wish, and think it my duty to wish, well to Ireland, and even to Scotland, as well as to England.[1]

Amongst the multifarious duties which fell to Wake's lot as archbishop of Canterbury, none were more vexatious and harassing than his visitatorial relations with some colleges of the universities of Oxford and Cambridge. The early years of his primacy, indeed, involved many difficulties with the universities, which were rent by political and academic strife. So grave were the political heats and suspicions of Jacobitism that, as has been already observed, Wake was prepared for a considerable degree of governmental control of the more important university and college appointments for a period of years, such as was proposed in the abortive University Bill. The controversies within colleges centred more in personal jealousies and rivalries, though this factor did not render them easier of composition. Merton College, indeed, during the quarter of a century's wardenship of Dr John Holland from 1709 to 1734, had the unusual distinction of being a hotbed of Whiggism; and one of its fellows in particular, Richard Meadowcourt, was fined 40*s*. in 1716, his name entered in the Black Book and he himself kept back for two years from proceeding to his master's degree by proctorial authority, as punishment for an ebullition of Hanoverian loyalty in celebration of George I's birthday. The college had its domestic disputes also, concerning the number of fellows to be maintained and the precise value of a benefice which would disqualify its holder from retaining his fellowship. In 1711 Archbishop Tenison on appeal had raised this value from £8 (fixed by Archbishop Laud) to £50, strictly enjoining at the same time that this limit should be rigidly enforced.[2] Disputes continued, however, concerning the number of fellows and the body qualified to make elections to fellowships; so that in 1716 recourse was had to Wake as Visitor. On 3 August 1716 he transmitted to the college his determination of these matters; confirming as Visitor the election to fellowships of Meadowcourt and five others; decreeing that elections to fellowships should be made by the Warden and the thirteen senior fellows (except in the eventuality of the college's desiring

[1] King Correspondence. Wake to King. 7 March 1722.

[2] B. W. Henderson, *Merton College*, pp. 153–9.

to increase its customary total of twenty-four fellows, in which case all the fellows should be summoned to make the new elections); that henceforth no elections should be made of less than three fellows, nor should elections be delayed beyond five vacant fellowships; and that such elections should be fixed by the Warden within twenty days of the fifth vacancy, and if, after fixing the date of such election, further fellowships should fall vacant, elections should be made to bring the total to twenty-four fellows.[1] This appeared to determine two of the points at issue, by requiring the number of fellows to be maintained at twenty-four, and by vesting the power of normal elections in the Warden and the thirteen seniors.

Now, however, the exuberant Hanoverianism of Merton was in danger of expressing itself by the election to fellowships of divines tinctured with Hoadleian principles of church and state! Dr David Wilkins, chaplain to Wake, wrote on 16 April 1719 to Thomas Herne of Merton (one of the suspects), to express his grace's concern at the spread in the college of loose opinions inimical to the Church of England. The Archbishop

> must not betray the constitution of the Church, nor the fundamentals of Christianity either to preserve any one's friendship or for fear of anyone's displeasure. Nor by the grace of God will he ever do it. But as he has hitherto endeavoured not to please men, but faithfully to discharge the part of a true, primitive bishop, so I would have you be fully persuaded that he will always countenance those that are sincere members of the Church established, and discourage in a most effectual (though prudent) manner those that go astray and turn aside from her.[2]

These paternal, if prudent, admonitions had their effect in due season; for on 12 January 1720/1 the Warden reported to the Visitor the election of five fellows of sound principles both in church and state, to whom the Archbishop in reply was able to give his cordial approval.[3] It was indeed of this election that the industrious, if indiscreet, collector of Oxford gossip, Dr Stratford of Christ Church, reported that

> the Bangorians were jockeyed yesterday at Merton at the election which they had for five fellows. They like the saints who are privileged, had agreed to cheat their own brother Whigs and the Warden too, and to bring in, without communicating with the others, all five of their own principles. The Warden smells this, and secretly treats with the poor remnant of Tories there, and at the election joins his Whigs to the Tories, and excludes all the Bangorians and brings in every man he had agreed on with the Tories.[4]

The episode had reverberations nearly three years later when charges of bribery in the election were freely made and letters of accusation and denial

[1] Arch. W. Epist. 16, f. 112 *bis*. (The foliation of this volume proceeds regularly to f. 209; and then changes at the next item to f. 110. I have referred to these later items as '*bis*'.)

[2] *Ibid.* f. 116 *bis*.

[3] *Ibid.* ff. 123, 124, 131 *bis*.

[4] Portland MSS. VII, 287. 12 January 1720/1.

flowed into Lambeth, involving particularly Meadowcourt and John Russell. Wake referred the matter for investigation to the Dean of Arches, Dr John Bettesworth, who reported that the evidence was insufficient for any animadversion on either fellow; and therewith the storm subsided.[1]

The Archbishop could combine peremptory with paternal counsels when occasion demanded, as was seen in his trenchant rebuke of Russell for deferment of institution to a benefice, in order to secure the profits both of his fellowship and of the living. Russell was presented in February 1721/2 by the dean and chapter of Peterborough to the rectory of Fiskerton in the diocese of Lincoln. By the college statutes a fellow presented to a living of sufficient value to require the resignation of his fellowship, might, with the consent of the patron, the diocesan bishop and the archbishop of the province, defer his institution for a year and a half, thereby gaining two and a half years' grace instead of the one year allowed for the resigning his fellowship. On 22 January 1722/3 therefore Wake wrote to Russell in direct terms to remind him of his duty and obligations.

> When Dr Ibbetson acquainted me with your desire, I could not but freely declare to him that I wondered you could let pass the whole last summer without taking institution to a living, to which you had been presented at so good a season for it. But that, however, if you were now truly let by sickness from coming to town, I should be willing to allow you a reasonable time to get well, without taking any advantage of the lapse; but that I could not consent to run on your delay of institution to the end of another six months.
>
> I must now take the liberty to add more; and profess myself scandalised at so unwarrantable a procedure; which I cannot but see has been made for the sake of breaking the statutes of your college, by getting two and a half years of grace, instead of one; a thing of very bad example, and such as my relation to that college must make very uneasy to me.
>
> The only reparation you can make for both these irregularities will be to hasten your institution as much as possible. The bishop of Lincoln is in town; a journey to London will be very easy as soon as your cold is off; and I hope I shall hear from his lordship that you have been instituted in a very little time. This as it will well become you, so will it be no less acceptable to me.

To this missive in the style of 'a true, primitive bishop', the culprit replied on 24 January that he would 'next week proceed by the first coach to institution'; and, being as good as his word, received institution on 31 January.[2] The protracted college disputes, however, culminated in a formal visitation by Archbishop Potter in 1737 and his issue of a series of injunctions.

But the troubles of Merton were a storm in a teacup compared with the tempests which raged in All Souls' and involved frequent intervention on the part of the Visitor. Indeed, as has been justly observed, during the

[1] Arch. W. Epist. 16, ff. 164–92 *bis*. [2] *Ibid*. ff. 161–2 *bis*.

wardenship of Bernard Gardiner from 1702–26 'the storms are so furious that we might imagine there was nothing else going on', and 'the college seems to live in the courts of the Visitors'.[1] Trouble had been already brewing during the primacy of Tenison and in the reign of Anne. The Warden had resolved to use his veto to prevent the violation of the founder's statutes by the encroachment of non-residence and the decline of the clerical element amongst the fellows. 'The clerical element was gradually disappearing; and under various pretexts the college was becoming a sort of thinly inhabited club, the occasional resort of non-resident laymen.'[2] By the terms of the statutes all the forty fellows were to be *clericales*, and *ad sacerdotium habiles et dispositi*; whilst the twenty-four artists were to take holy orders within two years, and so many of the sixteen jurists also as did not publicly give proof of their embracing the study of the civil law and take degrees therein. Gardiner determined to put a stop to the laxity by which these statutory responsibilities were evaded, whether by the profession of physic or by using that vocation as a shield for membership of the House of Commons or service of the Crown in various capacities. Unfortunately for himself and the success of his endeavours, the formal visitation held by Tenison in 1710 through the agency of his Dean of Arches, led to the abolition of the Warden's veto on dispensations for non-residence granted by the fellows, which had hitherto been held to be a corollary of his veto upon elections to fellowships. Not even the restriction of the number of 'physic places' to four and the requirement of *bona fide* devotion to the study and practice of medicine, could compensate for the loss of the veto. Although the disputes and storms of the college continued when George I succeeded Anne and Wake followed in the chair of Tenison, the pugnacious Warden was henceforth deprived of his most powerful weapon alike of defence and attack. Gardiner and Wake moreover had already exchanged correspondence with each other, when the latter threatened to support the University Bill of the Whig administration in reprisal for Oxford Jacobitism.

The problems to be settled were both general and specific. In addition to the growing non-residence and laicisation of the college, discipline was lax amongst even the resident clerical fellows.

I will give Your Grace as little trouble for the future as is consistent with the express words of my oath to the college [wrote the Warden on 1 October 1717]. Nevertheless I must humbly acquaint you that on Michaelmas day just past there was a Sacrament in our chapel but no sermon, as by order and ancient usage there ought to have been. The duty of preaching is to be performed by such of the fellows as shall partake of the chapel-money; but there being no fellow to undertake the

[1] Montagu Burrows, *All Souls' Worthies*, p. 348; C. Grant Robertson, *All Souls' College*, p. 161; to which this account is much indebted.

[2] Burrows, *op. cit.* p. 352.

reading surplice prayers this year and consequently to receive the chapel-money... there was therefore no one to preach the sermon. A chaplain assisted me at the Communion, as on Whitsunday when for lack of a fellow I preached myself.[1]

To this the Archbishop replied, assuring the Warden that 'it is so highly reasonable that you should observe not only the express words of your oath to the college, but the true intent and meaning of it, that I shall never account it any trouble to be informed by you of anything which you shall think yourself obliged by such a sacred tie, to lay before me'. After citing the relevant portions of the college statutes, however, he observed that

in all this I do not see that you need my assistance either to oblige your fellows to do their duty, or to inflict proper penalty upon them for their neglect of it. But... I must add that if in this matter my help be wanting to you, you shall readily have it; it being my sincere desire that all who by virtue of your statutes ought to enter into holy orders, should be obliged to do so; that if any hold any fellowship in your college who either by their estates or preferments ought to be dismissed from them, their places should be declared void; and if any neglect to reside upon your college or to perform the duties of it at such times and in such manner as your statutes require, they shall be admonished of their duty and be required to comply with such their statutable attendance. In all this my help shall not be wanting to you, if you shall have occasion for it, as far as by your statutes I am empowered to afford it; which is as much as either you can desire or I offer.[2]

Amongst specific difficulties, there was the complex case of Mr John Stead, who had been dispensed from taking holy orders by a majority of the fellows, notwithstanding the Warden's dissent; who had married subsequently, and had been elected by a majority vote to the office of bursar of arts. The Warden contended that his right of veto on election to fellowships applied also to the office of bursar; and accordingly appeal was made to the Visitor by both parties to the dispute. On 11 March 1716/17 Wake determined in favour of the legality of Stead's election; whereupon after being admitted by the Warden, he left the college and its bursarial duties to take care of themselves.[3]

Encouraged by the Archbishop's promises in his letter of 12 October 1717, the Warden resolved to invite him as Visitor to settle all the questions at issue between the fellows and their head. Unfortunately further delay was caused by the insistence of the Dean of Arches, Dr Bettesworth, that Gardiner must adopt a regular method of procedure either by appeal or petition under the seal of his office, whilst the Warden deemed it sufficient to send 'a suggestion or complaint in a private letter, containing a variety of other things'. This, Dr Bettesworth emphasised, was not

my opinion singly, but I have therein the concurrence of several of the most eminent civilians, judges and advocates, such as have often been engaged in visitation work

[1] Arch. W. Epist. 15, n.f. Gardiner to Wake. 1 October 1717.
[2] *Ibid.* Wake to Gardiner. 12 October.
[3] *Ibid.* A series of documents.

either as assessors or counsel and therefore best acquainted with it; that Your Grace as Visitor cannot take notice of anything there transacted wherein the rights, interest or privilege of any one member are concerned but by visitation of the place by appeal or proper petition in form, and of the last they remember but one single instance. They are likewise of opinion that if either of the latter methods be made choice of, Your Grace not only may but must, as they conceive, be under an unavoidable necessity of citing up the several parties concerned, however unusual it may seem to the Warden.

The hearing these complaints at Lambeth would in all probability be more satisfactory to Your Grace, less expensive to the college and much more easy and agreeable to those who have the honour of serving you; but if those are not the only matters that want redress; if as the gentlemen on the other side say, nothing short of a visitation can set them right, if the use of the negative in elections and the power of inspecting, the scrutiny, as managed by him are as great grievances as ever, if all the late injunctions are broke through, as they suggest, I am afraid that trouble sooner or later cannot well be avoided.[1]

Confronted by this opinion, the Warden on 17 April 1719 under seal of his office formally laid his complaints before the Visitor; who decided that the visitation should be held at All Souls'; where on 30 June Dr Bettesworth arrived at 5 p.m. and forthwith proceeded to the college chapel, opened his commission, swore the fellows and administered the interrogatories, to which he required answers by 9 o'clock the following morning.

The Dean solemnly assured the society that the Archbishop's intention 'was nothing more than to remove the differences now on foot, by explaining what is doubtful and rectifying what was amiss, and putting the college upon such a bottom as may if possible prevent all future complaints'; and that he had 'the welfare and prosperity of the college very much at heart'. Finally he appealed in the discussion of differences for 'decency and respect to each other', and care 'to avoid all such terms as might provoke or exasperate, and must needs, considering whom he had the honour to represent on this occasion, be very shocking and disagreeable'.[2] The enquiry uncovered a sorry state of affairs; and the resultant injunctions were not issued until the following March. They tightened the rules of residence, limiting the period of absence allowed to fellows to sixty statutable days save for causes defined in the statutes and by licence of the Warden, deans and bursars, and ordering that not more than twenty fellows should be allowed leave of absence at one and the same time. In regard to dispensations from taking holy orders, unanimity of the Warden, deans and bursars was to be requisite for their issue, instead of as formerly a simple majority. A scale of fines was fixed for absence from chapel thrice a week or oftener; and for failure to receive the Sacrament four times a year. The Warden's sole right of allotting chambers

[1] Arch. W. Epist. 16, f. 117.

[2] *Ibid.* f. 123.

was confirmed, and his right of veto on elections to fellowships reaffirmed; but his veto upon the annual election of college officers was taken away.[1] The historians of the college concur in interpreting the result as a setback for Gardiner. 'It was tantamount to another defeat for the courageous Warden'; and again, 'It does appear at this distance of time to go somewhat harder against the Warden than the evidence warrants.'[2] The Archbishop on the other hand was convinced of the justice of his decision.

> I have spared no trouble, I have stuck at no cost to get the best advice and direction I could; and I have clearly satisfied my own conscience that I have done impartially what I thought truth, justice and the welfare of that Society required. I am sure whoever considers the whole, will see that I have favoured no party; but indeed was prepared to hear that I had offended all.[3]

It was hardly surprising, however, that Gardiner appealed for some archi-episcopal preferment to remove him from the scene of strife and to enable him to end his days in peace.

> Now that I have stood the test of two visitations without any accusations (as I verily believe) of neglect of duty, or of any conduct but what becomes an uncorrupt governor and a good Christian, I am not without hopes that Your Grace will bestow some marks of your favour upon me. If anything offers to make my family some amends for parting with my headship, I purpose to make room for someone who may do that good here, which I have attempted to do, but have failed of it. The truth is the expense I have been put to several times has been so very burthen-some as to make the place hardly worth my keeping for some years past, if I could with reputation have quitted it till these trials were over.[4]

Unfortunately no sign of favour was vouchsafed; and the Warden had to be content with his vicarage of Ambrosden and his rectory of Hawarden.

Instead, a further occasion of controversy arose in 1723 concerning the claim of Mr Robert Wood to admission as a fellow on the ground of founder's kin. In this episode the society found itself enjoying that magic elixir which maketh men to be of one mind in an house; for both Warden and fellows were unanimous in rejecting the plea. Wake as Visitor pronounced however in favour of Wood; and forced him on the college. The case was attended, as contemporary accounts related, with some accompaniments of comedy; for 'no sooner was the import of this sapient decree—that the Visitor pronounces for his own jurisdiction—communicated to a crowd of purple slaves attending in the antechamber, but mutual and cordial congratulations ensued, because, as they rightly observed, "My Lord hath got his cause"'.[5] On 16 July 1723 the Warden informed the primate that 'Mr Wood was this

[1] *Ibid.* f. 149. [2] C. G. Robertson, *op. cit.* p. 167; M. Burrows, *op. cit.* p. 378.
[3] Ballard MSS. III, f. 162. Wake to Charlett. 8 March 1719/20.
[4] Burrows, *op. cit.* p. 380. [5] *Ibid.* p. 383.

day admitted; a certificate in form shall be transmitted as soon as the mandates can be registered. We hope, since Your Grace's pleasure is fulfilled in this point, that Mr Wynne may not lose his scholarship.' In reply it was graciously allowed that 'if it be the desire of yourself and the fellows of the college that I should nominate Mr Wynne to the other scholarship, as soon as your return is made to me I shall be very willing to gratify you in that matter'.[1]

This interchange of civilities did not obscure the fact that the college resented both the verdict and the means by which it had been secured; and also the loss of £700 in pleading their cause. Accordingly the historians of All Souls' have borne hardly upon the Archbishop for his action.

> Wake was technically right, but, as Blackstone afterwards showed, in reality wrong; and as he made use of the expression more than once that his wife was of founder's kin and placed his own son in the college on that account, he has been accused of partiality. Certainly he proceeded on opposite principles from those which had guided him in the recent visitation.

Or again,

> The result was a foregone conclusion. Wake, who had placed his own son in All Souls' by the 'right of the founder's kin', naturally decided for his own jurisdiction....One more defeat for the gouty old Warden! Wood was admitted, the college sulkily recording a protest that 'it was compelled thereto by the mandate of the visitor, but reserved any right to further remedy'.[2]

Unfortunately Wake's son had died in infancy, at much too tender an age to be entered upon the books of any college, much less to enjoy the *otium cum dignitate* of a fellowship at All Souls'. In 1718, on the other hand, the Archbishop had induced his secretary, Richard Chicheley, to resign his fellowship in that College; hoping thereby to

> put an end to some reflections which were little deserved by me. Had the Warden thought fit, as being a person of the direct name and family of their founder, and secretary and kinsman to their Visitor, to have shewn him the same favour he did to another worthy gentleman but who had not the like pretensions to it, I believe nobody could have justly condemned him for it, nor would his Society have suffered by it. In the meantime I hope I shall take such care of him that he shall not repent of the resignation he has made, chiefly to justify me from some imputations which I as little value as I ever deserved them.

At least, Wake concluded, it would now be publicly known 'that my secretary no longer helps to keep that college in disorder'.[3]

In view of his difficulties with colleges to which he stood in the relationship

[1] Arch. W. Epist. 16, f. 194.
[2] M. Burrows, *op. cit.* pp. 382–3; C. G. Robertson, *op. cit.* p. 168.
[3] Rawlinson MSS. D. 472, f. 2. Wake to Charlett. 20 November 1718.

of Visitor, it might have been expected that the Archbishop would exercise the utmost caution against being involved in the protracted polemics which characterised the Mastership of Richard Bentley at Trinity College, Cambridge. The conflict between Master and Fellows, which embraced also the dispute concerning the relative powers as Visitor of the Bishop of Ely and the Crown, had seemed on the point of determination after an enquiry by Bishop Moore of Ely, when his death in 1714 prevented the publication of his verdict. His successor, Bishop Fleetwood, declined to intervene until the issue had been decided by the King. At this juncture Wake gratuitously allowed himself to be drawn into the *mêlée* through his acquaintance with Philip Farewell, a junior fellow and a supporter of Dr John Colebatch against the Master. The Archbishop expressed the opinion that the college could not continue to endure the arbitrary proceedings of Bentley, advised the presentation of a petition to the King in Council, and promised that he himself would both second such a request and also propose the appointment of a royal commission to visit the college. After a preliminary enquiry of Lord Townshend as to the most suitable method of procedure, nineteen fellows signed on 18 May 1716 a short petition, simply requesting a determination of the visitatorial power. Before the petition was heard in council on 26 October, however, further and (if it were possible) even fiercer disputes had arisen between Master and Fellows concerning the election to offices and fellowships; which, when reported to Wake, evoked his observation that Bentley was 'the greatest instance of human frailty that he knew of, as with such good parts and so much learning he could be so insupportable'. The petition was referred to the attorney-general, Sir Edward Northey, who had not reported on it when in 1718 he gave place to Sir Nicholas Lechmere.[1]

In that same year Bentley was involved in even graver disputes in the university with its Vice-Chancellor, Dr Thomas Gooch, Master of Caius, who, sitting with six heads of houses as assessors, declared the Master of Trinity to be suspended from all his degrees. This sentence having being confirmed in both the non-regents' and the regents' houses, Bentley appealed to the Crown as Visitor; and on this occasion himself wrote to Wake, asking his 'patronage and protection' when the matter came before the King in Council, 'so far as my case will there appear to be just and right', adding, not unjustly, that 'a sentence of suspension or degradation *ab omni gradu suscepto* pronounced upon a trifle, without citation or summons, or the least opportunity of defence, upon a Regius Professor and Master of the greatest College here, is a thing unprecedented from the foundation of the University'.[2] At the same time Colebatch renewed his request to the Archbishop for a reconsidera-

[1] J. H. Monk, *Life of Richard Bentley* (2 vols. London, 1833), vol. I, chs. xi and xii.
[2] Arch. W. Epist. 16, f. 22.

tion of the petition from nineteen fellows of Trinity College in 1716 and for a decision concerning the visitatorial authority. Wake replied dissuading Colebatch from this complication of the issue, and his advice was accepted.[1] The appeal of Bentley was therefore read at the meeting of the Council on 30 October, and the vice-chancellor was ordered to attend on 6 November to present his case for the degradation. The Council thereupon referred the matter to a committee for report, which though prepared on 10 December, did not receive consideration until 9 May 1719; when it was agreed 'that His Majesty hath an undoubted right to visit the said two universities of Oxford and Cambridge', and a committee was appointed 'to consider of a form of a commission for visiting the university of Cambridge'.[2] At this juncture also Colebatch renewed his request that the Council should include within the ambit of their deliberations the petition from Trinity College; and the Archbishop counselled him to approach Lord Sunderland on the matter. On 26 May therefore the Regency Council considered the petition and referred it to the committee charged with preparing the form of visitatorial commission, of which Wake was a member.[3] This double threat drove Bentley to effect a strategic retreat, by which, having made a composition with his opponents in the college, the petition of the nineteen fellows was withdrawn; and the wily Master thereby disencumbered himself of the more dangerous of his opponents. On the other hand the *vis inertiae* characteristic of the age, brought to nothing the ambitious project of a royal visitation of the university.

Wake indeed became involved in conflict with Bentley on one further occasion, concerning the college librarianship; the appointment to which lapsed to the archbishop of Canterbury if the master and seniors failed to fill the office within fourteen days of its being vacant. In 1716 Wake had already exercised this right; but in 1729 the situation was complicated by the non-residence of the librarian and his breach of the statutes by proceeding to a degree higher than that of Master of Arts, and by the circumstance that the offender, Thomas Bentley, was a nephew of the master. The episode produced a spirited correspondence between primate and master, in which the former's attitude was characterised by 'a liberal and candid consideration for all parties, a clear-sighted penetration and an anxiety to act rightly under embarrassing circumstances'.[4] The matter was referred for decision to the attorney-general, now Sir Philip Yorke, and was finally settled by a curious compromise, whereby the librarian resigned his office and was succeeded by two librarians,

[1] Arch. W. Epist. 16, ff. 23, 24.

[2] *Ibid.* f. 26.

[3] Monk, *op. cit.* vol. II, pp. 79 *seq.*

[4] Monk, *op. cit.* vol. II, pp. 275–9. The correspondence is printed in *The Correspondence of Richard Bentley*, ed. Christopher Wordsworth (2 vols.), vol. II, pp. 680–98, 823.

Mr Sandys Hutchinson, appointed by Wake, and Mr William Gossip, elected by the master and seniors as 'additional library-keeper with a salary from the college'. Thereby, at long last, the Archbishop was delivered from the contentiousness of colleges, after suffering the particular misfortune to find both All Souls' College in Oxford and Trinity College in Cambridge undergoing one of their most litigious periods.

During his tenure of the primacy Wake's thoughts turned back to the project which he had formed whilst rector of St James', Piccadilly, of completing his collection of English ecclesiastical records, so as to extend Spelman's *Concilia*. The first-fruits of his researches had been garnered in his *State of the Church and Clergy of England* in 1703; and the work was to reach its fulfilment in Wilkins' *Concilia Magnae Britanniae et Hiberniae* more than thirty years later in 1737. It had been his pristine hope by his own hand, as he explained to Professor Pictet of Geneva, to add a third and possibly a fourth volume to the two of Spelman.[1] But meantime the duties of episcopal office, and still more those of the archbishopric, for which neither his energy nor time were sufficient and which left no leisure from public business, had engaged him (as he confided also to Leibnitz in 1716). Nevertheless with the help of his learned and laborious librarian, David Wilkins, he had hopes of finishing the task.[2] This would appear to be the first mention of Wilkins in connection with the ambitious scheme entertained by Wake; and, though the relationship between primate and librarian has been sketched by Professor E. F. Jacob in a fascinating fascicule,[3] it may be permissible to enlarge somewhat upon it here, so far as concerns the Archbishop himself.

The indefatigable repository of learned lore, Hearne, caught a first whisper of the design in 1725; and in 1732 heard that Wilkins' *Councils* 'are the archbishop of Canterbury's own collections'; to which the later information was added that

> what I was lately told of an edition of our *English Councils* by Dr Wilkins is well grounded. He is now employed in that work by the archbishop of Canterbury, Dr Wake, first entrusted with Dr Walker, who being better qualified for classics,

[1] 'Plurima ad historiam Ecclesiae nostrae et praesertim ad publicos ejusdem conventus spectantia e tenebris eruerim; quae si huic tantum mihi otii deinceps largitus fuerit, possunt aliquanto in lucem proferri; et concilia nostra, duobus jam voluminibus, omnino imperfecte edita, in tria vel quatuor non absque aliqua literati orbis utilitate, augere.' Arch. W. Epist. 25, f. 51. 30 September 1717.

[2] 'Speraveram aliquando Historiam Ecclesiasticam gentis nostrae ac praecipue Synodalem non inutilem neque parvam orbi literato proponere. Sed obstitit huic incepto brevi postea superveniens munus episcopale; obstat multo magis quo nunc implicor archiepiscopi opus...cui soli exequendo nec vires nec tempus sufficiunt. Si quid tamen otii a negotiis publicis? Possim fortasse diligentis nec minus literati Bibliothecarii mei D. Wilkinsii auxilio, etiam haec aliquando praestare.' *Ibid.* f. 24. 1716.

[3] E. F. Jacob, 'Wilkins' *Concilia* and the Fifteenth Century'. *Transactions of the Royal Historical Society*, 4th ser. vol. XV (1932), pp. 91–131.

has dropt it and left it to Dr Wilkins, who is an industrious man and is skilled in Saxon &c; but his materials are the Archbishop's own collections, who some time sent Mr Baker a catalogue of the particulars which are very considerable, and it thence appears to be a great work if well digested.[1]

A year later Hearne had been

told that Dr Wilkins is publishing in folio all the British, Saxon and English councils and synodical Decrees, wherein will be included both Sir Henry Spelman's volumes. I find Archbishop Wake intended this work and made collections for it near thirty years ago. I am sure Wilkins was upon it himself in Queen Anne's time, perhaps by the countenance of Wake, but was then hindered, being not thought to be a proper person.[2]

Hearne was surprisingly accurate in his information, though warped in judgment where Wilkins was concerned. Wake had begun his accumulation of materials in the days of his convocation writings.

I have entered on a new work, though part of an old design, since my coming to town [he confided to Thomas Tanner]. I have collected together all that my own books afford for a collection of ecclesiastical and concilliary affairs from the beginning of King Henry VIII's reign. I shall have finished my own collection by the end of this month. It is larger than I had expected, and yet I doubt not will be much increased when you men of manuscripts and curiosities come to see my catalogue. I have at present no other thought but of putting them together for my own use. Yet if once my collection be perfected, I shall by degrees as I have leisure, collect the public acts with a short breviate of the history of the Church to make them the more intelligible; and if I finish them, they may in time serve for public use. But this is so remote that I make no account of it. In the meantime I will endeavour in about three weeks' time to send you a perfect catalogue of what I have got together and entreat you to consider yourself and to advise with any others you shall think fit, to make what additions our university may afford to it. But suppress my name, unless to a particular friend. I have amassed a good quantity of Convocation Acts together, and am in pursuit of more; which may afford matter for a discourse on that subject. I have also epitomised the Acts of Parliament from Magna Charta to this day that respect ecclesiastical affairs. All to Henry VIII I shall set at the head of my Collection; The rest shall follow among the other public Instruments in their respective years. Together I shall make two (if not more) large volumes in quarto.[3]

There, unfortunately, thanks to the intrusion of those thieves of learned leisure, the duties and responsibilities of episcopal office, the matter rested until as archbishop he began to use his chaplains and librarian for the

[1] Hearne, *Collections*, vol. VIII, p. 385; vol. XI, pp. 119, 123.
[2] *Ibid.* vol. XI, p. 285.
[3] Bodleian Tanner MSS. XXII, f. 154. 10 January (no year).

resumption of the work. To Mr Thomas Baker of St John's College, Cambridge, he wrote on 20 January 1725:

> I once had a design to have not only published a new edition of Spelman's *Councils*, 2 volumes, the 2nd much corrected, as indeed it needs, but to have added enough to make a 3rd volume if not more. I've most of the materials ready by me; but I am too old and engaged in other business too much to carry on such a design. Had I been able to do this, I would have sent my Index of what I have to you, and desired you to add under their proper years, what you had that would have been proper to add that I had not met with. But at present I must not think of this.[1]

In the following autumn he reported further steps towards realisation of the project.

> The 2nd volume of Spelman's *Concilia* being grown very scarce, and as by examination I have found, very inaccurate and imperfect, I have long had it in my thoughts to set out a new and more perfect edition of it. Having at last determined to set my chaplain, Mr Walker, about it, I've given him my catalogue of what instruments and materials I have ready for the improvement of such a work, besides the many corrections I have made from the original records and manuscripts of those already published in my copy of that book. Mr Walker designs to wait upon you next week and communicate that catalogue to you, and ask the favour of you to look it over, and make what additions you can to it; which Mr Walker will get some proper person to copy at my expense under your direction. My design is to collect whatever may seem to illustrate the doctrine and discipline of our English Church in a constant succession from the Conquest to the Reformation. My collections are in the way of annals; several years have nothing at all in them; in these I would chiefly desire your assistance; in others any supply of materials to what I already have. You will see that though I chiefly look to synodical acts, yet I do not so much stick to them as not to take in all other public acts and monuments relating to the Church. Your comprehensive search after all these matters will much oblige my enquiries; which after your assistance will terminate in my friend Dr Tanner, for what concerns this province.[2]

In thanking Baker for his help, the Archbishop avowed on 11 October,

> I have deferred the work I now resume—too late—several years, hoping for more leisure and better help. I am now too far gone to do much myself, but if Mr Walker will go heartily about it, my collections, my purse and my own poor assistance as far as I am able, shall be ready for the furthering of it. I should hope now the materials are brought pretty near together, he may with the more ease carry on such work and finish it in a short time.[3]

The project, indeed, had not been forgotten during the long years of preoccupation with ecclesiastical duties. Whilst dean of Exeter, Wake had made extracts from the records of that see; Tanner and Gibson had contributed their meed, as also had Nicolson; whilst Wilkins himself during the early years

[1] Bodleian MSS. Eng. Hist. d. I. 29781, f. 77 (3). [2] *Ibid.* f. 78 (4). [3] *Ibid.* (5).

of Wake's primacy had been a researcher in Oxford and elsewhere. The result of this co-operative effort is represented by twenty-four volumes among the manuscripts left by the Archbishop to Christ Church, chiefly concerned with Convocation Records of both provinces. It is not possible to ascertain precisely when Wilkins became the principal and finally the sole editor. John Walker became chaplain to Wake in 1727, having been preferred by the primate to the rectory of Bocking two years previously; and he was clearly entrusted with the preliminaries as late as the autumn of 1726. But the project was completed by Wilkins, who finished his edition of Selden's works in 1726. Like his master, he sought and obtained the assistance of many churchmen in his task. Professor Jacob has shown that he was no mere redactor; but that he brought an independent judgment to bear on the construction of the work. 'The work therefore is in a sense a great co-operative continuation of Spelman, originally planned by an English primate and completed by an archdeacon who began life as a Prussian stranger working for pay.'[1] Perhaps the greatest tribute to its importance may be seen in the fact that after the lapse of two centuries a panel of expert medieval scholars has embarked upon a revision and expansion of Wilkins' *Concilia*, as Wake and his librarian did of Spelman.

Another exercise of Wake's primacy was of a more strictly recreative character, namely his collection of medals and coins. He owed the stimulus to this diversion, no less than his continuing interest in the enterprise once begun, to his Swiss protégé, J. H. Ott.

> Mr Otte has lately tempted me at a very unseasonable time of my life [he averred to Turrettini on 3 September 1720] to begin a small collection of Medails; which indeed I do rather to leave behind me as a proper ornament of the archiepiscopal library, than for any great improvement I shall make in that study myself. I believe I should have done better had I followed your example and bought a good collection at once. But Mr Otte took the other way; and I am now too far in it to retreat. So that I must perfect my small treasure the best I can. I have got about 1000; and most of these are of a good sort. I meddle not with any modern pieces. If I should meet with a collection of such together, I would at once furnish myself with them.[2]

L'appétit vient en mangeant; and the Archbishop's interest and enthusiasm grew with the extension of his collection. The letters written by Ott during his travels abroad, were punctuated with descriptions and prices of medals seen on his way. Indeed his patron considered him to have 'a particular genius for the study of medals', since he had picked 'a greater collection than I could have expected or should ever otherwise have had'.[3] Further evidence of Wake's zeal for, and of the expansion of, his hobby was given in a letter

[1] E. F. Jacob, *op. cit.* p. 104. Wake preferred Wilkins to the archdeaconry of Suffolk in 1724.
[2] Geneva MSS. Inventaire 1569, f. 81.
[3] *Ibid.* f. 139.

of 2 February 1726/7 to the antiquarian, physician and divine, Dr William Stukeley, whom he had admitted to holy orders.

I believe I once acquainted you that I had been endeavouring to gather a perfect collection of our English money, of all metals, from the Conquest to the present times. I am almost perfect from King Henry VII inclusive; but want several of the more antient reigns. If it should lie in your way to meet with any of them, and you would be so kind as to think of me, I would most thankfully receive them at any reasonable rate you could get them for me. I have some of William the Conqueror, Henry II, Edward I, II, and III, Henry IV, V, and VI, Edward IV; none of any others before Henry VII. You will have the goodness to excuse this liberty, and impute it to the desire I have to finish a collection, intended for the use of the public when I myself have done with it.[1]

Instead of adorning Lambeth Palace library, however, the collection was bequeathed together with his manuscripts to Christ Church, where it remained until transferred on loan to the Ashmolean Museum; of which it now constitutes an item of not inconsiderable value and importance.

It seems clear that the year 1730 marked a landmark in the life of the ageing Archbishop. Until that time he retained much of his vigour and interest in public affairs. In 1729, thanks to the impending vacancy of a prebend of Westminster, which he had long coveted for his son-in-law, Dr Lynch, his desire in this respect seemed at long last about to be fulfilled. The Duke of Newcastle informed him that the King would bestow the preferment on Lynch, provided the beneficiary would resign his prebend of Canterbury; and if this dignity should be in the Archbishop's gift, he would appoint to it whomsoever His Majesty should nominate. The sting of the offer lay in its tail; since Lynch was the butt of contemporary satirists for his pluralism. 'The King thinks that the holding of two prebends in the great cathedrals by his means, would be so ill a precedent and so prejudicial to his service, that His Majesty for this reason makes this condition.'[2] With a sudden resurgence of his old spirit, Wake declined the proposal; even though, as he confessed, a prebend of Westminster 'would indeed be more acceptable to me for him than any other preferment of much greater value'. But the condition imposed was altogether unacceptable.

I was not aware when I begged His Majesty's favour to him for Westminster, that I had asked anything contrary to His Majesty's good liking; such a preferment being no more than what has commonly gone with a prebend of Canterbury heretofore. The very statutes of that Church in the chapter *De Qualitatibus Canonicorum* cap. x, particularly provide for the qualifying the king's chaplains to hold a prebend of Westminster or Windsor with a canonry of Canterbury.

[1] J. Nichols, *Literary Illustrations of the Eighteenth Century*, vol. II, p. 784.
[2] S.P. Domestic. George II. Vol. 16, f. 5. 4 November 1729.

Various examples of such pluralism were adduced; which had made the Archbishop hope 'that a prebend of Canterbury might have been allowed to take a prebend of Westminster with it; but since it is not His Majesty's pleasure, I can only say I am sorry I did not know it; and hope His Majesty will forgive my mistake. I humbly beg Your Grace to lay these reasons before His Majesty as my apology for my conduct.'[1]

About the same time, moreover, Wake took the opportunity to rap ministerial knuckles because of irregularities in the form of donation used in royal presentations to prebends of Canterbury. It was not the first time he had protested against these forms. On 3 August 1723 he had pointed out that a patent had been presented to him

in such a form as is utterly inconsistent with the statutes of our Church and wholly different from the patents that have always been drawn for any dignities in it. It is not directed to me as Bishop of the Church, nor am I once mentioned in it. There is no order for me to give institution; but the King wholly collates to it as a mere donative. There is no power left me, after institution, to order an induction; but the King grants a separate patent to the Dean and Chapter for instalment. Every circumstance of which is expressly repugnant to our statutes and the immemorial practice of our Church.[2]

Five years later a further protest was called for.

Our statute is as express as words can make it, that the Canons shall be presented to the Archbishop by the King *per Literas Patentes magno sigillo nostro aut successorum nostrorum sigillatas*. I beg your lordship to let this matter be settled in such a way as may hereafter avoid these difficulties, occasioned only by the clerk's returning to their old, improper forms after others had been corrected and adapted to our statutes and practised for many years last past; and for what reason I cannot tell.[3]

Notwithstanding these remonstrances and an express promise of amendment, the very same errors recurred 'either by ignorance or carelessness'; so that on 18 February 1729/30, Wake once more despite his 'present weakness and indisposition', wrote a strong letter of protest. In a recent patent,

I am not once named in it, nor have I any command from His Majesty either to institute or grant a mandate for instalment,...and I should be glad to know from Mr Attorney [General] whether I can do either of these without any commission, order or direction of the King to that purpose. In a donative of a common patron to a living, the bishop cannot (I think) by law give an institution which would injure the patron and make his church become presentative; whether I can legally give an institution to a donative of the King without any licence of or authority from the King I wish Mr Attorney would please inform me.

Once more the Archbishop recited the statutes of his cathedral and also forms correctly drawn; and reminding the minister of his former promise to

[1] S.P. Domestic. George II, vol. 16, f. 6. 5 November 1729.
[2] *Ibid.* George I. Vol. 44, f. 115.
[3] *Ibid.* George II. Vol. 7, f. 269.

amend the procedure, begged that this should be done 'and thereby prevent any further trouble of this kind'.[1] Certainly this letter suggested no failing of Wake's intellectual powers. Nor was there any lack of vigilance or vigour in his defence of the clergy of his diocese against a charge of Jacobitism forwarded to him by Lord Townshend in November 1729. 'Pursuant to my promise I wrote to my archdeacon to make the best enquiry he could into the complaint made to your lordship against the clergy of my diocese as to their disaffection to His Majesty's government, which I verily believe the anonymous correspondent would be hard put to, to make any tolerable proof of.' Enclosing the detailed report of the archdeacon, he fully endorsed its conclusion that 'the information is not only absolutely false but groundless; and that this diocese is in as good a temper and as well-affected towards His Majesty as it has been at any other time, and as any other diocese in this kingdom, which is the very lowest I can say of this clergy'.[2]

In 1730, however, Wake suffered the most serious of his succession of illnesses, which henceforth gravely disabled him. 'I have for a long time been laid up with a fever', he informed Thomas Baker on 7 June; 'which has not only deprived me of all my strength, but, which is worse, has almost beyond what I can express, impaired my memory and my understanding.' A few days later he confessed that the illness had 'so impaired all my faculties that I am to seek for my own books, manuscripts and others, by a decay or almost loss of memory; and have not strength to search for what I want and can remember somewhat of'.[3] In the following year his wife died on 15 April; and nearly two years later on 15 February 1732/3 he informed his old friend Browne Willis that 'my long-continued sickness and weakness, both increased by the misfortune I have had in losing my wife, has so broken me and lost me the use of my own eyes, that I do with great difficulty write to you'.[4] The few letters extant in his own hand after this date tell their own tale of infirmity. Henceforth he withdrew from public affairs to complete retirement. The last occasion on which he officiated at the consecration of bishops was on 23 January 1732 when he consecrated his friend Thomas Tanner to St Asaph and Nicholas Claggett to St David's. In the political sphere it was remarked that in the famous division in the House of Lords on 24 May 1733, when the Walpole administration was saved from defeat by 24 episcopal votes cast for it, only the Archbishop of Canterbury was absent without a proxy.[5] The ministry took alarm and pressed him therefore to lodge his proxy for the ensuing session with his brother of Durham. But all that his son-in-law,

[1] *Ibid.* Bundle 17, f. 124. Wake to Townshend.
[2] S.P. Domestic, George II. Vol. 16, ff. 31–2, 35. 27 November 1729.
[3] Bodleian MSS. Eng. Hist. d.1. 29781, f. 79 (10) and f. 80 (11). 7 and 11 June 1730.
[4] Bodleian MSS. 16328, f. 2d. Browne Willis MSS. 36, f. 247.
[5] Hist. MSS. Comm. Earl of Carlisle MSS. 118.

Dr Lynch, could reply was that 'Her Majesty and Your Grace will recollect what I had the honour to say to you both upon this subject, was only that I would endeavour to persuade the Archbishop if the court at any time was hard pressed in any particular point, to make a proxy to serve them in that vote'.[1]

Apart from incidental references in his correspondence, hardly any information can be gathered about his wife and family. His six surviving daughters all married,[2] and contemporary criticism fastened on his dependence in his declining years upon his son-in-law, Dr Lynch, whose name became a byword for rapacity and pluralism.[3] With the progressive decline of his faculties during the last few years of his life Wake fell into increasing infirmity of mind. Finally, as his Act Book recorded,

> on Monday the 24th day of January 1736/7, between the hours of 2 and 3 of the clock in the afternoon of the same day, in a certain chamber within Lambeth House, the Most Reverend Father in God, William Wake, Lord Archbishop of Canterbury, Primate of All England and Metropolitan, departed this life in the presence of Mr John Catlin one of his gentlemen and others of his servants, and of me, R. Chicheley, Notary Public.[4]

He died within two days of his eightieth birthday; and was buried on 9 February in Croydon parish church, in the south chancel (sometimes called the Bishops' chancel) where stood the monuments of Whitgift and Sheldon among his predecessors and where his successors Potter and Herring were likewise to rest. His tomb and that of his wife were marked by a simple inscription: 'Depositum Gulielmi Wake Archiepiscopi Cantuariensis: Qui obiit 24 Januarii A.D. 1736 Aetatis suae 79; Et Ethelredae uxoris ejus Quae obiit 15 Aprilis 1731.'[5]

[1] B.M. Add. MSS. 32689, f. 142. Lynch to duke of Newcastle. 15 January 1733/4.

[2] Wake's eldest daughter, Amy, married Henry Seymour, Esq., of Handford, Dorset; the second, Ethelred, married Thomas Bennett, Esq., of Norton Bavant, Wiltshire; the third, Hester, married first Richard Broderip, Esq., of Mapperton, Derbyshire, and next Thomas Strode of Parnham in the same county; the fourth, Dorothy, married James, eldest son of Sir James Pennyman, Bart, of Ormsby, Yorkshire; the fifth, Magdalen, married William Churchill, Esq., of Hanbury, Dorset; and the sixth, Mary, married Dr John Lynch. The Master of Whitgift's Hospital at Croydon, Henry Mills, described Mrs Wake as 'the best of wives, the tenderest of mothers, the most respectful to her relations and friends, the best of mistresses and the most obliging to her neighbours'. Further, 'her time was not spent in mirth, jollity and pleasure; but every hour of the day (as I am informed) was allotted for its peculiar business'. *An Essay on Generosity and Greatness of Spirit.* Dedicated to Archbishop Wake, p. lvii.

[3] Cole MSS.; B.M. Add. MSS. 5841, f. 21; Egmont MSS. (Hist. MSS. Comm.) II, 333.

[4] Lambeth Act Books, VIII, f. 67.

[5] D. Lysons, *Environs of London* (4 vols. 1786), vol. I, p. 184.

EPILOGUE

'Omnium consensu capax imperii nisi imperasset.' The apophthegm of Tacitus springs as swiftly as spontaneously to mind in considering the contrast between the high anticipations entertained at the outset of Wake's primacy and his total eclipse after only seven years by Gibson, and demands consideration of the justice of its application. Must his tenure of the archbishopric be written down as a failure; and if so, were the causes personal to himself? From the political standpoint there can be no doubt that the bright hopes with which his friends hailed his succession to the chair of St Augustine, and even the more moderate optimism with which he himself looked forward to its responsibility, were soon and sadly belied by the issue of events. The alliance of churchmen with the Whig administration, on which the security both of the new dynasty and of the established church seemed to depend, quickly broke down so far as Wake was concerned; and the task of repairing the breach was confided to the more energetic hands of Gibson. In great part, however, this was due to the ineptitude (not to say imbecility) of the ministers of state in promoting Hoadly to the see of Bangor (and thence in rapid succession to Hereford and Salisbury during the first septennium of Wake's primacy), and also to their consequent blunders in suppressing Convocation because of its threatened censure of Hoadly's opinions and in dismissing from the rota of royal chaplains those divines who entered the literary lists against him. Such actions revealed not only an alarming irresponsibility but also a complete incomprehension of the ecclesiastical situation. To give this affront to a new primate at the very beginning of his succession was an act of political unwisdom amounting to foolhardiness. On the other hand, the Archbishop's *volte-face* in regard to the repeal of the Occasional Conformity and Schism Acts was equally disconcerting from the standpoint of his would-be political allies; for the Whigs were bound to do something for the Dissenters and the repeal of these offending statutes (themselves the symbol of the Tory and high church reaction during the last four years of Anne's reign) was the minimum with which both the administration and the Dissenters could be content. After this episode, relations between Wake and the ministry went from bad to worse. Here again, the personal traits of the Archbishop's character were a contributory factor to the series of misunderstandings and resentments. With the advent of Walpole and Townshend to power and the former's immediate and instinctive choice of Gibson as ecclesiastical adviser, Wake's short period of influence was ended. It is therefore important to remember that Gibson in turn, despite his tougher fibre and greater ability to withstand the rough and tumble of political manœuvre, found the Whigs impossible allies and after the episode of the Quakers' Tithe Bill in 1736, during Wake's own lifetime, likewise threw in his hand. Even he could not create and animate the hybrid of a 'Church-Whig'. Perhaps Augustine Birrell was nearly right in designating the eighteenth-century lay Whigs 'as irreligious a set of dogs as ever barked at a cassock', who 'treated their spiritual brethren with a contempt they took no pains to conceal'; and in adding (no doubt from his own knowledge) that 'this Whig mode of treating bishops continued down to our own time, and would continue now, only there are no Whig lords left'. With the fate of Gibson in mind and the semi-approving comment of Birrell, Wake may be acquitted of the major share of blame for the failure of his political ventures.

A more serious charge was levelled against other aspects of his policy by his immediate successor at Canterbury, John Potter.

> Archbishop Wake had greatly too much timidity about him in many cases, and too little vigilance for the good of the Church, though otherwise a very good man and a well-wisher to good men and good principles. But, for want of discernment of one side and attention of spirit of the other, he suffered many bad things to be done, and several unworthy men to be highly preferred, without showing due care and encouragement of better men, though he often had it in his power to do the last and prevent the former. This Archbishop Potter (then bishop of Oxford) took the freedom one day to represent to him, and desired him to look round and see how little regard had been shown for so many years past by the great men to a number of eminent divines, while others of a different character found every advancement. The Archbishop was moved extremely with this representation, and pleaded only for himself, that really he had not observed or considered so much the state of things before, but he would be more attentive for the future. His Grace [Potter] added to me that the truth was, Archbishop Wake was not deep enough in theology and learning, especially antiquity, to know how to fix a proper rule of acting in his station, and therefore had not a proper firmness and steadiness in his conduct. That, moreover, he was chiefly influenced by Bishop Trimnell as long as he lived, who had too much regard to some great men of the laity, to do the Church much service.[1]

This indeed is a criticism of equal comprehensiveness and gravity, to which the eminence of its author adds further weight. It suffers from the evident defect of vagueness and generality, and fails to adduce any specific examples either of persons or episodes against which its censure is directed. Consequently it is not easy, for lack of concrete evidence, adequately to ponder its authority or to refute its judgments.

In respect of episcopal promotions during the period from Wake's succes-

[1] *The Christian Remembrancer*, vol. III, January–December 1821; June 1821. 'We are able to present our readers with the following Notes, copied verbatim from a manuscript in the handwriting of Dr Chapman, the learned author of Eusebius. He was the domestic chaplain and intimate friend of Archbishop Potter.' The extract (pp. 336b–338b) is headed: 'Memorandums of Things which I have heard in private from Archbishop Potter's own mouth, as certain Truths.'

sion to Canterbury in 1716 to his eclipse in 1723 by Gibson, the list numbers only eleven names; including Gibson himself, Hoadly, Blackburne, Chandler, Kennett, Boulter, Green, Reynolds, Wilcocks, Bowers and Baker. Of these Gibson and Kennett were indubitably Wake's own choice, and both would have been eminent in any age of the church. Chandler had written meritoriously in defence of orthodoxy against Deism; Green had been a model archdeacon of Canterbury, in which recognised stepping-stone to preferment he was succeeded by Bowers; and they, together with Reynolds, illustrated Thomas Fuller's dictum that 'the general weight of God's work in the church lieth on men of middle and moderate parts'. Boulter was raised to the episcopate by the favour of Gibson and was very shortly to become a notable primate of Ireland. Hoadly was certainly not Wake's nominee, but Blackburne was; and, though innocent of the baser charges levelled against him, was hardly suitable for the primacy of York (to which indeed he was advanced during Gibson's control of ecclesiastical preferment). Wake was responsible, however, for his elevation to the deanery and see of Exeter, and must bear responsibility thus far. Wilcocks owed his promotion to the circumstance of his having attended George I as chaplain to Hanover, whilst Baker was rewarded for the still more curious reason that he had been disappointed of a Hanover journey. The total of these promotions was comparatively few; and it must be remembered that Wake never enjoyed the monopoly of power which fell to Gibson's lot at any rate during the first quinquennium of his admission to the firm of Townshend and Walpole, when Townshend counselled an aspirant to preferment 'to apply to the bishop of London, for the court would not make a bishop against his inclination'.[1] In particular Wake was well aware of the intimate relationship between Bishop Trimnell of Norwich and Townshend, and that Trimnell had run him close for the succession to the primacy; so that not unnaturally he was careful to secure his rival's concurrence in the measures which he urged upon the ministers of state. So far as episcopal nominations go, therefore, Potter's charge has little substance.

Moreover it is informative to follow the course of the critic's own fortunes after he had succeeded Wake at Canterbury. Bishop Sherlock observed mordantly of him that 'I take the archbishop's principle to be, to go on with everything as he found it, *et non movere quieta*; for the present unsettled state of things it may perhaps be the wisest method. As to an influence in preferments, he looks upon that, I believe, to be so much his province that he will be hardly prevailed on to admit *socios imperii*.'[2] Despite this resolve, Potter was soon lamenting his lack of influence, particularly in regard to his especial

[1] Portland MSS. VII, 413.
[2] B.M. Add. MSS. 32701, f. 95. Sherlock to the Duke of Newcastle. 4 September 1743.

favourite, Dr George Sayer, archdeacon and prebendary of Durham. In November 1743 he complained to Newcastle that, although he had several times recommended Sayer 'to Lord Carteret when abroad, having never obtained any answer to those parts of his letters wherein this was done, he had cause to suspect it was never during His Majesty's absence properly laid before him'.[1] Accordingly Newcastle repaired the omission, only to report to the Archbishop that, when the King's decision was known, 'he would not flatter his grace with the expectation of its being what would be most agreeable to him'.[2] When the recommendation was renewed in the following January, it was accompanied by the intimation that failure in this case would make the Archbishop 'for the future despair of having it in his power to assist his grace and the rest of the administration, or even to be useful to His Majesty's government'.[3] Actually Potter found himself eclipsed, as Wake had done before him, by the still formidable Gibson, to whom the administration once more turned for advice and to whom they actually offered the succession to Canterbury on Potter's death. So deep was the Archbishop's disfavour that George II called him 'proud priest' and other harsh words, and even twice refused him an audience.[4] His own experience of the difficulties, both ecclesiastical and political, of high office therefore, furnished little support for his criticism of Wake. Rather it recalled the advice of Lord Hervey to Walpole on the death of Wake 'to take some Greek and Hebrew blockhead that had learning enough to justify the preferment and not sense enough to make him repent of it'; with the specific rider that Potter was one whose 'capacity was not so good nor his temper so bad as to make him apprehend any great danger from his being there'.[5]

With regard to the observation that Wake 'had greatly too much timidity about him in many cases and too little vigilance for the good of the church', it may be allowed that, in some sense, he was timid, though this was combined with a certain imperiousness of character and temper, which found expression in the repeated complaint of desertion, if not worse, by those bishops who differed from him in policy. It is hardly possible, for example, to imagine him as the author of such bold schemes as the Whitehall Preacherships and the Regius Professorships of Modern History and Languages, conceived and executed by Gibson as means of reconciling the universities to the Hanoverian dynasty and its Whig administration. In another direction, his timidity was

[1] B.M. Add. MSS. 32701, f. 278. Potter to Newcastle. 28 November 1743.

[2] *Ibid.* f. 322. Newcastle to Potter. 23 December.

[3] *Ibid.* 32702, f. 3. Potter to Newcastle. 2 January 1743/4.

[4] N. Sykes, *Edmund Gibson*, p. 379.

[5] Lord Hervey, *Memoirs of the Reign of George II*, vol. II, p. 108. Cf. the Duke of Richmond to Newcastle. 18 October 1747. 'I think the Archbishop died in good time, for I believe he was growing an old rogue.' B.M. Add. MSS. 32713, f. 277.

seen in his shrinking from the *mêlée* of politics and in his hyper-sensitive reaction to the painful episodes of conflict therein with his episcopal brethren. Indeed he admitted to the Archbishop of Dublin in 1719 that the approach of a parliamentary session always filled him with anxious fears.

> It is a time of trouble to me beyond any other. I can neither well bear the attendance it requires, nor be easy at the many difficulties and controversies which almost unavoidably arise in the prosecution of the great affairs of it. I am old and more infirm than most men are at my age. I love quiet above all things. And my duty is never so uneasy to me as when it obliges me to differ from, and perhaps have thereupon some kind of scuffle with my friends, whose affection I should be glad, on any other terms, to preserve without interruption.

It was evident that Wake felt deeply the breach of his long-standing friendship with Gibson, his ally in the Convocation controversy and his successor, chosen by himself, in the see of Lincoln. Moreover he was plainly the antithesis of Dryden's *Achitophel*,

> A daring pilot in extremity,
> Pleased with the danger when the waves went high,
> He sought the storms.

Wake certainly never sought the storms; but his lot was cast in an age when alike for churchmen and statesmen they could not be avoided.

The criticism of Potter, however, implied that he was also 'for a calm unfit'; and that his 'too little vigilance for the good of the church' was due to his not being 'deep enough in theology and learning, especially antiquity', with the result that he did not 'know how to fix a proper rule of acting in his station, and therefore had not a proper firmness and steadiness in his conduct'. This was perhaps a natural prejudice of a former regius professor of divinity at Oxford and the author of an authoritative *Discourse on Church Government* against a primate whose chief distinction lay in the field of English church history. But professional jealousy does not of itself establish the truth of a charge. It was indeed a fact that Wake was not a professed theologian; though this did not imply lack of a sufficient knowledge of theology. His early experiences in controversial exchanges with the redoubtable Bossuet were evidence no less of considerable theological knowledge than of ability to defend the position of the Church of England against the most renowned contemporary apologist of Rome. Nor did the series of tracts and sermons which he published during the reigns of James II and William III suggest inability to discharge the duty of *fidei defensor*. It is true that he withheld his pen from participation in the Socinian and Trinitarian controversies and contented himself with plain parochial sermons to instruct his flock rather than academic tomes of theology. But the reader of these sermons and of his translation of the Apostolic Fathers (together with his visitation charges of 1706 and 1709) cannot doubt his competent, if unostentatious, knowledge of patristic antiquity. It was, however, the spate of controversy which vexed Wake after his succession to the archbishopric, which constituted at once the test and the occasion of criticism of his ability to deal with theological issues. Indeed the flood of polemics—from the Bishop of Bangor's attack on the fundamentals of church government to the Trinitarian disputes arising from Dr Samuel Clarke's speculations, and from the Deists' disparagement of revelation as contrasted with natural religion to their direct challenge to the authenticity of the Old Testament prophecies and the New Testament miracles—was sufficient to try the mettle of any primate.

The primary objective of Wake was to preserve the traditional latitude of the *Ecclesia Anglicana* without allowing liberty to degenerate into licence. To Le Clerc he wrote in glowing terms of comprehensiveness as practised in the Church of England:

> Whether you regard its ancient, or more properly its apostolic, government; or the moderation of its Articles of Religion which the clergy must subscribe; or the liberty allowed to its other members to enquire, determine and even believe in matters of faith (always provided that nothing is publicly set forth which would disturb the peace and tranquillity of the church): I doubt if it does not excel greatly all the other reformed churches.[1]

Further, he avowed himself to the same author to be a sincere friend of liberty of thought. 'Liberty of prophesying, provided it be pious and sober, joined to charity and courtesy, nor contrary to the analogy of that faith once for all delivered to the saints, I consider not to be denounced but rather to be approved.'[2]

In seeking a solution of the theological controversies which vexed the church, his maxim therefore was *garder la paix sans gêner les consciences.* This did not mean, however, encouragement of divines holding Arian or Socinian opinions. On the contrary Wake was determined not to suffer heterodoxy to become a qualification for preferment. Potter himself related how, when there was 'a formed design' to bring Samuel Clarke on the bench and Bishop Trimnell 'came over to Archbishop Wake in order to get his acquiescence in it', the stiffness of the primate's refusal, as expressed by his determination to incur a *Praemunire* rather than consecrate Clarke, was

[1] Arch. W. Epist. 25, f. 52. 25 October 1717. 'Quod sive gubernationem ipsius spectes veterem seu potius Apostolicam; sive moderationem in Articulis Religionis a clero subscribendis; sive libertatem caeteris suis membris concessam inquirendi, judicandi etiam et credendi in rebus fidei (modo nihil in publicum proferatur quod paci et tranquillitati ecclesiae obstet) nescio an non alias omnes ecclesias reformatas plurimum antecellat.'

[2] *Ibid.* f. 9. 29 March 1716. 'Libertatem prophetandi, modo pia ac sobria sit, cum charitate ac mansuetudine conjuncta, nec contra Analogiam Fidei semel sanctis traditae, adeo non vituperandam ut potius probandam, censeam.'

responsible for the dropping of the proposal. Here at any rate was no weakness in giving way to pressure from Trimnell. Wake was willing to allow the suspect presbyter to continue in possession of his present preferment, provided always that he kept his promise not to write or speak further on these dangerous subjects. In the case of Hoadly, his episcopal status and above all the support which he enjoyed from the court and administration prevented the Archbishop from placing upon him any public mark of censure; but he was resolved not to allow others of like opinions to come on the bench. On the other hand he had striven, in respect of both Clarke and Hoadly, to safeguard the Convocation from the perils attending a direct censure of the persons, though ready to concur in a condemnation of their conclusions. Like Dryden's Zadoc,

> The Sanhedrin long time as chief he ruled,
> Their reason guided and their passion cool'd.

Or at least he sought to do so; and the suspension of sitting convocations was the result of defiance by the Lower House of the prudent counsels of the Upper. With regard to the publication of heretical books, Wake exerted his influence, not without effect, to prevent this when possible; or to suppress their circulation when published, and to forward legal prosecutions for this end. By these means he hoped to assuage the storm which was raging and to maintain in the Church the unity of the Spirit in the bond of peace.

At the same time he realised that the best defence of orthodoxy lay in refutation of heretical opinions by scholarly demonstration of their inadequacy. Like Potter himself, he delivered visitation charges against them; and he sought out and encouraged divines to answer their arguments. Potter's own solution for the complex of problems was set forth in a letter of 18 September 1717.

> There is no man who doth more heartily concur with Your Grace in lamenting the present unhappy state of the church than myself, when so many of chief note, even among the clergy, do either openly oppose or covertly undermine as well her principal doctrines as the most essential parts of her authority; but as to the power of requiring all persons who are admitted into holy orders or ecclesiastical benefices to give proper assurances of their sincerity and orthodoxy in the Christian faith, this is so clear in itself and so universally practised in all churches both of the present and former ages, that I can scarce conceive it to be denied by any sensible man, unless on one of these two accounts, viz. either that he thinks the church to be no true society nor to have any power over its own members; or that he disbelieves some of the doctrines to which his assent is required. As to the former of these I have said a great deal in my book of church government; and though in the writings of the Bishop of Bangor and others there may be several tacit objections against some parts of it, I have not yet seen any one of so much weight but that I should willingly leave it to the judgment of any impartial reader who would be at the pains

of comparing my book with it. As to the latter sort, among whom I reckon Dr Clarke because his book against the Christian Trinity is introduced with a prevaricating method of eluding subscription, it seems to me wholly in vain to endeavour to answer them any other way than by confuting their false doctrines; for whatever opinion such men may have of the church's authority to require subscriptions, they will never be easy whilst they look upon those doctrines to be false to which their subscription is required. If Dr Clarke had not first disbelieved the doctrine of the Trinity or some others received in the church, it seems probable to me that we should never have heard anything of his peculiar way of subscribing. I confess it seems to me no small disgrace to us that after the doctrine of the Trinity (to say nothing of others) hath been so publicly attacked for so many years together, though some replies have been made which perhaps neither Dr Clarke, Mr Whiston nor any other can fully answer, yet no just treatise hath been published on that subject; and though I am highly sensible of my own inability, I could hardly have allowed myself to be silent on this and perhaps several other occasions, if I could have hoped to complete any treatise which would have been of the least service to the church by the help of my own eyes; but the depending on other men's eyes is a disadvantage so great as hath discouraged me from undertakings of this nature....

I should humbly propose to Your Grace whether it may not be convenient that some person should write a short and plain discourse which should not exceed the length of an ordinary sermon to shew how reasonable and necessary it is that all clergymen before their admission to any place of trust in the church, should give some proof as well of their sincerity in believing the Christian religion and its chief doctrines as of their good life and behaviour....I should the rather incline to this method because the controversy concerning the church's authority having been sufficiently treated of by several writers not many years since, there seems the less reason to renew it at this time, especially since considering the present disposition it ought to be managed with the utmost prudence and tenderness, and many will sooner be influenced by other arguments than those which are fetched from the church's power which they do not love to hear much of, and which perhaps may as well be taken for granted as called into question without absolute necessity.[1]

It is difficult to find any positive counsels in this lengthy survey of the position which Wake did not carry out to the best of his ability. His support of the abortive Blasphemy Bill was designed to enforce subscription and to make it more of a reality than it had been found to be. When this failed he fell back on a royal order to the bishops to the same end. Nor was he inactive in promoting answers to heretical books in the form of erudite defences of orthodoxy.

I have sent you but a few books out of many [he wrote to Professor Pictet on 8 March 1720], so that it may be clear to yourself and your friends that the orthodox faith is no less strenuously defended from these shores by our sons than you have heard it to be attacked by its enemies. Every day more defenders of the true religion arise; and although, granted the liberty which we enjoy, it is not possible that

[1] Arch. W. Epist. 7. Canterbury II. Potter to Wake. 18 September 1717. Cited in A. W. Rowden, *The Primates of the Four Georges*, pp. 126–7.

pernicious books should not be published daily, yet we have this consolation that scarce any of them are issued with impunity, for they are all examined with the same boldness with which they are written.[1]

Certainly Waterland furnished the 'just treatises' which Potter desired; and Gibson's pastoral letters provided the shorter and more popular defences. In striving to steer between the Scylla of unrestrained licence and the Charybdis of heresy-hunting, Wake may be deemed to have followed both a steady and an even course. Perhaps it may even be claimed for him that he combined the zeal for comprehensiveness of a later primate confronted by a similar storm of controversy, Randall Davidson, together with the historical insight into the character of the Church of England of Mandell Creighton. Perhaps also it was less a deficiency of theology or of knowledge of antiquity than a better understanding of the *via media* which led him even in the heat of conflict to seek peace and ensue it.

From a positive standpoint moreover his own contribution to the good estate of the *Ecclesia Anglicana* was both massive and many-sided. Pre-eminently he left behind him a definitive history of English Convocations and gathered the materials for Wilkins's *Concilia*, an achievement in itself sufficient to establish his reputation as a historical scholar. If Stubbs could aver of the Convocation controversialists that 'the very dust of their writings is gold', Wake could claim to be the master-goldsmith of the company. Indeed in the range and depth of his historical erudition he may challenge comparison with Stubbs. Furthermore he provided the ammunition, both historical and liturgical (for his correspondence shows him to have been no mean student of liturgies), for Le Courayer's defences of Anglican ordinations; and his own printed visitation charges as bishop of Lincoln offer further evidence of the breadth of his learning. In undertaking the office and work of a bishop and thereby the opportunity of translating precept into practice, he more than fulfilled the exhortation given to Superintendents of the Church of Denmark 'qui non vocantur ad canonicale otium sed ad ingentes labores'. During the ten years of his oversight of the large and laborious diocese of Lincoln indeed he was exemplary in visitation, confirmation and ordination; and in the pastoral and judicial aspects of his office also he strove, not without success, to blend in due proportion mercy and justice in dealing with scandalous offenders amongst his clergy. As archbishop he was equally diligent in the administration of his much smaller diocese; whilst as primate and metro-

[1] Arch. W. Epist. 25, f. 169. 'Ego sane paucos e pluribus libros ad te misi, ut tibi et tuis pateat, fidem orthodoxam in his nostris oris non minus strenue a filiis suis tueri, quam ab inimicis ejus impugnari audiveritis. Plures quotidie exsurgunt verae religionis defensores; et quanquam in hac nostra, qua fruimur, libertate, fieri non potest, quin malos quotidie libros edi videamus, id tamen solatii habemus, quod vix ulli impune publicentur, sed eadem omnes παρρησίᾳ examinentur qua scribuntur.'

politan he upheld worthily the dignity of the chair of St Augustine. There was truth as well as foresight in the remark attributed to Samuel Clarke on the day when Wake kissed hands for the archbishopric, that 'we have now an archbishop who is priest enough'.[1] But this proper sense of the dignity of his office did not prevent him from showing a gracious condescension to his clergy and to the visitors who thronged his 'public days'. An archbishop of his times was necessarily much given to hospitality; and Wake was notable for his invariably kind reception of his multifarious guests. Furthermore he was a bountiful repairer of his official residences. It was related of him that he had spent £11,000 on the archiepiscopal houses; and not content with this, he rebuilt the vicarage house at Croydon in 1730 for the benefit of the incumbent at a cost of £700.[2] Croydon indeed was his favourite residence; and he reported to White Kennett in 1721 that 'the house is good, though old; it has cost above £3000 already in repairs; and will require a further charge before one can make it tolerably convenient. But then, I think, it will, to old-fashioned people as we are and bishops ought to be, prove a very pleasant and convenient dwelling.'[3]

As a spiritual lord Wake was conscientious in the discharge of his parliamentary duties, as was sufficiently testified by his minutely scrupulous analysis of his conduct during the proceedings for the impeachment of Oxford and Bolingbroke. Moreover he was evidently also a speaker of force. His destructive criticism of the Vestry Bill left it without defender and nothing more was heard of it. Nor was he ever lacking in courage to defend what he conceived to be the true interests of the church. His speech against the repeal of the Occasional Conformity and Schisms Acts was influential in reducing the scope of the projected measure by the excision of the clauses relating to the Sacramental Test, and was delivered in defence of the interest of the established church as at that time he saw the issue. Admittedly this is the most difficult of his public actions to explain or justify. There can be little doubt, however, that on the one hand alarm at the rising storm of controversies within the church and on the other hand anxiety for the success of his approaches to foreign churches, led him to rely and fall back upon adventitious props for the unity of church and realm. Similarly his opposition to the Quakers' Affirmation Bill proceeded from his fear of encouraging the pretensions of enemies of the established church. It was, moreover, a misfortune that his experiences in these episodes led to a growing neglect of parliamentary

[1] J. Nichols, *Literary Anecdotes*, vol. IV, p. 720.

[2] Henry Mills, *An Essay on Generosity and Greatness of Spirit*. Dedicated to Archbishop Wake (London, 1732), p. lv.

[3] B.M. Lansdowne MSS. 1016, f. 5. 20 September 1721. *The Gentleman's Magazine*, 1737, p. 61 averred that Wake at his death was 'worth upwards of £100,000'. It should be remembered that the revenues of the see of Canterbury were over £30,000 per annum.

attendance; for thereby the House of Lords was deprived of a powerful and important, if not always persuasive or compliant, voice.

A contemporary panegyrist ascribing to Wake the virtues of charity, meekness, patience and great humility, pointed particularly to his voluminous correspondence as their best expression and illustration. This indeed would appear to have reflected one of the most remarkable traits of his character. Whether his correspondents were the diocesan clergy at Lincoln or Canterbury, or S.P.G. missionaries in the plantations, or S.P.C.K. agents at Tranquebar, or his brethren of the English and Irish benches, he was indefatigable in answering their letters and prodigal in according his counsel, advice and exhortation. In great measure perhaps his vast correspondence compensated for the comparative paucity of his close friendships; for he seems to have been apter by pen than in more intimate personal relationships. Occasionally his letters contained illuminating *obiter dicta*; as when he gave Le Courayer his opinion of English church historians: 'Strype is honest though not entertaining, and always writes upon good authority. Bishop Burnet's records are faithfully collected and his *History* must be tried by them; Heylin is rash and often mistaken; Fuller not to be relied upon; Collier writes all for a party, but I have not read enough of him to judge of his care.'[1] But amongst the volumes of his correspondence the most remarkable collection is that to and from his foreign friends, written either in Latin or French (for he confessed to one of his German-speaking Swiss correspondents that to himself *lingua vestra penitus incognita est*), and often affording clues to not a few important and otherwise enigmatic incidents of his public career. To a not inconsiderable degree, indeed, Wake is mirrored best in his letters, especially his foreign correspondence.

It is little surprising therefore that the most outstanding of his achievements, as it was the foremost of his interests, was his oecumenical programme for the union of the churches. Herein he stands almost without peer in the long succession of holders of the see of St Augustine. For whilst some of his predecessors like Laud had maintained a vigorous controversial exchange with Roman Catholic polemists and others like Sancroft had shown great friendship to members of the foreign Reformed churches; and whilst a distinguished Irish primate, Bramhall, had laid the foundations of the defence of Anglican Orders, Wake was unique in combining all these aspects. Great courage indeed was needed to embark upon a correspondence with the divines of the Sorbonne. For the anti-popery cry was still powerful in England, where the Jacobite rebellion of 1715 was a recent memory and the banishment of Atterbury lay in the near future. Moreover Wake risked the potentially dangerous consequences, emphasised by the refusal of the

[1] *Biographia Britannica*, vol. VI, part 2, 4093b.

Archbishop of Paris to authorise officially the interchange of letters or to commit himself in writing to a single sentence of approval, of engaging in written discussion with private theologians of the Gallican Church, who might be disavowed at a stroke by all the authorities, ecclesiastical and political, of their kingdom. Although Cardinal De Noailles declined to write directly to Wake *calumniae metu*, the English primate did not shrink from incurring that opprobrium. If more than two centuries later Archbishop Davidson experienced parallel difficulties in authorising the Malines conversations and was subjected to the like criticism and censure, how much greater were the risks resolutely undertaken by Wake. Nor did he escape a meed of condemnation. Archdeacon Francis Blackburne in the preface to *The Confessional* thus stigmatised his eirenic endeavours.

> What a door is here opened for reflexion! A Protestant archbishop of Canterbury, a pretended champion too of the Protestant religion, sets on foot a project for union with a popish church and that with concessions of the grossest superstition and idolatry; and this represented as the spirit of the established Church of England in relation to those who dissent from its rule of doctrine and government.

The author admitted indeed that he was not 'sufficiently informed of the circumstances of this transaction of Archbishop Wake to know what progress he had made in it'; but, taking it for granted 'that, before he could bring it to bear, it must have passed through other hands', averred that he remembered

> enough of the times when Dr Wake figured at the head of the church, to be very certain that it would *then* have been lost labour to solicit the consent of a majority even of the members of the Church of England to an union with the Gallican (that is, the French popish) Church, even though all the bishops upon the bench had recommended it.[1]

In fact, the primate's position was more precarious than this antagonist imagined; for few even of his episcopal brethren would have ventured openly to support his action, and certainly not the aggressively insular Bishop Gibson. When in the course of the negotiation Du Pin's correspondence was seized and the doctor himself interrogated, the ominous possibilities were evident for his English correspondent, who had received neither the concurrence of his suffragan bishops nor the permission of the civil authorities to engage in such a delicate correspondence.

If Wake showed therefore great courage in embarking on the affair, so too he demonstrated his firm adherence to the Anglican position in sustaining it. His positive defence of the regularity and validity of Anglican orders, both in his own letters to the Sorbonne doctors and in the information which he

[1] Francis Blackburne, *The Confessional* (London, first ed., 1766), pp. lxii, lxiv.

contributed to Le Courayer's books, established conclusively the historical case for the consecration of Matthew Parker and adumbrated the lines of subsequent discussion of the theological issues concerning the Anglican doctrine of priesthood and sacrifice. Moreover he applied to the Gallican divines no less than to foreign Protestants his principle of differentiating between fundamental and non-essential doctrines. In the latter field he was ready to allow wide differences of belief and opinion; not denying to his Roman Catholic friends the liberty to accept transubstantiation, provided they granted the like freedom to disbelieve it to him, and even carrying his readiness to the extent of proposing the omission of the Black Rubric from the Book of Common Prayer. In his staunch insistence on the necessity of a disavowal of the claims of the contemporary papacy on the part of the Gallican Church, Wake was stating the historic Anglican position, whilst at the same time affirming his willingness to acknowledge a primacy of honour to the twin-apostolic see of the west upon the ground of ecclesiastical recognition, though not by dominical appointment. It may be a matter of opinion whether Wake 'showed himself singularly stiff and unyielding', or whether 'the only men who came at all well out of the business were the doctors of the Sorbonne'; but the perusal of the entire correspondence certainly does not support the conclusion that 'as a negotiation towards reunion the whole affair was somewhat unfortunate, and later historians have been wont to attach more importance to it than it really deserves'.[1] This verdict of a twentieth-century disciple of the Oxford Movement, by its fundamental misunderstanding of Wake's standpoint and lack of comprehension of the entire correspondence, at least serves to throw into stronger light the courage needed to undertake such an enterprise more than two hundred years ago. Nor has later history undermined the soundness of Wake's position. For although the political pretensions of the papacy which were foremost in his day no longer enjoy the same prominence, its fundamental claims both to *magisterium* and to infallibility as defined by the Vatican Council in 1870 have justified his refusal to concede to it more than a *primatus honoris*, as recognised by the oecumenical councils of the early church.

In his zeal to attain the union of Protestants, Wake belonged to a generation, embracing such churchmen as Molanus, Leibnitz and Jablonski, much concerned with this problem, amongst whom his own endeavours were outstanding. Moreover in this field he inherited a tradition of friendly relationship between his own church and the Protestant churches of the continent. To Lutheran and Reformed theologians alike he affirmed his principles of distinguishing between fundamentals and non-essentials, and being content with a common belief in the former and allowance of difference of opinion in

[1] H. R. T. Brandreth, *The Oecumenical Ideals of the Oxford Movement* (London, 1947), p. 6.

the latter. To them also he continually commended the example of the wide latitude of opinion and comprehensiveness characteristic of the Church of England. There can be no doubt that he would have accepted the definition of Creighton that 'the formula which most explains the position of the Church of England is that it rests on an appeal to sound learning'; and he applied this maxim to its tolerance of divergence in matters of secondary importance. Moreover he would have agreed also with Creighton's rider that 'sound learning must always wear the appearance of a compromise between ignorance and plausible hypothesis.... It is the function of learning to assert what is known and to leave perverse ingenuity steadily alone.'[1] Nor did this caution apply only to disputed points concerning predestination, election and grace. It was relevant also to the question of episcopacy. Wake indeed never ceased to emphasise his conviction that an indispensable condition of corporate union was the restoration to, and acceptance by, the foreign Protestants of the historic episcopate; nor to insist upon the trust committed to his own Church in this respect by its possession of a continuous yet reformed episcopacy. But he held fast to the episcopal *regimen* on the ground that it was *plane Apostolicum*; that is, on the basis of history not of dogma. He anticipated indeed in action, and would have subscribed in belief, to Lightfoot's conclusion that

> if the preceding investigation be substantially correct, the threefold ministry can be traced to apostolic direction; and short of an express statement we can possess no better assurance of a divine appointment or at least a divine sanction. If the facts do not allow us to unchurch other Christian communities differently organised, they may at least justify our jealous adhesion to a polity derived from this source.[2]

In applying this principle to the foreign Reformed churches Wake followed the Elizabethan and Caroline tradition which recognised the validity of presbyterian orders where bishops could not be had, and accepted this ineluctable historical necessity in their cases. But he went further than either his predecessors or his successors by encouraging and authorising reciprocal intercommunion with the Lutheran and Reformed churches of Europe. If in so doing he advanced upon his own practice when chaplain in Paris during the reign of Charles II, he gave thereby practical expression to his recognition of the validity of their orders and sacraments. To his great disappointment these churches did not respond by taking episcopacy into their system of church government; and so, apart from an interchange of compliments and of good words for the Anglican reformed episcopacy, his cherished schemes for corporate union were not realised. Notwithstanding, he may justly claim to be judged according to the character of his aspirations and of the

[1] M. Creighton, *The Church and the Nation*, pp. 251, 259–60.
[2] J. B. Lightfoot, *Philippians*: excursus on 'The Christian Ministry', p. 267.

ideal which he put forward *ut omnes unum sint*; and pre-eminently in his oecumenical vision and in his indefatigable efforts towards its achievement (as also in other aspects of his life and work) he may challenge a place amongst the greatest of the successors of St Augustine.

If in his own times, as he lamented, the hardness of men's hearts frustrated his hopes and projects, the words of a collect which he wrote, entitled 'A Prayer for all the Reformed Churches' may be remembered as expressive of his unwearying zeal.

O God, who of thy great goodness hast united us into thy holy church, the mystical body of thy Son; we, as living members thereof, mourning with them that mourn and rejoicing with them that do rejoice, present our supplications and prayers at the throne of thy grace on behalf of all the Reformed churches; beseeching thee to look down in an especial manner, with an eye of mercy and pity, upon the sad and mournful estate of such of them as still labour under any troubles or persecutions for righteousness' sake. Suffer not thine enemies to triumph over thine heritage. Plead thy cause with them who corrupt thy truth, and afflict thy servants. Shew thyself to be their mighty deliverer, that all men may see it, and say, Verily there is a God that judgeth in the earth. Enlighten those who are in darkness and error, and open their eyes to the acknowledgement of thy truth; that so we may all become one flock under the one great Shepherd and Bishop of our souls, Jesus Christ our Lord. Amen.[1]

So too the epitaph on his own endeavours may best be written in the words of his last letter to Du Pin, in which he looked forward to the fullness and consummation of that unity of spirit to which they had attained here on earth, in the fellowship of the church triumphant hereafter.

I shall not cease to pray for you, most worthy brother, that the Holy Spirit of God may vouchsafe to indue you more and more with this mind. Do you intercede for me at the throne of grace that He may fashion the same mind in me; so that when we have both fulfilled this mortal life (which will shortly be) our friendship, which we have begun here far too late, may continue, flourish, increase and be fulfilled in heaven.[2]

Rogate quae ad pacem sunt Jerusalem: et abundantia diligentibus te.

[1] 'A Form of Prayer to be used in all Churches and Chapels throughout England and Wales, and the Town of Berwick upon Tweed, on Friday the Eighth Day of December, being the Day appointed by His Majesty for a General Fast and Humiliation, to be observed in a most Solemn and Devout Manner.' (London, 1721.) I owe this reference to my friend, Professor E. C. Ratcliff, Ely professor of divinity in the university of Cambridge.

[2] Ego pro te, frater dignissime, non desinam orare, ut hunc in te animum magis magisque efficere dignetur Sanctus Dei Spiritus. Tu pro me interpella ad Thronum Gratiae, ut eandem in me mentem efformare velit; utque mortali hac vita (quod brevi fiet) ab utroque peracta, amicitia nostra, sero hic nimis inchoata, in caelis permaneat, vigeat, augeatur, perficiatur.

BIBLIOGRAPHY

MANUSCRIPT SOURCES

In Wake's correspondence, the vast majority of the items are letters to him; and the minority consist of his rough drafts of replies. Especially in regard to his foreign correspondence, the *responsiones* in Epist. 25 and 26 are foul drafts, much corrected and with such abbreviations as to make them very difficult to decipher. The question therefore arises whether Wake despatched his fair copies in identical terms with the drafts. Fortunately the discovery of the originals of some of his letters to the Swiss churches at Geneva, Basle, Zürich and Lausanne, and of copies of the originals to his Gallican correspondents in the Bibliothèque Nationale, establishes the identity between rough draft and fair copy. It may with confidence therefore be affirmed that the drafts may be used as representing Wake's opinions even where the originals are not extant in foreign libraries. Similarly the volume of original letters from Wake to Professor Turrettini at Geneva and to Archbishop King of Dublin are invaluable in throwing light on many of his projects and purposes. Although only a small fraction of Wake's own letters has been preserved, it is sufficient, together with the correspondence received by him, to enable the reconstruction of at least an outline of his life and work.

Archbishop Wake's MSS. at Christ Church, Oxford; especially the volumes of his correspondence, as follows:

Arch. W. Epist. 1, Lincoln I: foliated.
Arch. W. Epist. 2, Lincoln II: foliated.
Arch. W. Epist. 3, Lincoln III: no foliation.
Arch. W. Epist. 4, Lincoln IV: no foliation.
Arch. W. Epist. 5, Lincoln V: no foliation.
Arch. W. Epist. 6, Canterbury I: no foliation.
Arch. W. Epist. 7, Canterbury II: irregularly foliated; stops at f. 187.
Arch. W. Epist. 8, Canterbury III: foliated.
Arch. W. Epist. 9, Canterbury IV: foliated.
Arch. W. Epist. 10, Canterbury V: foliated.
Arch. W. Epist. 11, Consecration of English Bishops: irregularly foliated.
Arch. W. Epist. 12, Ireland I: no foliation.
Arch. W. Epist. 13, Ireland II: foliated.
Arch. W. Epist. 14, Ireland III: foliated.
Arch. W. Epist. 15, Universities, Charities and Religious Societies to 1718: unfoliated.
Arch. W. Epist. 16, Universities, etc. from 1718: foliated.
Arch. W. Epist. 17, Miscellaneous I: foliated to f. 131.
Arch. W. Epist. 18, Miscellaneous II: no foliation.
Arch. W. Epist. 19, Miscellaneous III: no foliation.
Arch. W. Epist. 20, Miscellaneous IV: no foliation.

Arch. W. Epist. 21, Miscellaneous v: foliated.
Arch. W. Epist. 22, Miscellaneous vi: foliated.
Arch. W. Epist. 23, Miscellaneous vii: foliated.
Arch. W. Epist. 24, State of Religion in East and West Indies, Minorca Gibraltar, Isle of Man: foliated.
Arch. W. Epist. 25, Epistolae Latinae cum Responsionibus, 1716–21: foliated.
Arch. W. Epist. 26, Epistolae Latinae cum Responsionibus, 1721–6: foliated.
Arch. W. Epist. 27, Charities, Hospitals, Schools, Societies, French Refugees, Poor Proselytes: foliated.
Arch. W. Epist. 28, Foreign Churches and Ministers, 1715–18: no foliation.
Arch. W. Epist. 29, Foreign Letters: France and Flanders, 1717–21: foliated.
Arch. W. Epist. 30, Foreign Letters: France and Flanders, 1722–6: irregularly foliated.
Arch. W. Epist. 31, Foreign Letters: Italy, Switzerland, Germany, Holland: foliated.
Also Arch. W. 284–7; 297; 307–9; 330.
Matricula Ecclesiae Christi.
Chapter Act Books, nos. 39 and 40.

Bodleian Library:
Rawlinson MSS. A. 275; B. 376; B. 497; D. 472.
Tanner MSS. 21; 22; 23; 24.
MSS. Eng. Hist. d.1.29781.
MSS. 16328, Browne Willis MSS. 35.
MSS. 16335, Browne Willis MSS. 42.
Carte MSS. 224.
Add. MSS. A. 64; A. 269.
Ballard MSS. 3; 4; 5; 6; 7.
MSS. Oxf. Dioc. Papers. d. 106.

Geneva:
Bibliothèque Publique et Universitaire. MSS. Inventaire 1569. Collection J. A. Turrettini. Correspondance TAN-ZWI; Correspondance Ecclésiastique xxxix, MSS. Inv. 440.

Zürich:
Staatsarchiv des Kantons Zürich. E. 11.432; A. 222. 3, 4.
Zentralbibliothek. MS. H. 293.

Basle:
Öffentliche Bibliothek der Universitat in Basel.
MS. Fr. Gr. 111; MS. Ki. Ar. 26b.

Lausanne:
Letters to Professor J. P. de Crousaz; in the possession of Mlle B. de Crousaz, 6, Avenue de la Gare, Lausanne.

Berne:
Staatsarchiv B. 111. 98.

Paris:
Bibliothèque Nationale. MS. Lat. 17689.

Vatican:
Archives: MSS. Nunziatura di Francia. 234.

Dublin:
Trinity College Library, Correspondence of Archbishop King.
Exeter Cathedral Library:
Chapter Act Books, no. 3563 (1695–1708).
Lincoln:
Wake's Register, no. XXXVI.
St Andrews:
University Library. Gibson MSS. III and IV.
Canterbury:
Cathedral Library. Liber Tho: Green. Archidiac: Cantuar: 1708.
Somerset House:
Prerogative Court Registers: Chaynay and Mellershe, nos. 42 and 43.
Lambeth Palace Library:
Wake's Register, 3 vols.
Act Books VI–VIII.
Convocation Act Books, nos. 5; 18; 19; 21–3.
MS. 1133.
MSS. 930; 942.
MSS. 1079, A and B; 1081 (a).
MS. volume, containing the Wake-Beauvoir Letters and the *Commonitorium* of Du Pin.
Public Record Office:
State Papers, Domestic. George I and II.
British Museum:
Stowe MSS. 747.
Lansdowne MSS. 1016.
Add. MSS. 5841; 15521; 19399; 20105; 22880; 32686; 32701–2; 33924; 35585; 38889; 47030.
Privately owned:
Wake's Autobiography to 1705 and a Journal 1682–4 in the possession of J. T. Kirkwood, Esq., Warden, Dockland Settlement, no. 2, Isle of Dogs, London, E. 2.
Historical Manuscripts Commission:
7th Report. Appendix. MSS. of Sir Frederick Graham. Lord Preston's Letter Book.
12th Report. Appendix. Part VII.
Portland MSS. V; VII.
Earl of Carlisle MSS.
Egmont MSS. (Diary of Viscount Perceval, first earl of Egmont).

PRINTED WORKS

WORKS BY WAKE

An Exposition of the Doctrine of the Church of England in the several articles proposed by M. de Meaux (London, 1686).
A Defence of the Exposition of the Doctrine of the Church of England (1686).
A Second Defence of the Exposition, Parts 1 and 2 (1687).
Preparation for Death (1687).
A Discourse of the Holy Eucharist in the two great points of the Real Presence and the Adoration of the Host (1687).
Two Discourses of Purgatory and Prayers for the Dead (1687).
A Discourse concerning the Nature of Idolatry (1688).
A Continuation of the Present State of the Controversy between the Church of England and the Church of Rome (1688).
An Exhortation to Mutual Union and Charity amongst Protestants (1689).
The Genuine Epistles of the Apostolical Fathers, translated and published with a large Preliminary Discourse relating to the several Treatises here put together (London, 1693; 2nd ed. 1710).
Of our Obligation to put our trust in God (1695).
A Practical Discourse concerning Swearing (1696).
The Authority of Christian Princes over their Ecclesiastical Synods Asserted, with particular respect to the Convocations of the Clergy of the Realm of England (London, 1697).
An Appeal to all True Members of the Church of England in behalf of the King's Ecclesiastical Supremacy (London, 1698).
The Case of the Exiled Vaudois and French Protestants Stated (1699).
The Church of Rome no guide in matters of Faith (1700).
The Principles of the Christian Religion Explained, in a brief Commentary on the Church Catechism (1700).
The False Prophets tried by their Fruits (1700).
The State of the Church and Clergy of England in their Councils, Synods, Convocations, Conventions and other Publick Assemblies, historically deduced from the Conversion of the Saxons to the Present Times (London, 1703).
The Danger and Mischief of a misguided Zeal (1710).
Visitation Charges, 1706 *and* 1709 (London, 1707 and 1710).
The Bishop of Lincoln's Speech in the House of Lords, 17 March 1710.
Sermons and Discourses on Several Occasions (2nd ed. 1716).
A Brief Enquiry into the Antiquity, Honour and Estate of the Name and Family of Wake (1733).
Twenty-Two Sermons preached on Several Occasions (2 vols. 1737).

CONTEMPORARY WORKS

Atterbury, F. *A Letter to a Convocation Man* (1697).

—— *The Rights, Powers and Privileges of an English Convocation* (1st ed. 1700; 2nd ed. 1701).

—— *Epistolary Correspondence of* (3 vols. 1784).

Biographia Britannica, vol. VI, part 2.

Blackburne, F. *The Confessional* (1766).

Boulter, H. *Letters written by Hugh Boulter, Primate of All Ireland* (2 vols. 1769).

Brydges, Sir Egerton. *Restituta* (3 vols.).

Calamy, E. *A Historical Account of my own Life* (ed. J. T. Rutt, 2 vols. 1829).

Cave, W. *Apostolici, or The Lives of the Primitive Fathers for the first three ages of the Catholic Church* (1686).

Christian Remembrancer, The. Vol. III. June 1821.

Clarke, S. *The Scripture Doctrine of the Trinity* (1712).

Episcopal Opinions on the Test and Corporation Acts, as delivered in the House of Peers in December 1718 (London, 1780).

Evelyn, John. *Diary.* Ed. E. S. de Beer (6 vols. 1955).

Gibson, E. *Of Visitations Parochial and General* (1717).

—— *Synodus Anglicana* (1702).

—— *Codex Juris Ecclesiastici Anglicani* (2 vols. 1713).

Hardouin, Le P. *La Dissertation de P. Le Courayer sur la Succession des Évêques Anglais et sur la Validité de leurs Ordinations, réfutée* (Paris, 1724–5).

Hearne, T. *Collections* (Oxford Historical Society).

Hill, S. *Municipium Ecclesiasticum. A Vindication of the Authority of Christian Princes, to which are added Some Letters between Dr Wake and Mr Hill* (1701).

Hoadly, B. *The Nature of the Kingdom or Church of Christ* (1717).

Hody, H. *A History of English Councils and Convocations and of the Clergy's Sitting in Parliament* (1701).

Johnstone, H. J. *A Vindication of the Bishop of Condom's Exposition of the Doctrine of the Catholic Church* (1686).

Kennett, White. *Ecclesiastical Synods and Parliamentary Convocations* (1701).

Lafiteau, P. F. *Histoire de la Constitution* Unigenitus (2 vols. Liège, 1738).

Le Courayer, P. F. *Dissertation sur la Validité des Ordinations Anglais et la Succession des Évêques de l'Église Anglicane* (2 vols. 1723; English translation by D. Williams, 1725).

—— *Défense de la Dissertation* (2 vols. 1726).

Le Quien, M. *Nullité des Ordinations Anglicanes* (2 vols. 1725).

Mills, H. *An Essay on Generosity and Greatness of Spirit; dedicated to Archbishop Wake* (1732).

Mosheim, J. L. *Ecclesiastical History.* Trans. and ed. by A. MacLaine (5 vols. 1768).

Nichols, J. *Literary Anecdotes of the Eighteenth Century* (9 vols. 1812).

Nicolson, W. *Letters.* Ed. J. Nichols (2 vols. 1809).

Noble, M. *Continuation of J. Granger's Biographical History of England* (1806).

Spectator, The. No. 313. 28 February 1711/12.

Tenison, E. *A Protestation in behalf of the King's Supremacy* (1718).
Waterland, D. *A Vindication of Christ's Divinity* (1719).
—— *The Case of Arian Subscription considered* (1721).

SECONDARY WORKS

Barnes, A. S. *Bishop Barlow and Anglican Orders* (1922).
Beckett, J. C. *Protestant Dissent in Ireland*, 1687–1718 (1947).
Beeching, H. C. *Francis Atterbury* (1909).
Brandreth, H. R. T. *The Oecumenical Ideals of the Oxford Movement* (1947).
Burgess, M. A. *A History of Burlington School* (n.d.).
Burrows, M. *All Souls' Worthies* (1874).
Cardwell, E. *Documentary Annals of the Reformed Church of England* (2 vols. 1844).
—— *Synodalia* (2 vols. 1842).
Carlisle, N. *A Concise Description of the Grammar Schools of England and Wales* (1818).
Carpenter, E. F. *Thomas Tenison* (1948).
Cobbett, W. *Parliamentary History*.
Colligan, J. H. *The Arian Movement in England* (1913).
Cowie, L. E. *Henry Newman* (1956).
Cragg, G. R. *From Puritanism to the Age of Reason* (1950).
Dalton, H. *Daniel Ernst Jablonski* (Berlin, 1903).
De la Harpe, J. *Jean Pierre De Crousaz* (Geneva, 1955).
Douglas, D. C. *English Scholars* (1939).
Every, G. *The High Church Party, 1688–1718* (1956).
Fletcher, C. J. H. *A History of St Martin's Church, Oxford* (1896).
Frere, W. H. *Visitation Articles and Injunctions of the period of the Reformation*, vol. I (3 vols. 1910).
Gentleman's Magazine, The (1864).
Haddan, A. W. *Preface to Bramhall's Works*, vol. III (Library of Anglo-Catholic Theology, 1842–5).
Hart, A. T. *The Life and Times of Archbishop John Sharp* (1949).
Henderson, B. W. *Merton College* (1899).
Jacob, E. F. 'Wilkins' *Concilia* and the Fifteenth Century', *Transactions of the Royal Historical Society*, fourth series, vol. XV (1932).
Jenkins, C. *Bishop Barlow's Consecration and Archbishop Parker's Register, with some new Documents* (1935, from the *Journal of Theological Studies*, 1922).
Jones, M. G. *The Charity School Movement* (1938).
Jordan, G. J. *The Reunion of the Churches. A Study of G. W. Leibnitz* (1927).
Kemble, T. E. *State Papers and Correspondence* (1857).
Lewitter, L. R. 'Peter the Great and the Polish Dissenters', *The Slavonic Review*, vol. XXXIII, no. 80, December 1954.
Lightfoot, J. B. *The Apostolic Fathers*, part 2, vol. I (1889).
—— *The Epistle to the Philippians* (1879).
Lupton, J. H. *Archbishop Wake and the Project of Union between the Gallican and Anglican Churches* (1896).

Lysons, D. *Environs of London* (4 vols. 1786).
McLean, G. R. D. 'Archbishop Wake and Reunion with the Gallican Church', *Church Quarterly Review*, vol. CXXXI, no. 262, January–March 1941.
Mant, R. *History of the Church of Ireland* (2 vols. 1840).
Monk, J. H. *Life of Richard Bentley* (2 vols. 1833).
Notes and Queries. Seventh series, vol. XII.
Philipps, W. A. (ed.) *History of the Church of Ireland* (3 vols. 1933).
Pierling, P. *La Russie et le Saint Siège* (4 vols. Paris, 1907).
Powell, A. *John Aubrey and his Friends* (1948).
Préclin, E. *L'Union des Églises Gallicane et Anglicane: Une Tentative au temps de Louis XV: Pierre François Le Courayer et Guillaume Wake* (Paris, 1928).
Robertson, C. G. *All Souls' College* (1899).
Rowden, A. W. *The Primates of the Four Georges* (1916).
Sergeant, J. S. *Annals of Westminster School.*
Sharp, T. *Life of John Sharp, Archbishop of York* (2 vols. 1825).
Shirley, F. J. *Elizabeth's First Archbishop* (1948).
Staehelin, E., *Johann Ludwig Frey, Johannes Grynaeus und das Frey-Grynaeische Institut in Basel* (Basle, 1947).
Stromberg, R. N. *Religious Liberalism in Eighteenth-century England* (1954).
Sykes, N. *Edmund Gibson* (1926).
—— *Church and State in England in the Eighteenth Century* (1934).
—— *Old Priest and New Presbyter* (1956).
—— *Daniel Ernst Jablonski and the Church of England* (1950).
—— 'The Cathedral Chapter of Exeter and the General Election of 1705', *English Historical Review*, vol. XLV, no. 178, April, 1930.
—— 'Episcopal Administration in England in the Eighteenth Century', *ibid.* vol. XLVII, no. 187, July, 1932.
—— 'The Buccaneer Bishop: Lancelot Blackburne', *Church Quarterly Review*, April–June 1940.
—— 'Archbishop Wake and the Whig Party, 1716–23', *Cambridge Historical Journal*, vol. VIII, 1945, p. 2.
—— 'Bishop William Wake's Primary Visitation of the Diocese of Lincoln, 1706', *Journal of Ecclesiastical History*, vol. II, no. 2 (1951).
—— 'The Election and Inthronization of William Wake as Archbishop of Canterbury', *Journal of Ecclesiastical History*, vol. I, no. I (1950).
—— 'Ecumenical Movements in Great Britain in the Seventeenth and Eighteenth Centuries', in *A History of the Ecumenical Movement*, by R. Rouse and S. C. Neill (1954).
Vuilleumier, H. *Histoire de l'Église Réformée du Pays de Vaud sous le Régime Bernois* (4 vols. Lausanne, 1927–33).
Whitebrook, J. C. *The Consecration of Matthew Parker, Archbishop of Canterbury* (1945).
Williams, B. *Stanhope* (1932).
Williams, G. *The Orthodox Church of the East in the Eighteenth Century* (1868).

INDEX